THE FLETCHER JONES FOUNDATION
HUMANITIES IMPRINT

The Fletcher Jones Foundation has endowed this imprint to foster innovative and enduring scholarship in the humanities.

D0861086

The publisher gratefully acknowledges the generous support of the Fletcher Jones Foundation Humanities Endowment Fund of the University of California Press Foundation.

Food in Time and Place

Food in Time and Place

*The American Historical Association
Companion to Food History*

EDITED BY
Paul Freedman,
Joyce E. Chaplin,
and Ken Albala

UNIVERSITY OF CALIFORNIA PRESS

University of California Press, one of the most
distinguished university presses in the United States,
enriches lives around the world by advancing scholarship
in the humanities, social sciences, and natural sciences. Its
activities are supported by the UC Press Foundation and
by philanthropic contributions from individuals and
institutions. For more information, visit www.ucpress.edu.

University of California Press
Oakland, California

Library of Congress Cataloging-in-Publication Data

Food in time and place : the American Historical
Association companion to food history / edited by Paul
Freedman, Joyce E. Chaplin, and Ken Albala.
    pages   cm.
  Includes bibliographical references and index.
  ISBN 978-0-520-27745-8 (cloth : alk. paper)
  ISBN 978-0-520-28358-9 (pbk. : alk. paper)
  ISBN 978-0-520-95934-7 (ebook)
  1. Food—History. 2. Food habits—History. I.
Freedman, Paul H., 1949-, editor. II. Chaplin, Joyce E.,
editor. III. Albala, Ken, 1964-, editor.
  TX353.F644   2014
  641.309—dc23   2014014666

Manufactured in the United States of America

23 22 21 20 19 18 17 16 15
10 9 8 7 6 5 4 3 2

In keeping with a commitment to support
environmentally responsible and sustainable printing
practices, UC Press has printed this book on Natures
Natural, a fiber that contains 30% post-consumer waste
and meets the minimum requirements of ANSI/NISO
Z39.48–1992 (R 1997) (Permanence of Paper).

Contents

Illustrations

Acknowledgments

Food in Time and Place is intended to offer orientation to several fields within food history across geographical areas, chronological periods, and topics. There are, for example, chapters on Africa, on European cuisine before the modern era, and about immigrants and food. We have tried to achieve a balance among world cultures and historical periods. As a work intended for an audience interested in history, this collection emphasizes the past and the context it provides for present aspects of food consumption.

The impetus for this project came from the American Historical Association (AHA), particularly Professor Iris Berger, formerly the Association's elected vice-president for research, and former Executive Director Robert Townsend. The editors are grateful to them for their initiative and encouragement, as well as for the support of their successors, Professor John McNeil of the Research Division and current Director James Grossman.

The original intention of the AHA was to produce a book about teaching the history of food. While we have expanded in order to interest more general readers, not just teachers, we have tried to offer guidance to college and high school teachers about the state of various questions in the fields covered. The editors are grateful to Kate Marshall of the University of California Press not only for seeing this complicated work through to completion, but for suggesting that the scope of the volume be expanded and its chapters be broadened beyond pedagogy.

The editors acknowledge with thanks the careful readings of outside referees, Lizzie Collingham of the University of Warwick, Matthew Booker at North Carolina State University, and Daniel Bender from the University of Toronto. We are especially grateful to Agnieszka Rec, a doctoral student at Yale University, who tirelessly and meticulously edited the chapters and put them in consistent order to ready them for publication.

Our gratitude is particularly directed to our contributors, whose work has shown us, and will we trust show the reader, many unexpected and thought provoking aspects of food studies. The patience, dedication, and suggestions of our authors have benefited us and made us hope that this book will be a unique contribution to an increasingly busy field.

Preface

PAUL FREEDMAN

One expression of the recent surge of interest in the history of food is the appearance of many more books and essays on the subject than were available just a few years ago. The small number of large books surveying food history in a general way has now been supplemented by both more ambitious and more specialized works: multivolume treatments across an extensive chronology, studies of food history as part of the interdisciplinary field of food studies, even accounts of the historiography of food.[1] The purpose of the present book is somewhat different and twofold: first, to provide a convenient handbook presenting a geographically, chronologically, and topically broad range of food history, and second, to serve as a resource for teachers of food history, including those who are thinking about putting together such a course, those who have already taught one, and historians who would like to add or increase a food component in courses oriented towards one nation (e.g., French history), period (e.g., medieval history), or topic (e.g., history of immigration). This preface outlines the situation of a field that can no longer be described as "emerging," but that has achieved visibility and widely acknowledged importance. Here we want to suggest some aspects of the current situation of food history and look at how chapters in this book can contribute to its stated purpose.

. . .

In the past a preface of this sort would have advocated the importance of the field of food history to a presumably skeptical audience of historians who would have needed to be convinced of its seriousness. While famines, crop yields, and average caloric intake have long been considered respectable areas of social historical inquiry, anything involving food choice (what people at different times and places have preferred) tended until recently to be viewed as frivolous, antiquarian, or hobbyist, amounting to little more than the ephemeral ins and outs of fashion. Introducing a survey of food history published in 2007 I discussed this problem and distinguished between the history of food in terms of nutrition and survival, on the one hand, and the history of cuisine, which involves taste and discrimination, on the other. The latter seemed then to require justification as an academic subject of inquiry.[2]

The popularity of food history among students and the expansion of academic programs, journals, and conferences on the subject make it clear that there is a durable interest in food as an expression of culture, a sign of identity, and an index of social as well as technological change. Food stands at the junction of contemporary concerns such as environmental degradation, public health, gender roles, globalization, and the erosion or preservation of cultural products and collective traditions. Efforts to protect food products and social identity are exemplified by such phenomena as the 1970s Campaign for Real Ale in Britain, the international Slow Food movement, and the proliferation of farmers' markets in the United States. Historians have been able to show some of the origins or early evolution of contemporary problems such as the politics of farming and water consumption and also of cultural perceptions of dieting, obesity, and body image.

The relevance of food history to a number of intersecting topics explains the answer to the question posed by Warren Belasco in the first chapter of this volume, "Why has food studies taken off?" Yet it remains surprising that historians have been less receptive than social scientists to food as a subject of study. Belasco describes some of this resistance, and many of us of a certain age can recollect amused or slightly appalled responses to proposals to study restaurants, cooking styles, or immigrants' cuisine. Anthropologists, on the other hand, have always concerned themselves with the so-called foodways of the societies they live with, not just what is eaten but how food is distributed hierarchically and with what sorts of gestures it is consumed. Even anthropologists who were not writing exhaustive descriptions of material culture or kinship relations placed food at the center of their accounts. Clifford Geertz's classic study of symbolic anthropology, *The Religion of Java* (published in 1960), begins with the *slametan*, a ceremonial meal, as a key to Javanese views of the world of matter and spirit. The food is wrapped in banana leaves and served by women to men who are seated on the floor. This informal but ritualized meal marks good and bad events: births, deaths, misfortunes, escapes from danger, arrivals, departures.

The *slametan* might seem merely a small and uneventful collation—nothing is explicitly said during the meal about the reason for the ceremony—but it is an event at which, as one of Geertz's informants said, "all kinds of invisible beings come and sit with us and they also eat the food. That is why the food and not the prayer is the heart of *slametan*." Because of the spiritual participants, the human diners do not eat all the food. As Geertz goes on to show, the symbolic implications of the meal are a key to traditional Javanese ways of making sense of the world, from an oblique diffidence to a feeling of spiritual and material interpenetration.[3]

It was anthropologists rather than historians who called attention to the importance of seemingly trivial or frivolous food preferences as causes of significant, even cataclysmic historical shifts. In *Sweetness and Power* (published in 1985), Sidney Mintz showed how New World slavery was created in response to European demand for sugar, used in the seventeenth and eighteenth centuries to sweeten new drinks such as tea, coffee, and chocolate.[4] This nonessential commodity, consumed in unserious settings such as cozy afternoon teas, made and destroyed societies around the world.

Amid all the turns that have taken place in the study of history, that towards material culture has been the most important for the growth of interest in food.[5] The artifacts of everyday life include the somewhat ephemeral patterns of food consumption and the more durable evidence of cooking and serving utensils. Additionally there is an interest in the organization of consumption. Attention to shopping, household management, and women's spaces has influenced studies of the growth of modern cities and has demonstrated the existence of consumer desires and behavior in distant periods as well.[6]

A second factor in directing historians' interests is a fascination with social positioning and the marking of status by symbols and consumption. This includes flaunting possessions such as swimming pools or big cars, and also making less material displays of taste, knowledge, and discrimination.[7] The marshaling of precious objects, the symbolism of clothes, and the rituals of dining characterize the seemingly stable hierarchies of traditional societies. Medieval banquets and early modern European sumptuary laws ceremonialized and codified food. In the more fluid societies of modernity, the proof of taste through connoisseurship and the pursuit of business and romance through dining are fruitful lines of inquiry for food studies to contribute to the analysis of society.

There is also the food itself. Appetite and eating are quotidian concerns, but dining is an activity that can seem paradoxically all the more irrelevant because of its inexorable nature. One meal follows another, and the ubiquity of food and the brevity of its enjoyment render it conceptually less visible than more durable cultural expressions such as art, furniture, or even clothing. Ephemeral though it is, food is a vivid pleasure as well as a grim necessity; it can be the object of nostalgia not just personally, as with Proust's madeleine, but also culturally, as for the meals of one's childhood or the cooking of a distant homeland. A particularly poignant and disturbing example of the emotional power of food is a cookbook put together by women in the Theresienstadt concentration camp, in which recollections of recipes from a destroyed world of quiet comfort constitute an act of memory, solidarity, and defiance.[8]

One of the most interesting things about teaching courses on the history of food is the personal connection students have with food and their curiosity about it. They are absorbed by food not just as a way of understanding modern global problems, but also as an aesthetic experience. Perhaps this shouldn't be so surprising since there has been an obvious increase in discussion about restaurants, food tourism, or the cuisine of regions, such as Peru or Mozambique, previously ignored by the self-described global *cognoscenti*. Yet the media present high school and college students as obsessed by fad diets and food phobias, partial to binges and eating at odd hours, and willing to sacrifice quality to convenience (pizza delivered at 3 A.M.).

When I started to teach food-related courses in 2008 I expected that apart from the "fun" aspect (which I tried to combat by grave demeanor and threats), environmental preoccupations and interest in sustainable agriculture would be what drew those taking the class. In fact I was intrigued to find that a substantial number of students were simply interested in food itself.

Food is a way of looking at the history of societies and a facet of cultural habits and expressions. Teachers in various historical fields benefit from consideration of food in terms of standards of living, the environment, and class, but in addition to these material and social conditions food is important for cultural identity, colonization, and the implications of globalization. As already stated, this book is intended to be useful for students and an interested public, but it is also directed to teachers of history. It offers chapters in the food habits of particular cultures and societies (China, the Muslim Middle East), and suggests ways of thinking about food and transnational topics (popular culture, industrialization).

The chapters in this book do not follow a set template or uniform order. They are individual essays reflecting the author's outlook as well as the particular topic. Our intention in each chapter has been to provide an overview of the subject as well as a sense of the controversies and progress made in exploring it. This is not a book of historiography in the narrow sense, and we have attempted to emphasize the state of various fields rather than the totality of past or present approaches. Nevertheless, attention to how the area of interest is studied should, we hope, be useful to teachers preparing courses, students studying food history, and anyone interested in how to approach food and culture.

We have tried to be comprehensive, both geographically and topically, but of course many societies and their food and some practical and theoretical approaches to food history have been left out.

In the introduction, "Food History as a Field," Warren Belasco recalls the emergence of food history as an academic topic and some of the intellectual and institutional obstacles it had to overcome. He identifies two phases of the growth of interest in the field: one in the two decades before 2000 when historian-pioneers sought to legitimize the field as an area of research, and the other since 2000, an acceleration of interdisciplinary concern about food safety, sustainability, and obesity. Although these latter topics are often approached as policy or scientific problems, they also invite consideration of how, historically, we arrived at this point.

The subsequent chapters are divided into three sections. The first and largest group describes nations or cultural areas according to chronological periods, subdivided in the case of American history. The first of the areas and eras considered is the culinary world of premodern Europe. Ken Albala surveys the historical periods from classical Greece until the beginnings of modern European cuisine in the seventeenth century. He discusses approaches to the history of ancient Greece and Rome, the Latin Middle Ages, the Renaissance, and the early modern era and identifies pedagogical as well as historiographic issues. The elegant culinary tastes of these many centuries are at the same time alien to us and the basis for modern European and, in certain respects, international cuisine.

E.N. Anderson describes the Chinese culinary world, emphasizing the variation among its regions and time periods. There is a modern tendency to overemphasize the unity of aesthetic principles in Chinese cooking, both retrospectively and geographically. Anderson is particularly concerned to show that China was not a world set apart, impervious to outside influence. The impact of the Islamic Middle East in the medieval period and of the West in the modern era, especially with the initial globalization of trade and product exchanges, are emphasized. The nature of the sources and resources for study in English is also described.

India is also sometimes regarded as unchanging or as having a permanent set of basic principles, ingredients, religious laws, preparations, and serving styles. Here Jayanta Sengupta emphasizes the diversity of India across its regions. The influence of the Muslim Mughal style of dining, with its Persian components and enthusiasm for meat is set alongside vegetarian traditions, especially those associated with diverse religious teachings. The British colonial influence is examined not simply as an alien or temporary phenomenon, but rather as a component of modern Indian cuisine. Particular attention is given to the spread of Indian communities to other countries, both to the local effects on what is considered Indian diaspora cuisine and the reception of Indian food by foreigners.

If India and China tend to be credited with exaggerated continuity and unity, Africa is often wrongly considered marginal to global food trends and innovations. Jessica B. Harris sets out the diversity of the continent. Harris also points out how little there is in the way of unified food histories of Africa and notes some of the sources for putting together such an overview, including archaeology, the accounts of Arab and European travelers, records of colonial administrations, the documents left by the slave trade, and the identification of cuisine with nation in post-independence Africa. She sees European influence not merely as an attempt to ignore Africa by importing European practices to colonial centers, but also as one of the ways in which modern African cuisines have been formed.

Charles Perry defines the history of Middle Eastern food as far back as ancient Babylonia and emphasizes the significance of Persian and Turkish as well as Arab culinary standards. The establishment of the Abbasid Caliphate in Baghdad beginning in the eighth century created a court culture and cuisine combining Persian and Arab elements. The trendsetters in Baghdad were receptive to the products and cooking methods of regions further east, especially South Asia. The golden age of Middle Eastern cuisine from the point of view of cookbook production and the place of food in the cultural discourse of elites is the tenth through thirteenth centuries. Perry describes how this culinary tradition has been studied and its links to other aspects of Islamic culture, especially medicine.

Latin America is the subject of Jeffrey M. Pilcher's chapter, and he approaches it both thematically and chronologically. Here it is not only the geographical diversity of a vast territory that affects the region's food history, but also the layers of indigenous and colonial populations and the role of modern Latin America in a global food system, the "export liberalism" of the chapter title. Industrialized agriculture geared for the international market has displaced small-scale farmers (*campesinos*), but in certain instances has been effectively resisted by social movements that have led to a revival of indigenous and Creole traditions. The teaching of Latin American food history can thus reflect the class and gender conflicts of the continent as well as its changing place in the global economy.

Joyce E. Chaplin's chapter is in certain respects linked to the essay on premodern Europe by Ken Albala, as it begins with a consideration of the effects of European colonization of the New World and some of the food exchanges that resulted. Chaplin discusses colonial conditions and the expansion and acceleration of agricultural productivity in the eighteenth- and nineteenth-century United States. She shows how food both reflects and sheds light on problems of American history such as the image of abundance, notions of resource exploitation, and the persistence of an ideal of simplicity. The political and economic power of the United States is an outgrowth of its food history, but so is much of the formation of America's own self-imagination, from the agrarian yeoman ideal of Jeffersonian democracy to later ideas of westward expansion and agricultural productivity.

The modern results of American resources and ideologies are set forth in Amy Bentley and Hiʻilei Hobart's view of the integrated large-scale food industry. Well established ideas of agricultural plenty characterized twentieth-century America's self-image. These ideas were linked to the "rationalization" of agriculture into larger units, along with the integration of food producers into giant national enterprises. Consolidation created an inexpensive food supply, but one dependent on agricultural and transportation technology; intensive marketing; an emphasis on durability over flavor, availability over quality, processing over nature; and artificial inputs to compensate for nutritional degradation imposed by processing. The tastes of Americans could hardly escape being affected by this homogeneity, and what had been a diversity of regions and culinary practices yielded in the course of the twentieth century to what has become a famous or infamous model of sameness symbolized most effectively by the fast-food industry.

Two subsequent chapters, covering much of the same twentieth-century period, deal with the persistence of difference and the customs of people not entirely integrated into the industrial food structure. Frederick Douglass Opie's chapter connects not only with the others on American food history, but also with Jessica Harris's essay on Africa. Opie looks at the African diaspora, principally in the United States but also in the Caribbean and Latin America, as culinary regions that influenced each other and so should be considered together in diaspora history. Slavery and the subsequent presence of blacks in Southern kitchens influenced, when it didn't outright create, modern Southern food and through it what are regarded as typical American dishes. At the same time that the twentieth-century created an awareness and celebration of uniquely African American dishes, ingredients, and preparations, the impact of other black culinary traditions (those of the West Indies, for example) was underestimated along with the multiple ways in which dishes were imported and exported within a changing African American food landscape.

Like Opie, Krishnendu Ray analyzes issues of authenticity in his essay on the experience of immigrants to the United States. Here it is not only a question of the diversity of immigrant experiences, cuisines, and degrees of attachment to tradition but also of selective co-optation by the majority American-born population. The "ethnic" restaurant industry represents immigrant enterprise and profits from and to some degree manipulates ideas about authenticity. Americans have a simultaneous attachment to industrialized food (as Bentley and Hobart have shown) and to experimentation and eating different cuisines. The proliferation of Italian and Chinese restaurants shows the success of the ethnic restaurant model, while other groups have been less successful at marketing versions of their cooking. Ray resists conventional treatments of this subject by showing that immigrant restauranteurs have well-planned strategies and refusing to see their enterprises as unreflective manifestations of tradition and diversity.

While many chapters consider specific places and times, all of them deal with multiple influences and cross-cutting topics. The second section presents three treatments of culinary history that focus on how taste is formed and how choices are made about what sort of food is desirable or even fashionable.

The French culinary revolution of the seventeenth and eighteenth centuries defined modern European and eventually global high-end cuisine until the late twentieth century and represents the origin of much of what is valued by sophisticated modern palates. Priscilla Parkhurst Ferguson shows how the soft power of culture created cultural prestige that in some ways was more consistently effective in presenting an image of France than that country's wars and diplomacy. This is a question not only of tastes and cooking priorities, but also of the codification of rules and the professionalization of cooking and service. The French domination of culinary taste involved an ideology of the superiority of French models that would be imitated everywhere. Ferguson concludes with a guide to the major, accessible works and approaches to this field.

Among the most important modern food institutions developed by France is the restaurant in its modern form, discussed here by Paul Freedman. For the first time in Europe patrons could choose to dine out at a "destination" where they could choose their companions, time of service, and particular dishes from a menu. The restaurant can be understood as an instance of French sway internationally at the high end, but additionally as a form of culinary experimentation, visible especially in the sorts of ethnic restaurants set up, as Krishnendu Ray describes, by immigrants. Restaurants have a cultural and social function, facilitating business and personal interactions, but also affording opportunities for the display of knowledge and status. Unlike some of the other topics in this volume, the history of restaurants lacks much of an historiographic tradition.

The last chapter in this section examines one of the most important artifacts of culinary styles, both of elite and of ordinary people: the cookbook. Regarded until recently as a routine and essentially ephemeral object, the cookbook has, largely through Barbara Ketcham Wheaton's pioneering studies, come to be regarded as an essential reflection of culture, both aspirational and everyday. In the present outline of how cookbooks can be studied, Wheaton discusses the cookbook as both a physical, often cherished, object and as the outcome of thought, experimentation, and the customs of households and communities. Cookbooks are practical guides, but also ways of thinking about possibilities, in some cases even fantasies. They display taste preferences and traditions as well as a fondness for experimentation and anxiety about health.

The final three chapters look at analytic frames for thinking about food history, posing intriguing problems in food studies that concern the contemporary food landscape. Krishnendu Ray's chapter on immigration, though focused on the United States and thus placed in the first section, is in certain respects also concerned with a modern phenomenon that is not in itself exclusively a food topic.

Amy B. Trubek's "Revolt against Homogeneity" demonstrates responses to the industrial model presented by Bentley and Hobart. Looking particularly at wine, cheese, and coffee, Trubek examines how new producers and consumers have rejected the dominance of bland national and global brands by seeking out quality, variety, and artisanal origins. The efforts to create markets for high-quality artisanal products have ethical motives—related to environment, treatment of animals and land, and revitalization of particular local spaces—as well as aesthetic motives.

Popular culture of recent decades has often included food as symbolically important, especially the fast-food industry, where McDonald's has functioned as one kind of symbol, while globalization has also brought forward sushi and bubble tea as iconic international youth commodities. Fabio Parasecoli considers examples of discourse about high-end items (Champagne) and comfort products (Nutella). Food has an ideological content, not just in how it is advertised but also in how it is deployed by those advocating political and economic change. Popular culture is a representation of reality and lends itself to both idealized and especially satiric and critical uses. Parasecoli considers how students' familiarity with popular culture provides opportunities for teaching food history. At the same time, Parasecoli relates the study of food and popular culture to theoretical approaches involving symbols, words, and desire.

The final chapter, by Peter Scholliers, describes the speed and scale of change in Western food production and consumption since 1945. Using a food systems approach, Scholliers describes economic changes in Europe and America that have made food cheaper, as well as shifts in culture such as increased travel, the desire for experimentation, and the decline of family meals. Particular attention is given to dining out and its accelerating popularity since the end of the Second World War. This is a result not simply of affluence but of styles of food provision, patterns of socialization, and the development of both individual and corporate business structures.

. . .

The editors hope the following chapters will offer the student, teacher, and general reader a survey of the field of food history and suggestions for areas of interest and research. The field, as was remarked at the outset, can hardly be called new or emerging, but it remains one in which there is a need for considerable research, with tremendous possibilities in archival and other written evidence, archaeological reconstruction, and social research into changing food attitudes in light of historical traditions. We have intended to present the current situation as a product both of uniquely contemporary concerns and of a deep past of different but converging cultures that make up the current and future food scenes.

NOTES

1. Fabio Parasecoli and Peter Scholliers, eds., *A Cultural History of Food*, 6 vols. (New York; London: Berg, 2012). Kyri W. Claflin and Peter Scholliers, eds., *Writing Food History: A Global Perspective* (London; New York: Berg, 2012). Jeffrey Pilcher, ed., *The Oxford Handbook of Food History* (Oxford: Oxford University Press, 2012).

2. Paul Freedman, ed., *Food: The History of Taste* (Berkeley: University of California Press, 2007).

3. Clifford Geertz, *The Religion of Java* (Glencoe: Free Press, 1960), 11–15.

4. Sidney Mintz, *Sweetness and Power: The Place of Sugar in Modern History* (New York: Penguin Books, 1985).

5. See the six articles in "AHR Forum: Historiographic 'Turns' in Critical Perspective," *American Historical Review* 117 (2012), 698–813.

6. E.g. Evelyn Welch, *Shopping in the Renaissance: Consumer Cultures in Italy, 1400–1600* (New Haven: Yale University Press, 2005); Lisa Jardine, *Worldly Goods: A New History of the Renaissance* (New York: Doubleday, 1996), especially pp. 275–330; Susan Mosher Stuard, *Gilding the Market: Luxury and Fashion in Fourteenth-Century Italy* (Philadelphia: University of Pennsylvania Press, 2006).

7. See the work of Pierre Bourdieu, especially *Discrimination: A Social Critique of the Judgement of Taste*, trans. Richard Nice (Cambridge: Harvard University Press, 1984).

8. Cara DeSilva, ed., *In Memory's Kitchen: A Legacy from the Women of Terezin* (Northvale: J. Aronson, 1996).

Introduction

Food History as a Field

WARREN BELASCO

Perhaps the most personally useful historical lesson for students is that career paths are circuitous and unpredictable. Like most of my colleagues in this book, I am quite sure that as an undergraduate (in my case, in the late 1960s) I would have been very surprised to learn that over forty years later I would be writing an introduction to an AHA-sponsored collection on the state of food history. That I would turn out to be a historian would have been less surprising, as I had had good high school teachers who seduced us would-be intellectuals with soft paperback copies of Richard Hofstadter's contrarian critiques of American culture, particularly *Anti-Intellectualism in American Life* and *The Paranoid Style in American Politics*.[1] But food history? That would have seemed a major stretch.

Getting here did have a certain convoluted logic, however. I started college as a medievalist, a focus well adapted to my monastic life in a Midwestern Gothic academy. Transferring to a Big Ten public university exposed me to specialties unknown at my tiny former college, where one resourceful professor "did" all of U.S. history. Awakened by the counter-culture and New Left, I explored timely new emphases such as urban studies, slavery, gender, environmentalism, film, and the history of revolutions. Staying on for graduate study, I came under the tutelage of modern cultural historians, one of whom, when nudged for fresh dissertation topics, muttered "cars!" This became my equivalent of the famous "plastics!" moment in *The Graduate*, except that unlike Benjamin, Dustin

Hoffman's character, I actually followed orders. "Cars!" yielded a thesis and eventual book on the early days of U.S. auto tourism, with a focus on the emerging roadside industry of auto camps, motels, gas stations, and, yes, fast food restaurants.[2] While my research dealt mainly with tourist camps, it did unearth quite a lot of material on eating as well, and this eventually wound up in a 1979 article in the *Journal of American Culture*, "Toward a Culinary Common Denominator: The Rise of Howard Johnson's."[3] Three important notes about this first foray into culinary history: First, it appeared in one of the earliest journal issues devoted solely to food studies. Second, the bulky title was a common style in popular culture studies at that time, as if the approach to ordinary phenomena needed to be gussied up in hyperbolic language. And third, during the interview for my eventual job at the University of Maryland, Baltimore County, my vita induced my prospective dean to exclaim, "Howard Johnson's, Warren, for God's sake!" While this remark did not upset the deal, it confirmed my sense that the time (1979) was not yet ripe to foreground a scholarly curiosity about food history, particularly of the vernacular, roadside variety.

If anything, the early 1980s seemed a period of considerable cultural reaction—and for us radicals, disbelief. For an explanation of how capitalism could have survived the recent revolution, I turned to Gramscian hegemony theory, which suggested how dominant cultures tolerate, tame, and eventually absorb deviant subcultures. This inspired a new book project, *Retailing Revolt*, which proposed to illustrate the processes of appropriation and co-optation through several contemporary case studies, including blue jeans, rock and roll, and natural foods. After a brief overview of the evolution of blue jeans from working-class emblem to fashion statement, I turned to the history of natural foods— and never left food, as the subject was so rich and wide open. (Disclosure: I also had a personal stake in the subject, having become an organic-gardening, tofu-touting environmentalist about ten years earlier.) It did not take much time to work up the literature review for what became *Appetite for Change: How the Counterculture Took on the Food Industry* (1989), as there were few broad food history surveys— none by a living, tenured professor—and just a handful of works on food reformers, most of them ranging from bemused to hostile.[4]

For help I turned to other fields, mainly social sciences. Anthropologists provided definitions of cuisine, taboos, and "food habits"; folklorists were beginning to research "foodways"; sociologists offered observations about the social significance of meals; psychologists had interesting taste, flavor, and choice experiments; nutritional ecologists and rural sociologists were developing bold "food systems" analyses; and media scholars had done some of the spadework of applying hegemony theory to American popular culture.[5] Semiotician Roland Barthes offered suggestive hints in "Ornamental Cookery" and "Toward a Psychosociology of Contemporary Food Consumption."[6] According to other erudite essayists, American food was largely a topic for cosmopolitan satire, populist celebration, or moralistic scorn, though a few investigative journalists had begun to expose the corporate food industry in the 1970s.[7] But the most useful (for me) works of food history—by Sidney Mintz, Harvey Levenstein, Stephen Mennell, Joan Jacobs Brumberg, Margaret Visser, as well as a new journal dedicated to food history and culture, *Food and Foodways*—appeared only when *Appetite* was already well underway.[8] Like many of my colleagues, I was pretty much flying solo through most of the 1980s.

Whereas a prospective food historian starting out today faces a hefty reading list of impressive secondary works before daring to write a word, I started reading food history only after I'd written some myself. Everything has to start somewhere. The advantage of being there in the early stages is that there's little competition; the downside is that you don't know very much. As an odd duck, I did get asked out a lot, and these invitations to talk and synthesize forced me to figure out what I needed to know more about. A frantic period of keeping up with the rapidly emerging food studies literature ensued in the early 1990s. More on that efflorescence below.

More immediately pressing in the 1980s was the need to figure out how to teach food to my students, who have always served as useful first respondents to my research. Indeed I soon came to rely heavily on my students for first-hand dietary data, not only about their current practices and beliefs but also about their multigenerational family histories. One advantage of teaching commuter students who were deeply rooted in the immediate environs of my university was that it was easy to ask them to interview their grandmothers. But teaching food was not in my original job description, certainly not as an untenured assistant professor hired to teach high-enrollment surveys of American popular culture. My early years as professor of rock-and-roll and TV did serve my food research well, however, as they taught me much about the production of culture, mass marketing, and the main conventions underlying popular narratives.[9] Those early years teaching about the culture business were particularly valuable in exposing a treasure trove of market research on consumer needs and behavior—all very useful for learning about the food industry.[10]

My first "food course" appeared in 1986, after tenure, when I used my department's capstone research seminar to guide students through a rudimentary commodity chain analysis. Tracing a product from field to fork was—and still is—an intensely challenging experience, and it was definitely "historical" even if it was more within the purview of sociologists, geographers, and economists than of historians.[11] What could be more personal *and* political than tracing where dinner comes from? As students quickly learned by using Margaret Visser's *Much Depends on Dinner,* John McPhee's *Oranges,* or, later on, Elisabeth Rozin's *Primal Cheeseburger,* Mark Kurlansky's *Cod,* and Michael Pollan's *Botany of Desire,* the connections to fundamental facts of global history were startling. For example, twenty years before Pollan's bestselling *Omnivore's Dilemma,* Visser identified corn as "the driving wheel of the supermarket" and America's key post-1492 contribution to the world's diet. McPhee drew graceful connections from the modern Florida frozen orange juice industry back through crusader Richard the Lionhearted and then way back to Confucius. Deconstructing the basic cheeseburger-fries-soda meal, Rozin put meat at the center of human dietary aspirations and linked the bun to the Neolithic agricultural revolution. And Kurlansky located cod at the center of more key events in colonial North American history than any early modernist might have imagined.[12]

Even in our fumbling early attempts to sketch the provenance of mundane foodstuffs such as hot dogs, potato chips, "lite" beer, coffee, and Jell-O, my class felt privileged to take a peek at a dazzling parallel universe ignored in conventional historical narratives. This may be the appeal of one of the most popular forms of food writing, the single product history that channels and retells the history of the world through the tale of one foodstuff. If nothing else it certainly offers a tantalizing hook for skillful authors, as in Henry Hobhouse's introduction to *Seeds of Change: Five Plants That Transformed Mankind* (1987): "Why did the Mediterranean peoples cease to dominate Europe? What led Europeans subsequently to spread all over the globe in post-Renaissance times? The starting point for the European expansion out of the Mediterranean and the Atlantic continental shelf had nothing to do with, say, religion or the rise of capitalism—but it had a great deal to do with pepper."[13]

Similarly the personal food memoir, another very popular genre, may produce telling reflections on one's place in history. Indeed reading just a few lines of Marcel Proust's famous madeleine passage from the first volume of *Remembrance of Things Past* generated fascinating student papers about the histories of their families and communities.

As I just suggested, the 1990s were the take-off years for noticing food in almost every liberal arts discipline, conventional and not. Within history the convergence on food often came from other subjects—for historians of the arts, labor, family, business, science and technology, medicine, courtly behavior, nationalism, imperialism, protest, gender, consumer culture, race, class, and immigration, food offered fresh insights into their established specialties. Some of these returned to their home base after their "food book," while others, like me, stuck around in the new world. That decade also witnessed the establishment of several new graduate programs—especially at Boston University, New York University, and the University of Adelaide—and the maturation of informal scholarly associations, including the Association for the Study of Food and Society (ASFS), the Agriculture, Food, and Human Values Society (AFHVS), and the International Commission for Research into European Food History (ICREFH). These developments expanded in the early 2000s, as evidenced by the proliferation of panels, conferences, food series, textbooks, journals, reference books, concentrations, networks, web museums, blogs, and, perhaps most numerous, food-related courses at all levels, from high school and first-year surveys to doctoral seminars. My own all-purpose overview course, "American Food," first appeared in 1990 and became an annual staple through my retirement in 2011. As the course always filled—the bottom-line calculation in so much of higher education—it bought me opportunities to focus more directly on teaching food.

Viewing the rapid acceleration of activity since 1990, the historian naturally asks, "Why then? And why now?" What has encouraged such an outpouring of interest in food studies? Where is this all heading? And what does all this activity *mean?*

Given that some of the most influential food history has been written by nonhistorians—a reflection perhaps of our discipline's relative conservatism—it is appropriate to borrow anthropologist Sidney Mintz's basic distinction between "outside" and "inside" meanings.[14] The former entails the more distanced, theorized perspective of the hindsighted scholar, the latter the more subjective and idiosyncratic experiences of those who actually lived the history. The outside answer to "Why has food studies taken off?" might focus on the *-isms* and *-tions* that encapsulate or package trends. First should come feminism, especially women's studies, which foregrounded and largely legitimized previously ignored aspects of women's work, much of it food-related. While many first-wave and older second-wave feminists had deplored or down-played the confining, domesticated view of women "through the kitchen window," Arlene Avakian's 1997 collection by the same name helped to affirm the role of home food production in establishing women's power in families, relationships, and communities. Spreading that view, many of Avakian's contributors were themselves professors and writers work-ing on food projects.[15] Along similar lines, an emerging multiculturalism encouraged new attention to the myriad ways by which food practices construct ethnic, racial, regional, and class identities and borders.[16] Environmentalism—a key factor in the counterculture's original atten-tion to food system issues—revived in the 1990s, bringing new attention to the resource costs, ecological consequences, and future uncertainties of modern culinary abundance. Appropriately enough, my first class on "American Food" was keyed to respond to student fervor over the rebirth of Earth Day in April 1990; students were particularly impressed by the ecological case against industrial meat production, an argument voiced twenty years earlier by Frances Moore Lappe's *Diet for a Small Planet* and revived for the next generation in Jeremy Rifkin's popular history, *Beyond Beef: The Rise and the Fall of the Cattle Culture*.[17] (Pol-lan reiterated the same point fourteen years after Rifkin, in 2006.) This also coincided with the sensational rise of environmental history, much of it inspired by the food- and agriculture-centered work of Donald Worster, Alfred Crosby, and William Cronon.[18] Concerns about the macro environment were accompanied by a new wave of personal heal-thism, which intensified scrutiny of the body, with all its variations and vulnerabilities. In food studies this meant attention to the history of body image, fatness, dieting, alternative medicine, and nutritional sci-ence. Given worries about an imminent public health crisis due to rising obesity rates, some of that scholarship even received outside funding—a relatively rare phenomenon for historians—although quite a bit of the academic work went into questioning whether fatness was even a problem.[19]

At the same time the recombinant style of antimodernism sought to detach food production from the industrial modernist vision, which had projected a monolithic, streamlined future of ultra-efficient "pushbut-ton farms" producing raw materials to be spun into nutritionally enriched synthesized meals (ultimately, perhaps, the meal in a pill).[20] Whereas the generation that fought World War II came of age believing in "better living through chemistry," their children were more interested in revisiting what peasants grew, cooked, and ate. For my own cohort of Baby Boomers, modern food was dangerous and, perhaps worse, inauthentic. Our excavations of the preindustrial past exposed an array of niches for historical preservation, culinary tourism, neo-agrarianism, cultural strip mining, and hipster boutique entrepreneurship. In short, in the highly segmented world of post-Fordist food marketing, history had commercial value, especially if delivered in nostalgic fragments to an upscale clientele. One example was the rash of gentrified urban "marketplaces" that followed the Rouse Company's dramatically successful repurposing of Boston's Quincy Market. Another was the commodification of *terroir,* the taste of "place" and "tradition" that however invented and vague, adds considerable value for its savvy purveyors, who have significant political clout, especially in Europe, where the sale of historical "authenticity" has long been a major industry.[21]

While antimodernism flirted with the archaic and local, new focus on globalization encouraged a fresh look at fascinating transnational culinary connections and processes, such as the Columbian Exchange (a topic with special popular resonance in the commemorative year of 1992), McDonaldization (the worldwide spread of American fast food culture), biological imperialism (the conquest of indigenous ecosystems by invasive species), and glocalization (the adaptation of transnational corporate practices to local conditions). Studying globalization meshed well with the comparative, integrative sweep of the new global history, which sought to transcend the confines of tired, arbitrarily-defined nation-states in search of broad, big-picture insights into world systems.[22] While grand thinkers like Fernand Braudel and Immanuel Wallerstein touched on the more quantifiable aspects of food production and consumption only in passing, food history had its own transatlantic, multicentury epic in Sidney Mintz's classic story about sugar, slavery, and the Industrial Revolution, *Sweetness and Power* (1986), which may be said to have launched a thousand ships exploring global food networks and routes, past and present.[23]

Some critics have also seen an element of neoliberalism in the rise of conscientious consumption, a key component of environmental ethics, animal rights, healthism, locavorism, and other varieties of principled hedonism, as the erosion of public culture and governmental authority appeared to put a premium on personal responsibility to save the world, or at least oneself.[24] Schooled in Hofstadter's examination of the role of laissez-faire ideology in U.S. reform movements, I would argue that individualism has long been a staple of American thought. Nor is there anything new, remarkable, or even especially American about people channeling social anxieties, conflicts, and frustrations into a heightened concern about what they put into their bodies.[25] But I will allow that the neoliberal hypothesis has certainly grabbed the attention of a whole generation of graduate students. And, returning to my initial interest in hegemony theory, there seems little doubt that capitalism has clearly survived, and perhaps even thrived on the food consciousness that we food scholars have helped to expand.[26]

The problem with the outside *-isms* is that real people and events get lost amidst the deterministic forces, which is why these explanations must be balanced with an inside perspective, particularly an understanding of the actual agents of change. Who did the work to bring all this about? In my own case, I credit the early encouragement offered by activists and social critics who were delighted to hear that a professor was trying to make sense of the reform movement that they were part of. Thanks also go to the interest expressed by food sociologists and anthropologists happy to see a rare historian joining the annual parties of the Association for the Study of Food and Society. Then again, was I truly a historian? Yes and no. I did have a history doctorate and like all historians screened the world through the three c's—change, continuity, and context. But I did not teach in a history department, but rather in a wholly independent and eccentric American Studies department. My first invitation to speak about food at a mainstream historical conference (the annual meeting of the Organization of American Historians) didn't come until 1994, by which time I had already been "doing food" for over fifteen years. My first food panel at the annual meeting of the American Studies Association came in 1996, of the American Historical Association in 1998. Had it not been for the exceptional freedom afforded me by my supportive chair and enthusiastic students, I might never have done much with food in the first place. So the bittersweet luck of being a benignly neglected outlier had something to do with it.

I mention this because I believe it also applies to many of my colleagues in the early stages of food studies. Rather than moving along secure tenure tracks in conventional departments in the elite research universities, where we might have been encouraged to pursue more "respectable" work, most worked somewhat outside the main line—in colleges of home economics, education, general studies, medicine, hospitality, and agriculture, or in small teaching colleges, or in nonflagship public universities and community colleges, many as adjuncts, visitors, temporaries, instructors, and other versions of the new academic proletariat. Along the same lines, it would be interesting to know how many of us came to food studies through vegetarianism, a dissident subculture that heightens awareness of hegemonic food habits, beliefs, and practices. To be sure, many of us would have remained isolated proletarians had it not been for the institutionalizing efforts of gifted academic entrepreneurs—the meeting mavens, dean-savvy horse-traders, program builders, and other senior patrons who saw value in this work and recruited us into their networks, book projects, panels, grants, special issues, and centers. Additional credit goes to the receptive deans who transcended their innate wariness—"Howard Johnson's, for God's sake!"—and supported innovative, interdisciplinary, cost-effective courses that always filled.

That food had market worth was evidenced by the exceptional attention paid to our books and conferences by enthusiastic journalists. When *Appetite for Change* appeared in 1989, I had over fifty press interviews. While some were of the drive-time radio, get-a-load-of-this-goofy-egghead variety, others were with knowledgeable food writers excited that academia was finally waking up to what they did for a living. The admiration was often mutual, as when I had several delightful conversations with Molly O'Neill of the *New York Times*, who gently cultivated a number of academic sources in the 1990s. A brief chat with the *Times*'s resident epicure, R.W. Apple was also memorable, as was the opportunity to dine with Julia Child just as she was working to establish Boston University's pioneering gastronomy program. Speaking appearances at food conferences in San Francisco, Santa Fe, Montreal, Ithaca, Ann Arbor, and Washington D.C. brought exceptional dining experiences. One should not underestimate the role of unusually good food in building the food studies field—and in a few cases building scholarly ties to commercial interests, as when culinary institutes and professional associations sponsored food history workshops, or olive oil marketers subsidized meetings that celebrated the "Mediterranean diet." Even the federal and foundation-sponsored "obesity epidemic" conferences of the early 2000s were smartly catered; such meals surpassed the usual academic conference fare which, apparently still wedded to the old mind-over-body hierarchies, remains largely indifferent to the benefits of commensality. Indeed, food was a rare scholarly field that could count on a commissary of enthusiastic chefs, many of them attuned to the key ideologies of the sustainable food movement. Some of them even crossed over to enroll in the new food studies programs. And the celebrity interactions more than compensated for the ironic smirks in the faculty dining room.

The publicity also encouraged risk-taking acquisition editors at major presses, both university and commercial, to fight with their stodgy boards and corporate overlords for still more book contracts for food scholars. By 2000 or so, those preliminary battles had been won, publishing opportunities abounded, and food panels were regularly scheduled at mainstream history conferences. Moreover, food history collections were being organized at major research libraries, museums, and online. Perhaps most significantly, with senior mentors no longer advising their juniors to wait to "do food" until tenure, the number of graduate students working on food in once conservative mainline programs increased noticeably.

We should beware of overhistoricizing the rise of food studies, however. Whether outside -isms or inside agents, these factors simply brought attention to food. Had the subject not been inherently interesting, the attention would have moved on to something else. In an era dominated by post-structuralist, social constructionist, antiessentialist paradigms, it's not often that we academics argue for the intrinsic worth of anything. And while as a historian I believe that meanings are subjective, relative, contested, and shifting, as a fan I'm not so sure. I use the sports word *fan* deliberately, as I first learned the meaning of "intrinsic" from my freshman year philosophy professor, who illustrated the concept by citing the pleasure of hearing the sound of a solidly hit baseball leaving the bat. Just as a baseball fan does not need to explain the delights of good wood, a food scholar should not need to explain a fascination with how people grow, cook, and eat their meals. While academics may have only recently begun to notice food, once they do notice it, they realize that humans have been thinking about food literally forever. Interest in food may be said to be archetypal, though the variety of ways that interest is expressed is almost infinite. That omnivorous variability, too, is interesting, even ennobling, as no other creature has invented so many ingenious ways to convert the raw into the cooked. No wonder cooking shows are so popular!

Whatever the reasons for the initial attention to food, by the early 2000s the academic infrastructure was almost ready to accommodate the second wave of interest in serious food issues, spawned by popularizers such as Michael Pollan, Eric Schlosser, and Carlo Petrini and reinforced by an infrastructure of restauranteurs, sustainable producers, and vendors who spread the word—and taste—of the "good food" movement across the gentrifying landscape.[27] So now that we have the public's attention, what can we tell them about food history?

Well, both quite a lot and not so much. Even a rudimentary historical overview of food production stands as a sobering corrective to much of the nostalgia found in popular discourse, especially the common assertion that "industrial agriculture" is largely a post-World War II invention—a reversible aberration in an otherwise benign narrative of small organic "family farms."[28] Tell that to the slaves described by Sidney Mintz in his seminal history of sixteenth- and seventeenth-century industrial sugar plantations, or to British peasants whose lands were enclosed in the same period, or to the opportunistic tobacco exporters who wrecked the Chesapeake Bay in the eighteenth century, or the nineteenth-century wheat farmers who ploughed up much of the world's dry lands to meet world demand for commercial bread.[29] Speaking of bread, historians can also contest popular myths of virtuous home-baking grandmothers. Similarly, family historians can challenge assumptions that all or even most mothers loved cooking from scratch, or that instructive, congenial "family meals" were timeless and universal until the 1960s ruined everything.[30] And they can question assertions that meat—or any other basic food—has "always" been the preference of all peoples—a claim voiced by a wide range of advocates, from radical environmentalists and reformers to diet doctors and cattlemen; conversely they can dispute current assertions that the "industrial meat" of "animal factories" is a particularly recent, North American, or wholly unfortunate development.[31] As every history student should know—and as the other essays in this collection will attest—it is a mistake to confuse an archetypal interest in food with a belief that particular modes of food production and consumption are also archetypal.

At the same, we historians should be humble when it comes to overstating what we know. Indeed, I can say that, after all the reading I've done since 1990, I am considerably less sure about food history than I was before 1990. The more local variations we uncover, the harder it is to synthesize, generalize, and moralize. This humility may be one of history's more useful benefits—a counter to conventional wisdoms and certainties. Loaded words like "traditional," "old," "timeless," "primal," "never," and "always" should be red flags to every historian. One of the most appealing aspects of our job as teachers is helping students to challenge such absolutes and thus be better armed for the battles of the family dinner table (or the op-ed columns). To be honest, we don't know really know what most people ate for most of history, nor do we know how they prepared it, whether they liked it, or what it tasted like. Since people lie, distort, or just can't remember, we don't even know much about current food behaviors, much less those of the past. Food history faces a fundamental source problem—the bane of all dissertation proposals. At the very basic level, our main data tend to be literary and idealized representations written for elites (or their servants). This is true even of contemporary marketing research, which is heavily skewed to the desires of the upper middle classes. One lesson I learned from spending twenty years researching and teaching about television is that you can't possibly understand TV's cultural appeal and influence if all you watch is PBS. Yet the culinary equivalent of *Masterpiece Theatre* is pretty much all that we food historians have available to scrutinize. This problem faces historians of all the senses: we also don't know what Beethoven's fortepiano sonatas really sounded like (of course, he didn't know either), or what Michelangelo's frescos looked like before electrical lighting and good eyeglasses. True, we can attempt to reconstruct those experiences, but the variables are daunting; try interrogating a New York bagel connoisseur's claim that "it's the water." At best we may hope for rough approximations which, while better than nothing, are still pretty rough. Archaeologists are adept at wringing the most meaning out of the least data, but the best of them wisely resist overextrapolation of the sort lampooned in David Macaulay's *Motel of the Mysteries* (1979), in which an overeager amateur archaeologist's 4022 A.D. excavation of a 1985 roadside site (the "Tootin' C'Mon Motel") yields speculations about artifacts such as "the Sacred Seal" (a "Do Not Disturb" doorhanger), "the Great Altar" (a television stand replete with containers for "libations and offerings"), and "the Sacred Urn" (a porcelain toilet bowl), souvenir replicas of which were available as a coffee set (one pitcher, four cups) in the museum shop.[32] To be sure, having just realized that Macaulay's spoof was published the same year as my own earnest roadside research, my dean's disbelief ("Howard Johnson's, for God's sake!") now seems more understandable than I'd originally thought. Sometimes it takes a while to put things in their historical context.

That's not to say that the quest is fruitless. It's the detective investigation, along with the debates over the meaning of the scant discoveries, that makes history such fun. Or as my countercultural informants said about the dense and often inedible loaves they baked in sketchy communal kitchens, it's the process, not the product.

NOTES

1. Richard Hofstadter, *Anti-Intellectualism in American Life* (New York: Knopf, 1963) and *The Paranoid Style in American Politics* (New York: Knopf, 1965).

2. Warren James Belasco, *Americans on the Road: From Autocamp to Motel* (Cambridge: MIT Press, 1979).

3. Warren James Belasco, "Toward a Culinary Common Denominator: The Rise of Howard Johnson's," *Journal of American Culture* 2 (1979): 503–18.

4. Warren James Belasco, *Appetite for Change: How the Counterculture Took on the Food Industry, 1966–1988* (New York: Pantheon Books, 1989). For examples of early work on food reformers, see Gerald Carson, *Cornflake Crusade* (New York: Rinehart, 1957) and Ronald Deutsch, *The Nuts Among the Berries* (New York: Ballantine Books, 1961). Three exceptions to the "nuts" theme: Stephen Nissenbaum, *Sex, Diet, and Debility in Jacksonian America: Sylvester Graham and Health Reform* (Westport: Greenwood Press, 1980); Harvey Green, *Fit for America: Health, Fitness, Sport, and American Society* (New York: Pantheon Books, 1986); and James C. Whorton, *Crusaders for Fitness: The History of American Health Reformers* (Princeton: Princeton University Press, 1982). The two most useful surveys at that time were written by nonacademics: Waverley Root and Richard de Rochemont, *Eating in America: A History* (New York: William Morrow, 1976) and Reay Tannahill, *Food in History* (London: Penguin, 1973).

5. E.g., Peter Farb and George Armelagos, *Consuming Passions: The Anthropology of Eating* (Boston: Houghton Mifflin, 1980); Joan Dye Gussow, ed., *The Feeding Web: Issues in Nutritional Ecology* (Palo Alto: Bull Publishing, 1978); Linda Keller Brown and Kay Mussell, eds., *Ethnic and Regional Foodways in the United States: The Performance of Group Identity* (Knoxville: University of Tennessee Press, 1984); Elisabeth Rozin, "The Structure of Cuisine," in *The Psychobiology of Human Food Selection,* ed. Lewis M. Barker (Westport: AVI Publishing, 1982), 189–203; Todd Gitlin, *The Whole World is Watching: Mass Media in the Making and Unmaking of the New Left* (Berkeley: University of California Press, 1980).

6. Roland Barthes, "Toward a Psychosociology of Food Consumption," in *Food and Drink in History,* ed. Robert Forster and Orest Ranum (Baltimore: Johns Hopkins University Press, 1979), 166–173; Roland Barthes, *Mythologies,* trans. Richard Howard and Annette Lavers (1972; repr. New York: Hill and Wang, 2012).

7. E.g., Calvin Trillin, *American Fried: Adventures of a Happy Eater* (New York: Vintage Books, 1979); John L. Hess and Karen Hess, *The Taste of America* (1977; repr. Urbana: University of Illinois Press, 2000); Jim Hightower, *Eat Your Heart Out: Food Profiteering in America* (New York: Crown, 1975).

8. Sidney Mintz, *Sweetness and Power: The Place of Sugar in Modern History* (New York: Penguin, 1986); Harvey Levenstein, *Revolution at the Table: The Transformation of the American Diet* (Berkeley: University of California Press, 2003); Stephen Mennell, *All Manners of Food: Eating and Taste in England and France from the Middle Ages to the Present,* 2nd ed. (1985; repr.

Urbana: University of Illinois Press, 1995); Joan Jacobs Brumberg, *Fasting Girls: The History of Anorexia Nervosa* (New York: Vintage, 2000); Margaret Visser, *Much Depends on Dinner: The Extraordinary History and Mythology, Allure and Obsessions, Perils and Taboos, of an Ordinary Meal* (New York: Collier, 1986).

9. Particularly helpful were Todd Gitlin, *Inside Prime Time* (Berkeley: University of California Press, 2000) and John G. Cawelti, *Adventure, Mystery, and Romance: Formula Stories as Art and Popular Culture* (Chicago: University of Chicago Press, 1976).

10. For food marketing data I relied heavily on trade publications such as *Advertising Age, Food Technology,* and *Nation's Restaurant News,* as well as readable introductory texts such as Philip Kotler, *Marketing Management,* 4th ed. (Englewood Cliffs: Prentice-Hall, 1980).

11. For a history of the commodity chains concept, see Shane Hamilton, "Analyzing Commodity Chains: Linkages or Restraints?" in *Food Chains: From Farmyard to Shopping Cart,* ed. Warren Belasco and Roger Horowitz (Philadelphia: University of Pennsylvania Press, 2009), 16–25.

12. Visser, *Much Depends on Dinner;* John McPhee, *Oranges* (New York: Farrar, Straus and Giroux, 2000); Elisabeth Rozin, *The Primal Cheeseburger: A Generous Helping of Food History Served on a Bun* (New York: Penguin, 1994); Mark Kurlansky, *Cod* (New York: Penguin, 1998); Michael Pollan, *The Botany of Desire* (New York: Random House, 2001).

13. Henry Hobhouse, *Seeds of Change: Five Plants That Transformed Mankind* (New York: Harper and Row, 1986).

14. Mintz, *Sweetness and Power,* 151–58.

15. The first reevaluations of women's work looked at the history of housework, with food chores just one part of women's domestic drudgery: see e.g., Susan Strasser, *Never Done: A History of American Housework* (New York: Pantheon Books, 1982); Ruth Schwartz Cowan, *More Work for Mother: The Ironies of Household Technology from the Open Hearth to the Microwave* (New York: Basic Books, 1983). Later studies tended to take a somewhat more positive view of women's foodwork: see Arlene Voski Avakian, ed., *Through the Kitchen Window: Women Writers Explore the Intimate Meanings of Food and Cooking* (Boston: Beacon Press, 1997); Avakian and Barbara Haber, eds., *From Betty Crocker to Feminist Food Studies: Critical Perspectives on Women and Food* (Amherst: University of Massachusetts Press, 2005). For more feminist recentering of food, see Brumberg, *Fasting Girls;* Amy Bentley, *Eating for Victory: Food Rationing and the Politics of Domesticity* (Urbana: University of Illinois Press, 1998); Anne L. Bower, ed., *Recipes for Reading: Community Cookbooks, Stories, Histories* (Amherst: University of Massachusetts Press, 1997).

16. Hasia Diner, *Hungering for America: Italian, Irish, and Jewish Foodways in the Age of Migration* (Cambridge: Harvard University Press, 2001); Donna Gabaccia, *We Are What We Eat: Ethnic Foods and the Making of Americans* (Cambridge: Harvard University Press, 1998); Jeffrey M. Pilcher, *¡Que Vivan Los Tamales! Food and the Making of Mexican Identity* (Albuquerque: University of New Mexico Press, 1998); Barbara G. Shortridge and James R. Short-

ridge, eds., *The Taste of American Place: A Reader on Regional and Ethnic Foods* (Lanham: Rowman & Littlefield, 1998); Peter Scholliers, ed. *Food, Drink and Identity: Cooking, Eating and Drinking in Europe since the Middle Ages* (Oxford: Berg, 2001).

17. Frances Moore Lappe, *Diet for a Small Planet* (1971; repr. New York: Ballantine Books, 1991); Jeremy Rifkin, *Beyond Beef: The Rise and the Fall of the Cattle Culture* (New York: Plume, 1992).

18. Donald Worster, *Rivers of Empire: Water, Aridity, and the Growth of the American West* (New York: Oxford University Press, 1992); Alfred W. Crosby, Jr., *The Columbian Exchange: Biological and Cultural Consequences of 1492* (1972; repr. Westport: Praeger, 2003); Alfred W. Crosby, Jr., *Ecological Imperialism: The Biological Expansion of Europe, 900–1900* (Cambridge: Cambridge University Press, 2003); William Cronon, *Nature's Metropolis: Chicago and the Great West* (New York: Norton, 1991).

19. For a discussion of healthism as well as a review of the "obesity epidemic" literature: Julie Guthman, *Weighing In: Obesity, Food Justice, and the Limits of Capitalism* (Berkeley: University of California Press, 2011). For histories of the body: Joan Jacobs Brumberg, *The Body Project: An Intimate History of American Girls* (New York: Random House, 1997); Peter N. Stearns, *Fat History: Bodies and Beauty in the Modern West* (New York: New York University Press, 2002); Hillel Schwartz, *Never Satisfied: A Cultural History of Diets, Fantasies, and Fat* (New York: Free Press, 1986).

20. Unlike modernism, which is one-directional—full speed ahead!—the recombinant style mixes and matches disconnected pieces of past and present into a picturesque and highly marketable collage of images, stories, and associations. My usage derives from Todd Gitlin's examination of how television programmers address viewers' ambivalent demands for shows that are both new and nostalgic, innovative and familiar. "The fusion of these pressures is what produces the recombinant style, which collects the old in new packages and hopes for a magical synthesis." Gitlin, *Inside Prime Time,* 78, quoted in Warren Belasco, *Meals to Come: A History of the Future of Food* (Berkeley: University of California Press, 2006), 220.

21. Amy Trubek, *The Taste of Place: A Cultural Journey into Terroir* (Berkeley: University of California Press, 2008); Kolleen Guy, *When Champagne Became French* (Baltimore: Johns Hopkins University Press, 2003).

22. Raymond Grew, ed., *Food in Global History* (Boulder: Westview Press, 1999); Jeffrey M. Pilcher, *Food in World History* (New York: Routledge, 2006); Kenneth F. Kiple and Kriemhild Conee Ordelas, eds., *The Cambridge World History of Food,* 2 vols. (Cambridge: Cambridge University Press, 2000). On McDonaldization and glocalization, see James L. Watson, ed., *Golden Arches East: McDonald's in East Asia* (Palo Alto: Stanford University Press, 2006).

23. For pre-1990s European historiography: Scholliers, "Twenty-five Years of Studying *un Phénomène Social Total:* Food History Writing on Europe in the Nineteenth and Twentieth Centuries," *Food, Culture and Society* 10 (2007): 449–71. For an overview of Mintz's influence: Amy Bentley, ed., "Special Issue: *Sweetness and Power:* Rethinking Sidney Mintz's Classic Work," *Food and Foodways* 16 (2008).

24. The best and most recent presentations of this critique are Guthman, *Weighing In,* and Josée Johnston and Shyon Baumann, *Foodies: Democracy and Distinction in the Gourmet Foodscape* (New York: Routledge, 2010).

25. Richard Hofstadter, *The Age of Reform: From Bryan to F.D.R.* (New York: Knopf, 1955); Green, *Fit for America;* Nissenbaum, *Sex, Diet and Debility;* Levenstein, *Revolution at the Table;* Madeleine Ferrières, *Sacred Cow, Mad Cow: A History of Food Fears,* trans. Jody Gladding (New York: Columbia University Press, 2006).

26. Belasco, *Appetite for Change;* Johnston and Baumann, *Foodies;* David Kamp, *The United States of Arugula: The Sun Dried, Cold Pressed, Dark Roasted, Extra Virgin Story of the American Food Revolution* (New York: Random House, 2007); Samuel Fromartz, *Organic, Inc.: Natural Foods and How They Grew* (Orlando: Harcourt, 2006).

27. Michael Pollan, *The Omnivore's Dilemma: A Natural History of Four Meals* (New York: Penguin, 2006); Eric Schlosser, *Fast Food Nation: The Dark Side of the All-American Meal* (Boston: Houghton-Mifflin, 2001); Carlo Petrini, *Slow Food: The Case for Taste,* trans. William McCuaig (New York: Columbia University Press, 2001).

28. Peter D. McClelland, *Sowing Modernity: America's First Agricultural Revolution* (Ithaca: Cornell University Press, 1997); Steven Stoll, *The Fruits of Natural Advantage: Making the Industrial Countryside in California* (Berkeley: University of California Press, 1998); Cronon, *Nature's Metropolis;* David B. Danbom, *Born in the Country: A History of Rural America* (Baltimore: Johns Hopkins University Press, 1995).

29. Mintz, *Sweetness and Power;* Lois Green Carr, Russell R. Menard, and Lorena S. Walsh, *Robert Cole's World: Agriculture and Society in Early Maryland* (Chapel Hill: University of North Carolina Press, 1991); Donald Worster, *Dust Bowl: The Southern Plains in the 1930s* (New York: Oxford University Press, 1979).

30. Tracey Deutsch, "Memories of Mothers in the Kitchen: Local Foods, History, and Women's Work," *Radical History Review* 110 (Spring 2011): 167–77; Katherine Leonard Turner, "Buying, Not Cooking: Ready-to-Eat Food in American Urban Working-Class Neighborhoods, 1880–1930," *Food, Culture and Society* 9 (2006): 13–39; Rachel Laudan, "A Plea for Culinary Modernism: Why We Should Love New, Fast, Processed Food," *Gastronomica: The Journal of Food and Culture* 1 (Winter 2001): 36–44; Alice Julier, "Family and Domesticity," *A Cultural History of Food in the Modern Age,* ed. Amy Bentley (London: Berg, 2012), 145–64; Marc Jacobs and Peter Scholliers, eds. *Eating Out in Europe: Picnics, Gourmet Dining and Snacks since the Late Eighteenth Century* (Oxford: Berg, 2003).

31. A good compendium of such claims can be found in Lierre Keith's *The Vegetarian Myth: Food, Justice, and Sustainability* (Crescent City: Flashpoint Press, 2009), and it is a fundamental premise of Michael Pollan's *Omnivore's Dilemma.* On meat history: Jeffrey M. Pilcher, *The Sausage Rebellion: Public Health, Private Enterprise, and Meat in Mexico City, 1890–1917* (Albuquerque: University of New Mexico Press, 2006); Roger Horowitz, *Putting Meat on the American Table: Taste, Technology, Transformation* (Baltimore: Johns Hopkins

University Press, 2006); Paula Lee Young, ed., *Meat, Modernity, and the Rise of the Slaughterhouse* (Durham: University of New Hampshire Press, 2008).

32. David Macaulay, *Motel of the Mysteries* (Boston: Houghton Mifflin, 1979). For a good sample of rigorous food archaeology: Martin Jones, *Feast: Why Humans Share Food* (Oxford: Oxford University Press, 2007).

SELECTED BIBLIOGRAPHY

Barlösius, Eva. "The history of diet as a part of the *vie matérielle* in France." In *European Food History: A Research Review,* edited by Hans J. Teuteberg, 90–108. Leicester: Leicester University Press, 1992.

Belasco, Warren. "Food Matters: Perspectives on an Emerging Field." In *Food Nations: Selling Taste in Consumer Societies,* edited by Warren Belasco and Philip Scranton, 2–23. New York: Routledge, 2002.

Bender, Daniel, and Jeffrey M. Pilcher. "Editor's Introduction: Radicalizing the History of Food." *Radical History Review* 110 (Spring 2011): 1–7.

Claflin, Kyri W., and Peter Scholliers. "Introduction: Surveying Global Food Historiography." In *Writing Food History: A Global Perspective,* edited by Kyri W. Claflin and Peter Scholliers, 1–8. London: Berg, 2012.

Coclanis, Peter. "Breaking New Ground: From the History of Agriculture to the History of Food Systems." *Historical Methods* 38 (2005): 5–13.

Ferguson, Priscilla. "Review article. Eating Orders: Markets, Menus, and Meals." *Journal of Modern History* 77 (2005): 679–700.

Fitzgerald, Gerard J., and Gabriella M. Petrick. "In Good Taste: Rethinking American History with Our Palates." *Journal of American History* 95 (2008): 392–404.

Freedman, Paul. "Introduction: A New History of Cuisine." In *Food: The History of Taste,* edited by Paul Freedman, 7–33. Berkeley: University of California Press, 2007.

Grew, Raymond. "Food and Global History." In *Food in Global History,* edited by Raymond Grew, 1–29. Boulder: Westview Press, 1999.

Scholliers, Peter. "Meals, Food Narratives, and Sentiments of Belonging in Past and Present." In *Food, Drink and Identity: Cooking, Eating and Drinking in Europe Since the Middle Ages,* edited by Peter Scholliers, 3–22. London: Berg, 2001.

———. "Twenty-five Years of Studying *un Phénomène Social Total*: Food History Writing on Europe in the Nineteenth and Twentieth Centuries." *Food, Culture and Society: An International Journal of Multidisciplinary Research* 10 (2007): 449–71.

Smith, Andrew F. "Historiography," In *The Oxford Encyclopedia of Food and Drink in America,* edited by Andrew F. Smith, 1: 669–76. New York: Oxford University Press, 2004.

PART ONE

Regional Histories

CHAPTER I

Premodern Europe

KEN ALBALA

In the two thousand year span on which this chapter focuses, there is scarcely a topic that cannot be discussed as essentially concerned with food. This is hardly surprising since growing, processing, and consuming food has been the preoccupation of most people on earth until very recently. Nonetheless, the traditional historical focus on topics such as war, the rise and fall of empires and great leaders, social strife, and great intellectual movements has obscured the fact that human history is at its very core about obtaining basic nourishment. This is true not only of ordinary people but even of powerful rulers whose attempts to expand borders, seek new trade routes for exotic goods, and conquer colonial outposts are more often than not motivated by the need either to feed people with common staples or to entice them with rare edible luxuries. The ancient Greek city-states spreading in search of fertile arable land on which to grow wheat, medieval merchants carrying spices grown halfway around the earth, or Portuguese colonists manning their sugar plantations in Brazil with African slave labor—all these can be told as food histories. When examining these topics through the lens of food, what might have seemed to be familiar terrain suddenly seems new, and new vistas are opened both for teachers and for students.

Consider first one of the most momentous events in European as well as global history: the encounter of Europeans with Native Americans beginning with Columbus. The story can be told many different ways: Columbus the explorer and expert navigator, Columbus the

Christ-bearer carrying the cross over the ocean to civilize the native populations, or Columbus the inept greedy ruler whose cruelty led to the decimation of millions of humans.[1] Each version is both politically charged and historiographically situated in a particular time and place with its own unique concerns. Since the publication of Alfred Crosby's *Columbian Exchange,* historians have increasingly seen these events as essentially a food narrative.[2] Columbus was clearly seeking a westward route to Asia to trade in spices and other luxuries. His journal is filled with reports of culinary and medicinal plants he expected to encounter in Asia, and to his dying day he never realized he had discovered a new continent. More importantly, American plants and animals, rather than Asian spices, were brought to Europe: the tomato, chili peppers, maize, chocolate, squashes, and potatoes, as well as turkeys. Conversely European species such as wheat, pigs, cows, and chickens were brought to the Americas. Of course European diseases were also brought to the New World and had a devastating impact on native peoples.

Further research in the past few decades has complicated the story. Europeans did not immediately accept many American plants; it took centuries to adopt the tomato and potato.[3] Moreover, European settlers in the New World were reluctant to give up their wheat bread and European recipes, and corn remained the staple of the impoverished Native Americans, creating social and ethnic divisions based on diet.[4] It took much longer than might be supposed for cuisines incorporating ingredients from both sides of the Atlantic to develop.

This is merely the best known of subjects retold as a food story, and it has generally made its way into textbooks and curricula in grade schools and colleges. But there are many other narratives that can be recast in terms of food history to excellent effect.

The most profitable way to approach this vast expanse of time, from ancient to early modern civilizations, is by focusing on several interconnected themes. A useful first theme is the examination of how foodways and culture are shaped by the ways in which people interact with their geographical setting, how they exploit natural resources, and what technologies they employ in processing food. The gradual expansion of trade networks is a natural extension of this topic. So too is the social meaning of individual ingredients and recipes, and the discussion of cuisine as an expression of cultural, political, and artistic values. This might lead to examining the impact of ideas—philosophical, religious, and scientific—upon eating habits and prohibitions. What follows is a chronological discussion of how these various food-related themes relate to successive periods in premodern history and how historians have dealt with these topics. Each section begins with a discussion of historiography then proceeds to pedagogy.

Most food historians speak of the relative newness of the field, how perhaps twenty years ago the topic of food history raised suspicious eyebrows or uncomfortable laughter. There certainly were people who did not consider it part of a serious curriculum. We can be grateful that that has changed, and dramatically—hence the proliferation of books and courses offered in universities across the country and abroad. But this narrative of sudden efflorescence can be countered with examples of what is undeniably food history written before the twentieth century, to show that current scholarship did not sprout up spontaneously without precedent, and that there have always been serious scholars writing about what undeniably has been a central concern to all people throughout history.

The pedagogical discussion within each section briefly recounts the major themes and sources so that interested historians unfamiliar with food history can better incorporate it into the classroom. Teaching strategies per se are not discussed, but incorporating primary documents for analysis, looking at images, and discussing influential ideas are, as with any historical topic, paramount.

ANCIENT GREECE

While the cultural, artistic, and economic accomplishments of ancient Greece are a well traversed subject, how these achievements relate to food culture is less familiar and rarely covered in the curriculum today. On the other hand, food in antiquity was among the first topics studied from a historical vantage point. As the father of history in the Western tradition, Herodotus recorded many of the food habits of places he visited, especially Egypt. His comments on the bounty of the Nile are justly famous.[5] Even more important is the *Deipnosophists* by Athenaeus, written in Naucratis in the early third century C.E. and essentially a compendium of food references in ancient Greek literature. Many writers in late antiquity were concerned with the food habits of the past; particularly good examples are Iamblicus and Porphyry, third-century A.D. philosophers who described the vegetarianism of Pythagoras, who preceded them by seven hundred years.

The systematic study of ancient foodways with an objective historical bent really began in the Renaissance, as scholars recovered ancient texts and began to comment on them critically.[6] The first editions of classical food texts, most notably the Latin cookbook of Apicius, were also published in this era, giving readers a direct glimpse at ancient cuisine.[7] It was also in this era that the first food encyclopedias were written about food habits around the known world.[8] Unlike works on most other food history topics, such world food encyclopedias have been in constant production for the past five centuries, reaching a peak perhaps in the late nineteenth century, though the flow of such works is by no means abated today.[9]

To grapple in the classroom with this vast literature, the geography of Greece is a good place to start. Greece is a mountainous appendage dangling from the southeast edge of Europe and scattered on islands stretching across the Aegean Sea. Difficult terrain meant that political unification was correspondingly difficult, especially when compared with other ancient civilizations such as Sumer and Egypt. This may account for the development of independent city-states. More importantly, with the rise in population that preceded the classical era, finding enough arable land for growing wheat became a problem for most cities. On the other hand being situated near the sea meant that most cities developed naval technologies for fishing and traveling. Founding colonies was the natural solution to the problem of insufficient grain production. The Athenians founded cities around the Black Sea; other city-states spread to the southern Italian peninsula, Sicily, and as far as Massila (Marseilles in modern France). The Greek terrain and climate was also ideally suited to grape and olive production, both products that could be transformed into easily transported goods—wine and oil—and carried by Greek merchants.

The proliferation of wealthy citizens to a great extent necessitated the development of political systems that afforded them participation, democracy included. The interaction through trade with people across the Mediterranean gave the Greeks a cosmopolitan outlook. Most importantly, having wealth relatively evenly spread among the populace provided opportunities for patronage of the arts, theater, literature, and of course cooking. The professional cook was a stock figure in Greek drama. The Greeks also created the earliest known cookbooks, fragments of which survive in the work of Athenaeus.[10] Principal among these is *Hedypatheia* of Archestratus, probably composed in Gela on the southern coast of Sicily.[11] Archestratus's knowledge of where the best fish and bread could be found throughout the Mediterranean attests not only to wide trade networks and a Greek propensity to travel, but also to a certain connoisseurship among the Greeks. His criticism of those who ruin good ingredients with fussy preparation or overseasoning suggests that most people thought such dishes were a mark of distinction, but the true gourmand understood better.

In all cultures the appearance of culinary literature is matched by its ideological opposite: how to eat well in the interest of health. The dietary literature of the Greeks forms the foundation for all Western medicine. The Hippocratic authors devoted significant space to humoral physiology, but its fullest expression was in the works of Galen of Pergamum.[12] Galen classified every known food according to its digestibility, usefulness for treating various disorders, and, most importantly, its propensity to increase particular humors within the body (blood, phlegm, bile, and melancholy). Since health was considered a balance of the four humors, diet was typically the first recourse for any distemperature. Food was considered an integral and essential part of the overall regimen for maintaining health in this holistic system. From these ideas about food we get a better appreciation for the Greek attention to the body, beauty, and physical strength since there are diets appropriate for athletes as well as dietary distinctions on the basis of age, gender, and occupation.

Even the great philosophers paid attention to food issues, most infamously Plato who considered cooking a form of pandering to base appetites, and much less noble than medicine, which as an art taught patients to eat well. Plato's denigration of the animal functions of the human body and praise of intellectual pursuits arguably left a long legacy to Western culture, in which eating has been considered mere maintenance, something one should not expend too much energy considering. The fact that Plato could take the normally raucous symposium, usually enlivened with naked flute girls and drinking games and turn it into a philosophical discourse, gives some indication of his influence over ideas about food and drink. Other philosophical schools were equally influential. The Stoics maintained that remaining dispassionate in the face of life's travails gave one inner strength and virtue, and therefore detachment from pleasures such as food made one stronger: the sober and abstemious life was to be preferred. The Epicureans too, despite their reputation through the ages, thought of happiness in life as characterized by maximizing pleasure and avoiding pain. This translated into a lifestyle that was exactly the opposite of sybaritic, since luxuries make one dependent. We can never be sure of finding them, the Stoics concluded, thus the greatest happiness is found in a simple diet.

The fact that so many thinkers recommended abstemiousness suggests that at a certain point the simple Greek diet based on grain, vegetables, pulses, dairy, and olive oil gradually grew more luxurious and wealthy people were eventually able to use food as a mark of distinction. This was certainly true in the Hellenistic world, in the wake of Alexander's conquests, when a common language and currency facilitated trade across a much broader region. Most importantly, trade routes with the East opened up, new fruits such as oranges, peaches, and apricots appeared, followed by the trees that produce them, including trees that require grafting such as the apple. Spices too arrived from India, pepper as well as cinnamon and a new sweetener which remained a rarity in antiquity but would have an enormous impact in later centuries—sugar.[13]

ROME

Food scholarship on ancient Rome, like food scholarship on ancient Greece, was pursued by later historians of later times, including the Renaissance, though Rome was given precedence, given their greater familiarity with Latin. Thus early editions of the primary sources discussed below were among the first books in print, notably the cookbook of Apicius; the medical works of Celsus, which were rediscovered in the Renaissance; the agricultural manuals of authors like Cato, Varro, and Columella; and the *Satyricon* of Petronius, rediscovered in the seventeenth century. These works and many others, including Virgil's *Georgics,* Juvenal's *Satires,* and Martial's *Epigrams,* laid the foundation for an excellent understanding of Roman foodways among scholars. Starting in the Renaissance, archaeology added to this, though it did not reach a scientific stage until the nineteenth century. By the twentieth century, new approaches to history in general had an effect on the study of food in ancient Rome, most notably social and economic history, the history of women, and culinary history.[14]

In the classroom, discussing the history of Rome through food offers countless possibilities. Imperial Rome engulfed the Hellenistic world and adopted its values alongside its luxurious imports. But in the early Republican period that preceded the conquest of Greece, Roman culture was quite different. Perhaps it is an exaggeration to characterize the early Romans as a fierce people, concerned mostly with conquest and farming. It is nonetheless true that the earliest prose work in Latin is the farming manual of Cato the Elder.[15] It is essentially a guide to investing in land and exploiting it to maximize profits, which in his day meant concentrating on value-added crops like grapes and olives that could be processed and sold in cities. Valuable fruits and vegetables were culti-vated as was anything that could turn a profit. The farms Cato describes are not the massive slave-run plantations *(latifundia)* that would later supply the army of the Roman Empire with grain, but rather fairly small operations using a few slaves and hiring workers for the harvest.[16]

With the expansion of the empire, great fortunes were to be made, especially in grain production. Huge *latifundia* using slave labor pro-duced grain, which was then ground in great quantities to feed both armies and growing cities. As Juvenal quipped, bread and circuses (i.e., chariot racing) were enough to keep the masses contented.[17] Juvenal's *Satires* are an excellent way to introduce the social meaning of food in later Roman culture. In one, Juvenal berates his friend for accepting an invitation to a dinner where the host eats fine delicacies and drinks excellent wine while the friend is given scrappy leftovers. Presumably the insult was intentional, to demean the guests. In another satire, Juve-nal invites his friend to his country house to eat homegrown natural and rustic foods of the finest quality. This is a type of gastronomy that deval-ues the extravagant and elite, in favor of true good taste.

The feast of Trimalchio in Petronius's *Satyricon* is among the most fascinating sources in all of food history.[18] In it, the upstart host tries to throw a lavish banquet that ends up as an embarrassing disaster, in the worst taste imaginable. Dormice dipped in honey and sprinkled with poppy seeds are served, among other culinary perversities. Petronius was himself a wealthy patrician and the arbiter of taste under Nero, and this story appears to be a warning to the newly rich not to try to pretend to have taste, which mere money cannot buy. On the other hand, some of Trimalchio's dishes bear a close resemblance to the recipes found in Apicius.[19] There we find dormice, sow's wombs, flamingo tongues, and a riot of contrasting flavors in each dish: *garum* (a salty fermented fish sauce), honey, *sapa* (boiled-down grape must), pepper, and other exotic spices. There are also simpler dishes, but it is difficult to determine to what extent these recipes reflect common Roman taste of the time when the historical figure Apicius lived, the first century C.E., or were merely recipes compiled several centuries later, perhaps even as a primary source for food history. After all, thanks to this cookbook, Apicius's name became a byword for extravagant luxury in the ancient world.

Food references run throughout the comedies of Plautus and are found in the letters of Seneca and the epigrams of Martial—it is fairly safe to say that eating was one of the major preoccupations of the Romans, including the emperors themselves. Although it is certainly written with an ideological bent and intended as a negative lesson, the biography of Heliogabalus attributed to Aelius Lampridius is remarkably detailed about that emperor's deranged customs.[20] Among these are banquets with fake food; food of all one color; food from the same ingredients served in every meal for days and days; and strange foods like camel's heels, cockscombs taken from living birds, and peacock's tongues—dishes Apicius is also said to have served. The account is probably not strictly true, but it makes for an excellent exercise in interpreting historical sources.

CHRISTIANITY AND THE EARLY MIDDLE AGES

Not surprisingly, the history of the early Church was well documented by early historians and theologians beginning in the New Testament and extending to the present. Food was of central concern, first in distinguishing Christians from Jews (by their abandonment of kosher food regulations), and eventually in defining Christian food practices such as fasting. Saint Basil and Saint Jerome are excellent sources for this topic. Medieval theologians commented on food practices extensively, and the entire system of fasting for Lent was reassessed during the Reformation, essentially as a result of historical criticism, since Protestants emphasized the Bible as having greater authority than tradition. Ulrich Zwingli is the best example of reinterpreting the meaning of the Eucharist and fasting by reference to practice in the scriptures. Modern scholarship is also rich in regards to the food practices of Jews at the time of Jesus and thereafter, as well as to the transition to Christianity.[21]

Any discussion of the food history of the early Church must naturally take account of Jewish food rituals and observances, in particular the sacrifice of animals to atone for sins, the complex Levitical laws defining clean and unclean meats, and the role of fasting as an act of penitence both on special holy days like Yom Kippur and for emergencies like impending battle. The early followers of Jesus did not cast these food practices aside entirely—often, they reinterpreted them. Though Christians proclaimed that the Age of Grace had superseded the Age of Law, they believed that food laws continued to be necessary, though in a different form. Avoidance of unclean animals, most notably pork, was abrogated. The sacrifice of Jesus on the cross was said to replace temple sacrifice, for the expiation of sins. But the case of fasting was a little more complex, since like Old Testament figures like Moses and David, Jesus and the apostles fasted. The question was whether communal fasting was required on a regular basis or only during special occasions to appease God's wrath. Eventually the Christian church adopted set dates for fasting, most notably Lent, Saturdays, and the vigils of saints' days, and defined fasting as eating just one meal per say, and abstaining from meat and animal products, rather than complete abstention from food. The original logic was primarily medical in origin. Since meat was believed to be the most nourishing substance, it was understood to be most readily transformed into flesh, blood, and ultimately sperm, in both men and women (both of whom were believed to have sperm). This, they felt, stimulated the libido and inclined people toward sin. Therefore a humorally colder and drier diet, composed of vegetables and bread, was better suited for atonement. There was not, as might be supposed, any real concern for animal welfare in these injunctions.

Fasting was also a particular concern for clergymen and ascetics, who intended to stay celibate year round. Neither the Church nor individual orders within it could forbid meat since many passages in the New Testament insist that all food is good, yet severely limiting it became an ideal. Some ascetics undertook extraordinary feats of self-abnegation, not only bringing themselves to the brink of starvation, but going without sleep and other physical comforts.[22] Monasticism took a more balanced approach, and the Rule of St. Benedict offers a glimpse of the practical compromises made in the feeding practices of a working monastery, including allowing wine for the monks.

Of course not all concerns in these centuries were holy minded. These were also extraordinarily tumultuous years that witnessed invasions of Germanic tribes, the disintegration of the Empire in the west, and serious famines. Massimo Montanari has also described a profound cultural shift from the neat, well-manicured wheat fields of the Romans to the Germanic love for forests themselves as well as hunting and the gathering of wild food.[23] Indeed much of Europe reverted to forests during this period, the population declined, and farming receded onto the best land. This general dearth is perhaps reflected in Charlemagne's *Capitularies,* which ordered regions throughout his empire to grow specific foods so his army would have something to eat when they passed through. Intellectually this era has also usually been characterized as relatively barren, and certainly as regards food writing, dietary, agricultural, and botanical knowledge it is fairly bereft. One exception is the work of a Greek physician in the classical tradition, Anthimus, who visited the court of the Franks in the sixth century and composed a little book about the properties of foodstuffs. He made great concessions to local customs including eating raw bacon and drinking beer, but otherwise the bulk of classical learning regarding food was lost.[24]

THE MIDDLE AGES

Compared to other subfields in the history of food, the Middle Ages have enjoyed a long and sustained record of scholarship. Deep interest began in tandem with the formation of nation-states, when scholars sought to learn the history of their native folk customs and elevate them as worthy of equal reverence beside classical civilizations. This meant publishing new editions of medieval cookbooks and studying food from the antiquarian's perspective, not always very sympathetically.[25] Early commentators could not appreciate the medieval aesthetic for heavily spiced, sweet-and-sour concoctions. In the words of one historian, "These spices played, alas! a great role in the abominable ragoûts in which our forefathers delighted."[26] By the twentieth century a wide array of scholars took direct interest in medieval food, the nutritional status of medieval people, the systems by which they farmed, and food as an essential part of the economy.[27] Food was studied from nearly every angle except the actual cooking and eating of it. This trend continued among Annales School historians who not only wanted to get a better sense of ordinary people's lives over long periods of time, but also approached the topic scientifically, preferring to bolster their arguments with statistical analysis.[28] More recently European scholars have focused more on the cultural side of medieval food history, how food was used as a marker of distinction, what motivated the far-flung trade in spices, and what the many medieval cookbooks really meant.[29] Translation of cookbooks has also been a major part of the scholarship on medieval food.[30] There are many excellent overviews of medieval cuisine as well, from both national and international perspectives.[31]

The so-called high and later Middle Ages (1000–1500), offer an excellent opportunity to introduce the topic of climatic change and demographics across a long period. In a nutshell, Europe grew warmer from the year 1000 until the fourteenth century. The longer growing season and expanded arable space to the north stimulated greater production of food, which in turn led to population growth. Quite simply, when opportunities are positive, people get married and set up households earlier, which expands the fertile years for childbearing, while better nutrition lowers the infant mortality rate. All these phenomena are ultimately connected to food, as are technological innovations such as improved plows that could cut through the heavier soils of Northern Europe; the horse collar, which made the horse a viable plow animal; and crop rotation systems, which require less fallow and provide fodder for animals and fertilizer in the form of manure. Improved waterwheel and windmill technology made possible the grinding of greater quantities of grain, which in turn supported greater populations and the growth of cities. Of course this general pattern is oversimplified here, but it places food at the center of the narrative.

The most prevalent system of exploiting the land was serfdom, at root a system of land tenure whereby a village farmed scattered plots collectively and paid a landlord to whom they were personally subordinate. This payment could take the form of labor service (several days of the week devoted to working the agricultural property, or *demesne,* of the lord of the manor), or fees paid in money to the lord in order to inherit land, to marry, and, sometimes, to use the mill. Another way of extracting revenue from serfs was to take a portion of what they harvested. Whatever the form of tribute they paid, serfs were legally bound to the soil and could not leave at will. Their methods also tended to be traditional: since this was essentially subsistence farming, taking risks and failing could mean starvation. There were many different forms of serfdom throughout Europe. Its dominance was seriously challenged by the arrival of bubonic plague in 1348. The plague was so devastating that it reduced the European population by one third. This completely reversed the demand for labor: peasants could increasingly dictate terms since landlords were desperate to keep them on the land. The initial reaction of the nobility was to pass laws tightening their hold on peasants as well as on laborers in cities, and this prompted rebellions everywhere. In the long run, feudalism changed, rents replaced services owed, and there was greater freedom of enterprise.

Since labor was scarce in the years after the bubonic plague, wages were generally high, and so was the standard of living of survivors. The amount of household income spent on meat increased. In many respects this was the golden age of meat, and this is reflected in cookbooks that contain many recipes for preparing it. It is not that wealthy people did not eat vegetables, they most certainly did, but they could also afford more expensive meats and could prepare them and dress them in ways that were aspirational, often in imitation of their superiors, and which incorporated exotic spices and sugar.[32]

While the Crusades were one impetus for the revival of the spice trade, growing wealth back in Europe also provided incentive for spices and luxury items to be imported from the East, carried primarily by Muslim merchants from Asia and Venetians and Genoese in the Mediterranean. Spices were used for several reasons. As quasi-medicinal drugs they could be used to correct foods and were incorporated in composite pharmaceuticals. Most importantly they were symbols of status, and as middling ranks of people began to take notice, the upper classes had to invent new recipes to maintain their distinction. This is a prime impetus for fashions to change. It is also the reason cookbooks began to proliferate, as a way to teach the latest culinary fashions to up-and-coming chefs.

The most famous cookbook of this era was attributed to Guillaume Tirel, nicknamed Taillevent, who was chef to King Charles V of France. He was even ennobled for his services, with a coat of arms bearing stewpots. Many of his recipes can also be found in earlier cookbooks, so the text of his cookbook, known as the *Viandier*, is not exactly original. Even more interestingly, the recipes are copied in later cookbooks, such as the guide written for a young bride by the anonymous author of *Le Ménagier de Paris*, who was perhaps a lawyer or professional. This suggests that people down the social scale were indeed emulating their superiors and trying to recreate elegant meals, though perhaps without such great expense or in such enormous quantities. Other cookbooks were composed, such as the English *Forme of Cury* written at the court of Richard II, the Catalan *Libre de Sent Sovi*, and several anonymous Italian cookbooks.

The late Middle Ages also witnessed a revival of classical learning, much of the material for which came via Arabic translations from Greek, which were in turn translated into Latin. Aristotle was the most important text used in the new universities, but medical literature like Galen's work and Arabic texts based on it by authors such as Avicenna, Rhases, and Isaac Judaeus initiated the revival of ancient dietary medicine. Agricultural texts which revived many classical practices were also composed, among them Pietro Crescenzi's.[33]

Finally, the impact of religion on eating habits was no less profound than in other eras. Not only was fasting thoroughly entrenched, but exemptions could be purchased by individuals or even whole cities, permitting them, for example, to eat butter or other animal products during fasting periods. How people, and in particular religious women, interpreted these strictures has been the subject of many detailed studies, some suggesting that ascetic women suffered from a form of ano-rexia.[34] The motivation to fast as well as to take the Eucharist as nour-ishment must be understood in historical context, which of course is totally different from the context that produces modern eating disor-ders.

THE RENAISSANCE

Historiographically, the Renaissance was an invention of nineteenth-century scholars and remains problematic as a distinct time period eco-nomically, socially and indeed culinarily. As an intellectual movement, recovering ancient texts, reading them in Greek, and publishing them doubtless marked a major reorientation. Galen, for example, was read in the original, and there was a major revival of his writings, and there-after the Hippocratic corpus. Many new dietary writings were written in the Renaissance as well, and they eventually departed from Greek medical orthodoxy. Apicius, as has been mentioned, was rediscovered in two manuscript copies made at Fulda in the ninth century. How schol-ars of the era interpreted this cookbook is not entirely clear, but they probably did not imitate it as they did other classical arts. The first librarian of the Vatican, Bartolomeo Sacchi, known as Platina, who was also among the first to read Apicius for many centuries, wrote in his own cookbook and dietary that modern cuisine was decidedly superior. After a recipe for *blancmanger*, a thoroughly medieval dish of pounded chicken, sugar, rosewater, and almond milk bound with rice starch, he says, "I have always preferred this to Apician condiments, nor is there any reason why the tastes of our ancestors should be preferred to our own, for even if we are surpassed by them in nearly all the arts, never-theless in taste alone we are not vanquished."[35] On the other hand, this comparison suggests that he may have tried the old recipes.

As for modern scholarship on food in the Renaissance, which in this case extends into the sixteenth century and beyond, there are specialized studies of dietaries and fine dining, as well as food from a literary angle, and modern translations of Renaissance-era cookbooks.[36] In terms of the lives of ordinary people, the social and political structure and virtu-ally all other topics relating to food, the Renaissance is merely an exten-sion of the Middle Ages, and the decisive changes occurred in the six-teenth century, which ushered in the early modern period. For the most part even works with the title Renaissance in them are about the early modern era.

THE EARLY MODERN PERIOD

In traditional historiography, three major events signal the passage into the early modern period—the discovery of the New World by Europeans, the Reformations of the Church, and the development of the nation-state. Each is in its own way related to food, as the example of Columbus at the start of this essay shows. Food scholarship on this period has been divided between the quantitative analyses of nutrition, trade, and food regulations on the one hand, and the more cultural studies of consumption, social history, and ideas about food that dominate more recent work. Interestingly, much of the best work has not been done by historians, but in related fields, by anthropologists and sociologists. Sidney Mintz's influential *Sweetness and Power* and Stephen Mennell's *All Manners of Food* are two of the best examples.[37] The former traces the impact of sugar production on the world economy, slavery, diet, and a host of other topics. Mennell compares English and French cookbooks as reflections of each country's unique social and political structure, the English based more on land with a representative government, while the French court, being more centralized, monopolized standards of taste. As with other periods, the culinary history of early modern Europe has also emerged as a distinct subfield.[38]

The most important factor separating the early modern era is a shift in the economy, prompted by a demographic surge. The rise in population drove down the demand for labor and wages sank. The gap between rich and poor widened, and the social meaning of food according to class intensified in line with increased stratification. Not everyone suffered and in fact industrious protocapitalists and nobles fared well, especially in procuring foodstuffs or luxury items. This was a time of agricultural innovation—introducing new crops and using new rotation systems, intensive cultivation, and irrigation systems—and an awakened interest in agriculture in general.[39] There were also numerous agricultural treatises composed in this era.[40]

The development of the modern nation-state also figures prominently in the food history of this era, partly in the emergence of distinct national cuisines, but also in the elaboration of manners, which are said to have become more complex and refined as the state increasingly monopolized violence. Hence the banishment of sharp knives from the table, the introduction of forks, and the proliferation of books on manners like Erasmus's *De Civilitate Morum Puerilium*, so up-and-coming young men could fit into polite courtly society.[41]

The Reformation also directly affected consumption, especially regarding fasting prohibitions. When early reformers examined the Bible closely they realized that although Jesus and his disciples, like Old Testament figures, did fast, these were voluntary fasts undertaken for special occasions. These fasts might be either private or public, but were always designed to appease God's wrath in an emergency or atone for sins in hope of forgiveness. They were not regularly scheduled, and they did not involve merely giving up meat. The latter were traditions added in the early Middle Ages, and at least according to the more fundamentalist sects, they needed to be abandoned. Martin Luther was characteristically uninterested in such outward forms of devotion and believed they could be useful exercises for the faithful, but were not essential for salvation. But for the Reformed tradition, springing from theologians like Ulrich Zwingli, these arbitrary fasting rules had to be abandoned, especially since they were so often abused by means of purchased dispensations. In the end, the Reformed churches did not entirely abolish fasting, they merely restored the Biblical form, especially public fasting during times of distress.

Perhaps more importantly, the Calvinist churches favored frugality and abstemiousness year round, as opposed to the fast and feast mentality of the Middle Ages. Exactly how dour the Puritans really were is still a matter of debate, as even the strictest of Puritans—English, Dutch, or Scottish—still kept wine cellars and drank beer for breakfast. Alcohol was simply too deeply ingrained in this culture to even think about abandoning it.[42] Nonetheless gastronomic simplicity, very much akin to that of the ancient Stoics who influenced Calvin, remained an ideal.

Most importantly the Reformation reexamined the central food ritual of Christianity, the Eucharist. The Reformed Churches insisted that Jesus was merely speaking metaphorically when he said "This is my body," and that therefore the bread is merely a memorial of his sacrifice. The Catholic Church upheld the doctrine of transubstantiation, which posits that the substance of the bread miraculously transforms into the body of Jesus and the wine into his blood, even though the accidents or external form remain as bread and wine. Luther adopted a position somewhere between the two, called consubstantiation, including both the real presence of Christ and the presence of wine and bread. It was these doctrines as well as the maintenance of all the fasting regulations among Catholics, that proved to be the most divisive issues, permanently rending Christianity into separate sects in this period.[43]

The early modern period also witnessed the transformation of nutritional theory and the gradual if not complete breakdown of humoral physiology. Scientific approaches to the study of food and the body were evident in two distinct schools. The iatromechanical school was inspired by the work of Santorio Santorio, who attempted to quantify nutrition by carefully weighing all the food he ingested and excreted for many years to determine which foods were best for the maintenance of weight and health. The iatrochemical school, inspired by Paracelsus and van Helmont, began to think of digestion and other bodily processes in chemical terms, substituting sulfur, mercury, and salts for the four humors. In practice these separate medical systems were jumbled and no truly scientific study of nutrition emerged until the nineteenth century, leaving great room for rampant quackery as well as weight loss diets and religiously inspired diets—none of which entirely disappeared with the advent of modern nutrition.[44]

Lastly, the topic of globalization can also be told as a food story. It begins not with Columbus, but with the Portuguese and their contacts with East Africa in the course of the fifteenth century. Here the slave trade began, and presaged the sugar plantations of the Caribbean and Brazil. By the time Bartholomeu Dias had reached the Cape of Good Hope, it was clear that traveling directly to Asia across the Indian Ocean was possible, which would cut out the Venetian middlemen in the spice trade with Asia. In other words, the Portuguese had found what Columbus was looking for, a direct sea route to Asia. They set up outposts in India, Indonesia, China, and for a while Japan, until the Dutch stole many of these colonies in the seventeenth century. In the wake of Columbus, other Europeans, financed by large nation-states as well as new corporate bodies like the Dutch East India Company, entered into the business of colonization. The English eventually settled along the Eastern coast of North America, the Dutch in New Amsterdam, and the French in Quebec. Most of these new colonies were founded specifically to produce and export luxury items, including tobacco, or to carry new drinks like coffee, tea, and chocolate. It has been argued that caffeinated stimulants were the perfect drink for business-minded nations, and they eventually replaced beer and alcohol for morning and midday refreshment, sweetened, of course, with sugar.[45]

The transition to the modern era can also be told largely in terms of food history. Agricultural innovations in eighteenth-century Europe, the earliest stages of industrial food production, the continuing globalization of the economy, and expansion of trade in consumable goods hinted at the momentous changes that would happen in the modern era.

In conclusion, the history of premodern Europe has always been about food production, processing, and consumption, and it has always been featured in historical works to some extent, though it is only in the past few decades that food is taking center stage in publishing and in the curriculum.

NOTES

1. Samuel Eliot Morison, *Admiral of the Ocean Sea: A Life of Christopher Columbus* (Boston: Little Brown, 1942). Larry Schweikart and Michael Allen, *A Patriot's History of the United States: From Columbus's Great Discovery to the War on Terror* (New York: Sentinel, 2004). Howard Zinn, *A People's History of the United States: 1492–Present* (New York: HarperCollins, 2003); David E. Stannard, *American Holocaust: The Conquest of the New World* (New York: Oxford University Press, 1993).

2. Alfred Crosby, Jr., *The Columbian Exchange: Biological and Cultural Consequences of 1492*, 30th anniversary ed. (Westport: Greenwood Press, 1972; Westport: Praeger, 2003).

3. David Gentilcore, *Pomodoro! A History of the Tomato in Italy* (New York: Columbia University Press, 2010).

4. Jeffrey Pilcher, *Que Vivan los Tamales! Food and the Making of Mexican Identity* (Albuquerque: University of New Mexico Press, 1998).

5. Herodotus, "On the Nile River," *Histories*, II: 19–31.

6. Johannes Wilhelmus Stuckius, *Antiquitatum convivalia libri III* (Zurich: C. Froschovius, 1582); Petrus Ciacconius, *De Triclinio Romano* (Rome: G. Ferrarium, 1588).

7. Apicius, *De re coquinaria* (Milan: Guillaume Le Signerre, 1498).

8. Jean-Baptiste Bruyerin-Champier, *De re cibaria* (Lyons: Sebast. Honoratum, 1560) is in many ways similar to the work of Alan Davidson in the *Oxford Companion to Food* (Oxford: Oxford University Press, 1999) as well as these other encyclopedias: Kenneth Kiple, ed., *The Cambridge World History of Food* (Cambridge: Cambridge University Press, 2000); Solomon H. Katz, ed., *Encyclopedia of Food and Culture* (New York: Charles Scribner's Sons, 2003); Ken Albala, *Food Cultures of the World Encyclopedia* (Santa Barbara: ABC-CLIO/ Greenwood, 2011).

9. Andrew Dalby, *Siren Feasts: A History of Food and Gastronomy in Greece* (London: Routledge, 1996); John M. Wilkins and Shaun Hill, *Food in the Ancient World* (Oxford: Blackwell, 2006); Peter Garnsey, *Food and Society in Classical Antiquity* (Cambridge: Cambridge University Press, 1999); James Davidson, *Courtesans and Fishcakes: The Consuming Passions of Classical Athens* (Chicago: University of Chicago Press, 2011).

10. Athenaeus, *Deipnosophists*, trans. Charles Burton Gulick (Cambridge: Harvard University Press, 2011).

11. Archestratus, *The Life of Luxury: Europe's Oldest Cookery Book*, trans. John Wilkins and Shaun Hill (Totnes: Prospect Books, 1994); S. Douglas Olson and Alexander Sens, *Archestratos of Gela: Greek Culture and Cuisine in the Fourth Century BCE: Text, Translation, and Commentary* (Oxford: Oxford University Press, 2000).

12. Galen, *On the Properties of Foodstuffs: Introduction, Translation and Commentary*, trans. and ed. Owen Powell (Cambridge: Cambridge University Press, 2003).

13. Andrew Dalby, *Dangerous Tastes: The Story of Spices* (Berkeley: University of California Press, 2002).

14. For a general overview see Patrick Faas, *Around the Roman Table*, trans. Shaun Whiteside (New York: Palgrave, 2003); Joan Alcock, *Food in the Ancient World* (Westport: Greenwood, 2006); and Emily Gowers, *The Loaded Table: Representations of Food in Roman Literature* (Oxford: Clarendon, 1993).

15. Cato, *On Farming*, trans. Andrew Dalby (Totnes: Prospect Books, 1998).

16. Robert I. Curtis, *Ancient Food Technology* (Leiden: Brill, 2001); K.D. White, *Roman Farming* (London: Thames and Hudson, 1970).

17. Juvenal, *The Satires of Juvenal*, trans. Rolfe Humphries (Bloomington: Indiana University Press, 1958).

18. Petronius, *The Satyricon*, trans. J.P. Sullivan (London: Penguin, 2011).

19. Apicius, *Apicius: A Critical Edition with an Introduction and an English Translation of the Latin Recipe Text*, trans. Christopher Grocock and Sally Grainger (Totnes: Prospect Books, 2006).

20. Anthony Birley, trans., *Lives of the Later Caesars* (London: Penguin, 1976).

21. John Cooper, *Eat and Be Satisfied: A Social History of Jewish Food* (Northvale: Jason Aronson, 1993); Leonard Greenspoon, Ronald A. Simkins, and Gerald Shapiro, eds., *Food and Judaism* (Omaha: Creighton University Press, 2005); Jordan Rosenblum, *Food and Identity in Early Rabbinic Judaism* (Cambridge: Cambridge University Press, 2010). Gillian Feeley-Harnik, *The Lord's Table: The Meaning of Food in Early Judaism and Christianity*, 2nd ed. (Washington, DC: Smithsonian Institution Press, 1994); Veronika E. Grimm, *From Feasting to Fasting, The Evolution of a Sin: Attitudes to Food in Late Antiquity* (London: Routledge, 1996); Susan E. Hill, *Eating to Excess: The Meaning of Gluttony and the Fat Body in the Ancient World* (Santa Barbara: Praeger, 2011); Teresa M. Shaw, *The Burden of the Flesh: Fasting and Sexuality in Early Christianity* (Minneapolis: Fortress Press, 1998).

22. Owen Chadwick, ed., *Western Asceticism* (Philadelphia: Westminster Press, 1958).

23. Massimo Montanari, *The Culture of Food*, trans. Carl Ipsen (Oxford: Blackwell, 1994).

24. Anthimus, *De observatione ciborum: On the Observance of Foods*, ed. and trans. Mark Grant (Totnes: Prospect, 1996).

25. Richard Warner, *Antiquitates Culinariae, or, Curious Tracts Relating to the Culinary Affairs of the Old English* (London, 1791); William Carew Hazlitt, *Old Cookery Books and Ancient Cuisine* (London, 1886); Taillevent, *Le Viandier de Guillaume Tirel*, ed. Jérôme Pinchon and Georges Vicaire (Paris: 1892), repr. with supplement, ed. Sylvie Martinet (Geneve: Slatkine Reprints, 1967).

26. Alfred Franklin, *La vie privée d'autrefois*, (1888; repr. Boston: Elibron Classics, 2005), 46.

27. Georges Duby, *Rural Economy and Country Life in the Medieval West*, trans. Cynthia Postan (Columbia: University of South Carolina Press, 1976); Marc Bloch, *Feudal Society* (Chicago: University of Chicago Press, 1974).

28. Robert Forster and Orest Ranum, eds., *Food and Drink in History,* Selections from the Annales, Économies, Sociétes, Civilisations, vol. 5 (Baltimore: Johns Hopkins, 1979).

29. Paul Freedman, *Out of the East: Spices and the Medieval Imagination* (New Haven: Yale University Press, 2008); Jack Turner, *Spice: The History of a Temptation* (New York: Knopf, 2004); Michael Krondl, *The Taste of Conquest: The Rise and Fall of the Three Great Cities of Spice* (New York: Ballantine Books, 2007).

30. Rudolph Grewe and Constance B. Heiatt, eds. and trans., *Libellus de Arte Coquinaria: An Early Northern Cookery Book* (Tempe: Arizona Center for Medieval and Renaissance Studies, 2001); Constance B. Heiatt and Sharon Butler, eds., *Curye on Inglysch: English Culinary Manuscripts of the Fourteenth Century* (London: Oxford University Press, 1985); Joan Santanach, ed., *The Book of Sent Soví: Medieval Recipes from Catalonia,* trans. Robin Vogelzang (Barcelona: Barcino, 2008); Taillevent, *The Viandier of Taillevent,* ed. Terence Scully (Ottawa: University of Ottawa Press, 1988); Gina L. Greco and Christine M. Rose, eds., *The Good Wife's Guide: Le ménagier de Paris: A Medieval Household Book* (Ithaca: Cornell University Press, 2009).

31. Terence Scully, *The Art of Cookery in the Middle Ages* (Woodbridge: Boydell, 1995); Peter Brears, *Cooking and Dining in Medieval England* (Totnes: Prospect Books, 2008); Melitta Adamson, *Food in Medieval Times* (Westport: Greenwood Press, 2004).

32. Christopher Dyer, *Standards of Living in the Later Middle Ages: Social Change in England, c. 1200–1520* (Cambridge: Cambridge University Press, 1989).

33. Petri de Crescentiis, *Opus ruralium commodorum,* manuscript facsimile (Vicenza: Biblioteca Internationale La Vigna, 2010); Mauro Ambrosoli, *The Wild and the Sown: Botany and Agriculture in Western Europe, 1350–1850,* trans. Mary McCann Salvatorelli (Cambridge: Cambridge University Press, 1997).

34. Rudolph M. Bell, *Holy Anorexia* (Chicago: University of Chicago Press, 1985); Walter Vandereycken and Roth van Deth, *From Fasting Saints to Anorexic Girls: The History of Self-Starvation* (London: Athlone Press, 1994). But see Carolyn Walker Bynum, *Holy Feast and Holy Fast: The Religious Significance of Food to Medieval Women* (Berkeley: University of California Press, 1990) who strongly argues against facile comparison between medieval fasting girls and modern anorexia.

35. Platina, *On Right Pleasure and Good Health: A Critical Edition and Translation of De Honesta Voluptate et Valetudine,* trans. Mary Ella Milham (Tempe: Medieval and Renaissance Texts and Studies, 1998), 293. The recipes in this text were taken from Martino of Como, whose work has also been translated as *The Art of Cooking: The First Modern Cookery Book,* ed. Luigi Ballerini, trans. Jeremy Parzen (Berkeley: University of California Press, 2005).

36. Ken Albala, *Eating Right in the Renaissance* (Berkeley: University of California Press, 2002); Ken Albala, *The Banquet: Dining in the Great Courts of Late Renaissance Europe* (Urbana: University of Illinois Press, 2007). Joan Fitzpatrick, *Food in Shakespeare: Early Modern Dietaries and the Plays* (Burlington: Ashgate, 2007); Joan Fitzpatrick, *Renaissance Food from Rabelais to Shakespeare: Culinary Readings and Culinary Histories* (Burlington: Ashgate, 2010);

Robert Appelbaum, *Aguecheek's Beef, Belch's Hiccup, and Other Gastronomic Interjections: Literature, Culture, and Food Among the Early Moderns* (Chicago: University of Chicago Press, 2006). Bartolomeo Scappi, *The Opera of Bartolomeo Scappi: L'arte et prudenza d'un maestro cuoco: The Art and Craft of a Master Cook*, trans. Terence Scully (Toronto: University of Toronto Press, 2008).

37. Sidney Mintz, *Sweetness and Power: The Place of Sugar in Modern History* (New York: Viking, 1985); Stephen Mennell, *All Manners of Food: Eating and Taste in England and France from the Middle Ages to the Present* (Oxford: Basil Blackwell, 1985).

38. Barbara Wheaton, *Savoring the Past: The French Kitchen and Table from 1300 to 1789* (Philadelphia: University of Pennsylvania Press, 1983); Gilly Lehmann, *The British Housewife* (Totnes: Prospect Books, 2003); Jean-Louis Flandrin, *Arranging the Meal: A History of Table Service in France*, trans. Julie E. Johnson (Berkeley: University of California Press, 2007).

39. Slicher van Bath, *The Agrarian History of Western Europe, AD 500–1850*, trans. Olive Ordish (London: Edward Arnold, 1963); Marcel Mazoyer and Laurence Roudart, *A History of World Agriculture from the Neolithic Age to the Current Crisis*, trans. James H. Membrez (New York: Monthly Review Press, 2006). See also Joan Thirsk, *Food in Early Modern England: Phases, Fads, Fashions, 1500–1760* (London: Hambledon Continuum, 2007), wherein an agricultural historian tackles the subject of food.

40. Charles Etienne and Jean Liebault, *Maison Rustique, or the Countrey Farme*, trans. Richard Surflet (London: John Islip, 1616); Thomas Tusser, *A hundreth good pointes of husbandrie* (London: Richard Tottel, 1557); Olivier de Serres, *Théâtre d'agriculture et mesnage des champs* (Paris, 1600); Vincenzo Tanara, *L'Economia Del Cittadino in Villa* (Venice: Stefano Curti, 1674); William Ellis, *The Country Housewife's Family Companion*, 1st ed. 1750 (Totnes: Prospect Books, 2000).

41. Desiderius Erasmus, "De Civilitate Morum Puerilium" [On Good Manners for Boys], trans. Brian McGregor, in *Collected Works of Erasmus*, ed. J.K. Sowards, vol. 25 (Toronto: University of Toronto Press, 1985), 269–89; Norbert Elias, *The Civilizing Process*, trans. Edmund Jephcott, rev. ed. (Oxford: Blackwell, 2000).

42. A. Lynn Martin, *Alcohol, Violence and Disorder in Traditional Europe* (Kirksville: Truman State University Press, 2009).

43. See Ken Albala and Trudy Eden, eds., *Food and Faith in Christian Culture* (New York: Columbia University Press, 2011).

44. Anita Guerrini, *Obesity and Depression in the Enlightenment: The Life and Times of George Cheyne* (Norman: University of Oklahoma Press, 2000); John Coveney, ed., *Food, Morals, and Meaning: The Pleasure and Anxiety of Eating* (London: Routledge, 2000); Christopher Forth, *Cultures of the Abdomen: Diet, Digestion, and Fat in the Modern World* (New York: Palgrave Macmillan, 2005).

45. Wolfgang Schivelbusch, *Tastes of Paradise: A Social History of Spices, Stimulants, and Intoxicants* (New York: Vintage, 1993); Marci Norton, *Sacred Gifts, Profane Pleasures: The History of Tobacco and Chocolate in the Atlantic World* (Ithaca: Cornell University Press, 2008).

CHAPTER 2

China

E. N. ANDERSON

The recorded history of food in China may be said to go back to ancient times, when somewhat folkloric stories of famous chefs were enshrined in the standard histories written in the Warring States period (481–221 B.C.E.). Serious, detailed attention to food continued throughout Chinese history.

Chinese food is traditionally divided into northern and southern, the north being wheat based (with noodles, dumplings, and breads), the south rice based. The south is then subdivided into three: east, west and south. The core of the east is the Yangzi Delta, with a variety of sea foods and a tendency to use sugar a good deal. The west centers on Sichuan and Hunan, home of food made scorching hot with chile peppers and other spices. (Chiles came from the New World in the sixteenth or seventeenth centuries, but there were plenty of native spices before that.) The south centers on Guangdong and especially the great city of Guangzhou, home of Cantonese food. Other provinces, such as Shandong (north) and Fujian (south), have distinctive cuisines of their own.

Within these regions, every city has distinctive foods. Unique cuisines heretofore unimagined outside their homes are now being described. Xu Wu chronicles the previously unrecorded *hezha* cooking of a remote montane area of Hubei.[1] The American scholar Jacqueline Newman has set herself to giving short but extremely accurate, insightful, and scholarly descriptions of Chinese local and minority foodways in the journal *Flavor and Fortune* (which is under her editorship).[2]

In addition to region and ethnicity, religion affects Chinese food. Every festival has its own dishes and traditions. Serious interpretive research on Chinese religious foodways has its own long and complex history, with most of the materials scattered in monographs on Chinese ritual and religious practice; papers by James and Rubie Watson provide a good entry point.[3]

Food in Chinese History is the basic reference on Chinese food history.[4] Like most works on Chinese history, it is arranged by dynasty. Experts on each period wrote accounts of its foods; these remain standard, and the relevant chapters should be a first resort for anyone researching food in the dynasties discussed below. In *Food in Chinese History*, E. N. Anderson has provided a comprehensive history with anthropological and cultural-ecological interpretations.[5]

EARLY CHINA

Earliest East Asia—the million years or so of human occupation before writing appeared—is known only from archaeology. Strictly speaking, one cannot really speak of "China" at that time, because the political-geographic entity we know as "China" was created by and takes its name from the Qin Dynasty (221–207 B.C.E.; "qin" is pronounced "chin"). Before that, we use the word in a rather loose and strictly geographical sense.

Recent archaeological research has pushed back the date of earliest agriculture. What is now China had the earliest agriculture in the world outside the Near East. Millets were domesticated by 8000 B.C.E.; "millet" is an English term for any small-seeded grain, the ones in question here being foxtail millet (*Setaria italica*) and broomcorn or panic millet (*Panicum miliaceum*). Meanwhile, wild acorns and other nuts, fruits, and seeds were gathered and small animals and fish were caught. Rice was almost certainly cultivated in this early period, but the evidence is equivocal before 6000 B.C.E. Dogs were probably domesticated by then. Pigs and chickens were domesticated by 4000 B.C.E. Chickens are native to China; linguistic evidence suggests they were probably domesticated by Thai speakers. A wide range of fruits and vegetables were domesticated around 4000 B.C.E. Wheat and barley came from the Near East by 2000 B.C.E. For more on the origins of Chinese food, a good introduction is *The Chinese Neolithic* by Li Liu.[6]

Writing, and with it the first historical accounts, appeared quite suddenly on the scene in the Shang Dynasty (ca. 1600–ca. 1050 B.C.E.).

Chinese writing appears to be a strictly local invention, though writing had long been known in the Near East. Imported goods from the Near East, such as the horse, were known in Shang, so an alien origin for writing is not entirely ruled out. In any case, Chinese writing soon recorded a great deal about food.[7] Much of this comes to us in the form of inscriptions on bronze vessels used in great feasts and sacrificial rites. Recent studies of food residues in archaeologically recovered bronze vessels show that they did indeed contain the foods and drinks that their inscriptions, or later traditions, said they did: stews, ale, grain, and so on. ("Ale" is used here for the Chinese word *jiu,* "alcoholic liquor." The word is usually translated "wine," but true wine was unknown or rare in the early dynasties, which used the word for a fermented grain drink. Later, *jiu* included ale, beer, wine, distilled liquor, and even medicinal tinctures, thus confusing the translator.)

The Zhou Dynasty (ca. 1050–221 B.C.E.) was divided by the fall of its capital in 771 B.C.E. and the consequent move of the capital to the east. There the dynasty weakened, leading eventually to the Warring States period, in which the Zhou state controlled only a small area, while a number of independent states controlled the rest of the landscape. Finally Qin—the state occupying the old Western Zhou heartland—conquered the rest, establishing China in name and reality. An enormous amount of textual material and archaeological excavation has brought this period into clear light. Zhou foodways have been especially well described by Roel Stercx.[8] Lothar von Falkenhausen's great study of Zhou archaeology has much to say about bronze and ceramic vessels and their contents.[9] In addition to many late Zhou and Han texts, the early *Book of Songs* names some fifty-two cultivated and wild food plants, all native to north China, except wheat and barley.

A specialized journal, *Early China,* covers this period; it appears as a single large volume per year.

THE HAN DYNASTY (206 B.C.E.–220 C.E.)

The Han Dynasty (206 B.C.E.–220 C.E., with some interruptions and crises) saw the first clearly documented contacts with the Western world; envoys reached the Roman Empire (or at least got near it) and brought back alfalfa and the grapevine. Buddhism became known late in Han, bringing with it a vegetarian ideology. Tea may have begun its slow conquest of China.

A very important development from the historian's point of view has been a recent flood of major translations of foundational Chinese works. These works date to the Warring States period, but many of them were edited and greatly augmented in Han. Short, culturally enshrined works like Confucius's *Analects*, Zhuang Zhou's *Zhuangi*, and the mythical "Laozi's" *Dao De Jing* have long been available in dozens of translations, but more comprehensive, ambitious early works were rarely translated. Several have now been issued in new, complete, scholarly translations: *Guanzi, Xunzi Mozi Huainanzi,* and others.[10] The particle *–zi,* literally "son," meant in this context a scholar who advised statesmen and rulers on how to manage their realms. The books were not usually written by the scholars in question, but were compilations of their sayings and of later works following their ideas. Thus the *Guanzi,* for instance, includes not only the few known writings of Guan Zhong, but also a vast amount of material related to his writings that accumulated over the succeeding several centuries. Guanzi is particularly valuable for its attention to food. It describes agricultural practices, soil knowledge, seasonal hunting and fishing rules, conservation methods, feasting and feast behavior, and a large range of other food-related activities. The other longer works treat these matters to varying degrees.

TIME OF TRIAL: CHINA DISUNITED (220–589)

In 220 C.E. Han broke up into the famous "Three Kingdoms." The nearest thing China has to an epic is the great novel *The History of the Three Kingdoms.* After this came the long period of "Northern and Southern Dynasties," when north and south China were ruled separately.[11] During much of this period, the north was ruled by the Toba or Tabghach Turks, whose dynasty was called Wei. They introduced Western and Central Asian culture, probably including a great deal of foodways, to northern China. We know little about this, because the constant wars and accidents of the period destroyed much documentation.

Buddhism, already known in China, had by this time become prevalent in Central Asia, and the Wei Dynasty greatly increased its presence in China. This led to vegetarianism, previously almost unimagined, becoming common. Over the centuries, a specialized Buddhist cuisine has developed, with imitation meats made from soybean products or wheat gluten.

During this period and later, there was a great deal of mutual teasing between northerners and southerners, over food especially: the northerners were teased for their mutton and fermented dairy products, the southerners for their fondness for frogs and snails.[12]

A fascinating description of southeast Chinese and southeast Asian plants, the *Nanfang Caomu Zhuang (Account of the Southern Regions' Herbs and Trees)*, was written in 304 C.E. by Ji Han and has been ably translated in a convenient edition.[13] It has later additions, and thus cannot be used to prove a given plant was in China by the time of its first writing.

Later, in the sixth century, books began to survive in abundance. This period was marked by two of China's greatest scholars of the practical side of life. One was Jia Sixie, whose great work *Qi Min Yao Shu (Knowledge Needed by Ordinary People)* is now being studied by Françoise Sabban. Jia described food production, processing, and preparation with amazing thoroughness, making this book a world-class resource. Extracts of it occur in many Western sources, especially Bray and some other volumes of the series *Science and Civilisation in China*.[14] The other distinguished scholar was Tao Hongjing, a Daoist adept and polymath scientist who contributed to astronomy, chemistry, religious studies, and medicine, as well as to dietetics and nutrition. He wrote or edited a number of medical works that include a great amount of data on foods. One example is the *Shen Nong Bencao Jing (Shen Nong's Herbal)*, a Han Dynasty work that Hong reedited. Shen Nong (or Shen Nung) was a mythical god of agriculture, a giant with the head of an ox. He was assigned a "real" date corresponding to the 2700s B.C.E., and this is the source of the frequent claim in Western literature that this or that plant was known in China in 2737 B.C.E. The plants in question are mentioned in the herbal. Most of them are indeed very ancient in China, but in fact the herbal dates from about 100 C.E. with Tao's reediting around 550. It has been translated.[15]

REUNITED: THE TANG DYNASTY (620–907)

After the very brief Sui Dynasty, China settled down to relative peace and stability under Tang. A recent history by Mark Lewis, *China's Cosmopolitan Empire*, covers this period well and discusses food and agriculture.[16] The Tang Dynasty is often cited as imperial China's golden age, and was particularly noted for involvement with western and Central Asia.

Many western Eurasian plants first occur in Chinese literature in a Tang tribute list from 647 C.E. At least eight found their way into the great medical work, *Prescriptions Worth a Thousand Gold* by Sun Simiao, in 654. Sun also was apparently aware that western Asia saw "heating" and "cooling" as basic qualities of food and that this was a different medical realm from the Chinese *yin* and *yang*.[17] He briefly discusses different values for foods under different systems. His writings on food are available in English online. Berthold Laufer's *Sino-Iranica* (1919) remains the standard reference for Western plants arriving in China in Tang and other medieval dynasties.[18] Edward Schafer was the great authority on Tang foods and other material culture, and wrote several basic books and articles. Among Central Asian foods that appeared in the Chinese capital of Chang'an (now Xi'an) were Persian breads, ancestral to the *shaobing* of today.[19] Even central Asian foods like yogurt and cheese had a tremendous following in China, which through most of history has rejected dairy foods. More typical of east and south China were fish and other aquatic foods, including sliced raw fish dishes related to Japanese *sashimi*.

Evaluation of the degree to which Western medical and dietary thought influenced Tang China is sorely needed. The vast wave of west Asian influence evidently brought in some such influence (Sun refers to it and Tao Hongjing apparently did so even earlier), but little research exists.[20]

THE SONG DYNASTY (960–1279)

The Tang ended in a brief, but interesting time of disunion, the period of "Five Dynasties." This has recently become much better known to English-language readers through the translation of a great Song Dynasty historical work, Ouyang Xiu's eleventh-century *Historical Record of the Five Dynasties*.[21] The work has little about food, but provides insight into the thoughts of a leading moral philosopher evaluating the behavior of what was, in his time, the very recent past.

The Song Dynasty reunited China in 960, but never ruled anything comparable to the huge realms of Han and Tang: they never conquered the Central Asian or far northern parts of the old empires. Moreover, the northern part of the empire was soon lost to the Khitan people, who established the Liao Dynasty there. The Liao in turn lost it in 1115 to the Jurchen Tungus, who then drove the Song out of north China in 1127. The Jin established the Jin Dynasty—overthrown in its turn by the Mongols in 1234 (an easy date to remember). Song met the same fate only forty-five years later, when the Mongols managed to gain enough knowledge of river, lake, and sea warfare to conquer the Yangzi Valley and the coasts.

Chinese food as we know it appears to have taken shape under Song.[22] It was a period of extreme refinement and taste, as well-to-do merchants and traders developed a middle-class culture in the great cities.

THE YUAN DYNASTY (1279–1368)

The Yuan Dynasty brought a huge flow of knowledge from west and central Asia to China. This resulted in a court nutritional manual that included many Near Eastern, Central Asian, Indian, and even European recipes; it has been translated under the title *A Soup for the Qan.*[23] A vast encyclopedia of Near Eastern medicine, the *Huihui Yaofang,* written in Chinese but with Arabic and Persian glosses, included a huge section on foods and nutrition, but these parts of the work are unfortunately lost. Some sections of the work survive, however. They include a great deal on medicinal foodstuffs, especially spices.[24]

Of the many cookbooks surviving from Yuan, one by the great artist Ni Zan has been translated.[25] It reflects a much more purely "Chinese" food pattern.

THE MING DYNASTY (1368–1644)

The Ming Dynasty was a period of growth, refinement, and cultural development. Many novels, short stories, and plays date from this period. Ming food production is well covered by many historical sources, including local works, agricultural manuals, and herbals. Unique to this time is a guide to wild plants and uncommon domesticated ones that can be used by individuals in times of crop failure and famine. This famine herbal, the *Jiuhuan Bencao,* appeared in 1406 under the direction of a prince of the dynastic royal family—apparently the only time in premodern history when a royal prince compiled a food guide for his poorest and most desperate subjects.[26]

In Ming, the major New World food crops—maize, sweet and white potatoes, chiles, tobacco, and others—reached China.[27] They spread slowly at first, though later in Qing they rapidly took over vast tracts of land.

Ming foodways were sophisticated and refined even at quite humble levels. Descriptions of inns, restaurants, and strolling food-sellers show that even in modest towns there was a great variety and quality of food.

The novel *Jin Ping Mei* (variously translated) is famous primarily for its erotic adventures, but food runs throughout the work and indeed is often central to the erotic scenes. Another promising source is the work of late-Ming medicinal food writer Gao Lian, who wrote extensively on food—his food book has been translated but not published.

Ming and Qing are covered by a particularly lively journal, *Late Imperial China,* which very frequently has articles about food and other cultural delights. The journal has a long history of being both impeccably scholarly and a great deal of fun to read; many a rousing yarn has graced its pages. A food-related example is Tonio Andrade's tale of He Bin, an outrageous rogue and double agent who cornered the mullet tax in Taiwan in the seventeenth century.[28]

THE QING DYNASTY (1644–1911)

During the Qing Dynasty, China's population grew from fewer than one hundred million after the interdynastic wars at the end of Ming to four hundred million. These were the "teeming millions" of "crowded" China in the old travel books, but the population of the United States today is about as dense as China's was in Qing. Feeding this vast and rapidly increasing population was a challenge, and the study of Qing food production, distribution, and supply has become a highly controversial topic. On the one hand, it is clear that China's farmers had to work harder and harder on less and less land just to keep up.[29] This is a process known as "agricultural involution" or "the high-level equilibrium trap."[30] Involution contrasts with development: development means more production per capita, while involution means more production by the total system, and perhaps more total surplus, but with no increase in wealth per capita in the rural sector. Farmers worked harder and harder just to stay in the same place.

The system was based on relatively cheap labor in comparison to scarce land and inputs, which produced an agriculture targeted toward biological improvements: more crop species, better management of fields, more complex cropping systems. The United States, by contrast, had cheap land and relatively expensive labor, and thus turned to large machines.[31] Particularly important in all this was Qing's active continuance of the old Chinese pattern of favoring small independent farmers over large landlords; the latter often faced expropriation, legal or otherwise. Thus China could grow even sugar—elsewhere a plantation crop—as a smallholder crop.[32]

Qing farmers succeeded beyond all reasonable expectations, providing plenty of food, including a surprisingly large surplus in good years. F.H. King's description of China's agricultural system at the end of Qing has never been excelled.[33] It shows how fantastically elaborate, fine-tuned, and productive the food production system was—far in advance of the Western agriculture of that time. Kenneth Pomeranz has emphasized the success of the Chinese economy (not just in agriculture), maintaining that through the eighteenth century the Chinese were doing about as well as Europeans.[34] This has attracted some controversy, and the issue of Chinese rural welfare remains a topic of debate.[35] Sober documentation, such as Philip Huang's or Kathryn Bernhardt's, can play either way; it shows a world of very small farmers, seriously exploiting family labor, but having enough to eat and wear unless major problems occurred.[36] However, much of this documentation is from the relatively rich Yangzi Delta or from the virgin soil of recently settled Manchuria, and we lack equally thorough work on poorer and more marginal regions.[37]

Lillian Li's decades of research on famine in modern China culminated in a major monograph.[38] Studies of famine relief and food aid by the Qing Dynasty led to the finding—rather surprising to some—that Qing had invested major effort, with very considerable success, in that area, and the Ming Dynasty has more recently been shown by Johanna Smith to have anticipated some of this effort by organizing local charity.[39]

As to foodways and food consumption, Qing patterns grade into modern practice, and descriptions are best found in good cookbooks. On the other hand, the great Qing novels, notably *The Story of the Stone* and *The Scholars,* are outstanding sources.[40] Yuan Mei, a poet and educator of the eighteenth century, wrote extensively on food, including a cookbook, as yet untranslated.[41] Many other cookbooks, including ones detailing imperial palace food, also appeared during this time.

AFTER THE END OF IMPERIAL CHINA

In the twentieth century food in China was sparse, but those who got an adequate diet were healthy. The grains were lightly milled, the oil unrefined, the vegetables fresh. The meat and fish were lean and local. The diet consisted almost entirely of grain and vegetables, with meat a rare luxury. The sugar, saturated fats, and other foods we now overconsume were almost unavailable. Trans fats did not exist. The diet was high in fiber, and those with some disposable income got enough vitamins and minerals, because vegetables were particularly high in these nutrients.

Research by T. Colin Campbell and collaborators in the midcentury showed incredibly low levels of blood cholesterol.[42] Obesity was rare and diabetes almost unknown.[43] Today sugar and fats are all too easily and cheaply available, and meat is abundant. The result has been an explosive increase in weight, and in diabetes, now affecting perhaps 10 percent of Chinese adults. Heart disease is now common.[44]

Of course, the old days may have been better for the fortunate few, but they were terrible for many. Famine continued through most of the twentieth century.[45] It has been eliminated in the last forty years.

China's worst famine was caused by Mao Zidong's Great Leap Forward in 1958–62. This has received full treatment in *Mao's Great Famine* by Frederick Dikötter.[46] Frequently described, with widely differing estimates of the death toll, this famine is now definitively presented in Dikötter's work.

Several more specialized and interpretive studies of twentieth-century China have recently appeared. Tea is ever fascinating, not only for its medicinal and stimulant value but also as a subject for art and refinement of life.[47] It also was a social lubricant. Wang Di found that teahouses in China were as noted for vibrant debate and dissent as coffee houses were and are in Europe.[48] Joanna Waley-Cohen has written a brilliant short essay on balance in food appreciation by Chinese gourmets.[49]

CHINESE FOOD GOES INTERNATIONAL

"Globalization" has been the big news in food studies in the last few decades. China was far ahead of the game. The Mongol Empire spread Chinese foodways west while it was introducing west Asian foodways to China. A steady flow of foods west across Asia has continued, but has been dwarfed in recent centuries by Chinese expansion to Southeast Asia.

More recently, we have seen the globalization of Chinese food, especially restaurants. This has been widely chronicled, especially by Sidney Cheung, Tan Chee-beng, and David Wu.[50] Their work covers not only expansion to the Western world, but the earlier spread of Chinese foodways and influences all over East, Northeast, and Southeast Asia.

Chinese trade with Southeast Asia led to massive mutual influence from the dawn of history onward. Chinese were already using cloves—from the Moluccas in what is now Indonesia—in the Zhou Dynasty. In Song and especially Ming, vast trading expeditions went back and forth, and large settlements of Chinese developed all over Southeast Asia.

Many Chinese foods and food words were established there, in the Hokkien language, which is distinct from both Cantonese and Mandarin. One such word went worldwide: the Hokkien Chinese word *ke tsiap*, "fruit sauce," came to be applied to soy sauce in Indonesia (where it is now spelled *kecap*). This word in turn was borrowed into English for a range of soy-based or soy-like fermented sauces. Tomato ketchup emerged in the last century or two. Other Hokkien loanwords like *tauhu* for bean curd and *tauge* for soybean sprouts remain confined to Malaysian and Indonesian languages.

From the 1400s on, entire fusion cuisines developed: the *nonya* cooking of Malaysia and Singapore, and the *peranakan* cuisine of Indonesia. Influences returned to the homeland with returning merchants, and one is surprised to find "sand tea sauce" in China until one learns that "sand tea" in Hokkien is pronounced *sa té*, referring here to the famous satay of Indonesia. The urban cuisine of Bangkok is similar, a Chinese-Thai rather than a Chinese-Malaysian fusion. Calling cuisines of the area "hybrid" is inappropriate, because the cuisines of China and the Nanyang (Southeast Asia) have never been separate in the first place. *Nonya* cooking declined in Singapore during the late twentieth century, but has recently had a major revival. One can also find every imaginable accommodation between *nonya* styles and more recent cuisines introduced from China in the last 150 years.

Vietnam too has been greatly influenced by Chinese food, with merchant settlements of Chinese again being important culture-bearers. Disentangling cultural influences leads to a study of how people have creatively experimented with food, how they have experienced it over the years, and how it takes on a local identity; Nir Avieli's book-length study of food in Hoi An, Vietnam, is a major recent effort in this regard.[51]

Since the late nineteenth century, Chinese cuisine has taken the world by storm. The beginning was not particularly hopeful: tiny restaurants and markets serving "coolie" workers in the Americas and Europe. ("Coolie" is a South Indian word for a day laborer. It was ironically glossed by the Chinese as *gu li*, "bitter strength.") However, good restaurants soon appeared, and Chinese food became popular, especially in the United States.

The story of chop suey and other American Chinese foods has been told by Andrew Coe in *Chop Suey*.[52] There are several "origin myths" about this food, most of them claiming that some restauranteur in California could not turn away rowdy latecomers and was reduced to cooking up the day's leftovers; "chop suey" is Cantonese *tsap suei*, "miscellaneous leftovers." In fact the dish was a vegetable growers' dish from Guangdong province. Growers had various small but succulent leaves, sprouts, and shoots left over at day's end, and cooked them up for dinner.[53] That version of the dish could be very good, but the American versions became variously altered in ways that did not necessarily improve it.

Similar fates betook fried noodles (chow mein, Cantonese *chau mien*) and other foods; all too often they were altered in the direction of blandness and poor-quality ingredients. Origin myths have attached themselves to some of these dishes too. Yangzhou fried rice is sometimes claimed as a Hong Kong or even a U.S. invention, in spite of the name, which correctly implies a long history in Yangzhou—though it took a more bland direction in America.[54] Sweet-sour pork is a more recent invention, again from Hong Kong or North America; it is an adaptation of a Cantonese fish dish, made when cooks realized that Europeans and Americans liked sweets much more than the Chinese traditionally did. The name in Cantonese is *gu lou yuk,* "murmuring and muttering meat," supposedly from the sound of frying, but there is a long-standing theory that it really derives from *guai lou yuk,* "meat for foreign devils."

The old-fashioned "chop suey house" is far from extinct in North America. Its South American equivalent, the *chifa* (presumably from the Mandarin *chi fan,* "eat rice"), flourishes greatly, especially in Peru. These eating houses had the appeal of providing extremely cheap, filling food while seeming homelike to members of the diaspora and "exotic" to Westerner. (The lure of the exotic should not be exaggerated however; early-day Chinese restaurants appealed largely to a Chinese clientele, and Westerners who frequented them were often both quite used to them and more interested in the price and convenience than in the "exotic." Occasional suggestions that these restaurants merely pandered to "romancing the exoticized other" do not survive the light of research.)

In Great Britain, a parallel phenomenon took place as Hong Kong Cantonese moved to England and then to other parts of the British Isles and Europe. Many of these emigrants were members of the Man lineage, from a single village area in rural Hong Kong. They moved into the chop suey house world, but quickly diversified into Chinese takeout stores, fish and chips shops, and more serious Chinese restaurants. Their story has been told by anthropologists James and Rubie Watson.[55]

Today, Chinese restaurants are worldwide. One finds them in the Arctic, in remote South American towns, in every part of Africa. They are established enough in India to have produced distinctive traditions there. Restaurant guides throughout the world classify local restaurants by type of cuisine. There is almost always a section for "Chinese."

With the liberalization of immigration in the Americas and Europe after 1960, mass emigration from Taiwan, Hong Kong, and mainland China populated the world with well-to-do, food-conscious Chinese, and the restaurant business expanded and improved accordingly. Today, there are Chinese restaurants in even the smallest communities in the English-speaking world, and one can eat almost as well in California, New York, London, or Amsterdam as in China itself. Specialty restaurants—ranging from Zhuang cuisine to medicinal-herb foods—can be found.

Chinese food in the West is often highly creative, yet within the traditional parameters of the food. Chinese cuisine has always been innovative and novelty-conscious. We are now seeing "fusion" restaurants in both the West and China itself, where one can find *haute cuisine* mixing Chinese ideas with every sort of Western and Asian tradition.

Westernization came to China, as we have seen, thousands of years before the empire, and it continued to propagate, especially in the Tang and Yuan Dynasties. The rapid but little-recorded spread of American food plants to China was first studied by Ping-ti Ho and has received attention since then, as more and more plants flow in; Shiu-Ying Hu's *Food Plants of China* is almost definitive, but I have seen additional records of the arrival of American foods in China.[56] Beer came in the nineteenth century with German port concessions. Other drinks followed. American foodways have recently spread to China, led by beer and orange soda, then cola drinks, and finally hamburgers and other fast foods. The spread of McDonald's to China cannot be ignored as a part of modern history.[57] Other transnational food chains, including Starbuck's, have followed. Today, most of the world's major cuisines are easily found in Taiwan and Hong Kong, and mainland China is catching up.

However, the chance that this will all end in one homogenized, tasteless, synthetic, or genetically engineered cuisine is exceedingly small. Encounters between cultures have led to great increases in national pride as well as in cross-cultural experimentation. People want their own cuisine, well-presented, and many of them also want to try everyone else's.

STUDYING CHINESE FOOD: CURRENT DIRECTIONS

The most immediate and pressing question of Chinese food history is simple documentation. We know amazingly little about the actual recipes and culinary *practice* of even the most well-known Chinese cuisines. There are vast areas of China whose foodways have never been documented at all. Entire nationalities—minorities with their own languages, cultures, and foodways—are culinarily unknown to the outside world.

In history, such simple facts as when particular crops reached China are still not well known. Specific crops deserve attention comparable to that noted above for sugar and for soybeans. Millets are the true Cinderella crops. They were China's major staples in the Neolithic, and comparable to or more important than rice in the early dynasties. They were the true foundation of China's early history. Yet they are almost out of cultivation now, and have received little historical attention. Minor but vitally important crops, such as fruits and vegetables, require more attention. Errors, such as the routine mistranslation of *mei* (flowering apricot) as "plum," or the assumption that New World crops like chiles and peanuts were found in ancient China, are still too common in the literature.

The history of Chinese food has been largely a Chinese preserve, with very little published in English by Chinese scholars and still less translated. The classic works exist in modern editions, with added translations from classical to contemporary Chinese, and often with scientific names of plants and animals or other scientific data; these are generally of high quality. Unfortunately, these items are rarely acquired by libraries in the Western world. Even more rare are the anonymous folk cookbooks that used to circulate widely, often carried in the packs of roving book-peddlers. These were prime sources for local cuisines.

Many of the best historical works tend to use the "food systems" approach, studying production, distribution, and consumption as one unit. There is clearly a need for more awareness of this approach and its advantages. On the other hand, more specialized studies, from work on the ecology of production to the phenomenology of consumption, are also appearing and are highly welcome.

The question of how successful China was at feeding itself, and how much of this success was due to involution rather than development, remains to be determined. Creative use of the sources is proving that the question can be answered up to a point, though perfect knowledge will remain elusive.

Interpretive studies of consumption, such as are common in studies of European food history, are rather few; Françoise Sabban is a clear leader here, and recently a number of papers on the subject have appeared.[58] More common are studies of food in its social context.

A large proportion of recent studies in Chinese food have dealt with internationalization or globalization, and this needs much more attention—especially the premodern globalization reflected in Yuan texts and Southeast Asian, Korean, and Japanese fusion cuisines.

RESOURCES: OVERVIEWS AND GENERAL WORKS

Every Chinese dynasty of note set about compiling an encyclopedic history of the one, or ones, it had replaced, and these histories pay varying degrees of attention to food. Gazetteers—reference books on counties and similar small areas—recorded local food production and consumption. Agricultural manuals, encyclopedias, and guides appeared throughout Chinese history. Countless cookbooks and dietetic and nutritional works were produced, but do not usually go into detail about history per se.

Traditional and modern books on Chinese medicine are also basic sources for research, especially *bencao,* "basic herbals." These are guides to herbal and other medicines and drugs. They contain long and detailed treatments of foods, since nutritional therapy has always been central to medical treatment in China. Medical books and herbals are historically valuable partly because they quote and cite earlier works; many are major works of historical scholarship. The acknowledged leader in this field, the *Bencao Gangmu* (*Compendium of Materia Medica*) by Li Shizhen, has been translated into English in six huge volumes.[59] There are also modern works in Chinese that identify and describe the plants mentioned in Chinese classical works such as the *Book of Songs*.

The present chapter confines itself to Western-language literature, primarily English, but the vast majority of works on Chinese food are (unsurprisingly) in Chinese. Many more are in Japanese, reflecting a centuries-old Japanese fascination with China. In recent years China has reissued the classic Chinese works on food, or on anything connected with food, and these are usually available widely in cheap editions.

The study of Chinese food as a technical subject for contemporary scholarly research has a respectable history of its own. It received a major stimulus from the work of Chang Kwang-chih (K.C. Chang), an archaeologist who developed an interest in the foodways of the earliest historic periods in China's past. He edited, and wrote several chapters in, *Food in Chinese History*. Chang went on to write several books on the Shang and Zhou Dynasties, including analysis of food vessels and food management in sacrifices and similar events.[60]

This book was soon followed by another landmark history from a different perspective: Francesca Bray's magisterial volume on the history of Chinese agriculture in Joseph Needham's *Science and Civilisation in China* series.[61] This too remains a standard reference. Bray made extensive use of classic Chinese materials and nothing since has even approached this work in combining scope and accuracy.

Since the 1990s, scholarly studies of Chinese food history have become much more numerous. Quickly emerging as a leader was Françoise Sabban.[62] In Germany, Thomas Gwinner chronicled the classic cookbook literature of China, with extracts from major works.[63] Frederick Simoons produced a major reference work on Chinese foods, with historical perspectives, especially for recent centuries.[64] Naomichi Ishige, Japan's leading expert on the history of East Asian cuisines, sometimes publishes in English on Chinese food.[65] Cookbooks also began to take a more sophisticated approach to Chinese food history.[66]

The above-mentioned works have encouraged a further wave of studies; high points will be cited here. H.T. Huang studied the history of fermentation technology, and his resulting volume for Joseph Needham's series remains particularly impressive.[67] Shiu-Ying Hu's encyclopedic reference, *Food Plants of China,* summarizes more than seventy years of field and herbarium research by this incredible scholar, still actively working (as of this writing) at well over one hundred years of age.[68] Sucheta Mazumdar devoted a monograph to the history of sugar in China, showing that China's management of sugar and the sugar industry was very different from, and very much less socially pathological than, the Western world's story of slavery and servitude in sugar production.[69] Independently, Sidney Mintz, the leading chronicler of the West's dark history of sugar, shifted to Chinese food as a focus at about the same time.[70]

Salt in Chinese culture has been the subject of a major monograph by Hans Ulrich Vogel; he reviews every aspect of its production and consumption in late Imperial times, and compares these with the contemporary European world.[71] Vogel notes, sympathetically, that the Chinese add deep-drilling—perfected for salt wells—to the list of the greatest inventions China has given the world, along with paper, printing, the compass, and gunpowder.[72]

Significantly, many of these works take the "food systems" approach. Mintz was one of the pioneers of this approach, and his influence has been strong, especially within anthropology; but historians such as Lillian Li and biologists such as H.T. Huang have used it to advantage.[73] On the other hand, studies focusing on consumption—especially, interpretive studies of Chinese attitudes and feelings about food—have also been prominent.

One organization, the Foundation of Chinese Dietary Culture, based in Taiwan, specializes in Chinese food history; it holds regular conferences and publishes a scholarly journal (largely in Chinese).

For the wider historical framework, there exist specialized works on all the dynasties. The *Cambridge History of China* has been slowly appearing in many huge volumes. Harvard has recently published a competing series, shorter but still massive.[74] For the nonexpert looking for an authoritative overview, Patricia Ebrey's *Cambridge Illustrated History of China* is recommended, especially if used with her *Chinese Civilization: A Sourcebook,* which covers food as well as other aspects of life.[75] Frederick Mote's great work *Imperial China 900–1800* is indispensable for the period it covers.[76] It discusses food production, but has little on consumption.

NOTES

1. Xu Wu, *Farming, Cooking, and Eating Practices in the Central China Highland: How Hezha Foods Function to Establish Ethnic Identity* (Lewiston: Edwin Mellen Press, 2012).

2. See also Jacqueline Newman, *Food Culture in China* (Westport: Greenwood, 2004).

3. James L. Watson and Rubie S. Watson, *Village Life in Hong Kong: Politics, Gender and Ritual in the New Territories* (Hong Kong: Chinese University of Hong Kong, 2004).

4. K.C. Chang, ed., *Food in Chinese Culture* (New Haven: Yale University Press, 1977).

5. E.N. Anderson, *The Food of China* (New Haven: Yale University Press, 1988).

6. Li Liu, *The Chinese Neolithic: Trajectories to Early States* (Cambridge: Cambridge University Press, 2004). See also Robert Bettinger et al., "The Transition to Agriculture at Dadiwan, People's Republic of China," *Current Anthropology* 51 (2010): 703–14.

7. K.C. Chang, *Shang Civilization* (New Haven: Yale University Press, 1980).

8. Roel Sterckx, *Food, Sacrifice and Sagehood in Early China* (Cambridge: Cambridge University Press, 2001); Roel Sterckx, ed., *Of Tripod and Palate: Food, Politics, and Religion in Traditional China* (New York: Palgrave MacMillan, 2005).

9. Lothar Von Falkenhausen, *Chinese Society in the Age of Confucius (1000–250 BC): The Archaeological Evidence* (Los Angeles: Cotsen Institute of Archaeology, UCLA, 2006).

10. W. Allyn Rickett, *Guanzi: Political, Economic, and Philosophical Essays from Early China,* vol. 1 (Princeton: Princeton University Press, 1985); vol. 2

(Princeton: Princeton University Press, 1998). Xunzi, *Xunzi*, trans. John Knoblock and Zhang Jue (Changsha; Beijing: Hunan People's Publishing House and Foreign Languages Press, 1999). Mo Di, *The Mozi: A Complete Translation,* trans. Ian Johnston (New York: Columbia University Press, 2010). Liu An, *Huainanzi,* trans. and ed. John Major et al. (New York: Columbia University Press, 2010).

11. Albert Dien, *Six Dynasties Civilization* (New Haven: Yale University Press, 2007).

12. For some slightly later examples, see Mark Edward Lewis, *China's Cosmopolitan Empire: The Tang Dynasty* (Cambridge: Harvard University Press, 2009), 127–31.

13. Li Hui-Lin, *Nan-fang Ts'ao-mu Chuang: A Fourth Century Flora of Southeast Asia* (Hong Kong: Chinese University of Hong Kong, 1979).

14. Francesca Bray, *Science and Civilisation in China,* vol. 6, *Biology and Biological Technology,* "Part II: Agriculture" (Cambridge: Cambridge University Press, 1984).

15. Yang Shou-Zhong, *The Divine Farmer's Materia Medica: A Translation of the Shen Nong Ben Cao* (Boulder: Blue Poppy Press, 1998).

16. Mark Edward Lewis, *China's Cosmopolitan Empire: The Tang Dynasty* (Cambridge: Harvard University Press, 2009).

17. Ute Engelhardt, "Dietetics in Tang China and the First Extant Works of *Materia dietetica,*" in *Innovation in Chinese Medicine,* ed. Elisabeth Hsu (Cambridge: Cambridge University Press, 2001), 173–91; Sun Simiao, *Recipes Worth a Thousand Gold,* trans. Sumei Yi, ed. E.N. Anderson (2007), http://www.krazykioti.com/articles/recipes-worth-a-thousand-gold/.

18. Berthold Laufer, *Sino-Iranica* (Chicago: Field Museum, 1919).

19. See especially Edward Schafer, *The Golden Peaches of Samarkand* (Berkeley: University of California Press, 1963); Edward Schafer, *The Vermilion Bird* (Berkeley: University of California Press, 1967); Edward Schafer, *Pacing the Void: T'ang Approaches to the Stars* (Berkeley; Los Angeles: University of California Press, 1977).

20. See Engelhardt, "Dietetics in Tang China."

21. Ouyang Xiu, *Historical Records of the Five Dynasties,* trans. Richard L. Davis (New York: Columbia University Press, 2004).

22. Michael Freeman, "Sung," in *Food in Chinese Culture,* ed. K.C. Chang, (New Haven: Yale University Press, 1977), 141–92.

23. Paul D. Buell, Eugene N. Anderson, and Charles Perry, *A Soup for the Qan: Chinese Dietary Medicine of the Mongol Era as Seen in Hu Szu-Hui's Yinshan Zhengyao* (Leiden: Brill, 2011).

24. Y.C. Kong, *Huihui Yaofang* (Hong Kong: Y.C. Kong, 1996).

25. Eugene N. Anderson, Teresa Wang, and Victor Mair, "Ni Zan, *Cloud Forest Hall Collection of Rules for Drinking and Eating,*" in *Hawai'i Reader in Traditional Chinese Culture,* ed. Victor Mair, Nancy Steinhardt and Paul R. Goldin (Honolulu: University of Hawaii Press, 2005), 444–55.

26. Bernard Emms Read, *Famine Foods Listed in the Chiu Huang Pen Ts'ao* (Shanghai: Henry Lester Institute of Medical Research, 1946).

27. Ho Ping-ti, "The Introduction of American Food Plants into China," *American Anthropologist* 57 (1955): 191–201; Sucheta Mazumdar, "The

Impact of New World Food Crops on the Diet and Economy of China and India, 1600–1900," in *Food in Global History*, ed. Raymond Grew (Boulder: Westview, 1999), 58–78.

28. Tonio Andrade, "Chinese Under European Rule: The Case of Sino-Dutch Mediator He Bin," *Late Imperial China* 28 (2007): 1–32.

29. Philip Huang, *The Peasant Family and Rural Development in the Yangzi Delta, 1350–1988* (Stanford: Stanford University Press, 1990).

30. Clifford Geertz, *Agricultural Involution: The Process of Ecological Change in Indonesia* (Berkeley: University of California Press, 1963); Huang, *Peasant Family and Rural Development*. Mark Elvin, *The Pattern of the Chinese Past* (Stanford: Stanford University Press, 1973).

31. Yujiro Hayami and Vernon Ruttan, *Agricultural Development: An International Perspective* (Baltimore: Johns Hopkins University Press, 1985).

32. Sucheta Mazumdar, *Sugar and Society in China: Peasants, Technology, and the World Market* (Cambridge: Harvard University Press, 1998).

33. F.H. King, *Farmers of Forty Centuries; or, Permanent Agriculture in China, Korea and Japan* (New York: Harcourt and Brace, 1927). See also Kenneth Ruddle and Gongfu Zhong, *Integrated Agriculture-Aquaculture in South China: The Dike-Pond System of the Zhujiang Delta* (Cambridge: Cambridge University Press, 1988); Wen Dazhong and David Pimentel, "Seventeenth-Century Organic Agriculture in China: I. Cropping Systems in Jiaxing Region," *Human Ecology* 14 (1986): 1–14; Wen Dazhong and David Pimentel, "Seventeenth-Century Organic Agriculture in China: II. Energy Flows through an Agroecosystem in Jiaxing Region," *Human Ecology* 14 (1986): 15–28.

34. Kenneth Pomeranz, *The Great Divergence: China, Europe, and the Making of the Modern World Economy* (Princeton: Princeton University Press, 2000).

35. Philip Huang, "Development or Involution in Eighteenth-Century Britain and China? A Review of Kenneth Pomeranz's *The Great Divergence: China, Europe, and the Making of the Modern World Economy*," *The Journal of Asian Studies* 61 (2002): 501–38; R. Bin Wong, *China Transformed: Historical Change and the Limits of European Experience* (Ithaca: Cornell University Press, 1997); see also Li Bozhong, *Agricultural Development in Jiangnan, 1620–1850* (New York: St. Martin's Press, 1998).

36. Huang, *Peasant Family and Rural Development*; Kathryn Bernhardt, *Rents, Taxes, and Peasant Resistance: The Lower Yangzi Region, 1840–1950* (Stanford: Stanford University Press, 1992).

37. James Lee and Wang Feng, *One Quarter of Humanity: Malthusian Mythology and Chinese Realities, 1700–2000* (Cambridge: Harvard University Press, 1999).

38. Lillian Li, *Fighting Famine in North China: State, Market, and Environmental Decline, 1690s-1990s* (Stanford: Stanford University Press, 2007).

39. On the Qing Dynasty, see Pierre-Étienne Will and R. Bin Wong, *Nourish the People: The State Civilian Granary System in China, 1650–1850* (Ann Arbor: Center for Chinese Studies, University of Michigan, 1991); on the Ming Dynasty, see Joanna Handlin Smith, *The Art of Doing Good: Charity in Late Ming China* (Berkeley: University of California Press, 2009).

40. Cao Xueqin and Gao E., *The Story of the Stone: A Chinese Novel in Five Volumes*, 5 vols., trans. David Hawkes and John Minford (Harmondsworth: Penguin, 1973–1986); Wu Ching-tzu, *The Scholars*, trans. Yang Hsien-yi and Gladys Yang (Beijing: Foreign Languages Press, 1973); mined in Anderson, *The Food of China* (New Haven: Yale University Press, 1988).

41. Arthur Waley, *Yuan Mei: Eighteenth Century Chinese Poet* (London: George Allen and Unwin, 1956).

42. T. Colin Campbell with Thomas M. Campbell II, *The China Study: The Most Comprehensive Study of Nutrition Ever Conducted and the Startling Implications for Diet, Weight Loss and Long-Term Health* (Dallas: Benbella Books, 2006); Chen Junshi et al., *Diet, Life-Style, and Mortality in China: A Study of the Characteristics of 65 Chinese Counties* (Ithaca: Cornell University Press, 1990).

43. Compare to Li Shu-Fan, *Hong Kong Surgeon* (London: Victor Gollancz, 1964).

44. Xaio-Ren Pan et al., "Impaired Glucose Tolerance and its Relationship to ECG-Indicated Coronary Heart Disease and Risk Factors Among Chinese: Da Qing IGT and Diabetes Study," *Diabetes Care* 16 (1993), 150–56; Frank B. Hu, "Globalization of Diabetes: The Role of Diet, Lifestyle and Genes," *Diabetes Care* 34 (2011), 1249–57.

45. Anderson, "Up Against Famine: Chinese Diet in the Early Twentieth Century," *Crossroads* 1 (1990): 11–24; Li, *Fighting Famine in North China*; Walter Mallory, *China, Land of Famine* (New York: American Geographic Society, 1926).

46. Frank Dikötter, *Mao's Great Famine: The History of China's Most Devastating Catastrophe, 1958–1962* (New York: Walker and Co., 2010).

47. Frederick R. Dannaway, "Placing a Mountain into a Valley: Microcosmic Aesthetics and the Arts of Tea," *The Art of Tea* 9 (2010): 88–91; Beatrice Hohenegger, ed., *Steeped in History: The Art of Tea* (Los Angeles: Fowler Museum at UCLA, 2009).

48. Di Wang, *The Teahouse: Small Business, Everyday Culture, and Public Politics in Chengdu, 1900–1950* (Stanford: Stanford University Press, 2008).

49. Joanna Waley-Cohen, "The Quest for Perfect Balance," in *Food: The History of Taste*, ed. Paul Freedman (Berkeley: University of California Press, 2007), 99–134.

50. Sidney C.H. Cheung and Tan Chee-Beng, *Food and Foodways in Asia: Resource, Tradition and Cooking* (London: Routledge, 2007); Wu Ching-tzu and Tan Chee-beng, eds., *Changing Chinese Foodways in Asia* (Hong Kong: Chinese University of Hong Kong, 2001); David Y.H. Wu and Sidney C.H. Cheung, eds., *The Globalization of Chinese Food* (Richmond: Curzon, 2002).

51. Nir Avieli, "Vietnamese New Year Rice Cakes: Iconic Festive Dishes and Contested National Identity," *Ethnology* 44 (2005): 167–87; Nir Avieli, *Rice Talks: Food and Community in a Vietnamese Town* (Bloomington: University of Indiana Press, 2012).

52. Andrew Coe, *Chop Suey: A Cultural History of Chinese Food in the United States* (New York: Oxford University Press, 2009).

53. Li Shu-Fan, *Hong Kong Surgeon* (London: Victor Gollancz, 1964), and my own field work.

54. Antonia Finnane, *Speaking of Yangzhou: A Chinese City, 1550–1850* (Cambridge: Harvard University Press, 2004).

55. James L. Watson, *Emigration and the Chinese Lineage: The Mans in Hong Kong and London* (Berkeley: University of California Press, 1975); James L. Watson and Rubie S. Watson, *Village Life in Hong Kong: Politics, Gender and Ritual in the New Territories* (Hong Kong: Chinese University of Hong Kong, 2004).

56. Ho, "Introduction of American Food Plants"; Shiu-Ying Hu, *Food Plants of China* (Hong Kong: Chinese University Press, 2005).

57. Watson, ed., *Golden Arches East: McDonald's in East Asia* (Stanford: Stanford University Press, 2006); Yan Yunxiang, "McDonald's in Beijing: The Localization of Americana," in *Golden Arches East,* ed. James L. Watson (Stanford: Stanford University Press, 2006), 39–76.

58. Françoise Sabban, "Milk Consumption in China: The Construction of a New Food Habit," in *Proceedings, 12th Symposium on Chinese Dietary Culture, Okinawa* (Taipei: Foundation for Chinese Dietary Culture, 2011), 397–420; Françoise Sabban, "Un savoir-faire oublié: Le travail du lait en Chine ancienne," *Zibun: Memoirs of the Research Institute for Humanistic Studies* 21 (1986): 31–65. Other recent articles include Waley-Cohen, "The Quest for Perfect Balance."

59. Li Shizhen, *Compendium of Materia Medica (Bencao Gangmu),* trans. Luo Xiwen (Beijing: Foreign Languages Press, 2003); Chinese original 1593.

60. Chang, *Shang Civilization;* K.C. Chang, *Art, Myth, and Ritual: The Path to Political Authority in Ancient China* (Cambridge: Harvard University Press, 1983); K.C. Chang, "China on the Eve of the Historical Period," in *The Cambridge History of Ancient China: From the Origins of Civilization to 221 B.C.,* ed. Michael Loewe and Edward L. Shaughnessy (Cambridge: Cambridge University Press, 1999), 37–73.

61. Bray, *Science and Civilisation in China.*

62. Françoise Sabban, "Forms and Evolution of Chinese Cuisine in France," in *Regionalism and Globalism in Chinese Culinary Culture,* ed. David Holm (Taipei: Foundation of Chinese Dietary Culture, 2009), 369–80; Françoise Sabban, "La diète parfaite d'un lettré retiré sous les Song du Sud," *Études chinoises* 16 (1997): 7–57; Françoise Sabban, "La viande en Chine: Imaginaire et usages culinaires," *Anthropozoologica* 18 (1993): 79–90.

63. Thomas Gwinner, *Essen und Trinken: Die Klassische Kochbuchliteratur Chinas* (Frankfurt am Main: Haag und Herchen, 1988).

64. Frederick J. Simoons, *Food in China: A Cultural and Historical Inquiry* (Boca Raton: CRC Press, 1991).

65. Naomichi Ishige, "East Asian Families and the Dining Table," *Journal of Chinese Dietary Culture* 2 (2006): 1–26.

66. E.g., Yan-kit So, *Classic Food of China* (London: MacMillan, 1992).

67. H.T. Huang, *Science and Civilisation in China,* vol. 6, *Biology and Biological Technology,* "Part 5: Fermentations and Food Science" (Cambridge: Cambridge University Press, 2000).

68. Hu Shiu-ying, *Food Plants of China* (Hong Kong: Chinese University of Hong Kong, 2005).

69. Mazumdar, *Sugar and Society in China.*

70. Sidney Mintz, *Sweetness and Power: The Place of Sugar in Modern History* (New York: Penguin, 1985). See e.g. his contributions to Christine M. Du Bois, Chee-Beng Tan, and Sidney Mintz, eds., *The World of Soy* (Urbana: University of Illinois Press, 2008).

71. Hans Ulrich Vogel, "Salt and Chinese Culture: Some Comparative Aspects," in *Regionalism and Globalism in Chinese Culinary Culture,* ed. David Holm (Taipei: Foundation of Chinese Dietary Culture, 2009), 181–248.

72. Vogel, "Salt and Chinese Culture," 185.

73. E.g. Anderson, *The Food of China;* Bray, *Science and Civilisation in China.*

74. E.g. Mark Edward Lewis, *China's Cosmopolitan Empire: The Tang Dynasty* (Cambridge: Harvard University Press, 2009).

75. Patricia Buckley Ebrey, *The Cambridge Illustrated History of China* (Cambridge: Cambridge University Press, 2010); Patricia Buckley Ebrey, *Chinese Civilization: A Sourcebook* (New York: Free Press, 1993).

76. Frederick W. Mote, *Imperial China 900–1800* (Cambridge: Harvard University Press, 1999).

BIBLIOGRAPHY

Anderson, E. N. *The Food of China.* New Haven: Yale University Press, 1988.
———. "Up Against Famine: Chinese Diet in the Early Twentieth Century." *Crossroads* 1 (1990): 11–24.
Anderson, E. N., Teresa Wang, and Victor Mair. "Ni Zan, *Cloud Forest Hall Collection of Rules for Drinking and Eating.*" In *Hawai'i Reader in Traditional Chinese Culture,* edited by Victor Mair, Nancy Steinhardt and Paul R. Goldin, 444–55. Honolulu: University of Hawaii Press, 2005.
Andrade, Tonio. "Chinese Under European Rule: The Case of Sino-Dutch Mediator He Bin." *Late Imperial China* 28 (2007): 1–32.
Avieli, Nir. "Vietnamese New Year Rice Cakes: Iconic Festive Dishes and Contested National Identity." *Ethnology* 44 (2005): 167–87.
———. *Rice Talks: Food and Community in a Vietnamese Town.* Bloomington: University of Indiana Press, 2012.
Bernhardt, Kathryn. *Rents, Taxes, and Peasant Resistance: The Lower Yangzi Region, 1840–1950.* Stanford: Stanford University Press, 1992.
Bettinger, Robert L., Loukas Barton, Christopher Morgan, Fahu Chen, Hui Wang, Thomas P. Guilderson, Duxue Ji, and Dongju Zhang. "The Transition to Agriculture at Dadiwan, People's Republic of China." *Current Anthropology* 51 (2010): 703–14.
Bray, Francesca. *Science and Civilisation in China.* Vol. 6: *Biology and Biological Technology.* "Part II: Agriculture." Cambridge: Cambridge University Press, 1984.
Buell, Paul D., Eugene N. Anderson, and Charles Perry. *A Soup for the Qan: Chinese Dietary Medicine of the Mongol Era as Seen in Hu Szu-Hui's Yinshan Zhengyao.* Leiden: Brill, 2011.

Campbell, T. Colin, with Thomas M. Campbell II. *The China Study: The Most Comprehensive Study of Nutrition Ever Conducted and the Startling Implications for Diet, Weight Loss and Long-Term Health*. Dallas: Benbella Books, 2006.

Cao Xueqin and Gao E. *The Story of the Stone: A Chinese Novel in Five Volumes*. 5 vols. Translated by David Hawkes and John Minford. Harmondsworth: Penguin, 1973–1986.

Chang, K.C. "Ancient China." In *Food in Chinese Culture*, edited by K.C. Chang, 23–52. New Haven: Yale University Press, 1977.

———. *Shang Civilization*. New Haven: Yale University Press, 1980.

———. *Art, Myth, and Ritual: The Path to Political Authority in Ancient China*. Cambridge: Harvard University Press, 1983.

———. "China on the Eve of the Historical Period." In *The Cambridge History of Ancient China: From the Origins of Civilization to 221 B.C.*, edited by Michael Loewe and Edward L. Shaughnessy, 37–73. Cambridge: Cambridge University Press, 1999.

———, ed. *Food in Chinese Culture: Anthropological and Historical Perspectives*. New Haven: Yale University Press, 1977.

Chen Junshi, T. Colin Campbell, Li Junyao, and Richard Peto. *Diet, Life-Style, and Mortality in China: A Study of the Characteristics of 65 Chinese Counties*. Ithaca: Cornell University Press, 1990.

Cheung, Sidney C.H., and Tan Chee-Beng. *Food and Foodways in Asia: Resource, Tradition and Cooking*. London: Routledge, 2007.

Coe, Andrew. *Chop Suey: A Cultural History of Chinese Food in the United States*. New York: Oxford University Press, 2009.

Dannaway, Frederick R. "Placing a Mountain into a Valley: Microcosmic Aesthetics and the Arts of Tea." *The Art of Tea* 9 (2010): 88–91.

Dien, Albert. *Six Dynasties Civilization*. New Haven: Yale University Press, 2007.

Dikötter, Frank. *Mao's Great Famine: The History of China's Most Devastating Catastrophe, 1958–1962*. New York: Walker and Co., 2010.

Du Bois, Christine M., Chee-Beng Tan, and Sidney Mintz, eds. *The World of Soy*. Urbana: University of Illinois Press, 2008.

Ebrey, Patricia Buckley. *The Cambridge Illustrated History of China*. Cambridge: Cambridge University Press, 2010.

———, ed. *Chinese Civilization: A Sourcebook*. New York: Free Press, 1993.

Elvin, Mark. *The Pattern of the Chinese Past*. Stanford: Stanford University Press, 1973.

Engelhardt, Ute. "Dietetics in Tang China and the First Extant Works of *Materia dietetica*." In *Innovation in Chinese Medicine*, edited by Elisabeth Hsu, 173–91. Cambridge: Cambridge University Press, 2001.

Finnane, Antonia. *Speaking of Yangzhou: A Chinese City, 1550–1850*. Cambridge: Harvard University Press, 2004.

Freeman, Michael. "Sung." In *Food in Chinese Culture*, ed. K.C. Chang, 141–92. New Haven: Yale University Press, 1977.

Gardella, Robert. *Harvesting Mountains: Fujian and the China Tea Trade, 1757–1937*. Berkeley: University of California Press, 1994.

Geertz, Clifford. *Agricultural Involution: The Process of Ecological Change in Indonesia*. Berkeley: University of California Press, 1963.

Gwinner, Thomas. *Essen und Trinken: Die Klassische Kochbuchliteratur Chinas*. Frankfurt am Main: Haag und Herchen, 1988.

Hayami, Yujiro, and Vernon Ruttan. *Agricultural Development: An International Perspective*. Baltimore: Johns Hopkins University Press, 1985.

Hohenegger, Beatrice, ed. *Steeped in History: The Art of Tea*. Los Angeles: Fowler Museum at UCLA, 2009.

Ho Ping-ti. "The Introduction of American Food Plants into China." *American Anthropologist* 57 (1955): 191–201.

Hu, Shiu-Ying. *Food Plants of China*. Hong Kong: Chinese University of Hong Kong, 2005.

Huang, H.T. *Science and Civilisation in China*. Volume 6: *Biology and Biological Technology*. "Part 5: Fermentations and Food Science." Cambridge: Cambridge University Press, 2000.

Huang, Philip. *The Peasant Family and Rural Development in the Yangzi Delta, 1350–1988*. Stanford: Stanford University Press, 1990.

———. "Development or Involution in Eighteenth-Century Britain and China? A Review of Kenneth Pomeranz's *The Great Divergence: China, Europe, and the Making of the Modern World Economy*." *The Journal of Asian Studies* 61 (2002): 501–38.

Ishige, Naomichi. "East Asian Families and the Dining Table." *Journal of Chinese Dietary Culture* 2 (2006): 1–26.

King, F.H. *Farmers of Forty Centuries; or, Permanent Agriculture in China, Korea and Japan*. New York: Harcourt and Brace, 1927.

Kong, Y.C. *Huihui Yaofang*. Hong Kong: Y.C. Kong, 1996.

Laufer, Berthold. *Sino-Iranica*. Chicago: Field Museum, 1919.

Lee, James, and Wang Feng. *One Quarter of Humanity: Malthusian Mythology and Chinese Realities, 1700–2000*. Cambridge: Harvard University Press, 1999.

Lewis, Mark Edward. *China's Cosmopolitan Empire: The Tang Dynasty*. Cambridge: Harvard University Press, 2009.

Li, Lillian. *Fighting Famine in North China: State, Market, and Environmental Decline, 1690s–1990s*. Stanford: Stanford University Press, 2007.

Li Bozhong. *Agricultural Development in Jiangnan, 1620–1850*. New York: St. Martin's Press, 1998.

Li Hui-Lin. *Nan-fang Ts'ao-mu Chuang, A Fourth Century Flora of Southeast Asia: Introduction, Translation, Commentaries*. Hong Kong: Chinese University of Hong Kong, 1979.

Li Liu. *The Chinese Neolithic: Trajectories to Early States*. Cambridge: Cambridge University Press, 2004.

Li Shizhen. *Compendium of Materia Medica (Bencao Gangmu)*. Translated by Luo Xiwen. Beijing: Foreign Languages Press, 2003. (Original 1593).

Li Shu-Fan. *Hong Kong Surgeon*. London: Victor Gollancz, 1964.

Liu An. *Huainanzi: A Guide to the Theory and Practice of Government in Early Han China*. Translated and edited by John S. Major, Sarah A. Queen, Andrew Seth Mayer and Harold D. Roth. New York: Columbia University Press, 2010.

Mallory, Walter. *China, Land of Famine.* New York: American Geographic Society, 1926.

Mazumdar, Sucheta. *Sugar and Society in China: Peasants, Technology, and the World Market.* Cambridge: Harvard University Press, 1998.

———. "The Impact of New World Food Crops on the Diet and Economy of China and India, 1600–1900." In *Food in Global History,* edited by Raymond Grew, 58–78. Boulder: Westview, 1999.

Mintz, Sidney. *Sweetness and Power: The Place of Sugar in Modern History.* New York: Penguin, 1985.

Mo Di. *The Mozi: A Complete Translation.* Translated by Ian Johnston. New York: Columbia University Press, 2010.

Mote, Frederick W. *Imperial China 900–1800.* Cambridge: Harvard University Press, 1999.

Newman, Jacqueline. *Food Culture in China.* Westport: Greenwood Press, 2004.

Ouyang Xiu. *Historical Records of the Five Dynasties.* Translated by Richard L. Davis. New York: Columbia University Press, 2004.

Pomeranz, Kenneth. *The Great Divergence: China, Europe, and the Making of the Modern World Economy.* Princeton: Princeton University Press, 2000.

Read, Bernard Emms. *Famine Foods Listed in the Chiu Huang Pen Ts'ao.* Shanghai: Henry Lester Institute of Medical Research, 1946.

Rickett, W. Allyn. *Guanzi: Political, Economic, and Philosophical Essays from Early China: A Study and Translation.* Vol. 1. Princeton: Princeton University Press, 1985.

———. *Guanzi: Political, Economic, and Philosophical Essays from Early China: A Study and Translation.* Vol. 2. Princeton: Princeton University Press, 1998.

Ruddle, Kenneth and Gongfu Zhong. *Integrated Agriculture-Aquaculture in South China: The Dike-Pond System of the Zhujiang Delta.* Cambridge: Cambridge University Press, 1988.

Sabban, Françoise. "Un savoir-faire oublié: le travail du lait en Chine ancienne." *Zibun: Memoirs of the Research Institute for Humanistic Studies* 21 (1986): 31–65.

———. "La viande en Chine: Imaginaire et usages culinaires." *Anthropozoologica* 18 (1993): 79–90.

———. "La diète parfaite d'un lettré retiré sous les Song du Sud." *Études chinoises* 16 (1997): 7–57.

———. "Forms and Evolution of Chinese Cuisine in France." In *Regionalism and Globalism in Chinese Culinary Culture,* edited by David Holm, 369–80. Taipei: Foundation of Chinese Dietary Culture, 2009.

———. "Milk Consumption in China: The Construction of a New Food Habit." In *Proceedings, 12th Symposium on Chinese Dietary Culture, Okinawa,* 397–420. Taipei: Foundation for Chinese Dietary Culture, 2011.

Schafer, Edward H. *The Golden Peaches of Samarkand: A Study of T'ang Exotics.* Berkeley: University of California Press, 1963.

———. *The Vermilion Bird: T'ang Images of the South.* Berkeley: University of California Press, 1967.

Simoons, Frederick J. "T'ang." In *Food in Chinese Culture,* edited by K.C. Chang, 85–140. New Haven: Yale University Press, 1977.

———. *Food in China: A Cultural and Historical Inquiry.* Boca Raton: CRC Press, 1991.

Smith, Joanna Handlin. *The Art of Doing Good: Charity in Late Ming China.* Berkeley: University of California Press, 2009.

So, Yan-kit. "A Study of Yuan Mei's Iced Bean Curd." In *Cookery: Science, Lore and Books: Proceedings of the Oxford Symposium on Food and Cookery, 1984 and 1985,* edited by Alan Davidson, 52–54. London: Prospect, 1986.

———. *Classic Food of China.* London: MacMillan, 1992.

Sterckx, Roel. *Food, Sacrifice and Sagehood in Early China.* Cambridge: Cambridge University Press, 2001.

———, ed. *Of Tripod and Palate: Food, Politics, and Religion in Traditional China.* New York: Palgrave MacMillan, 2005.

Sun Simiao. *Recipes Worth a Thousand Gold.* Translated by Sumei Yi, edited by E.N. Anderson. 2007. http://www.krazykioti.com/articles/recipes-worth-a-thousand-gold/

Vogel, Hans Ulrich. "Salt and Chinese Culture: Some Comparative Aspects." In *Regionalism and Globalism in Chinese Culinary Culture,* edited by David Holm, 181–248. Taipei: Foundation of Chinese Dietary Culture, 2009.

Von Falkenhausen, Lothar. *Chinese Society in the Age of Confucius (1000–250 BC): The Archaeological Evidence.* Los Angeles: Cotsen Institute of Archaeology, UCLA, 2006.

Waley, Arthur. *Yuan Mei: Eighteenth Century Chinese Poet.* London: George Allen and Unwin, 1956.

Waley-Cohen, Joanna. "The Quest for Perfect Balance." In *Food: The History of Taste,* edited by Paul Freedman, 99–134. Berkeley: University of California Press, 2007.

Wang, Di. *The Teahouse: Small Business, Everyday Culture, and Public Politics in Chengdu, 1900–1950.* Stanford: Stanford University Press, 2008.

Watson, James L. *Emigration and the Chinese Lineage: The Mans in Hong Kong and London.* Berkeley: University of California Press, 1975.

———, ed. *Golden Arches East: McDonald's in East Asia.* Stanford: Stanford University Press, 2006.

Watson, James L. and Rubie S. Watson. *Village Life in Hong Kong: Politics, Gender and Ritual in the New Territories.* Hong Kong: Chinese University of Hong Kong, 2004.

Wen Dazhong and David Pimentel. "Seventeenth Century Organic Agriculture in China: I. Cropping Systems in Jiaxing Region." *Human Ecology* 14 (1986): 1–14.

———. "Seventeenth Century Organic Agriculture in China: II. Energy Flows through an Agroecosystem in Jiaxing Region." *Human Ecology* 14 (1986): 15–28.

Will, Pierre-Étienne, and R. Bin Wong. *Nourish the People: The State Civilian Granary System in China, 1650–1850.* Ann Arbor: Center for Chinese Studies, University of Michigan, 1991.

Wong, R. Bin. *China Transformed: Historical Change and the Limits of European Experience*. Ithaca: Cornell University Press, 1997.

Wu, David Y.H., and Sidney C.H. Cheung, eds. *The Globalization of Chinese Food*. Richmond: Curzon, 2002.

Wu, David Y.H., Sidney C.H. Cheung, and Tan Chee-beng, eds. *Changing Chinese Foodways in Asia*. Hong Kong: Chinese University of Hong Kong, 2001.

Wu Ching-tzu. *The Scholars*. Translated by Yang Hsien-yi and Gladys Yang. Beijing: Foreign Languages Press, 1973.

Xunzi. *Xunzi*. Translated by John Knoblock and Zhang Jue. Changsha; Beijing: Hunan People's Publishing House and Foreign Languages Press, 1999.

Xu Wu. *Farming, Cooking, and Eating Practices in the Central China Highland: How Hezha Foods Function to Establish Ethnic Identity*. Lewiston: Edwin Mellen Press, 2011.

Yang Shou-Zhong. *The Divine Farmer's Materia Medica: A Translation of the Shen Nong Ben Cao*. Boulder: Blue Poppy Press, 1998.

Yan Yunxiang. "McDonald's in Beijing: The Localization of Americana." In *Golden Arches East: McDonald's in East Asia,* edited by James L. Watson, 39–76. Stanford: Stanford University Press, 2006.

CHAPTER 3

India

JAYANTA SENGUPTA

In India, as in other societies, food is one of the central elements of culture and reflects the social and economic structure of society. Any discussion of the subcontinent's food traditions, therefore, needs to be mapped onto its cultural, economic, environmental, and sociological features. India's great size and immense diversity belie broad generalizations. In geographical terms, it contains long stretches of coastal land, in conjunction with thickly forested inland regions, mountainous territories, arid deserts, and great stretches of plains crisscrossed by rivers—a diversity that has shaped food availability and agricultural techniques. Social and cultural diversity has contributed greatly to this mix. While the vast majority of the Indian population are Hindus, India also has the world's third largest Muslim population (after Indonesia and Pakistan). Vegetarianism is a religious practice among nearly 30 percent of Indians, while many among the Indian poor can little afford to consume nonvegetarian food. The contrast between India's poor—according a 2005 World Bank estimate, 42 percent of Indians live below the international poverty line[1]—and its fast-growing middle class, one of the largest in the world, also contributes to the divergence of food practices. And, despite the popularity of Indian restaurants in the West—where there prevails a widely shared perception of Indian food as spicy and primarily curry-based—the enormous variety of regional cuisine in India, too, cautions us against trying to generalize to any significant extent on a subject like food in the Indian subcontinent.

In the broadest terms, three distinct geographical regions divide the Indian subcontinent from north to south. Taking the western and eastern flanks together, the Himalayan mountain ranges constitute the subcontinent's northern boundary, separating it from China, blocking frigid arctic winds, bottling up monsoon winds, and sustaining a glacial system that feeds a number of major rivers. These latter flow into and around the Indo-Gangetic plains, stretching from the valley of the Indus River in Pakistan to that of the Brahmaputra in Assam and merging into the deltaic lowlands of Bangladesh. From the west to the east, these plains comprise much of India's rice- and wheat-producing grain belt, also containing within themselves the areas with the highest population density. Finally, to the south, peninsular India forms a huge inverted triangle surrounded by the Arabian Sea in the west, the Indian Ocean in the south, and the Bay of Bengal in the east. This region has long, narrow stretches of mountain ranges running along the eastern and western seaboards, enclosing a plateau heartland that is washed by a number of major rivers. One or more of these geographical features are shared with India by several other nation-states in South Asia—the Himalayan ranges and their foothills by Pakistan, Nepal, and Bhutan; the western portion of the Indo-Gangetic plains by Pakistan; and the eastern part of the Ganges-Brahmaputra delta by Bangladesh. As a result, insofar as food production and consumption patterns are shaped by distinctive geographical systems, the boundaries of Indian food overlap significantly with those of these neighboring nations.

Indian climate is dominated by the monsoon, which is the prime source of precipitation throughout the subcontinent. Hot summers in most of northern India lead to an intense low pressure belt, allowing the South Asian monsoon to reach an intensity unparalleled anywhere else. The extremely humid air contributes both to the high rainfall over much of tropical South Asia and to the extreme intensity of the rain storms that bring it.[2] Within this broad tropical climate, however, significant regional variations exist, evidenced in the stark contrast between the desert of Rajasthan in western India and the world's wettest zone in the Shillong Plateau in the northeast. In broad terms, precipitation diminishes from east to west. The temperature in the hot season comes down in a north-south gradient, while during the cold season this gradient is reversed.

There is little doubt that rainfall wields greater influence than temperature in the human geography of the subcontinent. The distinction between wet and dry seasons, therefore, is more important than that between hot and cold. Since the length of the growing season in South Asia is limited by low temperatures in only a few areas, precipitation is the principal climatic element affecting agriculture and hence the sustenance of human populations. The average annual rainfall is a major determinant not only of what crops can be grown (e.g., rice normally requires around one hundred centimeters), but also of the average yields to be expected. Typically in South Asia rainfall is heavy during a few months of the year. Inevitably, much of this concentrated precipitation is wasted as runoff from already saturated soil. The same quantity of rain distributed more or less evenly throughout the year (as is the case in much of Western Europe) would be far more beneficial for agriculture. As it is, in the absence of irrigation most of South Asia is limited, despite year-round warmth, to one crop a year. Over a very large area of South Asia, the pattern of variability of rainfall is of vital importance. Years of high rainfall may mean prosperity—unless the amounts are so high that flooding results—while years of low rainfall may bring famine. In the very high rainfall range, averaging more than two hundred centimeters per year, years dry enough to cause crop failure are virtually unknown, whereas toward the opposite extreme, in areas averaging less than thirty-five centimeters per year, crops cannot normally be grown without irrigation.

The basic division in scholarly discussion of Indian food lies in the examination of food as an aspect of material culture, on the one hand, and that of food as an entity endowed with cultural and moral characteristics, on the other. Intriguingly, these two approaches are informed by two virtually opposite ideas of India. Insofar as one seeks to write the history of Indian food as a temporal narrative of dishes and their ingredients and their evolution through the rise and fall of political regimes, social and cultural systems, and structures of economic production—best exemplified by the work of the Indian food historian K.T. Achaya—India invariably emerges as one of the most diverse societies in the world, having borrowed food ingredients and cooking styles heavily and openly from all corners of the world.[3] Indeed, "the story of Indian food," as Ashis Nandy reminds us, "is often the story of the blatantly exogenous becoming prototypically authentic."[4] On the other hand, a significant body of work—led by the research of the Indian anthropologist Ravindra S. Khare—examines what has been described as "gastrosemantics," namely, how the symbolism and communication involved in the cultural language of food link the worldly aspects of Hindu society with its otherworldly ones. While shedding important light on the ethnography of food as articulated in ideas of the cooked and the raw, the pure and the polluted, the sanctified and the profane, community and commensality, et cetera, such work has tended to exaggerate the pervasive cosmic presence of food in the Hindu moral universe and reinforce the Indological emphasis on India's exceptionalism and essential difference from the West.[5]

Evidence on patterns of food consumption in early India is primarily conjectural, confined mainly to tools excavated from archaeological sites, cave paintings, and surviving words in the ancient languages. Historians speculate that the first humans came to the Indian subcontinent by sea from East Africa and by land from East Asia at different times, and that their pointed stone tools indicated a mainly meat-based diet, possibly complemented with natural foods like honey, berries, fruits, roots, herbs, and nuts. The development of Neolithic tools starting about 5000 B.C.E. made possible the transition from hunting and gathering to agriculture, accompanied by new processes like the grinding of grain and spices. This soon led to the emergence of rice as a dietary staple, coupled with *ragi* (a kind of millet), lentils, pumpkin, eggplant, banana, coconut, pomegranate, jackfruit, oranges, limes, watermelon, gourds and squashes of various kinds, and the edible parts of the lotus plant. By this time, the domestication of animals like sheep, goats, and buffalos—for the purposes of farming, eating, and dairying—was a well-marked feature of the culture of the subcontinent.

The Harappan civilization, which flourished from 2500 B.C.E. to 1600 B.C.E. around the alluvial plains of the Indus River valley in modern Pakistan and in an extensive territory straddling the modern Indian states of Gujarat and Rajasthan, contributed richly to this developing mosaic of Indian food culture. Wheat and barley were the main crops grown by the Harappans, who prepared bread in round ovens similar to those used in the Middle East and Central Asia, and used animal fats for cooking. Among other foods consumed were rice, oats, peas, chickpeas, lentils, and fruits such as dates, pomegranates, and perhaps bananas. Bone remnants excavated from the Harappan sites indicate both extensive meat eating and the consumption of fish from the river and the Indian Ocean. During the ensuing thousand years or so, when groups of Indo-Aryan speakers from Central Asia gradually migrated into the subcontinent, cleared the thick forests of northern India, and settled along the valley of the River Ganges, consumption patterns did not undergo any dramatic changes, with the exception that sugar replaced honey to emerge as the major sweetening agent of food, and also as the key ingredient in sweet dishes that also used milk and rice and, occasionally, wheat bread. The other notable innovation of this period, growing out of the rising importance of the cow, was a significant consumption of milk and dairy products like butter, cream, yogurt, and clarified butter (*ghee*), which itself quickly became an important cooking medium. The use of the iron plough along with crop rotation and irrigation made it possible for the Indo-Aryans to produce enough food to sustain a rapidly growing population.

The really intriguing question with regard to food habits in ancient India is the emergence of the concepts of vegetarianism and abstinence as critically important ethical doctrines among significant sections of the Indian population, who came to avoid the consumption of food that necessitated the taking of life. This is a curious development, given that meat eating was widely prevalent in ancient India, both in the north and in the south. The researches of Om Prakash on food and drink in ancient India and of Jeannine Auboyer on daily life document a large variety of animals—including cows, sheep, goats, horses, swine, deer, and tortoises—whose flesh were consumed by Indo-Aryans in the Vedic period, often after ceremonial sacrifice, but also as part of more "regular" meals and as offerings made to guests.[6] The use of sacrificial meat continued in the period after 800 B.C.E., and even the Buddhist *Jataka* tales mentioned the practice of consuming the meat of the pigeon, partridge, monkey, and elephant. Indeed, Buddha did allow the consumption of meat, especially if it was offered as alms to monks. The most famous medical treatises of ancient India—the *Charaka-samhita* (circa the first century C.E.) and the *Sushruta-samhita* (first composed in the last centuries B.C.E. and fixed in its present form by the seventh century C.E.)—present formidable lists of edible meats that were deemed suitable for people of varying body types and health conditions. Francis Zimmerman's work on concepts of ecology and traditional medicine (*ayurveda*) among Hindus in ancient India contends that the Indian equivalent of what the Europeans called "the great chain of being" was a sequence of foods at the end of which were various cooked meats whose savors permeated the natural domain.[7] Recently, the eminent Indian historian D. N. Jha has scoured ancient Indian textual evidence to conclusively contend that the consumption of beef continued to be widely prevalent in post-Vedic India until the twelfth century C.E., and was practiced not only within the Hindu Brahmanical order but by Buddhists as well.[8] The book was declared "blasphemous" by Hindu extremists who have traditionally argued that it was only with the Muslim conquest that cows were first slaughtered in India.

However, early notions of vegetarianism were also developed in the midst of this widespread culture of meat eating, perhaps as early as the Vedic period itself, when the taking of life for food began to be questioned. A textual critique of meat eating began to develop in the later Vedic period, and is evident in the *Shatapatha Brahmana,* later in the *Dharma Sutras,* and then in the *Dharmashastras,* including *Manu Smriti.* The celebrated Indian food historian K.T. Achaya has shown that utilitarian economic needs—and not humanitarian impulses—led to early prohibitions on the slaughter of milk cows or draught oxen, and that a larger concern for the taking of animal life developed much later and as a gradual process.[9]

Eventually the Buddhists and the Jains prevailed in this campaign to put an end to Vedic animal sacrifices. If the unintentional killing of animals was acceptable to Buddha, the Jains were much stronger in their condemnation of the taking of life for food and went to extraordinary lengths to avoid injury to all living forms. The emergent concept of *ahimsa* or nonkilling gradually began to resonate with a significant number of people and was made into a moral compass of the state by Ashoka, the Buddhist emperor of the Maurya dynasty. This received strong endorsement from influential reformist and devotionalist schools of Hindu philosophy in early medieval India between around 800 C.E. and 1200 C.E., and consequently Brahmans—with the exception of those living in Kashmir, Bengal, and a part of Karnataka—were gradually obliged to become vegetarians. Although with time a few non-Brahman sections of Indian society took to vegetarianism as a symbol of Brahmanical prestige or piety, the lower castes were much less affected by the social taboo against meat-eating. Thus, while Chinese Buddhist travelers to India between the fifth and seventh centuries claimed that an almost universal vegetarianism prevailed in the subcontinent, al-Biruni—the Persian Muslim scholar who visited India in the early-eleventh century—was more accurate in observing that such strictures regarding a vegetarian diet were much less prevalent outside of the upper castes, mostly Brahmans.

Although the beginning of the Islamic influence in India can be dated back to the Arab conquest of Sindh in the eighth century, the Muslim presence only made itself felt with the raids of Mahmud of Ghazni in the early years of the second millennium C.E., and Islamic political influence did not establish itself until the early thirteenth century, with the foundation of the Delhi Sultanate, which was ruled by different Turkic and Afghan dynasties. The sultanate was overturned by a Mongol invasion in 1526 led by Zahir-ud-Din Mohammad Babur, who founded the powerful Mughal Empire, which ruled over the subcontinent through the sixteenth and seventeenth centuries, and was—along with the Ottoman and Safavid empires—one of the three most powerful Islamic empires of the early modern world. During the sultanate and the Mughal periods, agriculture remained the foundation of the economy, while trade, both overland and oceanic, continued with Africa, Asia, and Europe. It was the vast wealth of Mughal India that brought the Portuguese explorer Vasco da Gama to the southwestern coast of India in 1498.

Muslim influence on the style and substance of Indian food was profound. K.T. Achaya writes that the Muslims imported a new refinement and a courtly etiquette of both group and individual dining into the austere dining ambience of Hindu society.[10] Coming originally from modern Uzbekistan, Tajikistan, Kyrgyzstan, and Kazakhstan, the Mughals initially had a culinary style influenced by the nomadic lifestyle of the steppes, revolving around simple grilling and boiling. The later refinement, as Sami Zubaida contends, came mainly from Persian sources, especially after Babur's son, Humayun, came back to India after spending a long period of exile in Kabul and the Safavid imperial court in Iran. He brought with him an entourage of Persian cooks who introduced the rich and elaborate rice cookery of the Safavid courts to India, combining Indian spices and Persian arts into a rich fusion that became the iconic dish of Islamic South Asian cuisine, the biryani.[11] In general, during the centuries of Muslim rule food items native to India were enriched with nuts, raisins and other dried fruits, saffron, musk, asafetida and other aromatic spices, and liberal doses of clarified butter (*ghee*). These materials went into the making of meat and rice dishes (*pulao*), marinated meat (*kabab*) grilled usually in a clay oven traditionally sunk into the ground (*tandoor*), oven-baked or fried flatbreads (*naan* or *paratha*), spicy stews of rice and lentils (*khichri*), pastries with savory fillings (*samosa*), desserts (*halwa*), and sweetened drinks (*falooda*, *sherbet*).[12] It has been rightly said that by the time the Mughal Empire reached the peak of its power around the turn of the seventeenth century, royal cuisine "had been elevated to the level of a state concern," as indicated by the significant space that the Mughal emperor Akbar's famous court historian, Abul Fazl, devotes to it in the imperial gazetteer, the *Ain-i-Akbari*.[13] In reality, it was the Mughals who first gave shape to the concept of an Indian cuisine, though under them it never acquired truly pan-Indian proportions. And, although its close association with a feudal lifestyle and expensive ingredients made Mughal cuisine primarily an *haute cuisine,* pared-down versions gradually came to be adopted by the common people, especially in northern India.[14] In a regional variant that developed in the northern Indian kingdom of Awadh with its capital at Lucknow, local peasant cooking techniques were incorporated, resulting in dishes that were affordable to the poor.[15] Notwithstanding this concession to the poor, however, Awadhi cuisine has to this day remained the symbol of an aristocratic, highly sophisticated tradition of Islamic cooking marked by the subtle use of aromatic spices and the technique of *dum pukht,* the slow cooking of meat and rice in a round pot (*handi*) whose lid has been sealed with dough.[16]

The other decisive influence on Indian food habits in this period came from the contact with Europe and through it with the New World. In 1498, six years after Christopher Columbus set foot on the West Indies, the Portuguese seaman Vasco da Gama found the sea route to India and landed on the subcontinent's southwestern Malabar coast. The Portuguese were followed soon by the Dutch, French, and British trading companies, the last of which eventually established their political hegemony in the subcontinent in the second half of the eighteenth century. The Portuguese presence had by then become confined to their main outpost in Goa, on India's western coast, but not before they had used their series of forts and factories stretching from Brazil to Japan to create an extensive trading empire that ushered India into the Columbian Exchange—a global exchange of food crops, populations, ideas, and diseases between the New World and the Old World following Columbus's voyage to the Americas. The other factor contributing to a global exchange in India was the Spanish conquest of the Philippines in the 1560s, which made it possible for the goods of the New World to make their way into India from the opposite direction as well, across the Pacific and the eastern Indian Ocean.

In India, the Portuguese introduced a wide range of new foods, including potatoes, tomatoes, chili peppers, kidney beans, maize, tapioca, papayas, pineapples, guavas, sugar-apples, cashews, peanuts and sunflower seeds (both pressed for oil used in cooking), tobacco, and turkey from the New World; okra and coffee from Africa; and tea, soybeans, and litchis from China. The extent to which these products were assimilated in the regional cuisines was truly remarkable. In Goa itself, the interaction between the Portuguese influence and the local food of the Saraswath caste of western India gave rise to a distinctive cuisine. In Bengal in eastern India, the Portuguese generated a significant demand for cottage cheese, which was adapted by Bengali cooks as the chief ingredient of a wide range of sweetmeats. The potato quickly found general acceptance, and Indian cuisine gradually became one of the very few in the world to convert the potato from a side dish to the center-piece of many recipes. Kidney beans, cooked like lentils, also became one of the staple dishes of northern India.[17] And chilis, of course, became the iconic marker of the spiciness of Indian cuisine, as well as an easily affordable ingredient for the common people to add some flavor and taste to their diet.

Although the Portuguese were the first to arrive in India, it was the British East India Company that in the second half of the eighteenth century launched what would become a subcontinental colonial empire. The transformation of the company into an imperial power was, however, a drawn-out process that started in Bengal and gradually came to engulf virtually the whole subcontinent by the 1850s. Until the early nineteenth century, the British sought to rule India through an Indian idiom and, consequently, the Company's men in India often pursued a "native" lifestyle, learning Indian languages, taking Indian wives and mistresses, and eating spicy Indian food made by local cooks as well as hybrid dishes conjured up by the English lady of the house, including rice pulaos, biryanis, Indian-style pickles and relishes, and *kedgeree*—an anglicized version of the Indian *khichri*.

European attitudes towards India and its inhabitants were varied and often ambivalent, yet there was one basic assumption underlying all British colonial medical texts from the 1770s to the 1850s: a belief in the uniqueness of the Indian tropical disease environment and the need for a fundamental reappraisal of European medical knowledge in light of this. Most medical men believed that there was nothing inevitable about sickness in the tropics, and that it could be prevented by avoiding the inappropriate diet of Europeans, which revolved around an over-consumption of every sort of meat, including pork and beef, both roast and curried. Letters from Bengal written by the English traveler Eliza Fay reveal that, notwithstanding the oppressive heat of the tropics, their regular "bill of fare" in the afternoons consisted of "a soup, a roast fowl, curry and rice, a mutton pie, a fore-quarter of lamb, a rice pudding, tarts, very good cheese, fresh churned butter, fine bread, [and] excellent Madeira."[18] Indeed, as Elizabeth Collingham's work has shown, during the early decades of the British East India Company's rule in India, such ostentatious and unhealthy dining habits "served well to underline the status of the Company grandee in India." With the increasing racialization of colonial rule after 1858—when, following the suppression of the Indian Revolt of 1857, the Indian empire passed under the direct rule of the British Crown—the body of the colonial official in India became an even more powerful signifier of "British-ness," and diet and dress became, accordingly, cultural sites on which a sense of bodily difference between the British and their Indian subjects was maintained.[19] Though this entailed a refinement of eating etiquette compared to the meat-eating excesses of the earlier period, elaborate meals continued to be the norm, until at least the advent of the twenti-eth century, when lighter meals acquired increasing favor.[20]

Similarly, Dipesh Chakrabarty's work on the culture of managerial power in Bengal's jute mills around the turn of the nineteenth century shows that the lifestyle—and especially the food habits—of the British jute mill managers contained an element of spectacle as an important aspect of their physical superiority vis-à-vis the millhands. In such cir-cumstances, as Chakrabarty suggests, "eating was a ritualised expres-sion of a colonial ruling-class culture . . . signifying . . . excess and plen-itude." Thus an early-morning "small breakfast" (*chota haziri*) of a handful of pieces of toast, a few eggs, and a large pot of tea was duly followed by a regular breakfast consisting of "fish, stewed steak and onions, eggs, curried fowl and rice, with the usual addenda of tea or coffee, with bread, butter and jam." Some went further and gleefully downed a few pegs of whiskey and soda before going back to work.[21]

Just as these ostentatious eating habits were deployed as the cultural markers of a masculine, physically superior British Raj, the native kitchen or "cookhouse" was very bleakly portrayed as symbolic of all that was filthy, dirty, and uncouth about Oriental cultures. The author of a cookbook described a typical kitchen in an Anglo-Indian com-pound as "a wretchedly mean, carelessly constructed, godown [out-building] . . . inconveniently far from the house, and consequently open to every passer-by."[22] Further, because of inadequate equipment, the cook had to use "his cloth for a sieve, and his fingers for a spoon or fork."[23] Given this description, it is perhaps not surprising that yet another cookbook cautioned, "The native ways are not as our ways and the less you see of them over their cooking operations the more appetite you will have for the food set before you."[24]

Generally speaking, the gastronomic habits of the British in Bengal—including conspicuous consumption bordering on gluttony in the early days of Company rule, and more refined but elaborate meals in the sec-ond half of the nineteenth century—served as a metaphor for the racial and physical superiority of the Raj. Although such dietary habits were firmly castigated from the "scientific" viewpoint—most frequently by climatologists and medical men—the table manners of the Raj obviously valued symbolism over science. The Indian kitchen as an object of revulsion was the other part of the same worldview. The dark mysteries of the Orient manifested themselves within the cookhouse in many ways—through the heat, smoke, and filth, as well as through the cunning of foxy cooks or *bawarchis,* who pinched provisions, padded their accounts, and—worst of all—used their curry powder to enliven what a 1906 cookbook described as "superannuated fish or meat."[25]

Indeed, it was in such a hybrid world of cooking ingredients and styles that the concept of the "curry" was born and gained acceptance in Anglo-Indian cuisine in the late-eighteenth and through much of the nineteenth century. Towards the later part of that century its popularity went into a decline, though eventually—for most non-Indians—curry became a blanket catchphrase for every Indian dish. It has rightly been said that it was a British invention, both the word (adapted from the Tamil word *kari,* which means black pepper) and the ingredients that went into its making. As a generic term, curry designated a spicy stew of meat, fish, or vegetables, cooked in clarified butter or oil, with a large array of dry roasted whole or ground spices, frequently involving onions, ginger, and garlic, sometimes including tamarind and/or coconut milk or flesh, and typically eaten with rice. Colonial officials returning to Britain, no longer able to depend on Indian cooks, acquired commercial curry powder mixtures to try at home in the middle decades of the nineteenth century. Curry gradually became, as has been argued recently, "not just a term that the British used to describe an unfamiliar set of Indian stews and ragouts, but a dish in its own right, created for the British in India."[26]

One of the most dramatic moments in the history of the British Empire in India, the outbreak of violent and widespread revolt against British rule—the so-called "Mutiny" of 1857—is indelibly associated with the history of food taboos in India and the British insensitivity to them. Social unrest and political aggrandizement probably made the Mutiny inevitable, but the final trigger was the British disregard of forbidden foods: the cow, sacred to Hindus, and the pig, execrable to Muslims. Soon before the outbreak, a new weapon—the Enfield rifle—was introduced to the Indian soldiers of the British Indian army. The rifle cartridges had a protective coating of grease, and soldiers were required to bite the cartridge open for loading. The greasing agent was rumored to be beef and pork fat, which were intolerable to Hindus and Muslims respectively and spurred them on to a revolt that—though put down in about a year's time—rang the death-knell for the East India Company.

An important recent development in the field of Indian food history has been a growing interest in an examination of how themes related to cooking, food, nutrition, and the relationship between dietary practice and health came to preoccupy the intellectual worlds of the educated middle classes in many parts of colonial India. With the growth of English education among the primarily Hindu upper-caste, urban sections of the British Indian population, the articulation of a new set of values, prejudices, and tastes for these middle classes often came to be deeply implicated in thinking and discussion about modernity and nationalism. Though this emerging literature is less about food per se than about cooking and eating as cultural practices, it touches on several themes intimately connected with food—for instance, the relationship between food habits and the rise of the health sciences, ideas about an "appropriate diet" for different categories of Indians, debates about the place of cooking in the world of the educated, refined "New Indian Woman," and the emergence of a well-organized kitchen as the centerpiece of a new, reformed, efficient ideology of domesticity. This is a welcome development in the field, because it brings the history of Indian food squarely within the ambit of scholarship on the cultural politics of Indian modernity.[27] One of the most interesting instances of this literature is an examination of modern Indian cookbooks as cultural texts, leading to the argument that the making of a truly national Indian cuisine is a postcolonial process in which cookbooks have openly paraded the regional roots of their recipes, and so aided the "culinary cosmopolitanism" of a multiethnic, polyglot, consumerist Indian middle class whose very cultural identity is defined by an "interplay of regional inflection and national standardization."[28]

Within the very broad north-south division in Indian political and cultural geography, there is an enormous regional diversity in Indian cuisine that belies most broad generalizations and the popular identification of "Indian food" with the inauthentic, spiced-up Mughal-Punjabi fare dished out in the majority of Indian restaurants in the West. Outside the southern half of the subcontinent, there are well-defined regional food traditions in Kashmir, Punjab, Rajasthan, Gujarat, and Bengal, among other regions. The cuisine of Kashmir, India's northernmost state, characterized by a cold climate ideal for sheep-breeding, has a strong influence of Iranian and Afghan traditions. Essentially meat-based and centered on a main course of rice, Kashmiri cuisine is distinguished by the liberal use of dried fruits, nuts, and locally grown saffron. In the northwestern Indian region of Rajasthan by contrast, the hot and dry climate—especially in the desert—has often necessitated substituting water with milk, buttermilk, or *ghee* in the cooking process. In spite of the relative scarcity of fresh vegetables in the region, as much as 60 percent of the population are vegetarians, including the large group of the preponderantly mercantile Marwari community who have religious strictures against the taking of animal life. However, the long history of warrior traditions and hunting (*shikar*) by princely families has led to the popularity among Rajasthan's nonvegetarians of outdoor cooking—especially the grilling of marinated meats of poultry and game—often prepared by males. Punjab, partitioned between India and Pakistan in 1947, has virtually the same food on both sides of the border and lends its signature style to countless Indian restaurants in the West. Its prolific dairy farming leads to a liberal use of butter, *ghee*, yogurt, and curd cheese (*paneer*). Its abundant wheat crop—earning it the title "the granary of India"—gives a centrality in its cuisine to myriad unleavened and leavened flatbreads like *roti, naan,* and, most commonly, *paratha,* which is often stuffed with shredded seasonal vegetables and seasoned with herbs and spices. Among iconic Punjabi dishes—commonly featuring in Indian restaurants abroad—are *kaali daal* or *daal makkhani* (black lentils, often with a dollop of butter or cream); *palak paneer* (curried spinach with curd cheese); *makki roti* with *sarson ka saag* (cornbread with spicy mustard leaves, a winter favorite); and of course tandoori chicken (spicy marinated chicken roasted in a clay oven or tandoor and given the name "butter chicken" when placed in a curry sauce of butter, tomato puree, and spices).

Contrary to the common misperception that the largest concentration of India's vegetarian population lives in the southern region, that distinction actually belongs to the western state of Gujarat, where 69 percent of the state population are vegetarians, with many of them also avoiding onion and garlic. This is mainly due to the preponderance of people adhering to the Jain faith and a devotionalist strand of Hinduism, both of which place vegetarianism at the center of their religious lives. The percentage of vegetarians drops down to 30 percent as one travels south to Maharashtra. Further south in Goa one comes across a distinctive cuisine shaped by a long history of interaction between Portuguese and local influences. This is marked typically by a widespread consumption of pork—unique in India—and by the use of vinegar along with red chilies (and, often, coconut milk) to give a sour-hot taste to many of the region's iconic pork or chicken-based curry dishes like *vindaloo, sorpotel,* and *xacuti.*

Bengal, which like Punjab was partitioned in 1947 between India and Pakistan, shares with its eastern neighbor Bangladesh a strong emphasis in its cuisine on rice and fresh fish and on the use of mustard oil as a common cooking medium. It, along with Kerala, has the lowest proportion of vegetarians (about 6 percent) in any Indian region, and its Hindu Brahmans join their counterparts in Kashmir in eating meat and fish. The per capita consumption of potatoes in Bengal, though, is second only to that in Ireland.[29] A particularly notable contribution of Bengal to Indian cuisine is the wide range of sweets made with fresh, unripened curd cheese (*chhana*) and sugar—sometimes embellished with nuts and flavored with aromatic spices or date palm jaggery—most famously *sandesh* and *rasogolla.*[30]

The culinary traditions of India's four southern states—Tamil Nadu, Karnataka, Andhra Pradesh, and Kerala—are significantly different from those of the rest of the country. Together, they constitute India's oldest cuisine. There are important regional variations in the use of spices, but broadly speaking these states share an emphasis on rice and a wide variety of lentils; use coconut, tamarind, mustard seeds, and red chilies as ingredients in a wide range of dishes; use—with the exception of Kerala and parts of northern Karnataka—less of aromatic spices like cardamom, cinnamon, and clove common to north Indian cuisine; and show a marked preference for coffee over tea, a habit shaped undoubtedly by the presence of coffee plantations in India's peninsular south. Along with rice, however, the cuisine of Karnataka places equal weight on wheat and finger millet (*ragi*). Popular dishes common to all four states include the *dosa* (a fermented rice flour and lentil pancake); *idli* (steamed cakes of a fermented mixture of ground rice and split black gram); *sambar* and *rasam,* two varieties of a spicy lentil soup; and a mixture of boiled rice and plain or spice-tempered curd, eaten usually at the end of the meal with mango or lime pickle. The cuisines of Andhra and Tamil Nadu are the hottest in India, and during the period of colonial rule—when these states were part of the Madras Presidency—the British capitalized on this to create the hot and pungent spice mix they came to call hot Madras curry powder, which went on to become the chief flavoring agent in the classic Anglo-Indian hybridized dish called "Mulligatawny soup."[31]

Contrary to the popular perception of southern India as primarily a vegetarian area, the proportion of vegetarians in these states varies from 34 percent in Karnataka to 16 percent in Tamil Nadu and Andhra

Pradesh to only 6 percent in Kerala. Hyderabad in Andhra Pradesh, the core of a Muslim-ruled princely state in colonial India, continues to this day to be one of the country's foremost centers of Mughal-style cuisine adapted to local ingredients. It is famous especially for its signature dish *kachchi biriyani,* raw marinated lamb or goat meat cooked together with rice from the very beginning and flavored by fragrant spices—a process unlike the more conventional one of partially cooking meat and rice separately and then putting them together to finish off the dish by slow cooking. A wealthy Hindu mercantile community, the Chettiyars, has spawned another important local nonvegetarian cuisine in southeastern Tamil Nadu's Chettinad area, utilizing large amounts of pepper and savory meat and fish with aromatic marinades and broths, and producing classics such as the Chettinad chicken. The cuisine of Kerala, in keeping with its long history as a cultural "contact zone," is a rich medley of vegetarian and nonvegetarian dishes popular among its three major religious communities, Hindus (56 percent of the population), Muslims (25 percent) and Christians (19 percent). Kerala Brahmans are strict vegetarians but the other important Hindu caste, the Nairs, mostly eat meat and fish, while the Christians eat spicy offal, chicken, duck, fish, shellfish, beef, and wild boar. The Kerala Muslim population, most numerous along the southwestern Malabar coast and supposedly descended from Arab traders who settled there soon after the birth of Islam in the seventh century, has developed a cookery that blends local and Arab traditions in dishes like *alisa*—a porridge of ground wheat and meat that is analogous to the *harees* of the Muslim Middle East— and, of course, *biryani.* Common to the culinary traditions of all of these communities are the use of coconut milk as an ingredient and coconut oil as a cooking medium.[32]

The connection between the growth of a global Indian diaspora and the export of Indian food abroad is close, but often belies simple generalizations. Colleen Taylor Sen has shown that the first Indian restaurants—or "curry houses" as they were called in the early nineteenth century—were established in Britain as early as 1809, much before the formation of any significant Indian immigrant population. It was not however until the 1920s that Indian restaurants started increasing in popularity, eventually exploding in a remarkable boom from the 1980s onwards, as hordes of people from the South Asian nations—mainly India, Pakistan, and Bangladesh—began taking advantage of liberal immigration laws to make their way into Britain, hiking up the demand for "ethnic" food. Currently Indian food is a five billion dollar industry in Britain, and approximately eight thousand Indian restaurants in that country account for two-thirds of eating out, prompting the former British Foreign Secretary Robin Cook in 2001 to proclaim "chicken *tikka masala*"—marinated pieces of chicken grilled and then simmered in a spicy sauce—a "true British national dish."[33] By contrast in the United States, the relative affluence of Indian immigrants—who brought with them tastes quite distinct from those of the poorer, working-class immigrants to Britain—has prevented a "tandoori" or "tikka" revolution of the kind witnessed in contemporary Britain, where these budget restaurants are ubiquitous. Despite the relative growth of Indian restaurants in the United States in the last three decades, Indian food continues to lag far behind the most popular ethnic-restaurant options like Italian or Chinese. With a few notable exceptions, restaurants in both Britain and the United States have been largely unable or even unwilling to serve food that genuinely represents the huge regional diversity of Indian cuisine, relying instead on a kind of hybrid Mughal-Punjabi fare (in Britain, often accompanied by a Bangladeshi style) as their staple. This is only inadequately compensated for by the increasing availability of a wide array of regional specialty dishes in the form of precooked and packaged ready-to-eat single-serving meals manufactured by processed food companies like House of Spices, Deep Foods, MTR, and—increasingly in Britain—Patak's and the ethnic foods section of the supermarket giant Sainsbury's.

The influence of Indian cuisine is of course not limited to Britain and the United States. The cuisine of the British imperial settler colonies in Australia and Canada was influenced by India, so much so that as early as 1874 the Australian novelist Marcus Clarke proposed making a spicy curry made with goat meat, eggs, coconut, chilies, and pineapple "the base of our regenerated Australian food system."[34] Australians contributed to the development of curry by adding wattlebird and kangaroo tail to the list of meats that received the curry treatment.[35] The liberalization of Australian laws with regard to nonwhite immigration starting in the 1960s opened the way for a significant influx of people from India and Southeast Asia, and this revolutionized the ethnic food business. Indian restaurants run by first- or second-generation immigrants from South Asia are quite common in Australian cities now, and those offering regional or vegetarian food are gaining in popularity.[36] Similar changes in immigration laws in post-1962 Canada have contributed to a large and growing Indian diaspora in that country, leading cities like Toronto and Vancouver especially to sustain diverse Indian food cultures and a thriving restaurant business.[37]

In the Caribbean, the food practices of the Indian indentured laborers who came in the nineteenth century to work in the colonial sugar plantations have left an indelible imprint on the islands' foodways, especially in Trinidad and Guyana. The great majority of these immigrants came from northern India, but caste distinctions and taboos with regard to food were significantly modified in the Caribbean, where vegetarianism had very limited appeal. *Chappati* or *roti,* the traditional Indian rolled bread made with flour and water and baked on a special griddle (*tawa*), was introduced to the islands by these immigrants. It has since evolved into one of the most popular foods in the region, especially in Trinidad, where it is eaten with Indian-style lentil soup (*dahl*) or curried goat.[38] The mango, now one of the most common ingredients in Caribbean cooking, was brought from its native India by the Portuguese. Curry, considered "as much a part of Caribbean as of Indian cooking," has been the most powerful longstanding vehicle of "East Indian" influence on "West Indian" food.[39] Perhaps no less important a carrier of this influence is Trinidadian fast food—typically eaten with Indian-style chutney or condiments—especially *saheena* (very similar to Indian *pakoras,* fried vegetable fritters); "doubles," a sandwich made with a filling of Indian-style curried chickpeas (*chana*); and *kachowrie,* a local variant of the classic Indian spicy snack.[40]

The most significant concentrations of Indian immigrants in Africa are in South Africa and East Africa. In the former, poor laborers from the southern regions of India arrived in droves in the late-nineteenth century to work in the colonial sugar plantations and were subsequently followed by Gujarati businessmen and traders, many of them Muslim. Over time, Indian-style curries came to acquire a general popularity among all sections of the South African population, including Zulus. But the most famous culinary product of the Indo-South African cultural interaction turned out to be a spicy meat curry served in a hollowed-out loaf of Western-style bread, called "bunny chow," named after the Indian merchants of the Bania caste who served this dish clandestinely to blacks at small restaurants in Durban in the Natal province during the apartheid era. In East Africa, similarly, thousands of Indian laborers were recruited around the turn of the nineteenth century to work in the railways in the British protectorates of Kenya and Uganda. They were later followed by mainly Gujarati immigrants, who became important in retail trade and moneylending. Though the brutal Africanization programs of the 1970s drove most East African Indians to emigrate to Britain and North America, many have come back in more recent times and resumed business, including grocery stores and food stands. Indian restaurants in Africa, which initially began by catering to Indian immigrants, later expanded to serve the local clientele. This is particularly true of Durban in South Africa, Nairobi in Kenya, and Kampala in Uganda, all of which have a thriving Indian restaurant trade.[41]

Other than its obvious contribution to the growth of an Indian food business overseas, the Indian diaspora has also in recent times inspired some interesting new trends in the burgeoning field of Indian food history. The most significant of these has been an examination of how Indian immigrants seek to preserve their ties to a homeland—real or imagined—through their preservation of and participation in traditional customs and rituals of consumption. A number of studies attest to the strong connection between Indian ethnic food in the markets of the West and the national self-identification of diasporic Indians.[42] This connection has many facets—from the cooking of authentic Indian meals at home to the increasing number and popularity of Indian restaurants, to the growing availability of the specialized ingredients of authentic Indian cooking in ethnic grocery stores. An interesting recent addition to this literature is a genre that can be best described as "culinary nostalgia"—articulated through memoirs, written mostly by diasporic Indian authors, centered on the theme of food as a crucial catalyst of socialization, interspersed with recipes savored and learned in childhood.[43] Though framed as personal narratives, these memories are important documents for food historians, precisely because they help to explore the interstices of history and memory through the trope of food.

The teaching of Indian food history, especially in U.S. classrooms, raises several possibilities as well as challenges in terms of the placement of such food history courses in the overall curriculum and their relationship with more general or survey courses in Indian or South Asian history. In an ideal world, a course on Indian food history needs to establish a general familiarity with the history of the Indian subcontinent and the broad patterns discernible in its society, economy, and religious beliefs. This, of course, is easier said than done, even for survey courses dedicated to Indian or South Asian history. Across universities, there are relatively few takers for a genuinely comprehensive two-part survey of South Asian history. The majority of students in South Asia survey courses enroll for one semester only, often in order to complete an institution-wide general education requirement or a requirement within a history or Asian studies major. Given the "one and done" nature of the audience, a rigorous orientation to the key questions of Indian and

South Asian history is difficult to provide for such students, let alone for those who sign up for "food history" courses unconnected to surveys.

In such circumstances, one possible pathway into "foreign" students' appreciation of Indian history—indeed, a way of capturing their imagination—could be to begin with food history, or to consider it early on as exemplifying basic trends or characteristics of the society and culture of India. The question of comparing historical periods across cultures becomes particularly important here. In the teaching of Indian history, there is no consensus about standard periodization. Like the old, much-maligned division between the "Hindu," "Muslim," and "British" periods, the much more powerful convention of dividing survey courses on South Asian history into "before" and "after" Europe also does not make much sense any more. Viable alternatives do not abound. However, the Advanced Placement world history syllabus—which should be familiar to at least some of the students signing up for courses in Indian food history—splits the history of the world into five periods: 8000 B.C.E. to 600 C.E. (the "foundational" and "classical" periods), 600 to 1450 (imperial and "big" political systems), 1450 to 1750 (early modernity, the Columbian exchange, global trade, and major empires), 1750 to 1914, and 1914 onwards. Given that it avoids Eurocentrism, as well as theories of Indian and South Asian isolationism or exceptionalism, this periodization seems to be a reasonable one to adapt—with suitable adjustments—to courses on food history. In any case, there can be little doubt that those teaching South Asian food history should move towards a recalibrated periodization in which connections and synergies with Europe and the New World can be traced and plotted more clearly. This is not only more useful for American students, but is also more in keeping with modern research that places greater emphasis on such connections.

The most organic connection that Indian food history courses must maintain is with larger themes of global and transnational history, such as human migrations and settlements, trade, travel, imperialism, colonialism, modernity, and globalization. On the one hand, the study of Indian food has to be grounded in a history of India's evolving material culture, shaped invariably by its climate, social formations, patterns of state formation and economic production, historical contacts with the outside world, and the experiences of Muslim rule and British colonialism. However, food has also traditionally held many complex symbolic meanings in Indian society, and—in this particular sense—not only has its preparation, handling, and sharing shaped rules of inclusion and exclusion in social interaction, but it has also been fetishized into national cuisines and driven nostalgic recollections of lost pasts or imaginary homelands. A course on Indian food history must design itself to take both of these aspects into account.

A reasonable way to begin is by adopting brief survey texts on Indian history that give a good overview of India's demographic mix and the immense regional diversity of its social, economic, and religious life. Two that are particularly useful in this context are David Ludden's *India and South Asia: A Short History* and Thomas Trautmann's *India: Brief History of a Civilization*.[44] A good shorter substitute is *The Cambridge Encyclopedia of India, Pakistan, Bangladesh, Sri Lanka, Nepal, Bhutan and the Maldives,* especially the chapters on history, society, and religion.[45] Brief summaries of Indian food practices are available in *The Cambridge World History of Food* and the *Encyclopedia of Food and Culture*—both ill-served by a simplistic emphasis on a north-south division in Indian cuisine—as well as the third volume of *Food Cultures of the World Encyclopedia,* focusing on Asia and Oceania, which provides the best short overview.[46] Two literary anthologies that should be useful for a course on Indian food are *A Matter of Taste: The Penguin Book of Indian Writing on Food* and *The Table is Laid: The Oxford Anthology of South Asian Food Writing.*[47]

Selections from the ancient Indian ayurvedic texts—including dietary prescriptions—are available in English translation in *The Roots of Ayurveda*.[48] The collection offers excerpts from both *Charaka-samhita* and *Sushruta-samhita,* but more authoritative versions exist in *Caraka-saṃhitā: Agniveśa's Treatise Refined and Annotated by Caraka and Redacted by Dṛḍhabala: Text with English* and *The Sushruta Samhita: An English Translation Based on Original Texts*.[49] For references to food, especially meat-eating, in the Jataka tales, see *The Jatakas: Birth Stories of the Bodhisatta;* for Buddha's own observations on meat-eating, see *The Laṅkāvatāra Sūtra: A Mahāyāna Text* ("On meat-eating").[50] The best English translations of texts that develop a critique of meat-eating are the classics: books one and two of F. Max Müller and Julius Eggeling's edition of *The Satapatha Brahmana, Part I,* and Patrick Olivelle's *Manu's Code of Law: A Critical Edition and Translation of the Manava-Dharmasastra.*[51] Translations of the accounts of the Chinese traveler Fa Xian and the Persian traveler al-Biruni, appear in *A Record of Buddhistic Kingdoms, being an Account of the Chinese Monk Fa-Hien of his Travels in India and Ceylon* and *Alberuni's India.*[52] Two remarkable Indian historical texts from the twelfth and sixteenth century, respectively, that deal with food and drink and have been translated into English are *Mānasollāsa of King Bhūlokamalla Somesvara* (translated from Sanskrit) and *Culinary Traditions of Medieval Karnataka: The Soopa Shastra of Mangarasa III* (translated from Kannada).[53] For Muslim texts dealing with the cuisine of the Mughal Empire or regional Islamic polities, the most authentic editions are *The A'in-i Akbari by Abu'l-Fazl 'Allami* and Abdul Halim Sharar's *Lucknow: The Last Phase of an Oriental Culture,* both available in English translation.[54]

NOTES

1. World Bank, "New Global Poverty Estimates—What it Means for India," http://go.worldbank.org/51QB3OCFUo, accessed April 20, 2012.

2. Francis Robinson, ed., *The Cambridge Encyclopedia of India, Pakistan, Bangladesh, Sri Lanka, Nepal, Bhutan, and the Maldives* (Cambridge: Cambridge University Press, 1989), 16.

3. K.T. Achaya, *Indian Food: A Historical Companion* (Delhi: Oxford University Press, 1994).

4. Ashis Nandy, "The Changing Popular Culture of Indian Food: Preliminary Notes," *South Asia Research* 24, no. 9 (May 2004): 11.

5. R.S. Khare, *Culture and Reality: Essays on the Hindu System of Managing Foods* (Simla: Indian Institute of Advanced Study, 1976); R.S. Khare, *The Hindu Hearth and Home* (Durham: Carolina Academic Press, 1976); R.S. Khare, ed., *The Eternal Food: Gastronomic Ideas and Experiences of Hindus and Buddhists* (Albany: State University of New York Press, 1992); R.S. Khare and M.S.A. Rao, eds., *Food, Society, and Culture: Aspects in South Asian Food Systems* (Durham: Carolina Academic Press, 1986). For a similar study of food symbolisms—which compares Khare's work on northern Indian Brahmans with fieldwork conducted among Brahmans of Tamil Nadu in south India—see, Arjun Appadurai, "Gastro-Politics in Hindu South Asia," *American Ethnologist* 8, no. 3 (August 1981): 494–511.

6. Om Prakash, *Food and Drinks in Ancient India: From Earliest Times to c. 1200 A.D.* (Delhi: Munshiram Manoharlal, 1961); Jeannine Auboyer, *Daily Life in Ancient India, from Approximately 200 BC to 700 AD,* trans. Simon Watson Taylor (London: Weidenfeld and Nicolson, 1965).

7. Francis Zimmermann, *The Jungle and the Aroma of Meats: An Ecological Theme in Hindu Medicine* (Delhi: Motilal Banarasidass, 1999).

8. D.N. Jha, *The Myth of the Holy Cow* (London: Verso, 2002).

9. Achaya, *Indian Food,* 55.

10. Achaya, *Indian Food,* 154.

11. Sami Zubaida, "The Idea of 'Indian Food,' between the Colonial and the Global," *Food and History* 7, no. 1 (2009): 191–209.

12. Achaya, *Indian Food,* 154.

13. Hashi Raychaudhuri and Tapan Raychaudhuri, "Not by Curry Alone: An Introductory Essay on Indian Cuisines for a Western Audience," in *Food in*

Motion: The Migration of Foodstuffs and Cookery Techniques, ed. Alan David-son, Proceedings of the Oxford Symposium on Food 1981 (Leeds: Prospect Books, 1983), 45–56.

14. For detailed descriptions of the food habits of Mughal India, see Lizzie Collingham, *Curry: A Tale of Cooks and Conquerors* (Oxford: Oxford University Press, 2006), 13–45; Joyce Westrip, *Moghul Cooking: India's Courtly Cuisine* (London: Serif, 2005).

15. Collingham, *Curry,* 95–96.

16. Holly Shaffer, "Dum Pukht: A Pseudo-Historical Cuisine," in *Curried Cultures: Globalization, Food, and South Asia,* ed. Krishnendu Ray and Tulasi Srinivas (Berkeley: University of California Press, 2012), 110–25.

17. For the Portuguese contribution to Indian food, see Collingham, *Curry,* 47–80. For their impact on an important Indian regional cuisine, see Colleen Taylor Sen, "The Portuguese Influence on Bengali Cuisine," in *Food on the Move,* ed. Harlan Walker, Proceedings of the Oxford Symposium on Food and Cookery 1996 (Blackawton, Devon: Prospect Books, 1997), 288–98.

18. Eliza Fay, *The Original Letters from India of Mrs. Eliza Fay* (Calcutta: Thacker, Spink and Co., 1908), 140.

19. E.M. Collingham, *Imperial Bodies: The Physical Experience of the Raj, c. 1800–1947* (Cambridge: Polity Press, 2001), 13–116.

20. For the food habits of the British colonial ruling class, see Cecilia Leong-Salobir, *Food Culture in Colonial Asia: A Taste of Empire* (New York: Routledge, 2011), 12–38; David Burton, *The Raj at Table: A Culinary History of the British in India* (London: Faber and Faber, 1993); Collingham, *Curry;* Achaya, "The Coming of the Europeans," in *Indian Food,* 163–78.

21. Dipesh Chakrabarty, *Rethinking Working-Class History: Bengal 1890–1940* (Delhi: Oxford University Press, 1989), 167.

22. Wyvern [Arthur Kenney-Herbert], *Culinary Jottings: A Treatise in Thirty Chapters on Reformed Cookery for Anglo-Indian Exiles* (Madras: Higginbotham and Co., 1885), 499.

23. Wyvern, *Culinary Jottings.*

24. An Anglo-Indian [pseud.], *Indian Outfits and Establishments: A Practical Guide for Persons about to Reside in India* (London: L. Upcott Gill, 1882), 68.

25. Shalot [pseud.], *Things for the Cook: In English and Hindustani* (Calcutta: Thacker and Spink, 1906), 89. For a study of the deep-seated Anglo-Indian misgivings about the native 'bazar' and the Indian cook, see Mary Procida, "Feeding the Imperial Appetite: Imperial Knowledge and Anglo-Indian Domesticity," *Journal of Women's History* 15, no. 2 (Summer 2003), 123–49.

26. For the evolution of the curry as a culinary concept, see Collingham, *Curry;* Sen, *Curry: A Global History* (London: Reaktion Books, 2009); Leong-Salobir, "The Colonial Appropriation of Curry," in *Food Culture in Colonial Asia,* 39–58; and Shrabani Basu, *Curry: The Story of the Nation's Favourite Dish* (Stroud: Sutton, 2003).

27. David Arnold, "The 'Discovery' of Malnutrition and Diet in Colonial India," *Indian Economic and Social History Review* 31, no. 1 (October 1994): 1–26; Mary Hancock, "Home Science and the Nationalization of Domesticity in Colonial India," *Modern Asian Studies* 35, no. 4 (October 2001): 871–903;

Dipesh Chakrabarty, "The Difference-Deferral of (A) Colonial Modernity: Public Debates on Domesticity in British Bengal," in *Subaltern Studies VIII: Writings on South Asian History and Society*, ed. David Arnold and David Hardiman (Delhi: Oxford University Press, 1994), 50–88; Srirupa Prasad, "Crisis, Identity, and Social Distinction: Cultural Politics of Food, Taste, and Consumption in Late Colonial Bengal," *Journal of Historical Sociology* 19, no. 3 (September 2006), 245–65; Jayanta Sengupta, "Nation on a Platter: The Culture and Politics of Food and Cuisine in Colonial Bengal," *Modern Asian Studies* 44, no. 1 (January 2010), 81–98; Utsa Ray, "Eating 'Modernity': Changing Dietary Practices in Colonial Bengal," *Modern Asian Studies* 46, no. 3 (May 2012), 703–29.

28. Arjun Appadurai, "How to Make a National Cuisine: Cookbooks in Contemporary India," *Comparative Studies in Society and History* 30, no. 1 (January 1988), 3–24.

29. Felipe Fernández-Armesto, *Near a Thousand Tables: A History of Food* (New York: Simon and Schuster, 2004), 168.

30. Michael Krondl, *Sweet Invention: A History of Dessert* (Chicago: Chicago Review Press, 2011), 55–72; Chitrita Banerji, "How the Bengalis Discovered Chhana and its Delightful Offspring," in *Milk: Beyond the Dairy*, Proceedings of the Oxford Symposium on Food and Cookery 1999, ed. Harlan Walker (Blackawton, Devon: Prospect Books, 2000), 48–59; Colleen Taylor Sen, "Sandesh: An Emblem of Bengaliness," in *Milk*, ed. Harlan Walker, 300–8.

31. Leong-Salobir, *Food Culture in Colonial Asia*, 16–18.

32. For more detailed descriptions of the various regional food cultures of India, see Achaya, *Indian Food*, 117–41; Achaya, *A Historical Dictionary of Indian Food*; Colleen Taylor Sen, *Food Culture in India* (Westport; London: Greenwood Press, 2004), 81–125; Solomon H. Katz, ed., *Encyclopedia of Food and Culture* (New York: Scribner's, 2003), 252–66.

33. Sen, *Curry*, 36–51; Collingham, *Curry*, 215–43; Jo Monroe, *Star of India: The Spicy Adventures of Curry* (Chichester: Wiley, 2005).

34. Barbara Santich, *Bold Palates: Australia's Gastronomic Heritage* (Kent Town, Australia: Wakefield Press, 2012), 2, 15.

35. Beverley Kingston, "The Taste of India," *Australian Cultural History* 9 (1990): 45, cited in Collingham, *Curry*, 146.

36. Charmaine Solomon, "Australia's Asian Connection: Asian Immigration Has Had a Dramatic Culinary Impact," in *The Food of Australia: Contemporary Recipes from Australia's Leading Chefs*, ed. Wendy Hutton (Boston; Singapore: Periplus Editions, 1999), 19–21.

37. Sen, *Curry*, 63.

38. Lynn Marie Houston, *Food Culture in the Caribbean* (Westport: Greenwood Press, 2005), 22–4.

39. Linda Wolfe, *Recipes: The Cooking of the Caribbean Islands* (London: Macmillan, 1985), 66.

40. Sen, *Curry*, 69–74; Donald R. Hill, *Caribbean Folklore: A Handbook* (Westport: Greenwood Press, 2007), 63–64.

41. Sen, *Curry*, 81–88; Emma Mawdsley and Gerard McCann, eds., *India in Africa: Changing Geographies of Power* (Cape Town: Pambazuka Press, 2011), 92–100 passim.

42. Krishnendu Ray, *The Migrant's Table: Meals and Memories in Bengali-American Households* (Philadelphia: Temple University Press, 2004). Ketu Katrak, for instance, has written about how—on coming to the United States as a graduate student—her childhood uninterest in food "was transformed into a new kind of need for that food as an essential connection with home." See Ketu Katrak, "Food and Belonging: At 'Home' and in 'Alien-Kitchens,'" in *Through the Kitchen Window: Women Explore the Intimate Meanings of Food and Cooking,* ed. Arlene Voski Avakian (New York; Oxford: Berg, 2005), 263–75; Uma Narayan, "Eating Cultures: Incorporation, Identity, and Indian Food," in *Dislocating Cultures: Identities, Traditions, and Third-World Feminism* (London: Routledge, 1997), 159–88; Purnima Mankekar, "'India Shopping': Indian Grocery Stores and Transnational Configurations of Belonging," in *Cultural Politics of Food and Eating: A Reader,* ed. James L. Watson and Melissa Caldwell (Oxford: Blackwell, 2005), 197–214; and Sharmila Sen, "Indian Spices across the Black Waters," in *From Betty Crocker to Feminist Food Studies: Critical Perspectives on Women and Food,* ed. Arlene Voski Avakian and Barbara Haber (Amherst: University of Massachusetts Press, 2005), 185–99.

43. For typical representative samples, see Chitrita Banerji, *Life and Food in Bengal* (Delhi: Rupa, 1993); Chitrita Banerji, The *Hour of the Goddess: Memories of Women, Food, and Ritual in Bengal* (Calcutta: Seagull Books, 2006); Chitrita Banerji, *Feeding the Gods: Memories of Food and Culture in Bengal* (New York: Seagull, 2006); Shoba Narayan, *Monsoon Diary: A Memoir with Recipes* (New York: Villard, 2003); Raghavan Iyer, *The Turmeric Trail: Recipes and Memories from an Indian Childhood* (New York: St. Martin's Press, 2002). For a recent study on how food shapes the cultural imagination of diasporic populations, see Anita Mannur, *Culinary Fictions: Food in South Asian Diasporic Culture* (Philadelphia: Temple University Press, 2010).

44. David Ludden, *India and South Asia: A Short History* (Oxford: Oneworld, 2002). Thomas Trautmann, *India: Brief History of a Civilization* (Oxford: Oxford University Press, 2010).

45. Robinson, ed., *The Cambridge Encyclopedia of India, Pakistan, Bangladesh, Sri Lanka, Nepal, Bhutan and the Maldives.*

46. Kenneth F. Kiple and Kriemhild Coneè Ornelas, eds., *The Cambridge World History of Food,* vol. 2 (Cambridge; New York: Cambridge University Press, 1999). Katz, ed., *Encyclopedia of Food and Culture.* Ken Albala, ed., *Asia and Oceania,* vol. 3, *Food Cultures of the World Encyclopedia* (Santa Barbara: Greenwood, 2011).

47. Nilanjana S. Roy, ed., *A Matter of Taste: The Penguin Book of Indian Writing on Food* (Delhi: Penguin Books India, 2004). John Thieme and Ira Raja, eds., *The Table is Laid: The Oxford Anthology of South Asian Food Writing* (Oxford: Oxford University Press, 2009).

48. Dominik Wujastyk, ed. and trans., *The Roots of Ayurveda,* rev. ed. (London: Penguin Books, 2003).

49. Priyavrat Sharma, ed. and trans., *Caraka-saṃhitā: Agniveśa's Treatise Refined and Annotated by Caraka and Redacted by Dṛḍhabala: Text with English Translation* (Varanasi: Chaukhambha Orientalia, 2010). Kunjalal Bhishagratna, ed. and trans., *The Sushruta Samhita: An English Translation*

Based on Original Texts, 2nd ed. (Varanasi, Chowkhamba Sanskrit Series Office, 1963).

50. Sarah Shaw, ed. and trans., *The Jātakas: Birth Stories of the Bodhisatta* (London: Penguin Books, 2006). Daisetz Teitaro Suzuki, ed. and trans., "On Meat-Eating," in *The Lankāvatāra Sūtra: A Mahāyāna Text* (Delhi: Motilal Banarasidass, 2003; first published 1932), 211–22.

51. F. Max Müller, ed., and Julius Eggeling, trans., *The Satapatha Brahmana, Part I* (Books 1 and 2) (Whitefish: Kessinger Publishing, 2004; first published 1882). Patrick Olivelle, ed. and trans., *Manu's Code of Law: A Critical Edition and Translation of the Mānava-Dharmásāstra* (New York: Oxford University Press, 2004).

52. James Legge, ed. and trans., *A Record of Buddhistic Kingdoms, Being an Account by the Chinese Monk Fâ-Hien of his Travels in India and Ceylon (AD 399–414) in Search of the Buddhist Books of Discipline* (Oxford: Clarendon Press, 1886; repr., New York: Paragon Book Reprint Corp., 1965). Edward C. Sachau, ed. and trans., *Alberuni's India: An Account of the Religion, Philosophy, Literature, Geography, Chronology, Astronomy, Customs, Laws and Astrology of India,* 2 vols. (New York: Routledge, 2000; originally published 1910).

53. Gajanan K. Shrigondekar, ed. and trans., *Mānasollāsa of King Bhūlokamalla Somesvara* (Baroda: Oriental Institute, 1967). S.N. Krishna Jois, ed., and M. Konantambigi, trans., *Culinary Traditions of Medieval Karnataka: The Soopa Shastra of Mangarasa III* (Delhi: Intangible Cultural Heritage Division, Indian National Trust for Art and Culture Heritage and B.R. Publishing, 2012).

54. D.C. Phillott, ed., and H.C. Blochmann, trans., *The A'in-i Akbari by Abu'l-Fazl 'Allami,* vol. 1 (Calcutta: Asiatic Society of Bengal, 1927). Abdul Halim Sharar, *Lucknow: The Last Phase of an Oriental Culture,* ed. and trans. E.S. Harcourt and Fakhir Hussain (New Delhi: Oxford University Press, 1994).

BIBLIOGRAPHY

Achaya, K.T. *Indian Food: A Historical Companion.* Delhi: Oxford University Press, 1994.

———. *A Historical Dictionary of Indian Food.* Delhi: Oxford University Press, 1998.

Albala, Ken, ed. *Asia and Oceania.* Vol. 3 of *Food Cultures of the World Encyclopedia.* Santa Barbara: Greenwood, 2011.

Appadurai, Arjun. "Gastro-Politics in Hindu South Asia." *American Ethnologist* 8, no. 3 (August 1981): 494–511.

———. "How to Make a National Cuisine: Cookbooks in Contemporary India." *Comparative Studies in Society and History* 30, no. 1 (January 1988): 3–24.

Arnold, David. "The 'Discovery' of Malnutrition and Diet in Colonial India." *Indian Economic and Social History Review* 31, no. 1 (March 1994): 1–26.

Banerji, Chitrita. "How the Bengalis Discovered Chhana and its Delightful Offspring." In *Milk: Beyond the Dairy,* edited by Harlan Walker, 48–59. Proceedings of the Oxford Symposium on Food and Cookery 1999. Blackawton, Devon: Prospect Books, 2000.

Basu, Shrabani. *Curry: The Story of the Nation's Favourite Dish.* Stroud: Sutton, 2003.

Burton, David. *The Raj at Table: A Culinary History of the British in India.* London: Faber and Faber, 1993.

Collingham, E.M. *Imperial Bodies. The Physical Experience of the Raj, c. 1800–1947.* Cambridge: Polity Press, 2001.

Collingham, Lizzie. *Curry: A Tale of Cooks and Conquerors.* Oxford: Oxford University Press, 2006.

Fernández-Armesto, Felipe. *Near a Thousand Tables: A History of Food.* New York: Simon and Schuster, 2004.

Katz, Solomon H., ed. *Encyclopedia of Food and Culture.* New York: Scribner, 2003.

Khare, R.S. *Culture and Reality: Essays on the Hindu System of Managing Foods.* Simla: Indian Institute of Advanced Study, 1976.

———. *The Hindu Hearth and Home.* Durham: Carolina Academic Press, 1976.

———, ed. *The Eternal Food: Gastronomic Ideas and Experiences of Hindus and Buddhists.* Albany: State University of New York Press, 1992.

Khare, R.S., and M.S.A. Rao, eds. *Food, Society, and Cultures: Aspects in South Asian Food Systems.* Durham: Carolina Academic Press, 1986.

Kiple, Kenneth M., and Kriemhild Coneè Ornelas, eds. *The Cambridge World History of Food.* Vol. 2. Cambridge: Cambridge University Press, 1999.

Krondl, Michael. *Sweet Invention: A History of Dessert.* Chicago: Chicago Review Press, 2011.

Leong-Salobir, Cecilia. *Food Culture in Colonial Asia: A Taste of Empire.* New York: Routledge, 2011.

Nandy, Ashis. "The Changing Popular Culture of Indian Food: Preliminary Notes." *South Asia Research* 24, no. 9 (May 2004): 9–19.

Prakash, Om. *Food and Drinks in Ancient India: From Earliest Times to c. 1200 A.D.* Delhi: Munshiram Manoharlal, 1961.

Prasad, Srirupa. "Crisis, Identity, and Social Distinction: Cultural Politics of Food, Taste, and Consumption in Late Colonial Bengal." *Journal of Historical Sociology* 19, no. 3 (September 2006): 245–65.

Ray, Krishnendu. *The Migrant's Table: Meals and Memories in Bengali-American Households.* Philadelphia: Temple University Press, 2004.

Ray, Krishnendu, and Tulasi Srinivas, eds. *Curried Cultures: Globalization, Food, and South Asia.* Berkeley: University of California Press, 2012.

Ray, Utsa. "Eating 'Modernity': Changing Dietary Practices in Colonial Bengal." *Modern Asian Studies* 46, no. 3 (May 2012): 703–29.

Raychaudhuri, Hashi, and Tapan Raychaudhuri. "Not by Curry Alone: An Introductory Essay on Indian Cuisines for a Western Audience," in *Food in Motion: The Migration of Foodstuffs and Cookery Techniques,* edited by Alan Davidson, 45–56. Proceedings of the Oxford Symposium on Food 1981. Leeds: Prospect Books, 1983.

Sen, Colleen Taylor. "The Portuguese Influence on Bengali Cuisine." In *Food on the Move,* edited by Harlan Walker, 288–98. Proceedings of the Oxford Symposium on Food and Cookery 1996. Blackawton: Prospect Books, 1997.

———. "Sandesh: An Emblem of Bengaliness." In *Milk: Beyond the Dairy,* edited by Harlan Walker, 300–8. Proceedings of the Oxford Symposium on Food and Cookery 1999. Blackawton, Devon: Prospect Books, 2000.

———. *Food Culture in India.* Westport: Greenwood Press, 2004.

———. *Curry: A Global History.* London: Reaktion Books, 2009.

Sengupta, Jayanta. "Nation on a Platter: The Culture and Politics of Food and Cuisine in Colonial Bengal." *Modern Asian Studies* 44, no. 1 (January 2010): 81–98.

Shaffer, Holly. "Dum Pukht: A Pseudo-Historical Cuisine." In *Curried Cultures: Globalization, Food, and South Asia,* edited by Krishnendu Ray and Tulasi Srinivas, 110–25. Berkeley: University of California Press, 2012.

Westrip, Joyce. *Moghul Cooking: India's Courtly Cuisine.* London: Serif, 2005.

Zimmermann, Francis. *The Jungle and the Aroma of Meats: An Ecological Theme in Hindu Medicine.* Berkeley: University of California Press, 1987. Reprint, Delhi: Motilal Banarasidass, 1999.

CHAPTER 4

Out of Africa

A Brief Guide to African Food History

JESSICA B. HARRIS

Balkanized by Victorian politicians at the 1884 Berlin Conference, disparaged by ethnographers of the same period, and laid open to colonial acquisition and subsequent imperial incursions, the African continent remains under-acknowledged and unsung. The continent, though, provides some of humanity's earliest food history and also offers indications of some of the world's pressing contemporary food issues and innovative food solutions.

The African continent is one of astonishing diversity. It is made up of hundreds of ethnic groups speaking a Babel of languages and is of such a geographical vastness that no one can truly claim to understand the whole. Over the centuries, a combination of misconceptions, fanciful inventions, and trite inaccuracies has muddled the world's vision and come to represent the continent. The first step, therefore, is to return to a tabula rasa and begin anew.

A few basic facts:

1. Africa is a continent, NOT a country.
2. The African landmass is more than three times the size of Europe and four times that of the United States.
3. Madagascar, an island off the east coast of Africa that is culturally and historically considered part of the continent, is the fourth largest island in the world.

4. More than one thousand languages are spoken on the continent.

5. North Africa and sub-Saharan Africa share history and have long been in communication with each other.

Given the variety of climates and cultures, whatever sure knowledge exists about one part of the continent can be contradicted somewhere else on the continent. Africa has many entry points. Nowhere is its diversity better expressed than in the history of its food.

The African continent has a lengthy culinary history that stretches from earliest prehistory to current culinary developments. In *Africans: The History of a Continent,* John Iliffe notes that "there is evidence as early as 20,000 to 19,000 years ago of intense exploitation of tubers and fish at waterside settlements in southern Egypt near the First Cataract, soon followed by the collection of wild grain."[1] However, the early sources for agricultural history are few.

James C. McCann, in *Stirring The Pot: A History of African Cuisine,* underscores our relative ignorance: "While Africa is now universally understood to be the place of humankind's origin, our knowledge of its agricultural history of food is more limited than that of other world areas." He goes on to discuss Africa's "limited genetic endowments of the flora and fauna of food sources," but cautions that "Africa has always been part of a global system of biological and human exchange."[2] It is from these exchanges that the multiple cuisines of the continent grew.

Primatologist Richard Wrangham informs us, in his groundbreaking *Catching Fire: How Cooking Made Us Human,* that from earliest record, humans were using fire on the continent to cook food. Burnt shells and fish bones have been found near family-sized hearths at a coastal archeological site in Klasies River, South Africa, dating from sixty thousand to ninety thousand years ago and "charred logs, together with charcoal, reddened areas, and carbonized grass stems and plants [dating to] 180,000 years ago [have been found] at Kalambo Falls in Zambia."[3] These sites indicate that fires may have been used for weeks or months at a time to cook. Wrangham postulates that the softer, more nutritious food that cooking provided gave *Homo sapiens* advantages that resulted in the social development of humans as a species. Cooking allowed humans to devote less time and energy to digestion, allowing more scope for the development of the brain.[4]

The history of food on the African continent has also been studied by archaeologists. Certainly one of the most complete records of early foodways on the African continent is that of ancient Egypt. Several noted

Egyptologists have studied the food culture of Pharaonic Egypt using the abundant available remains. In Egyptian archaeological sites, food is featured prominently in wall paintings and reliefs of all periods. From funerary art we deduce that the ancient Egyptians were gourmets and indulged in a wide range of foods. It is believed that they were the first to make leavened bread as we know it, flavoring loaves with spices and honey. They also used bread to brew beer and sometimes drank to excess.

Archaeologists and art historians have also explored ancient Roman cuisine in North Africa by investigating a number of sources including excavations of floor mosaics that were features in the Hellenistic villas of the rich in Tunisia. The mosaics in the Bardo Museum in Tunis, for example, depict the detritus that would have remained on the floor after a feast ended: fish heads, eggshells, cherry pits, and other discarded food scraps. Other mosaics depict actual banquets with bibulous guests, providing food historians with a sense of how art can inform their research.[5]

Travelers' accounts of Africa are another useful source for understanding the continent's culinary history. Travelers think of food, both foods they have tasted and foods they have observed, and their writings have provided some of the best descriptions of the food and foodways of the premodern African continent. Leo Africanus and Ibn Battutta, two early Arab travelers who ventured into sub-Saharan Africa, offer their views of the food and foodways they observed in their travel books. Polish scholar Thadeusz Lewicki's *West African Food in the Middle Ages: According to Arab Sources* mines Arab travel literature in an attempt to reconstruct the food of the western part of the continent before European contact.[6] The work, however, is seen as flawed by contemporary scholars for its inaccurate identification of plant species based on flawed translations. It also demonstrates the difficulty of reconstructing the foodways of the past based on travelers' observations.

The voyages of exploration brought Europeans to sub-Saharan Africa. Accounts of meals abound in their travelogues. One such travel journal, the 1687 *Descrição Histórica dos Três Reinos do Congo, Matamba e Angola,* written by a papal envoy, describes in great detail the pomp and ceremony of the dining habits of the Mbundu queen Nzinga.[7] Other journals depict daily life through the lens of European travelers such as Abbé Boilat, who described life in eighteenth-century Senegambia. Most European travelers in the eighteenth century stayed on the coast and didn't venture inland. Only in the nineteenth century with the scramble for colonial empires did this change. Explorers and missionaries, travelers and traders all wrote about the foods they saw, the meals they ate, and the crops they encountered, both familiar and strange.

Along with the explorers and the missionaries came the slave traders. The history of enslaved Africans has long influenced the developed world's opinion and images of the continent. The transatlantic slave trade spread Africa's culinary legacy wider than that of almost any other continent and has made possible a geographically extensive study of African culinary history. Over the modern centuries, Africans in diaspora and their descendants have formed major segments of the population in virtually all the countries in the western hemisphere, Brazil leading with almost ninety-seven million people of full or mixed African descent and the United States second with forty-two million.[8]

This African diaspora transformed the food of the western hemisphere. The conditions of enslavement meant that for more than three centuries, enslaved Africans and their descendants were in charge of kitchens throughout the hemisphere. They were also involved in the agricultural pursuits and animal husbandry of the lands to which they journeyed. However there are virtually no culinary histories and few cookbooks that document the African contribution to what have become the national cuisines of many New World nations. This is most likely because in most cases the dishes prepared by Africans have become inseparable from the national cuisine. Some dishes, though, maintain a manifestly African character and in more than a few instances can be traced to specific points of origin on the African continent. Here historians have looked for information on the origins of slave ships and the destinations of captives to trace culinary connections between Africa and the New World.

Many in the West think of the African continent monolithically when it comes to culinary culture. While certain generalities can be drawn, the foods of the African continent that traveled to the Americas are as regionally distinctive as are those brought by European settlers. Details are offered by slavers' records like *A Slaver's Log* by Theophilus Conneau, as well as by ships' provisioning manifests and other crucial sources. Studies like *The Atlas of the Transatlantic Slave Trade* by David Eltis and David Richardson give a sense of the scattering of slaves and the surprising culinary connectedness of their cultures.[9] To be sure, not all of the enslaved who shipped from a given port were from the region of that port. Conversely not all who survived the voyage remained at or near their port of entry, or even in the country in which they first arrived. It is probable, however, that there were enough in one place from a particular ethnic group to ensure a cultural critical mass. To take one example, Senegambia, the Bight of Benin, Angola, and Cameroon further to the south are famed for their leafy green soupy stews commonly referred to as *sauce feuilles* (leaf sauce), *sauce gombos* (okra sauce), and *soupikandia* (*kandia* means okra in Senegal's Wolof language). Those regions sent many captives to Saint Domingue, Salvador da Bahia in Brazil, Martinique, Guadeloupe, and the Gulf Coast and Charleston in the United States.[10] It is not surprising then that green soups and stew-like dishes abound in these areas: the *efo* of Brazil, the *callaloo* of the southern English-speaking Caribbean, the *calalou* of the French-speaking Caribbean, and the gumbos of Charleston and New Orleans to name but a few. Some dishes like *efo, dukonoo* (from Jamaica), and *callaloo* even retain names that correspond to African points of origin.[11]

Along with green soupy stews came rice dishes. Low Country rice planters appear to have preferred slaves from rice-growing regions in western Africa, especially Liberia, Sierra Leone, Guinea, and southern Senegambia. These rice-growing regions have long had a considerable repertoire of rice recipes that are at the origin of some of South Carolina's favorite dishes. Along with the leafy greens and composed rice dishes, several other western and central African culinary paradigms apply in general throughout the western hemisphere and demonstrate how African culinary style influenced food culture in the Americas: the use of okra as a thickener, a taste for small pieces, a love of fritters, and a lively tradition of street vending.[12]

Along with key dishes and cooking techniques, the Americas also received plants and livestock from the African continent. Geographer Judith Carney's works investigate the botanical connections between the Old and New Worlds. Looking at plants in the Americas, she points out the African origins of several plants that have become emblematic of the African experience not only in the United States, but also throughout the Americas, and postulates several methods of plant transference.[13] Okra is perhaps a primary example, as the pod originates on the African continent and is a key ingredient in many African-inspired New World dishes. Rice however may be the most important contribution. West African rice *oryza glabberima* and a discussion of African-inspired methods of rice growing throughout the western hemisphere form the subject of Carney's first work, *Black Rice*.[14]

At the same time the continent was being depopulated by the transatlantic slave trade, exploration continued, along with trade and settlement. Again, travelers' tales, journals, and letters home from the likes of

Sir Richard Burton and René Caillié provide information about the interior of Africa. At the Berlin Conference of 1884, the map of the continent was redrawn, dominated by French Imperial turquoise and British Imperial pink. The Congo constituted an immense private possession of King Leopold of Belgium. The Congress preserved old, smaller holdings of the Portuguese and Spanish and confirmed new claims by Germany. Later the Italians would claim Somalia and Libya but fail to take over Ethiopia. Colonial divisions would leave marks on the food cultures of the continent that remain evident to this day and that have enriched the foodways of individual countries everywhere.

Colonization signaled the arrival of significant numbers of European women to Africa. They set up households and tried to recreate European life as they knew it in African urban centers as well as in more remote outposts of the continent. Cities were established on European models with special food markets catering to European colonists. Some, like Dakar's Marché Kermel, were designated for Europeans and differed from local markets in size and in the goods they carried. Trading posts grew into colonial stores bringing European products to Africa, and some cities saw the establishment of European-style restaurants. Cookbooks for departing colonial wives offered advice on purifying water by boiling it, de-contaminating fruit with potassium permanganate, and making substitutions with local products, such as using yams to replace mashed potatoes and plantains to make game chips to serve with the antelope that replaced venison on settlers' tables. These cookbooks also demonstrate that the resourceful colonial wives learned from their African cooks and houseboys and discovered that they could, for example, use papaya leaves as tenderizers and roselle pods instead of lemon juice. Some even feature adaptations of local dishes.

Colonial cookbooks offer a view into not only the larders and kitchens of colonial cooks, but also a vision of how households were run. More than a few of them deal with how to negotiate with recalcitrant houseboys and cooks. When they include traditional recipes from the colonial territories they also give a glimpse of what these traditional dishes were like at a given time (albeit through the eyes of the foreign other). Some examples of these books are: *The Kenya's Settlers' Book and Household Guide* published in 1928 by the Church of Scotland's Women's Guild; *A Household Book for Tropical Colonies* by E. G. Bradley, published by Oxford University Press in 1948; and Hildagonda Duckitt's *Hilda's Where Is It?*[15] This last is one of the oldest African colonial cookbooks. Born in 1840 in the Cape region of South Africa,

Duckitt collected recipes from her area of the country. The book, first published in 1891, is arranged in alphabetical order and offers a selection of European, Indian, Cape Malay, and other recipes from South Africa. There are also hints about food for invalids, and advice about how to make furniture polish and home remedies.

As colonial inhabitants migrated to other colonies and civil servants were transferred from post to post, culinary cross-fertilization took place as well. Workers too were transferred and South Africa's Durban, for example, took on an air of the Indian subcontinent. Soon Indians were middlemen shopkeepers in Uganda and Kenya, and Syrians and Lebanese became storeowners in the Ivory Coast and Senegal. Dishes like South Africa's bunny chow (bread hollowed out and filled with a kind of curry)—which may be named for the Indian Bania caste who originally prepared and consumed it—hark back to this era and tell their own culinary tale of diaspora.[16]

In English colonies, African home economists published books in traditional and colonial languages and crossed countries speaking to women's groups in an effort to improve sanitary conditions. They too influenced the cooking of the continent in that they relied heavily on European models and championed standardization, although they made a point of including traditional dishes in their collections. In the early twentieth century, the Players cigarette tin become a standard household measure in British colonies.

Independence for much of the continent began in 1957 when the Union Jack was lowered over the Gold Coast and the red, yellow, and green flag with its central black star proclaimed the birth of Ghana, a new nation and a new era for the continent. With independence came national pride and with national pride came a need to celebrate and codify traditional dishes like Ghana's jollof rice, a vegetable-filled rice dish made red with the addition of tomatoes, and the chicken and peanut-butter stew known as groundnut stew. In many of English-speaking countries, home economists continued their quest for food safety and hygienic conditions. In the English-speaking nations, books like Nigeria's *Miss Williams' Cookery Book* and the *Ghana Nutrition Cookery Book* (initially published in 1953) became staples among the emerging middle and upper classes.[17] In the French-speaking nations, Paris had been the focal point and Gallic culinary conventions became accepted for middle and upper class entertaining, albeit with traditional dishes filling the plates and bowls. Regardless of colonial language and country, throughout the continent and across classes, less formal meals were often eaten with the right hand from a communal bowl in the traditional style. Regional specialties developed into nationally beloved dishes across ethnic lines. The *soupikandia* of the Diola of southern Senegal became a dish served around the country along with the *thieboudienne* of the Wolof and the *mafe* that Senegal shares with neighboring Mali. *Soupikandia* is an okra-based soupy stew often served with rice. It is an ancestor to New World gumbo. *Thieboudienne,* the national dish of Senegal, is a red rice and fish dish, and *mafe* is a stew based on peanut butter, usually made with lamb.

The African American Civil Rights movement shared a kinship with the African independence movements. In fact, several of the leaders of the new emerging English-speaking nations had spent time in the United States. The first Black Arts Festival, convened in Dakar in 1966, brought a returning wave of Africans in diaspora from the United States, Brazil, and the Caribbean in what would signal the birth of cultural tourism.

Unlike previous tourists who had come in search of game preserves and safaris, these tourists came mainly to the western areas of Africa and were looking for cultural connections in all realms, including food. This period, which witnessed the first Peace Corps volunteers and groups such as Crossroads Africa, also saw the publication of some of the first national cookbooks designed for visitors. Monique Biarnès' *La Cuisine senegalaise* and other works like it codified national classics.[18] This epoch would expand even further with the airing of the television show *Roots* in 1977.

The 1970s and 1980s also saw the growth of African tourism agencies devoted to promoting tourism to the continent. Culinary endeavors formed a large part of their initiatives, and the resulting pamphlets on food and restaurants offer material for study. Hotel and tourism schools were also created. Untapped sources for study of this period include travel journals, cookbooks created by Peace Corps personnel for use by newly arriving volunteers, as well as restaurant information in contemporary African media. Publications like *Africa World News* and woman's magazines like *Amina* in the French-speaking countries offered recipes, and *Jeune Afrique* published a cookbook including recipes from all over the continent. Time Life included an African volume in its Foods of the World series (1970), written by Laurens Van der Post, a white South African who gave scant attention to the cuisines of West Africa.

The closing decades of the twentieth century saw an increasing number of African cookbooks in both French and English written by Africans, African Americans, and West Indians with connections to the continent. Books by authors ranging from Senegalese singer Youssou

N'dour and British television presenter Rosamund Grant, and African Americans such as Bea Sandler, Vertamae Grosvenor, and Jessica Harris explored the food of the continent, and its connections to the foods of the African diaspora. Former expatriates and those, like Fran Osseo-Asare, married to Africans, explored the cultures and cuisines of the part of the continent with which they were most familiar; still others, like Judith Carney, explored plant origins and diffusion to the New World from Africa.[19] Other writers present the food of specific regions.

In addition to its food history, the African continent has a great variety of beverages dating back to the ancient Egyptians. Wines are produced in the continent's temperate areas, notably in Tunisia, Morocco, and South Africa, and beer is common, both traditional styles prepared from millet and other grains and more European-derived styles. Ethiopia's *tej* is a variety of mead, and the country is also the birthplace of coffee. Roselle, called *bissap rouge* in Senegal and *karkade* in Egypt, is popular, as are a number of herbal teas and drinks both alcoholic and nonalcoholic, ranging from Benin's *sodabi* (fermented palm wine) to Morocco's *thé naanaa* (mint tea). Topics for possible study range from the importance of rum in the slave trade to the medicinal properties of Senegal's *kinkeliba* tea.

As the continent that evidences some of humankind's earliest food-ways, Africa also records some of the world's earliest documented famines, beginning with ancient Egypt. However, beyond mentions in early Egypt, there is little information about early famines. Accounts do exist of later food crises in medieval Egypt as well as in precolonial Zimbabwe, Nigeria, and Mali, and the continent remains one of those most at risk for famine in the twentieth century. Famine—its causes ranging from drought and crop failure to colonialism and genocide to the spread of the Sahara—has changed the face of the continent into modern times. Contemporary, haunting images of the starving define Africa and food for many.[20]

At the beginning of the second decade of the twenty-first century, a singular food history of the African continent remains to be written. The scope of the subject is vast, encompassing as it does not only sub-Saharan Africa but also North Africa, which is the southern rim of the Mediterranean basin. While the countries of North Africa have had more thorough individual documentation through the work of contemporary chroniclers, ethnographers, and food scholars, such as Moroccan writer Fatema Hal, and Americans such as Copeland Marks and Paula Wolfert, the ebb and flow of the food of the entire continent has yet to be covered in a single volume. But then again, few comprehensive volumes present the food of Europe, South America, or Asia. James C. McCann's previously cited work, *Stirring the Pot: A History of African Cuisine,* runs a scant 184 pages, of which about twenty deal with the African diaspora and forty with Ethiopia. McCann offers an overview as well as insights into the difficulty of attempting to write a comprehensive history of African cuisine. Some of the problems preventing such a volume include the difficulties of synthesizing multiple languages, cultures, and religions, and of writing history based on sources that are largely secondary accounts, as records of African food history often come from colonizers or visitors. Perhaps, it is best to hope for a multilingual series of volumes that might present the history of the food and foodways of individual countries or groups of people. What is clear is that there is ample material for study, a rich culinary matrix, and a need to understand better the food and foodways of a continent that has not only nourished itself for millennia, but has also had a major influence on the food of the western hemisphere.

NOTES

1. John Iliffe, *Africans: The History of a Continent* (Cambridge: Cambridge University Press, 1995), 12.

2. James McCann, *Stirring The Pot: A History of African Cuisine* (London: Hurst, 2010), 22–23.

3. Richard Wrangham, *Catching Fire: How Cooking Made Us Human* (New York: Basic Books, 2009), 84–85.

4. Wrangham, *Catching Fire,* 84–85.

5. Phyllis Pray Bober, *Art, Culture and Cuisine: Gastronomy Ancient and Medieval* (Chicago: University of Chicago Press, 1999), 134.

6. Tadeusz Lewicki, *West African Food in the Middle Ages: According to Arab Sources* (London: Cambridge University Press, 1974).

7. João Antonio Cavassi de Montecuccolo, *Descrição Histórica dos Três Reinos do Congo, Matamba e Angola,* vol. 1 (1687; Lisbon: Junto de Investigacoes do Ultramar, 1965), 139–40.

8. CIA, *World Factbook,* 11 March 2014.

9. David Eltis and David Richardson, *Atlas of the Transatlantic Slave Trade* (New Haven: Yale University Press, 2010), 87–137.

10. Gwendolyn Midlo Hall, *Slavery and African Ethnicities in the Americas: Restoring the Links* (Chapel Hill: University of North Carolina Press, 2007), 91, 93.

11. Jessica B. Harris, "Food of the Scattered People," in *Food and Drink: The Cultural Context,* ed. Donald Sloan (Abingdon: Goodfellows, 2013), 98–114.

12. Jessica B. Harris, *Beyond Gumbo: Creole Fusion Food from the Atlantic Rim* (New York: Simon and Schuster, 2003).

13. Judith Carney and Richard Nicholas Rosomoff, *In the Shadow of Slavery: Africa's Botanical Legacy in the Atlantic World* (Berkley: University of California Press, 2011), 123–34.

14. Judith Carney, *Black Rice: The African Origins of Rice Cultivation in the Americas* (Cambridge, MA: Harvard University Press, 2002).

15. *The Kenya Cookery Book and Household Guide* (Nairobi: Kenway Publications, 1970; first printed as *The Kenya Settler's Cookery Book* in 1928); E.G. Bradley, *A Household Book for Tropical Colonies* (Oxford: Oxford University Press, 1948); Hildagonda Duckitt, *Hilda's Where Is It of Recipes* (London: Chapman and Hill, 1891).

16. Brij V. Lal, ed., *The Encyclopedia of the Indian Diaspora* (Honolulu: University of Hawai'i Press, 2006).

17. Omosunlola R. Williams, *Miss Williams' Cookery Book* (1953; repr. London: Longmans, Green and Co., 1957).

18. Monique Biarnès, *La cuisine sénégalaise* (Dakar: Société africaine d'édition, 1972).

19. Carney and Rosomoff, *In the Shadow of Slavery;* Fran Osseo-Asare, *A Good Soup Attracts Chairs: A First African Cookbook for American Kids* (Gretna: Pelican Press, 1993).

20. Cormac Ó'Gráda, *Famine: A Short History* (Princeton: Princeton University Press, 2009).

BIBLIOGRAPHY

Africa News Service. *The Africa News Cookbook: African Cooking for Western Audiences.* Edited by Tami Hultman. New York: Viking, 1986.

Amina. www.amina-mag.com.

Biarnès, Monique. *La cuisine sénégalaise.* Dakar: Société africaine d'édition, 1972.

Boilat, Abbé David. *Esquisses sénégalaises.* 1853. Reprint, Paris: Karthala, 1984.

Bradley, E.G. *A Household Book for Tropical Colonies.* London: Oxford University Press, 1948.

Caillié, René. *Travels through Central Africa to Timbuctoo, and across the Great Desert, to Morocco, Performed in the Years 1824–1828.* 2 vols. 1830. Facsimile of the first edition. New York: Cambridge University Press, 2013.

Carney, Judith. *Black Rice: The African Origins of Rice Cultivation in The Americas.* Cambridge, MA: Harvard University Press, 2002.

Carney, Judith, and Richard Nicholas Rosomoff. *In the Shadow of Slavery: Africa's Botanical Legacy in the Atlantic World.* Berkeley: University of California Press, 2011.

Cavassi de Montecuccolo, João Antonio. *Descrição Histórica dos Três Reinos do Congo, Matamba e Angola.* 1687. 2 vols. Reprint, Lisbon: Junto de Investigações do Ultramar, 1965.

CIA. *The World Factbook,* 2014. www.cia.gov/library/publications/the-world-factbook/index.html.

The Church of Scotland's Women's Guild. *The Kenya Cookery Book and Household Guide.* Nairobi: Kenway Publications, 1970. First published as *The Kenya Settlers' Cookery Book,* 1928.

Conneau, Theophilus. *A Slaver's Log Book or 20 Years Residence in Africa: The Original Manuscript*. Englewood Cliffs: Prentice Hall, 1976.

Duckitt, Hildagonda. *Hilda's "Where Is It?" of Recipes*. 1891. Reprint, London: Chapman and Hill, 1914.

Eltis, David, and David Richardson. *The Atlas of the Transatlantic Slave Trade*. New Haven: Yale University Press, 2010.

Grime, William Ed. *The EthnoBotany of the Black Americans*. Algonac: Reference Publications, 1979.

Hal, Fatéma. *Les Saveurs et les gestes: Cuisines et traditions du Maroc*. Paris: Stock, 1995.

Harris, Jessica B. *Iron Pots and Wooden Spoons: Africa's Gifts to New World Cooking*. New York: Atheneum, 1989.

———. *Beyond Gumbo: Creole Fusion Food from the Atlantic Rim*. New York: Simon and Schuster, 2003.

———. *The Africa Cookbook: Tastes of a Continent*. New York: Simon and Schuster, 2010.

———. "Food of the Scattered People." In *Food and Drink: The Cultural Context*, edited by Donald Sloan, 98–114. Abingdon: Goodfellows, 2013.

Ibn Battuta. *The Travels of Ibn Battuta*. Translated by H.A.R. Gibb. 3 vols. Cambridge: Hakluyt Society; Cambridge University Press, 1958–2000.

Iliffe, John. *Africans: The History of a Continent*. Cambridge: Cambridge University Press, 1995.

Leo Africanus. *The History and Description of Africa*. Edited by Robert Brown. 3 vols. 1896. Reprint, New York: B. Franklin, 1963.

Lewicki, Tadeusz. *West African Food in the Middle Ages: According to Arabic Sources*. London: Cambridge University Press, 1974.

McCann, James C. *Stirring the Pot: A History of African Cuisine*. London: Hurst and Co, 2010.

Midlo Hall, Gwendolyn. *Slavery and African Ethnicities in the Americas: Restoring the Links*. Chapel Hill: University of North Carolina Press, 2005.

National Research Council. *Lost Crops of Africa*. Vol. 1. *Grains*. Washington, DC: National Academy Press, 1996.

N'Dour, Youssou. *Sénégal: La cuisine de ma mère*. Paris, Minerva, 2004.

Ó'Gráda, Cormac. *Famine: A Short History*. Princeton: Princeton University Press, 2009.

Osseo-Asare, Fran. *A Good Soup Attracts Chairs: A First African Cookbook for American Kids*. Gretna: Pelican, 1993.

Saffery, David, ed. *The Ghana Cookery Book*. 1953. Reprint, London: Jeppestown Press, 2007. First published as *The Gold Coast Cookery Book*, British Red Cross Society: Government Printing Office, Accra, 1933.

Williams, R. Omosunlola. *Miss Williams' Cookery Book*. London: Longmans, Green and Co., 1957.

Wilson, Hilary. *Egyptian Food and Drink*. Aylesbury, Bucks: Shire, 1988.

Wrangham, Richard. *Catching Fire: How Cooking Made Us Human*. New York: Basic Books, 2009.

CHAPTER 5

Middle Eastern Food History

CHARLES PERRY

The Middle East refers primarily to the Fertile Crescent of Syria and Iraq together with neighboring Turkey, Iran, and Egypt. Because of the cultural unity provided by Islam in this overwhelmingly Muslim part of the world, North Africa is regarded as part of the Middle East. Agriculture began in the Fertile Crescent, and early domesticates still predominate in the local cuisines. Wheat is still the chief grain (except in Iran and southern Iraq, where rice arrived in the early Middle Ages); sheep and goats are the primary meat and dairy animals; and chickpeas, lentils, and favas remain major sources of protein. Since most of these domesticates have reached Europe, Middle Eastern food may not seem as exotic to Westerners as some other cuisines.

This is also where writing began and where we find the oldest written recipes. It may be that recipes were occasionally written down in other places at other times, once literacy became sufficiently widespread, but have simply not survived to our time. The early Middle Eastern recipes date from two periods from which we have particularly abundant records: the seventeenth century B.C.E. and the eighth through thirteenth centuries C.E., the noonday of medieval Arab civilization.

The oldest recipes are recorded on three cuneiform tablets in the Yale Babylonian collection. In many ways they resemble recipes that might be written today. For instance, broth is made by boiling "fat" (probably fatty meat) with flavorings such as leeks and garlic. There are recipes for game meats, such as venison and gazelle, and a number of game birds.

Most ingredients appear to be local plants and animals, both domesticated and wild, though the exact species referred to is often uncertain.

Two dishes are identified as coming from Assyria and Elam, Babylon's great rivals, which suggests a certain degree of cosmopolitanism. There is one extremely long and complex recipe for a game bird and two recipes made in connection with religious sacrifices, but most seem to be the sorts of dishes that would be served in a well-to-do household of the time. In short, what we see in these recipes is somewhat familiar but with a strong whiff of the mysterious and archaic.

After these Babylonian writings, darkness descends for about 2,500 years. A few references in Latin and Greek literature cast a fitful light on Egyptian and Syrian breads, for instance, but the recipes for Parthian (northwest Iranian) and Numidian (Tunisian) chicken that appear in the second-century Roman cookbook of Apicius look thoroughly Roman to our eyes.

Eventually, in the eighth and ninth centuries, blazing light appears; by the end of the thirteenth century there would be six major recipe collections in Arabic, consisting of four hundred or more recipes each, and several smaller collections. During this period the Arabs were the only people in the world, so far as we know, who were writing cookbooks.

When Muslim armies from Arabia conquered Persia in 642–644, they found a highly developed cult of gastronomy in the Persian court. A clear picture of it is given by the short story "King Ḥusrav and His Boy" ("boy" in the sense of page or servant) written in Middle Persian. It tells the tale of an impoverished young nobleman who petitions the king of Persia (presumably Khusrau I, who reigned 531–579) for a position in his retinue on the grounds of his noble ancestry, wide learning, mastery of the martial arts, and above all, his discriminating taste. The king proceeds to quiz him on what is the finest in thirteen categories. The young man answers in a formulaic way: "May you be immortal! Such-and-such is good, such-and-such is good and such-and-such is good, but such-and-such is best." For instance, the finest fowl is a rooster fed on hemp seeds and olive oil, chased and frightened before killing, hung overnight and then roasted. In short, the story is really a handbook of gourmet opinions. And gourmet is really the word—nine of the thirteen categories concern food or drink.

Notice the extravagance and luxury that had so scandalized the Greeks about the Persians: a lamb is suckled on the milk of two mothers, a sweetmeat is made with the fat of the (proverbially lean) gazelle. Notice also the focus on hierarchical ranking of dishes: haute cuisine was a particularly strong marker of status in the aristocratic culture of pre-Islamic Iran. Gentlemen of the Sassanian court were expected to be knowledgeable about food, even to be able to cook—there are anecdotes of Persian kings organizing cooking contests among their boon companions, just as they organized competitions among the palace cooks. The crucial fact for food history is that Persian courtiers kept their own personal recipe collections, possibly including some unique dishes of their own, more likely versions of well-known dishes that they particularly fancied, probably taken down from the practice of the gentlemen's household cooks.

The Arabs were dazzled by all this wealth and sophistication and adopted many Persian practices. In the eighth and ninth centuries, the caliphs of Baghdad organized cooking contests among their companions, just as Persian kings had, and it was also fashionable among gentlemen of their court to keep their own personal recipe collections.

This period saw some new gastronomic elements. It was when wine was first drunk from glasses, rather than from bowls or cups, so Arabic developed a more detailed vocabulary for describing the colors of wine than the Greeks and Romans had known. Different words for "red" were applied to young and old red wines, and a light rosé was called 'ain al-dīk, "rooster's eye." Al-Hamadhani's tenth-century entertainment "The Wine Maqāma" gives an example of wine-connoisseur speech, featuring the roguish exaggeration dear to the medieval Arab taste. In this tale, a barmaid boasts thus of her aged wine: "Bidding farewell to age after age, a secret in the pocket of pleasure, it has inherited bounties and the days and nights have taken from it until there remain only fragrance and sunbeams and the aromatic herbs of the soul . . . . (it is) like incandescence in the veins and a cold wind in the throat, a lantern of thought and an antidote to the poison of time."[1]

So far as we know there had been no food poetry in pre-Islamic Persia, but ninth- and tenth-century Baghdad saw a vogue for it. Mostly the resulting poems are no more than courtly verse-making that mechanically compares every dish or ingredient to a precious stone, a fragrant flower, or a heavenly body, but some are more interesting, such as this verse by one of the leaders of the movement, Ibn al-Rumi:

> Never will I forget a baker I passed
> Who rolled out thin flatbread in the twinkling of an eye.
> Between seeing it as a lump in his hand
> And seeing it rolled out, a disk like the moon,
> Was no longer than it takes a ripple to spread
> In water where a stone has been tossed.[2]

We know a great deal about the courtly cuisine of this period because in the tenth century, a scribe compiled *Kitāb al-Ṭabīkh* ("The Book of Dishes"), the first recipe book in Arabic, at the behest of a patron who wanted to know the dishes "of kings and caliphs and lords and notables."[3] This unnamed patron was almost certainly Saif al-Daula, the prince of Aleppo, somewhat of an upstart who yearned to robe himself in the glory of aristocratic tradition. As for the compiler, his name—Ibn Naṣr ibn Sayyār—indicates that he was descended from a seventh-century Muslim governor of eastern Iran, and this family connection might have given him access to court circles. True to his assignment, Ibn Naṣr ibn Sayyār identified many dishes by their courtly provenance: "a *maḍīra* from the manuscript of Ibrāhīm ibn al-Mahdī," say, or "a *mulahwaja* which was often prepared for Hārūn al-Rashīd." The unascribed dishes doubtless also come from the recipe books of aristocrats, just not those famous enough for his patron to care about.

In the eighth and ninth centuries, Baghdad was probably the largest and richest city in the world, and its court cuisine was suitably aristocratic and recherché. Many of the dishes in *Kitāb al-Ṭabīkh* have Persian names and some come with anecdotes ascribing them to various Persian monarchs (these recipes are written in fairly bad Arabic, so they might actually have been translated from Middle Persian). Many more dishes were invented by Baghdad cooks, under heavy Persian influence, and have names taken from an ingredient or a cooking technique. Nine dishes are named after figures of the court, and some of the names are still current, such as the rice pudding *muhallabiyya,* named for a governor of eastern Iran, and *būrāniyya* (originally meaning fried eggplant but today the name for a wide range of dishes from stews of all sorts to cold vegetables dressed with yogurt), which was named for a caliph's wife.

The dishes include fried, stewed, and roasted meats, fish dishes, stews, condiments, pastries, puddings, and candies.[4] Like all medieval Arab cookbooks, *Kitāb al-Ṭabīkh* devotes the lion's share of its space to stews of various kinds. Mostly they call for "meat," which would have been either lamb or kid, though sometimes beef or game were called for. These are elaborate dishes flavored with nuts, spices, herbs (sometimes as many as four fresh herbs in a single dish), fruits, vegetables, and expensive aromatics like truffles and musk.

The appeal of these dishes to the book's social-climbing patron was apparently shared by many lower on the social ladder, because this book has survived in three complete manuscripts and recipes from it were copied into other books. But many of the dishes must have been beyond an ordinary household's abilities. For one, a large live fish is kept in a tank of grape juice in order to give its flesh a special savor. For another, the leg bones are removed from a calf so that each leg can be given a different sort of stuffing before it is roasted whole.

Still, *Kitāb al-Ṭabīkh* appears to have familiarized the Arabs with the idea of cookbooks. By the thirteenth century, there was a lively "publishing" industry in manuscripts, to judge from the fact that nearly all that have come down to us show evidence of multiple generations of copying.

The cuisine in these thirteenth-century books is by no means as aristocratic as that of *Kitāb al-Ṭabīkh* because there was no longer a metropolis of wealth and power comparable to ninth-century Baghdad in the now fragmented Islamic world. But their contents still tended to be special-occasion dishes designed to impress, and some texts offhandedly remark that the writer learned such-and-such a dish from a particular aristocratic household, so we may assume that social climbing was an enduring motivation for buying cookbooks. However, by this time there is also evidence of interest in food for its own sake, because people have written down recipes learned from unknown sources in the margins of nearly every manuscript. At all periods, there was interest in what were held to be the health effects of particular foods.

Cookbooks were being compiled in all the population centers of the Arab world in the thirteenth century. Two represent the cookery of North Africa and Moorish Spain: *Fuḍālat al-Khiwān (The Excellence of the Table)* and an anonymous and untitled manuscript generally known among food historians as the *Manuscrito Anónimo* after the edition published by a Spanish scholar.[5]

Such was the prestige of the Persian-inspired cuisine of Baghdad that North African cuisine has a clear family resemblance to that illustrated in the tenth-century book, despite the political separation of Moors from the Arab East, which began before Baghdad was the capital of the Caliphate. However, Moorish cuisine had a distinct culinary personality of its own.[6] A ninth-century musician and gourmet named Ziryāb, driven out of Baghdad by a rival, found a welcome home in Granada, where he introduced innovations including the idea of serving food in courses. The author of *Anónimo* writes, "Many of the great figures and their companions order that the separate dishes be placed on each table before the diners, one after another; and by my life, this is more beautiful than putting an uneaten mound all on the table, and more elegant, well-bred, and modern."

In the east, cuisine was beginning to feel the influence of the cuisine of the Turks, who would later dominate the region.[7] In the west, non-Arab and non-Persian influences came from the Berbers and the Spanish—the former seem to have invented couscous, the latter a sort of puff pastry. The Moors also developed stews and baked goods of their own.

Many Moorish stews were finished off by a procedure called *takhmīr;* in *Anónimo,* 128 out of the book's 420 recipes feature it. This word has puzzled scholars. It looks as if it is related to the Arabic word for yeast, so some have translated it as "to ferment," and it nearly always involves eggs, so others have imagined that it means "to thicken." Clumsy scribes sometimes wrote *takhmīr* in ways that could be read as "to brown" or "to drown," both regrettably plausible. In fact, *takhmīr* has the straightforward dictionary meaning "to cover" and it refers to a coating of eggs, or occasionally bread crumbs, that was applied to a stew before sending it to the oven for a final cooking. This tradition survives in Tunisia, where a stew called *tagine* is so often topped with eggs that tourist guides may refer to it as an omelet.

Meanwhile, in the east, there are three major thirteenth-century cookbooks, related to each other in varying degrees, sharing recipes and details of chapter organization. Manuela Marin and David Waines, editors of the Arabic text of *Kanz al-Fawā'id fī Tanwī' al-Mawā'id (The Treasury of Benefits regarding the Diversity of Tables)*, have identified it as being compiled in Egypt, while *Kitāb al-Wuṣla ila al-Ḥabīb (The Link to the Beloved)* is clearly Syrian and *Kitāb Waṣf al-Aṭ'ima al-Mu'tāda (The Description of Familiar Foods)* is from Baghdad, at least in part, because it consists of the text of a book written by a certain Muḥammad ibn al-Karīm al-Baghdādī, expanded a few years later by the addition of another 240 recipes.

The cuisine of these books continues in the same vein as *Kitāb al-Ṭabīkh,* though the percentage of Persian names declines relative to the Arabic names of newly developed dishes. The books are loyal to *jūdhāb* (or *jūdhāba*), the most esteemed dish of medieval Baghdad. For this dish, a chicken was roasted in a tandoor oven. When its juices started to drip, a tray of pudding—the *jūdhāb* proper—would be inserted under it to catch them, and the diner got a slice of this enriched pudding along with a piece of roast chicken. There were many *jūdhāb* recipes, such as bread, rice, or apricot pudding, even a tray of nut-stuffed crepes. This dish was scarcely known to the Moors, because they used the European-style brick oven rather than the tandoor, which is basically a large clay jug with a hearth at the bottom.

The easterners also continued to revere a Persian confection called *lauzīnaj,* which consisted of a cylinder of marzipan rolled up in a paper-thin pastry and stored in sesame oil. Poets praised its delicacy: "pearled with sesame oil, star-like in color, melting before it can be chewed."[8] As a measure of their pride in this pastry, when the Seljuk Turks conquered Baghdad in 1055, the city fathers presented a tray of *lauzīnaj* to the Seljuk chief, a rough nomad warrior named Toghril Beg, confident of impressing upon him the elegance and refinement of their civilization. They were dismayed when his response was "these are good noodles but they could use some garlic."[9] Fortunately, the Turks would learn to appreciate haute cuisine.

After the year 1300, the writing of cookbooks in Arabic virtually ceased; coincidentally, this is when cookbooks begin to be written in Europe. There might be many reasons. The region had seen war, famine, and plague, not to mention the obliteration of Baghdad by the Mongols, and economic life had begun to decline. The torch of Islamic civilization was passing from the Arabs to Turkic nations.

In Turkey and the Fertile Crescent, the dominant power came to be the Ottoman Turks. They revered *Kitāb Waṣf* and al-Baghdādī's book, probably as a precious link to the culture of the Baghdad of the caliphs. They preserved two manuscripts of *Waṣf* at the Topkapi Palace in Istanbul and al-Baghdādī's original manuscript was kept in the library of the Aya Sofya mosque. In 1438, a few decades before the Ottomans conquered Istanbul, Muhammed bin Mahmud Şirvani, the court physician of Sultan Murad II, translated al-Baghdādī into Ottoman Turkish, adding about sixty recipes of his own time, in the process creating the first Turkish cookbook.

In the next two centuries the Turks went on to create a new haute cuisine, the cuisine of stuffed vegetables, shish kebabs, and baklava-type pastries that dominates the eastern Mediterranean today. During the eighteenth century, they began writing cookbooks of their own, beginning in 1732 with Mehmet Kâmil's *Ağdiye Risalesı.* Over the next century and a half several other books appeared, first in manuscript and eventually in print, derived from Mehmet Kâmil's book, including Turabi Efendi's *Turkish Cookery Book,* the first published on the subject in English.

In the sixteenth century, the Ottomans began systematically conquering the Balkans and virtually the entire Arab world, with the exception of Morocco and desert Arabia. As a result there were no Arab courts to support haute cuisine outside Morocco, and no cookbooks were written

in Arabic until the nineteenth century. In fact, one of the first was *Malja'
al-Ṭabbākhīn* (1886–87), a translation of *Melceü't-Tabbahin,* one of the
descendents of Mehmet Kâmil's book.

Persian cuisine, which had such a great influence on Arab, Turkish,
Central Asian, and Indian cuisines, is regrettably ill-attested before the
sixteenth century, when two very valuable books were written by Nur
Allāh and Hājji Mohammad Ali Bavorchi Baghdādi.

HISTORICAL VIEWS OF MIDDLE EASTERN FOOD

The study of medieval Arabic cookbooks began in 1934 when the Iraqi
scholar Daoud Chelebi (Dā'ūd al-Chalabī) published the text of al-
Baghdadi. In 1939, A. J. Arberry, later to be one of the leading Middle
East scholars of the mid-twentieth century, translated it into English. In
1945, Maxime Rodinson published a major study of the cookery literature, "Documents arabes rélatifs à la cuisine," which included a study of
Kitāb al-Wuṣla. Ambrosio Huici Miranda published the Arabic text of
Anónimo in 1956. In general, these Western scholars showed a traditional academic attitude toward cookery manuscripts—they might have
been interested in them as texts, but they disdained recipes as such.
Arberry's and Huici Miranda's translations were perfunctory and rid-
dled with lazy errors. Rodinson was more interested in the recipes than
either of them, but having made his name as a scholar with his essay, he
never published a translation of *Kitāb al-Wuṣla.*

A serious problem with this textual approach is that many recipes
cannot really be understood by mere translation: they need to be tried.
For many years scholars remarked on the peculiar medieval recipes for
a condiment called *murrī,* which was made by infecting lumps of barley
dough with mold spores, rotting the barley for forty days and then
grinding and mixing it with water and salt and allowing it to rot for
another forty days or longer. Not until the recipe was tested was it discovered that it tasted like soy sauce, which is created by the same technique, although *murrī* was never made from soybeans or indeed any
legume, and it was always flavored with spices.

Likewise, the dish *sikbāj,* one of the most esteemed of the Middle Ages,
looks pedestrian on the page: lamb stewed with apparently any combination of fruits and/or vegetables and whatever flavorings you like, always
with saffron and a good deal of vinegar. Served hot, it can be repellently
sour, but when allowed to cool, it turns out that the sauce becomes a
jelly—that magical texture which was one of the glories of European

haute cuisine until the late nineteenth century, when packaged gelatin rendered it commonplace. Because of the vinegar, the dish is essentially a lamb aspic, and Anna Martellotti has even argued that the word "aspic" itself comes from *asicpicium,* one of the stumbling medieval attempts to spell *al-sikbāj* (pronounced *assikbīj* by the Moors) in Latin.

In the last twenty years, published Arabic texts and translations have been arriving at an increasing rate, but several medieval books await translation, notably *Kanz al-Fawā'id* and Shihāb al-Dīn Aḥmad b. Mubārak Shāh's *Zahr al-Ḥadīqa fi al-Aṭ'ima al-Anīqa (The Flower of the Garden on Elegant Foods).*[10] The latter, which may date from late in the thirteenth century, contains about 167 recipes, including a particularly large number of *murrīs,* vegetarian dishes, and dairy products. The French translation of *Fuḍālat al-Khiwān* by M. Mezzine and L. Benkirane is unaware of certain key features of the cuisine, such as the nature of *murrī* and the *takhmīr,* and deserves to be superseded. The late Rudolf Grewe produced an excellent translation of the *Manuscrito Anónimo* before his death, and this should be published at some point; at the moment it languishes in a modern sort of limbo—Grewe wrote it using a word processing program that has fallen out of use.

Şirvani's *Kitabü t-Tabih* deserves translation from Ottoman Turkish, or at least from the modern Turkish translation by Mustafa Argunşah and Müjgan Çakır, not only because of the unique fifteenth-century recipes appended to it but because the recipes Sirvani translated from the Arabic differ in details from those in the original al-Baghdadi manuscript, giving a picture of change in tastes during the intervening two centuries about which we are otherwise almost wholly ignorant.[11] In Turkey there is sufficient interest in this issue that the English translation of al-Baghdadi has been published in Turkish. Turkish scholars such as Turgut and Günay Kut, M. Nejat Sefercioğlu, and Priscilla Mary Işın have published significant essays on Turkish food history; Işın writes in English as well as Turkish.

Of immense interest and highly deserving of translation are the earliest recipe collections in Persian, Hājji Muhammad 'Ali Bāvorchi Baghdādi's *Kārnāmeh dar Bāb-e Tebākhi va Son'at-e Ān* (from the reign of Shah Ismail, 1501–1524) and *Māddet-ol-Hayāt,* by Nur Allāh, cook of Shah Abbas I (who reigned 1587–1629). The books show late-medieval Turkic influences such as the Central Asian pancake *chalpak* and the earliest recipes for the modern Middle Eastern staples baklava and *dolma* (stuffed vegetables). They were published together by Irāj Afshār under the title *Āshpazi dar Doureh-ye Safavi.*[12]

OTHER AREAS FOR STUDY

As more translations become available, there will be room for diachronic studies of the development of particular dishes and synchronic studies of their nature in the thirteenth-century books, particularly the three related eastern books. These studies will be able to speculate about local tastes and traditions, but they will have to proceed cautiously—the traditional way of writing a cookbook is what we would call plagiarism and most of the recipes in these books are drawn from various sources. Since it is possible that the scribes producing these books for sale felt it advisable to "pad" their volumes with more recipes, a book of, say, basically Egyptian provenance may include some undigested lumps of Baghdad.

Other natural subjects include what these books reveal about cooks in their time. Some recipes are phrased as neutral descriptions ("water is boiled"), some as instructions which may have been taken down from an illiterate cook ("you boil water"), some as instructions for the householder to pass on to the cook ("let him boil water"). *Kitāb al-Ṭabīkh* and *Kitāb al-Wuṣla* mention some household cooks by name, mostly women.

An important subject is the mutual influence of Persian, Arabic and (in the thirteenth century and later) Turkic cuisines, particularly in the technology of grain foods and dairy products. There were also regional foreign elements, such as Berber and Spanish influences on medieval Moorish cuisine and traces of the Copts of Egypt and Aramaic-speaking Christians of the Fertile Crescent in the east. *Kitāb al-Ṭabīkh* connects certain dishes with the provincial Persian aristocracy (*dihqān*) and *Anónimo* gives dishes of the *ṣaqāliba*, a class of European slaves in Moorish Spain.

A very rich subject would be the recipes that appear in Arab medical writings, above all Yaḥyā ibn Jazla's eleventh-century medical encyclopedia *Minhāj al-Bayān,* which was heavily plagiarized by Arab cookbook writers. Anna Martellotti's *Il* Liber de Ferculis *di Giambonino da Cremona* studies one collection of recipes from the *Minhāj* which was translated not only into Latin but also Middle High German, and it indicates a number of medical sources in Arabic that deserve study from a culinary history standpoint.

NOTES

1. *Maqāmāt Badī' al-Zamān al-Hamadhānī* (Beirut: Dar al-Mashriq, 1973), 61. English translation by Charles Perry in Maxime Rodinson, A.J. Arberry, and Charles Perry, *Medieval Arab Cookery* (Devon: Prospect Books, 2001), 271.

2. Ibn Sayyār al-Warrāg, *Kitāb al-Tabīkh*, Kaj Öhrnberg and Sahban Mroueh, eds. (Helsinki: Seuran Toimituksia, 1987), 36. English translation by Charles Perry.

3. The English translation of this important book by Nawal Nasrallah is generally reliable and equipped with extensive glossaries but is somewhat marred by naïve linguistic speculation.

4. Baghdad seems to have been the first place where cooks experimented with the higher densities of sugar syrup, making possible candies, taffies, and nougat-like sweetmeats. The recipes for them in medieval books are rather uniform, perhaps because of the nature of sugar work but perhaps also reflecting the traditional secretiveness of Middle Eastern confectioners—these might be the only recipes that escaped their freemasonry.

5. *Traducción Española de un Manuscrito Anónimo del Siglo XIII sobre la Cucina Hispano-Magribi*, a Spanish translation that appeared in Madrid in 1966 under Huici Miranda's byline, is regrettably unreliable. Some years ago the author of this chapter agreed as a favor to a historical recreationist group to vet their translation of the Spanish. In the end he produced virtually a complete new translation directly from the Arabic, serviceable but lacking scholarly apparatus. He elected to allow the Society for Creative Anachronism to publish it themselves online. In time this translation should be supplanted by Rudolf Grewe's.

6. Because of the relative abundance of texts from the east, writings about Arab food history have paid less attention to Moorish cuisine. A useful corrective is Lilia Zaouali, *Medieval Cuisine of the Islamic World: A Concise History with 174 Recipes,* trans. M.B. DeBevoise (Berkeley: University of California, 2007). However, Lucie Boelens, *La Cuisine andalouse, un art de vivre: XIe-XIIIe siècle* (Paris: Albin Michel, 1990), must be approached with caution, because Boelens relies largely on the notoriously error-ridden Spanish translation of *Anónimo* and is rather credulous toward certain food myths, such as the idea that the word *qahwa* already referred to coffee in sixth-century Damascus.

7. Contrary to the widespread belief that the Turkish peoples ate nothing but yogurt and shish kebab when they were nomads in Central Asia, their staff of life had been the grain they obtained by trade with settled people. Turkish grain cookery later influenced the cuisines of many settled peoples, particularly in the case of certain noodle products and the layered bread *yufka* which led in Ottoman times to the development of baklava. See Charles Perry, "Grain Foods of the Early Turks," in *A Soup for the Khan: Chinese Dietary Medicine of the Mongol Era As Seen in Hu Sihui's* Yinshan Zhengyao, eds. Paul Buell and Eugene Anderson (Leiden: Brill, 2010).

8. Maxime Robinson, "Studies in Arabic Manuscripts Relating to Cookery," trans. Barbara Inskip, in *Medieval Arab Cookery. Medieval Arab Cookery* (Totnes, Devon: Prospect Books, 2000), 271. The Arabic text appears in Al-Hamadhānī, *Maqāmāt Badī' al-Zamān al-Hamadhānī* (Beirut: Dar al-Mashriq, 1973), 61.

9. D.S. Richards, trans., *The Annals of the Saljuq Turks: Selections from the al-Kāmil fi l-Ta'rīkh of 'Izz al-Dīn ibn al-Athīr* (London: RoutledgeCurzon, 2002), 40.

10. Manuela Marin and David Waines, eds., *The "Treasury of Benefits": Kanz al-Fawā'id* (Wiesbaden: Franz Steiner Verlag, 1993). Erfurt, Forschungs- und Landesbibliothek Gotha, MS Orient., A1344.

11. Mustafa Argunşah and Müjgan Çakır, *15. Yüzyıl Osmanlı Mutfağı* (Istanbul: Gökkübbe, 2005).

12. Irâj Afshâr, *Âshpazi dar Doureh-ye Safavi* (Tehran: Sada va Sima, 1981).

BIBLIOGRAPHY

Ahsan, M.M. *Social Life Under the Abbasids*. London: Longman, 1979.

Al-Baghdadi, Muhammad b. al-Hasan al-Warraq. *A Baghdad Cookery Book*. Translated by Charles Perry. Totnes, Devon: Prospect Books, 2005.

Bottéro, Jean. *The Oldest Cuisine in the World: Cooking in Mesopotamia*. Translated by Teresa Lavender Fagan. Chicago: University of Chicago, 2004.

Hājji Mohammad Ali Bavorchi Baghdādi. "Kārnāmeh." In *Āshpazi-ye Doureh-ye Safavi*, edited by Irāj Afshār. Tehran, Sadā ve-Simā, 1981.

Al-Hamadhānī. "The Wine Maqāma," translated by Charles Perry. In *Medieval Arab Cookery*, 269–72. Totnes, Devon: Prospect Books, 2000.

Ibn Naṣr ibn Sayyār, Abū Muḥammad al-Muẓaffar. *Kitāb al-Ṭabīkh*. Edited by Kai Öhrnberg and Sahban Mroueh. Helsinki: Finnish Oriental Society, 1987.

Işın, Mary. *Sherbet and Spice: The Complete Story of Turkish Sweets and Desserts*. London: I.B. Tauris, 2012.

Maḥjūb, Sulaima, and Durriyyah al-Khaṭīb, eds. *Kitāb-al-Wuṣla ilā āl Ḥabīb fī Waṣf al-Ṭayyibāt wal-Ṭīb*. Aleppo: Institute for the History of Arabic Science, 1987–88.

Martellotti, Anna. *Il Liber de Ferculis di Giambonino da Cremona*. Faisano, Bari: Schena, 2002.

Miranda, Ambrosio Huici, ed. "Kitāb al-Ṭabīkh fi al-Maghrib wal-Andalus fī 'Aṣr al-Muwaḥḥidīn li-Mu'allif Majhūl." *Revista del Instituto Egipcio de Estudios Islámicos en Madrid* 9 (1961): 16–255. A translation by Charles Perry under the title *An Anonymous Andalusian Cookbook of the Thirteenth Century* is available online at www.daviddfriedman.com/Medieval/Cookbooks/Andalusian/andalusian_contents.htm.

Nasrallah, Nawal, trans. *Annals of the Caliphs' Kitchens: Ibn Sayyār al-Warrāq's Tenth-Century Baghdadi Cookbook*. Leiden: Brill, 2007.

Nur Allāh. "Māddet ol-Hayāt." In *Āshpazi-ye Doureh-ye Safavi*, edited by Iraj Afshar. Tehran, Sadā ve-Simā, 1981.

Perry, Charles. "Grain Foods of the Early Turks." In *A Soup for the Qan: Chinese Dietary Medicine of the Mongol Era As Seen in Hu Sihui's* Yinshan Zhengyao, edited by Paul D. Buell and Eugene N. Anderson, 617–38. Leiden; Boston: Brill, 2010.

———, trans. "The Description of Familiar Foods (*Kitāb Waṣf al-Aṭ'ima al-Mu'tāda*)." In *Medieval Arab Cookery*, Maxime Rodinson, A.J. Arberry and Charles Perry, 273–466. Totnes, Devon: Prospect Books, 2001.

Rodinson, Maxime. "Études sur manuscrits arabes rélatifs à la cuisine," *Révue des Études Islamiques* (1948): 95–165. Translated by Barbara Inskip under the title "Studies in Arabic Manuscripts Relating to Cookery," in *Medieval Arab Cookery*, Maxime Rodinson, A.J. Arberry and Charles Perry, 91–163. Totnes, Devon: Prospect Books, 2001.

Tujibi, Ibn Razin. *Fuḍālat al-Khiwān fī Ṭayyibāt al-Ṭa'ām wal-Alwān*. Translated by M. Mezzine and L. Benkirane. Fez: Publications Fès-Saïs, 1997.

Turabi Efendi. *Turkish Cookery Book*. London: W.M. Watts, 1864. Reprint, Rottingdean, Sussex: Cooks Books, 1987.

Unvala, J.M. *The Pahlavi Text "King Ḥusrav and His Boy."* Paris: P. Geuthner, 1921.

Zaouali, Lilia. *Medieval Cuisine of the Islamic World: A Concise History with 174 Recipes*. Translated by M.B. DeBevoise. Berkeley: University of California, 2007.

CHAPTER 6

Latin American Food between Export Liberalism and the *Vía Campesina*

JEFFREY M. PILCHER

Latin America is widely regarded as a land of exotic civilizations and export agriculture. The Aztecs, Maya, and Inka are renowned for their ancient grandeur, while bananas, coffee, and chocolate from the region appear regularly on the breakfast table. These are just stereotypes, but they do illustrate a central theme of Latin American history: the exploitation of indigenous communities in order to produce commodities that are consumed somewhere else. Indeed, that story of oppression is about the only mention that Latin America receives in many world history textbooks.[1] Yet there are more positive lessons that can be learned by studying the history of Latin American food. As citizens of the developed world begin to question the healthfulness and sustainability of industrial food systems, they are taking renewed interest in the *vía campesina,* literally, the way of the rural worker, the knowledge of food and farming accumulated by agrarian societies. Moreover, in a time of social and religious strife, Latin America provides telling examples of how food can contribute to the forging of multicultural societies. Finally, food can offer new perspectives on Latin America's foundational narrative of conquest and exploitation, thereby helping to think in new ways about globalization and power.

Rural societies in Latin America have been divided since the sixteenth century between commercial plantations—known variously as haciendas, fazendas, and estancias—and subsistence-oriented *campesino* communities, both indigenous and of mixed race. Whereas haciendas generally produced market crops such as sugar, wheat, livestock, coffee, and bananas, peasants fed themselves with the dependable indigenous staples maize, potatoes, and manioc. Because *campesinos* grew most of their own food and fought regularly with neighboring *hacendados* over access to land, water, and other resources, they have often been portrayed as isolated and suspicious of outsiders. Nevertheless, peasants participated in the expanding global economy through tribute payments, market sales, and migrant labor. As a result, they were far more knowledgeable about the wider world than Europeans often acknowledged. From the sixteenth century to the present, campesinos have recognized the impact of global commodity production on the food choices they make and their ability to support themselves on the land. But although food reformers have recently sought to revalorize peasant diets and traditional farming—in contrast to the industrial food system—the ceaseless hard labor and risk of harvest failure held little romance for campesinos themselves.

Food also helped to shape multicultural societies in Latin America. The renowned scholar Fernando Ortiz compared Cuban national identity to the cooking of *ajiaco,* an African stew of starchy tubers, indigenous *ají* (chiles), and Spanish beef. Likewise, Mexicans considered *mole de guajolote,* a mixture of New World turkey and chile peppers with Old World spices, as a representation of their "mestizo" national identity as the offspring of Spanish conquistadors and Indian women.[2] Inclusive nationalist ideologies of the twentieth century have highlighted the contributions of women and non-Europeans, but foods have also served to exclude groups. The colonial system of castes, a racial hierarchy separating European elites from Indians, Africans, and mestizos, was based as much on cultural attributes such as food, dress, and language as on skin color. Independence leaders abolished the legal segregation of the caste system, but informal discrimination remained widespread. Nineteenth-century racial science even blamed indigenous poverty on poor diets rather than on the lack of educational and economic opportunities. Meanwhile, new immigrants from Asia and the Middle East were often stigmatized with references to their supposedly unwholesome foods.

A history that focuses on the kitchen and the dinner table can also provide new perspectives on relationships between the global and the local. Although globalization is often perceived as a tool of the powerful—Iberian conquistadors in the sixteenth century, liberal oligarchs in the nineteenth century—African slaves and Asian indentured servants also have contributed to the global transformation of Latin America.

Today, indigenous groups are pursuing a global agenda of food sovereignty, using the Internet to build alliances and to share seeds and farming techniques with peasants around the world. Even nineteenth-century liberals, who imported ideas and technology from Europe in the hopes of stimulating national development, felt a nostalgic attachment to local foods, however unfashionable they might have appeared. Such culinary patriotism has been revived in the past few decades by the *cocina novoandina* and the *nueva cocina mexicana* (nouvelle Andean and Mexican cuisines). These gourmet movements have drawn international attention, but despite the supposed pre-Hispanic roots of these fashionable cuisines, indigenous communities have not shared equally in the profits.

The balance between global market production and local subsistence consumption has swung back and forth over the course of the national history of Latin America. Enlightenment reforms and population growth in the late eighteenth century created an increasingly commercialized and unequal distribution of food. The growing inability of subsistence communities to support themselves on the land contributed in multiple ways to the coming of independence. Peasant communities gained a brief respite from hacienda encroachments during the unrest around the wars of independence, from 1810 to 1824. By the mid-nineteenth century, however, liberal oligarchies had consolidated power and placed renewed emphasis on export agriculture. Campesinos and urban workers who suffered under global boom and bust cycles joined revolutionary nationalist movements of the early twentieth century. By the Great Depression, liberal oligarchies had been overthrown and discredited throughout the Americas. Populist regimes then took power, seeking to foster national industries and local consumption, but they likewise foundered with the global economic malaise of the 1970s and 1980s. These new crises allowed the restoration of "neoliberal" regimes, dedicated to free market ideology, which sought to privatize state firms and dismantle welfare programs built by their populist predecessors. Neoliberalism, in turn, inspired a new wave of social movements, often based on indigenous populations, who demanded cultural autonomy and food sovereignty. Thus, the historical struggles between the global and the local and between market and subsistence have persisted in the twenty-first century.

THE CREOLE LEGACY

The contours of Latin American cuisines were shaped by the encounter of the Mediterranean diet with American staples. Despite broad commonalities across Latin America, however, there was also pronounced culinary regionalism; for example, the *carne asada* (grilled meat) of northern Mexico differs from the Mayan cuisine of the southeastern state of Yucatán, as do the *churrascuria* (grilled meat) of southern Brazil and the African-influenced dishes of the northeastern state of Bahia. Although these differences reflected long histories of climate and human settlement, the late eighteenth century was a particularly formative moment in the regional cuisines of Latin America, as population growth and commercialization transformed the availability of foods in a highly unequal fashion.

During this time, hybrid cuisines, known as creole (*criollo*), or mestizo in Mexico, became the basis for local diets, particularly among the lower classes. These cuisines were founded on sturdy New World staples, often supplemented by animal proteins from the Old World. Cooks blended pork fat into the indigenous Mesoamerican corn tamales, they stuffed Colombian and Venezuelan *arepas* (cornmeal pancakes) with cheese, and they added beef to the Andean *papa rellena* (stuffed potato). Creole cuisines were based on labor-intensive indigenous cooking techniques, including hand-grinding maize and grating and soaking manioc to remove cyanide. African slaves also contributed cooking techniques and foodstuffs such as plantains, yams, and greens to the creole diet. The archaeologist Daniel Schávelzon has attributed the origins of South American *locros* (stews) to distinctive African earthenware cooking pots. In addition, many creole specialties such as sausage, cheese, dried beef, and candied fruit arose from the need to preserve perishable foods.

Modern nationalists have exalted these creole or mestizo cuisines as early examples of racial mixing, but the colonial system of castes identified indigenous and African foods with the lower classes. Early modern social hierarchies separated elites and commoners through culture as well as appearance, and European settlers went to great lengths to retain a Mediterranean diet based on wheat bread. Nevertheless, the Portuguese in Brazil, unable to obtain sufficient wheat flour, substituted *farofa,* toasted manioc meal that resembled bread crumbs, to thicken stews and to add a tasty crust to cooked meat and vegetables. Europeans also acquired a taste for native beans and chile peppers. Native Americans, who rarely ate wheat, raised chickens and planted European vegetables in their kitchen gardens.

Commercial plantations and subsistence agriculture had struggled with one another for resources since the conquest, but this balance shifted in many places during the late colonial era. In the Caribbean, expansive sugar plantations imported of tens of thousands of African slaves, which sparked numerous slave rebellions. In 1804, rebels in the French colony of Saint-Domingue founded Latin America's first independent republic, Haiti. Freed blacks proceeded to destroy the sugar mills and divide the land into small plots to ensure that plantation slavery never returned to the island. Haitian farmers thereby reverted to subsistence farming, improving their diets in the process, though they also grew coffee and cacao for export markets.

Although the threat of similar uprisings led planters to accept the abolition of slavery throughout most of the region, the island of Cuba was transformed from a backwater of subsistence rice farmers and cattle ranchers into the most profitable sugar export colony of the nineteenth century. The transformation had begun already in 1762, when the English imported new slaves and technology during their brief occupation of Havana in the Seven Years' War. The booming sugar industry also attracted European migrants and foreign investment, including Latin America's first railroad, which was built in the 1830s.

In South America, peripheral regions began to benefit from commercial agriculture at the expense of the viceregal capital of Lima. Cacao exports enriched the northern cities of Caracas and Guayaquil; the future liberator Simón Bolívar, for example, was heir to a cacao mercantile fortune. In the Southern Cone, Buenos Aires became a major exporter of cattle products, primarily hides during the eighteenth century, although new technologies of meat salting introduced after independence spurred the production of beef jerky.

The spread of Enlightenment ideas also commercialized domestic food supplies, leading to widespread food riots. In early Latin America, as in medieval Europe, food provisioning was governed by what the historian E. P. Thompson called a "moral economy," a set of principles that held local elites responsible for the wellbeing of their communities in times of famine.[3] Thus, municipalities regulated the sale of grains, maintained a public granary called an *alhóndigas,* and contracted out meat supplies at fixed prices through a monopoly known as the *abasto.* Eighteenth-century economists called for the abolition of such restrictions and the distribution of food through free markets. Richard Graham has described the effects of such policies in Brazil, where the removal of marketplace controls led not to abundance but rather to rising prices that harmed the most vulnerable members of society.

Likewise in New Spain, as colonial Mexico was known, population growth and the commercialization of agriculture led to widespread hunger in the countryside and among poor urban dwellers when harvests failed in the final decades of the eighteenth century. By contrast, in the far northern provinces of Sonora and New Mexico, commercial prosperity allowed farmers to retain a part of their wheat harvest, rather than selling the grain to urban markets and relying for subsistence on the more dependable maize. Rural women, without access to expensive ovens, began to make wheat flour tortillas, creating a northern Mexican culinary icon in the process of raising their families' social status by consuming the European grain.[4]

Enlightenment thought came to dominate food politics, but new trends in European cookery did not gain a comparable influence in colonial Latin American kitchens. No cookbooks were published in Latin America before independence, limiting our knowledge of culinary technique. But a study of manuscript cookbooks by José Luis Juárez López has suggested that although late colonial dishes often had French names, the actual recipes bore scant resemblance to the nouvelle cuisine that Parisian chefs were developing in the eighteenth century.[5] Indeed, *mole de guajolote*, with its bold use of chiles and spices, had become a distinct anachronism compared with the "subtle" and "natural" flavors fashionable in Europe. Although the creole cuisines of the colonial era diverged from developments elsewhere in the early modern world, the rise of liberal oligarchies brought Latin America to the center of global food history.

FOOD IN THE AGE OF EXPORT LIBERALISM

The nineteenth-century liberals who governed Latin America until the Great Depression eagerly embraced the newly emerging industrial food system. Britain, at the center of this global network, used financial and technological means to funnel resources from around the world to feed its industrial working classes. France dominated the era gastronomically, thereby profiting from the global sale of luxury goods such as Champagne and canned asparagus. Proletarian migrants also contributed to this nineteenth-century era of globalization by building infrastructure, processing food, and establishing what would come to be known as ethnic cuisines. Under these circumstances, Latin American campesinos fought to preserve their cultural and dietary autonomy.

Many of Latin America's leading agricultural exports came to prominence during the liberal export boom. Brazil became the world's leading coffee producer, with giant *fazendas* worked largely by slaves until abolition in 1888 and by tenant farmers thereafter. By contrast, independent smallholders in Colombia and Costa Rica could compete with plantations because of the careful attention needed to produce high-quality coffee. Argentina experienced a "revolution on the pampa," in the words of James Scobie, after the expulsion of nomadic Indians made room for cattle ranching and wheat farming on the South American plains. In Central America, the United Fruit Company purchased huge tracts of fertile soil to grow bananas, reducing the amount of land available for local food production. Latin American bird waste was exported to benefit European agriculture; Peruvian and Chilean merchants exported guano fertilizers, composed of shorebird dung that had been preserved for centuries in deserts along the Pacific. Yet another global commodity chain, documented by Sterling Evans, began in the Yucatán peninsula with agave plants grown for their fiber, which was used on the plains of North and South America as binding twine for harvesting wheat, which was then baked into bread in London, Paris, and New York.

While European and North American consumers enjoyed the fruits of global commodity production, Latin Americans paid the price of environmental degradation. Brazilian coffee planters contributed to the destruction of the South Atlantic tropical forest, an ecosystem that once rivaled the Amazon basin in size and biodiversity and has now almost completely vanished. The spread of cattle across the South American pampa brought thistles and other invasive species, even before the land was plowed to grow wheat. Banana enclaves in Central America suffered from rampant Panama disease because of the use of monoculture to supply overseas markets with uniform products. Companies therefore maintained vast reserves of idle land for periodic replanting, leaving even less land available to grow food for local consumption. And in the Yucatán, *henequen* planters cleared corn fields and scrub forest to make way for rectilinear rows of agave plants.

Campesinos throughout Latin America struggled to adapt to the labor and resource demands of the expanding capitalist food system. Studies by John Coatsworth and Vincent Peloso have pointed to dietary declines in Mexico and Peru during the nineteenth century, although economic historians debate the regional effects. The transfer of land to commodity production not only reduced the supply of local foods, it also sometimes affected their quality. When sugar and coffee displaced rice cultivation in Puerto Rico, campesinos responded by eating more rice and beans in place of meat and vegetables, using wages to buy imported grain. The historian Cruz Miguel Ortiz Cuadra has observed that this machine-milled imported rice had fewer nutrients than hand-milled local varieties. Nevertheless, export commodities such as coffee did percolate into local diets, albeit via inferior beans that were passed over by foreign merchants. A distinctive version of *café con leche* (coffee with milk), sweetened generously with sugar, became a pan-Caribbean pick-me-up from Havana to Cartagena.

Proletarian migrants, whose labor helped to build global commodity chains, also enriched the cuisines of Latin America. After the suppression of the Atlantic slave trade in the mid-nineteenth century, tropical planters sought out new sources of labor from Asian indentured servants. Violating contracts that required them to return home, many Chinese became truck farmers, grocers, and restaurateurs in Cuba and Peru, just as South Asians settled with their curry sauces in Trinidad. Meanwhile, migrants from southern and central Europe introduced pasta and wienerschnitzel to more temperate regions of South America. Internal and regional migration also shaped emerging national cuisines. A turn-of-the-century industrial boom gave rise to the Mexico City taco shop, which catered to laborers from the provinces and helped to build a cosmopolitan, working-class version of the national cuisine. The historian Patricia Vega Jiménez has likewise traced the introduction of Afro-Caribbean rice and beans to Costa Rica and Nicaragua by migrant railroad workers. Known as *gallo pinto* (spotted rooster), the cheap, nutritious combination became a national symbol in both countries during the Great Depression.

Latin Americans participated in nineteenth-century intellectual debates about nutritional and racial science, advancing distinctive interpretations based on social conditions. Latin American intellectuals rejected eugenicist ideals of racial purity and advocated European migration to "whiten" and "improve" the mixed-race masses. Influenced by French positivism, Latin American elites attributed lower-class poverty not as Anglos did, to social Darwinist theories of genetic inferiority among Native American or African populations, but rather to environmental causes, particularly inadequate diets. In 1896, the Dominican intellectual José Ramón López blamed Caribbean backwardness on plantains and tubers, while his Mexican contemporary, Francisco Bulnes, made similar claims about the supposed deficiencies of maize. Although their nutritional calculations were flawed, these authors clearly understood that campesinos who could support themselves growing maize or plantains would not voluntarily accept the exploitation of early industrialization.[6]

Latin American nutritional discourse thus reflected the elite belief that to become modern, Latin Americans simply had to adopt European culture. The wealthy dined at exclusive social clubs and restaurants such as the Mexico City Jockey Club or the Harrod's department store café in Buenos Aires. The middle classes could purchase imported wine and ham for special occasions or even hire an immigrant cook from Italy or Spain. Cookbooks provided another point of entry for aspiring social climbers wishing to reproduce exotic dishes at home. The first Mexican volumes, published in the 1830s, were filled with European recipes, while the Brazilian O Cozinheiro imperial (The Imperial Chef, 1840) was largely copied from the Portuguese Lucas Rigaud's Cozinheiro moderno (The Modern Chef, 1785). Sarah Bak-Geller Corona has noted that Parisian publishing houses dominated the market for Latin American domestic manuals for the rest of the century, creating a culinary form of pan-Americanism in the effort to extend sales throughout the region.

Yet nineteenth-century liberal elites balanced their desire to appear cosmopolitan with a sense of culinary patriotism. Mexican cookbook authors balanced continental dishes with local favorites and defended the use of chile peppers from European detractors. Even the Jockey Club, with its renowned French chef and wine cellar, employed a cook from the city of Puebla to satisfy the members' hunger for *mole de guajolote*. Cookbooks in Argentina, Cuba, and other countries included recipes for creole dishes. While displays of culinary patriotism have been seen as precursors to twentieth-century populist revolutions, they more properly indicate the desire felt even by elites to balance foreign fashions with local foods.

THE TASTE OF REVOLUTIONARY NATIONALISM

Unequal access to land and food ranked high among the grievances that inspired a wave of popular rebellions in early twentieth-century Latin America. Campesino leaders such as Emiliano Zapata in Mexico and Augusto Sandino in Nicaragua fought to reclaim communal land from liberal oligarchs and foreign investors. Meanwhile, presidents Juan Domingo Perón in Argentina and Luis Sánchez Cerro in Peru mobilized factory workers with promises of affordable food. By mid-century, corporatist regimes had shifted many Latin American economies from raw material exports toward industries geared for domestic consumption. Rising middle classes, empowered by new economic opportunities,

helped to construct self-consciously national cuisines, while nevertheless importing the latest culinary fashions and developmental and nutritional discourses. Modernity remained the Latin American ideal,
although Coca Cola replaced Champagne as its global icon.

Political expediency often limited the effectiveness of Latin American
populist reforms in improving the welfare of citizens. Paulo Drinot has
demonstrated that *restaurantes populares* established in Lima during
the Great Depression sought not only to improve urban diets but also to
demonize Chinese-Peruvians, whose inexpensive restaurants, called *chi-
fas,* were portrayed as unhygienic and immoral. The Peronista government in Argentina likewise established its populist credentials by limiting exports to Britain and by creating an entitlement to beef for
working-class constituents, known as *descamisados* (shirtless ones). The
plan failed, as Natalia Milanesio has shown, when drought devastated
the livestock industry around 1950. Enrique Ochoa has analyzed Mexico's food welfare regime, first established in the late 1930s in part to
bolster the revolutionary credentials of the ruling party (PRI), but also
to subsidize domestic industrialization by helping to restrain wage
demands among factory workers.

Reconciling the goals of social justice and industrial development was
even more difficult in the countryside. Bolivia, Cuba, and Mexico enacted
sweeping land reform programs, while smaller-scale distributions were
carried out in Nicaragua, Peru, Venezuela, and several other countries.
Yet land alone was not enough to ensure success if farmers could not
obtain seeds, water, and other resources. Mexico shifted priorities during
World War II from agrarian reform to agricultural modernization in
order to supply the Allied war effort. Scientists from the Rockefeller
Foundation worked with Mexican plant breeders to develop hybrid
seeds, which became the basis for the so-called Green Revolution. Mexican farm productivity soared in the 1950s and 1960s, but the profits
went primarily to large commercial farmers, who had access to fertilizers, pesticides, and irrigation. Campesinos' incomes plummeted, forcing
many to abandon their small plots to search for work in the cities. Even
in Cuba, the government of Fidel Castro turned away from distributing
land to smallholders and toward Soviet-style collectivization following
the United States' aborted Bay of Pigs invasion in 1961. Whether under
capitalism or communism, Latin American land reform served less to
support peasant farms than to modernize the hacienda system.[7]

Food processing formed an important part of the import-substitution
industries that arose in twentieth-century Latin America. The roots of

regional industrialization reach back to late-nineteenth-century liberal oligarchs, who sought to import technologies such as canning and brewing to further the spread of European culture. Populist regimes gave impetus to the mass-production of creole dishes as part of a wider effort to develop domestic industry. The Mexican government encouraged the development of tortilla factories and subsidized research for a dehydrated tortilla flour industry. Entrepreneurs in Brazil and the Caribbean meanwhile sought to mechanize the laborious work of processing manioc. Nevertheless, much of the impetus for industrialization continued to come from abroad. Coca Cola was a major investor in Latin America, not only to obtain raw materials such as sugar and coca-leaf extract but also to encourage local consumption. Pedro Marcos Noriega, founder of the Mexican snack giant Sabritas, began frying potato chips in his kitchen in the 1940s and went national in the 1960s through a distributorship deal with PepsiCo.

International discourses of nutrition and development also continued to influence Latin American governments. Nationalist ideologies replaced the Eurocentric notion of whitening that had dominated liberal oligarchies in the previous century. "Indigenista" movements in many countries sought to incorporate Indians into the national life, while Brazil proclaimed itself a "racial democracy" in contrast to the discrimination prevalent in the United States. Nevertheless, as Sandra Aguilar-Rodríguez has recently shown, health officials promulgated European and North American dietary staples such as milk, even to lactose-intolerant children, just as Green Revolution agricultural policies sought to transform campesinos into agribusiness workers.

Yet this influence did not go all in one direction; migrants from Mexico and the Caribbean had already introduced their cuisines to the United States in the nineteenth century. Although chili con carne and tamales were quickly appropriated by packing companies, Latino cooks continued to invent distinctive cooking styles, combining Latin American sensibilities with ingredients from the U.S. food processing industry. By the 1940s, Mexican Americans had invented the "taco shell," the U-shaped, pre-fried tortilla that defined U.S. Mexican food in the postwar era. Once again, businessmen outside the ethnic community sought to profit from these innovations. Taco Bell founder Glen Bell even claimed to have invented this Mexican American recipe, which he then marketed to non-Mexican audiences. Competition between entrepreneurs inside and outside the ethnic community helped Latino foods gain acceptance within the U.S. national cuisine.

Although national dishes were important to the emerging middle classes of Latin America, middle-class women were perhaps even more concerned about changing social relationships around domestic labor. Advice on elegant, affordable cookery proliferated in books and media, including the region's first televised cooking shows broadcast in the 1950s. In Argentina, for example, Doña Petrona C. de Gandulfo insisted that abundant, home-cooked food was essential to middle-class status, even as Argentine women were increasingly working outside the home. As Rebekah Pite has shown, Doña Petrona's popular television show, costarring a loyal assistant named Juanita Bordoy, became the focus of a national conversation about relationships of domestic service. Meanwhile in Communist Cuba, where renowned cookbook author Nitza Villapol chose to remain even after her middle-class audience had gone into exile, the "new revolutionary woman" sought to find a new answer to the question "Who will cook under socialism?" According to Marisela Fleites-Lear, it was far easier for Villapol to introduce substitutes for foods made scarce by the U.S. trade embargo than it was for Cuban women to change patriarchal gender ideals. Indeed, Latin American populist regimes often fell short of expectations, even before they were undermined by the global economic crisis of the 1970s.

NEOLIBERALISM AND THE *VÍA CAMPESINA*

Whereas democratic capitalism had been the premise of nineteenth-century liberalism, at least in theory, twenty-first-century neoliberalism has advocated a system of authoritarian capitalism. Neoliberal reforms, known as "structural adjustment programs," sought to privatize civil society, devalue wages through economic "shock therapy," abolish public social safety nets, and criminalize union organizing. The Chilean military dictator Augusto Pinochet pioneered these supply-side policies in the 1970s, anticipating the governments of Margaret Thatcher and Ronald Reagan. By the turn of the century, governments throughout Latin America had largely dismantled populist welfare programs, spreading misery and inspiring food riots in working-class communities.[8] Paradoxically, this was also a time when Latin America experienced a culinary renaissance. International recognition followed in part from the migration of hard-pressed workers, whose family restaurants showed European and North American consumers that Latin American food was not all canned chili con carne and fast food taco shells. At the same time, classically trained chefs from the region were reinterpreting pre-Hispanic and creole dishes for discerning diners. Thus, two separate forms of globalization coexisted: the *nouvelles cuisines* served to affluent tourists and the popular food sovereignty movement opposing neoliberalism.

The international student movement of the 1960s provided the basis for contemporary Latin American gourmet revivals. Youth from Europe and North America began to seek out peasant cuisine as a more authentic alternative to the modern industrial food system. Meanwhile, Latin America students sought to share in a cosmopolitan counterculture while at the same time asserting their nationalist roots; in Mexico, they called themselves *xipitecas* (pronounced "hippie-tecas," as in Aztecas). Thus, the ancient Maya and Aztecs inspired *nueva cocina mexicana* chefs such as Patricia Quintana, while the *cocina novoandina* celebrity chef Gastón Acurio reinterpreted Peruvian creole dishes such as ceviche (seafood "cooked" in lime juice). One goal of this movement was to achieve acceptance for long-scorned indigenous foods in order to preserve endangered species such as Mexican *gusanos* (agave worms) and Peruvian anchovy. The latter, which had been overfished to provide animal feed, were presented as expensive haute cuisine in the hopes of ensuring more sustainable harvests. Nevertheless, one result of this new popularity was that campesinos could no longer afford their own food traditions.

Even while elites consume nouvelle peasant food, campesinos suffer the effects of neoliberal privatization in a number of ways. The loss of welfare programs and the reversing of land reform in the name of free markets have redirected agriculture away from food crops for local consumption toward exports. New forms of biotechnology have also had an impact on the region. Opponents of genetically modified organisms often focus on potential harms, particularly in important areas of biodiversity, such as southern Mexico, where maize was first domesticated. Campesinos have also suffered from the effects of "biopiracy," the granting of legal patent protection to supposed innovations that may have been unknown in the global North but were common knowledge among campesinos in the global South. In essence, international property law has allowed giant seed companies to take freely from genetic material developed by small farmers and sell it back to them at a profit.[9]

Neoliberalism has also transformed the retailing of food in Latin America. The first supermarkets began to open in the 1950s in affluent neighborhoods of Buenos Aires, Mexico City, and São Paulo, but mass markets emerged with the arrival in the 1990s of Walmart, which has become the largest private employer in Mexico. Not only did the company open vast numbers of outlets, allegedly bribing officials to speed approval, but also it provided a model of proprietary supply chains that was taken up by local competitors. A collaborative study led by James Biles observed that Walmart has contributed to a growing privatization of food distribution at a time of neoliberal disinvestment in public wholesale markets that serve the lower classes.

Campesinos adopted a variety of organizing strategies to resist these neoliberal policies. The Zapatista Army of National Liberation took up arms in Chiapas on January 1, 1994 to coincide with the inauguration of the North American Free Trade Agreement. Their military struggle, however, was secondary to an Internet campaign seeking to gain international support for their protest against unequal trade and to demand indigenous rights. La Vía Campesina was founded in 1993 as an international alliance of peasant groups from around the world dedicated to the goal of food sovereignty, defined as culinary and agricultural self-determination. The group organized protests against international bodies such as the World Trade Organization, which they saw as infringing those rights. Another international organization, Campesino a Campesino, sought to build alliances not for political protest but to employ peasant-based farm extension services, in order to encourage agroecological farming techniques as a sustainable alternative to the Green Revolution. Yet another Latin American social movement, Brazil's Movemento Sem Terra (Landless Workers Movement), established in 1984, advocated direct action to challenge social inequality by way of land occupations and democratic community building.[10]

One curious point to observe in works on the food sovereignty movement is that many have little to say about actual food as something to be cooked and eaten. They focus instead on planting and farming activities that are gendered male. This is not to say that there are no female activists; in fact, they often take leading roles, while still facing institutional barriers to making their voices heard. Moreover, even sympathetic outsiders may overlook the culture and community work of food preparation. Annette Aurélie Desmarais noted that the Vía Campesina Women's Assembly "encouraged numerous cultural exchanges—particularly dances, music, and song"—but apparently not recipes.[11] By failing to hear women talk about food, interlocutors are leaving it to the European-trained nouvelle chefs to define Latin America's campesino cuisines.

In addition to political organizing, campesinos have sought to gain more leverage in international markets. Fair trade initiatives now give consumers in the global North the opportunity to support ecologically beneficial practices such as shade-grown coffee. Critics of such initiatives object that merchant intermediaries retain the bulk of the premiums paid by shoppers, passing on only a small proportion of the money to impoverished communities. Terroir, a French term meaning "taste of place," offers another strategy for increasing the value of products from particular regions, for example, Oaxacan chocolate processed using traditional indigenous techniques. Although many European subregions have benefited from such initiatives, the success of these special designations depends on agricultural extension and marketing support that is rarely available from Latin American governments. Many communities have sought to develop culinary tourism, often as an adjunct to ecological or ethnic tourism initiatives. Such approaches have often benefited campesino participants, even while remaining within the dominant neoliberal paradigm.

Perhaps the most common strategy for campesinos has been labor migration, but this also brings with it risks for the long-term survival of communities. New urban consumption patterns have begun to displace traditional diets. Today, festival foods such as Mexican *mole de guajolote* or the Andean *pachamanca* (a communal barbecue of meat, potatoes, and corn) remain a source of communal identity and female status. Nevertheless, on an everyday basis, industrial junk foods have become an increasingly important part of working-class diets. Rates of obesity have grown rapidly, even as many still continue to suffer from diseases of poverty such as anemia. Health officials have begun to call for a return to campesino diets as a healthier alternative, thus seeking to reverse more than a century of faith in dietary modernization. It remains to be seen whether the change will come quickly enough to benefit the masses.

TEACHING LATIN AMERICAN FOOD HISTORY

Food has enormous pedagogical potential as a topic of inquiry in its own right, as a lens to analyze categories such as gender or class, and "as a uniquely multi-sensory tool with which to investigate history, culture, and society."[12] The Latin American perspective offers food historians of other regions a more complete view of the often hidden links of global commodity chains and labor supplies that enable North American food systems. Yet it is equally important to remember that Latin Americans are not simply exploited workers, but rather active participants in shaping modern cuisines. Food can also enrich general Latin American history classes with insights on material culture and social history that is particularly revealing about the lives of working-class women.

Culinary historians have developed methodologies for analyzing cookbooks by tracing the genealogies of recipes, setting them in social and historical context, and interpreting the intentions and aspirations of authors and audience. Scholars have also studied cookbooks as a genre of female autobiography and as an archive of social networks that often extended beyond domestic production to embrace political movements as well.[13] Numerous historical cookbooks are available both in facsimile and digital form. Perhaps the largest culinary archive is the Latin American collection of the American Institute of Wine and Food, now housed in the special collections library at the University of California, San Diego. Dan Strehl has made Latino culinary traditions available to non-Spanish speakers through a fine translation of Encarnación Pinedo's *El cocinero español* (*The Spanish Chef*, 1898), which provides rich material for students and scholars alike on California-Mexican cookery and on the travails of an elite Mexican family under U.S. occupation.

Valuable references to food are also spread generously through a range of other sources. Travel accounts, particularly those written by women, such as the Mexican letters of Fanny Calderon de la Barca, describe culinary culture in rich detail colored by European sensibilities. The Latin American literary movements of *costumbrismo* (local color) and modernism also used food to drive their plots; for example, the heroine of Jorge Amado's *Gabriella, Clove and Cinnamon* (1958) seduces the reader with her creole beauty and cooking, thereby giving literary expression to Afro-Brazilian society and the ideals of racial democracy. Providing context without sensationalism—even when the stories are quite sensational—is always important for teaching the works of another culture in an empathetic fashion.

Latin American scholars have also contributed theoretical perspectives that may be useful to students elsewhere in the world. The Yucatecan anthropologist Steffan Igor Ayora-Diaz has suggested an approach to understanding the formation of regional cuisines. Regional cuisines have often been treated by social science as the "historical past," a traditional society viewed in opposition to modern changes that are more often the focus of study.[14] Ayora-Diaz, by contrast, argues for a historical process he calls the "naturalization of taste," whereby the ongoing exchange of foods, repeated through cycles of everyday and festive meals, serve to institutionalize the recognition of certain ingredients and combinations as "Yucatecan," even while allowing for the creativity of individual cooks as well as the incorporation of new foods and flavors.

Food can also offer an entrée into difficult questions in the classroom such as race. Latin American perceptions of human difference such as the colonial system of castes or positivist theories of nutritional backwardness can help North American students to see their own racial histories in new ways. Moreover, knowledge of Latin American conceptions of racial democracy, and of its practical limitations, can help to overcome legacies of segregation and encourage acceptance of diversity.

Latin American food can also be used to rethink unequal global power relations, and in particular to challenge a common North American perspective that dismisses the region for its supposed inability to build proper nations or industries.[15] In my research on early attempts to build a Mexican meatpacking industry, I argued that Hispanic taste preferences for freshly slaughtered meat contributed to a rejection of the Chicago model of centralized slaughter and refrigerated transport. Although this could be seen as an example of industrial failure, small-scale local livestock production and reduced animal protein consumption might in fact offer a healthier and more sustainable model. Likewise, my global history of Mexican food seeks to reverse theories of cultural imperialism and McDonaldization by arguing that Mexican Americans actually developed the technology for fast food taco shells. Racial segregation rather than Anglo-Latino cultural differences explain the initial success of firms like Taco Bell in mass-marketing Mexican food. Moreover, the pursuit of authenticity is increasingly drawing consumers away from fast food toward the regional cuisines of Mexico.

The contemporary idealization of taco trucks contains its own dangers of racial stereotyping and peasant essentialism, the tendency to view campesinos as unchanging relics of the past rather than as historical actors fashioning modern lives. Nevertheless, the entrepreneurial energy of migrant restaurateurs—and the delicious food they serve—is helping to change the image of Latinos in North America.

CONCLUSION

The basic themes of food history in North America and Europe over the last two hundred years, including the industrial diet and nutritional science, commodity chains and environmental change, global migration and ethnic eating, have all left their mark on Latin America as well. By examining the patterns these themes have taken, we can not only perceive more about Latin American history, but also better understand our place in the global food system. The long coexistence of hacienda and campesino holds lessons for attempts to develop alternatives to industrial agriculture. The fluid boundaries of race in Latin America can help us to move past a black-and-white binary that never adequately captured North American social reality. And an examination of creole foods can show the ways in which the lower classes have not only preserved their diets but seduced otherwise disdainful elites with the piquant tastes of popular cuisines. More work remains to be done, particularly to redress regional inequalities. The historiography contains far more on Mexico, Argentina, and Brazil than on the rest of Latin America put together. We also know much less about the food cultures of the lower classes than about the better-documented kitchens of the elite, but that is a common problem for the entire field of food studies. By peering into the cooking pots of Latin American campesinos, researchers can help to develop a more equitable and sustainable food system for all.

NOTES

1. Susan K. Besse, "Placing Latin America in Modern World History Textbooks," *Hispanic American Historical Review* 84, no. 3 (2004): 411–22.

2. Fernando Ortiz, "Los factores humanos de la cubanidad," in *Etnia y sociedad*, ed. Isaac Barreal (Havana: Editorial de Ciencias Sociales, 1993), 1–20; Jeffrey M. Pilcher, *¡Que vivan los tamales! Food and the Making of Mexican Identity* (Albuquerque: University of New Mexico Press, 1998), 25–27.

3. E.P. Thompson, "The Moral Economy of the English Crowd in the Eighteenth Century," *Past and Present* 50 (February 1971): 76–136.

4. Amílcar E. Challú, "The Great Decline: Biological Well-Being and Living Standards in Mexico, 1730–1840," in *Living Standards in Latin American History: Height, Welfare, and Development, 1750–2000*, eds. Ricardo D. Salvatore, John H. Coatsworth, and Amílcar E. Challú (Cambridge: Harvard University David Rockefeller Center for Latin American Studies, 2010), 23–67; Jeffrey M. Pilcher, *Planet Taco: A Global History of Mexican Food* (New York: Oxford University Press, 2012), 46–75.

5. Jean-Louis Flandrin, "Introduction: The Early Modern Period," in *Food: A Culinary History from Antiquity to the Present*, eds. Jean-Louis Flandrin, Massimo Montanari, and Albert Sonnenfeld, trans. Clarissa Botsford (New York: Columbia University Press, 1999), 362–73.

6. Lauren Derby, "Gringo Chickens with Worms: Food and Nationalism in the Dominican Republic," in *Close Encounters of Empire: Writing the Cultural*

History of U.S.-Latin American Relations, eds. Gilbert M. Joseph, Catherine C. LeGrand, and Ricardo D. Salvatore (Durham: Duke University Press, 1998), 454; Pilcher, *¡Que vivan los tamales!,* 193–216.

7. William C. Thiesenhusen, *Broken Promises: Agrarian Reform and the Latin American Campesino* (Boulder: Westview Press, 1995).

8. John Walton and David Seddon, *Free Markets and Food Riots: The Politics of Global Adjustment* (Oxford: Blackwell, 1994); David Harvey, *A Brief History of Neoliberalism* (New York: Oxford University Press, 2005).

9. Jack Kloppenburg, *First the Seed: The Political Economy of Plant Biotechnology, 1492–2000,* 2nd ed. (Madison: University of Wisconsin Press, 2004).

10. For a comparative discussion, see Eric Holt-Giménez, "From Food Crisis to Food Sovereignty: The Challenge of Social Movements," in *Taking Food Public: Redefining Foodways in a Changing World,* eds. Psyche Williams-Forson and Carole Counihan (New York: Routledge, 2012), 592–602.

11. Annette Aurélie Desmarais, *La vía campesina: Globalization and the Power of Peasants* (Halifax: Fernwood Publishing, 2007), 161–89, quote from 187–88. See also Carole Counihan, "Gendering Food," in *The Oxford Handbook of Food History,* ed. Jeffrey M. Pilcher (New York: Oxford University Press, 2012), 99–116.

12. Jonathan Deutsch and Jeffrey Miller, "Teaching with Food," in *The Oxford Handbook of Food History,* ed. Jeffrey M. Pilcher (New York: Oxford University Press, 2012), 191.

13. See Ken Albala, "Cookbooks as Historical Documents," in *The Oxford Handbook of Food History,* ed. Jeffrey M. Pilcher (New York: Oxford University Press, 2012), 227–40; Janet Theophano, *Eat My Words: Reading Women's Lives through the Cookbooks They Wrote* (New York: Palgrave, 2002); Donna R. Gabaccia and Jane Aldrich, "Recipes in Context: Solving a Small Mystery in Charleston's Culinary History," *Food, Culture, and Society* 15, no. 2 (2012): 197–221.

14. See, for example, Sidney Mintz, *Tasting Food, Tasting Freedom: Excursions into Eating, Culture, and the Past* (Boston: Beacon Press, 1996), 96.

15. Inspiration for this argument came from Micol Seigel, "World History's Narrative Problem," *Hispanic American Historical Review* 84, no. 3 (2004): 431–46.

BIBLIOGRAPHY

Aguilar-Rodríguez, Sandra. "Nutrition and Modernity: Milk Consumption in 1940s and 1950s Mexico." *Radical History Review* 110 (Spring 2011): 36–58.

Amado, Jorge. *Gabriela, Clove and Cinnamon.* Translated by James L. Taylor and William L. Grossman. New York: Vintage, 2006.

Arcondo, Aníbal. *Historia de la alimentación en Argentina: Desde los orígenes hasta 1920.* Buenos Aires: Ferreyra Editor, 2002.

Ayora-Diaz, Steffan Igor. *Foodscapes, Foodfields, and Identities in Yucatán.* New York: Berghahn Books, 2012.

Bak-Geller Corona, Sarah. "Los recetarios 'afrancesados' del siglo XIX en México: La construcción de la nación mexicana y de un modelo culinario nacional." *Anthropology of Food* S6 (December 2009), http://aof.revues.org /index6464.html. Accessed December 7, 2010.

Bank Muñoz, Carolina. *Transnational Tortillas: Race, Gender, and Shop-Floor Politics in Mexico and the United States.* Ithaca: Cornell University Press, 2008.

Bauer, Arnold J. *Goods, Power, History: Latin America's Material Culture.* Cambridge: Cambridge University Press, 2001.

Biles, James J., Kevin Brehm, Amanda Enrico, Cheray Kiendl, Emily Morgan, Alexandra Teachout, and Katie Vasquez. "Globalization of Food Retailing and Transformation of Supply Networks: Consequences for Small-scale Agricultural Producers in Southeastern Mexico." *Journal of Latin American Geography* 6, no. 2 (2007): 55–75.

Calderón de la Barca, Fanny. *Life in Mexico.* Berkeley: University of California Press, 1982.

Caldo, Paula. *Mujeres cocineras: Hacia una historia sociocultural de la cocina argentina a fines del siglo xix y primera mitad del XX.* Rosario: Prohistoria, 2009.

Christie, Marie Elisa. *Kitchenspace: Women, Fiestas, and Everyday Life in Central Mexico.* Austin: University of Texas Press, 2008.

Clarence-Smith, William Gervase. *Cocoa and Chocolate, 1765–1914.* New York: Routledge, 2000.

Coatsworth, John. "Anotaciones sobre la producción de alimentos durante el Porfiriato." *Historia Mexicana* 26, no. 2 (1976): 167–87.

Corcuera, Sonia. *Entre gula y templanza: Un aspecto de la historia mexicana.* Mexico City: Universidad Nacional Autónoma de México, 1981.

Cotter, Joseph. *Troubled Harvest: Agronomy and Revolution in Mexico, 1880–2002.* New York: Praeger, 2003.

Desmarais, Annette Aurélie. *La Vía Campesina: Globalization and the Power of Peasants.* Halifax: Fernwood Publishing, 2007.

Drinot, Paulo. "Food, Race, and Working-Class Identity: Restaurantes Populares and Populism in 1930s Peru." *The Americas* 62, no. 2 (October 2005): 245–70.

Evans, Sterling. *Bound in Twine: The History and Ecology of the Henequen-Wheat Complex for Mexico and the American and Canadian Plains, 1880–1950.* College Station: Texas A&M University Press, 2007.

Fitting, Elizabeth. *The Struggle for Maize: Campesinos, Workers, and Transgenic Corn in the Mexican Countryside.* Durham: Duke University Press, 2011.

Fleites-Lear, Marisela. "Mirrors in the Kitchen: The *New Cuban Woman* Cooks Revolutionarily." *Food, Culture, and Society* 15, no. 2 (June 2012): 241–60.

Graham, Richard. *Feeding the City: From Street Market to Liberal Reform in Salvador, Brazil, 1780–1860.* Austin: University of Texas Press, 2010.

Holt-Giménez, Eric. *Campesino a campesino: Voices from Latin America's Farmer to Farmer Movement for Sustainable Agriculture.* Oakland: Food First, 2006.

Jaffee, Daniel. *Brewing Justice: Fair Trade Coffee, Sustainability, and Survival.* Berkeley: University of California Press, 2007.

Juárez López, José Luis. *La lenta emergencia de la comida mexicana: Ambigüedades criollas, 1750–1800.* Mexico City: Miguel A. Porrúa, 2000.

Lovera, José Rafael. *Historia de la alimentación en Venezuela: Con Textos Para Su Estudio.* Caracas: Monte Avila Editores, 1988.

Milanesio, Natalia. "Food Politics and Consumption in Peronist Argentina." *Hispanic American Historical Review* 90, no. 1 (February 2010): 75–108.

Ochoa, Enrique C. *Feeding Mexico: The Political Uses of Food Since 1910.* Wilmington: Scholarly Resources, 2000.

———. "Political Histories of Food." In *The Oxford Handbook of Food History,* edited by Jeffrey M. Pilcher, 23–40. New York: Oxford University Press, 2012.

Ortiz Cuadra, Cruz Miguel. *Puerto Rico en la olla: ¿Somos aún lo que comimos?* Madrid: Ediciones Doce Calles, 2006.

Otero, Gerardo, ed. *Food for the Few: Neoliberal Globalism and Biotechnology in Latin America.* Austin: University of Texas Press, 2008.

Peloso, Vincent. "Succulence and Sustenance: Region, Class, and Diet in Nineteenth-Century Peru." In *Food, Politics, and Society in Latin America,* edited by John C. Super and Thomas C. Wright, 46–64. Lincoln: University of Nebraska Press, 1985.

Pilcher, Jeffrey M. *¡Que vivan los tamales! Food and the Making of Mexican Identity.* Albuquerque: University of New Mexico Press, 1998.

———. *The Sausage Rebellion: Public Health, Private Enterprise, and Meat in Mexico City, 1890–1917.* Albuquerque: University of New Mexico Press, 2006.

———. *Planet Taco: A Global History of Mexican Food.* New York: Oxford University Press, 2012.

Pinedo, Encarnación. *Encarnación's Kitchen: Mexican Recipes from Nineteenth-Century California: Selections from Encarnación Pinedo's El Cocinero Español,* edited and translated by Dan Strehl. Berkeley: University of California Press, 2003.

Pite, Rebekah. "Entertaining Inequalities: Doña Petrona, Juanita Bordoy, and Domestic Work in Mid-Twentieth Century Argentina." *Hispanic American Historical Review* 91, no. 1 (February 2011): 96–128.

Schávelzon, Daniel. *Historias del comer y del beber en Buenos Aires: Arqueología histórica de la vajilla de mesa.* Buenos Aires: Aguilar, 2000.

Soluri, John. *Banana Cultures: Agriculture, Consumption, and Environmental Change in Honduras and the United States.* Austin: University of Texas Press, 2005.

Vega Jiménez, Patricia. *Con sabor a tertulia: Historia del consumo del café en Costa Rica (1840–1940).* San José: Editorial de la Universidad de Costa Rica, 2004.

———. "*El Gallo Pinto:* Afro-Caribbean Rice and Beans Conquer the Costa Rican National Cuisine." *Food, Culture, and Society* 15, no. 2 (June 2012): 223–40.

Warman, Arturo. *Corn and Capitalism: How a Botanical Bastard Grew to Global Dominance.* Translated by Nancy L. Westrate. Chapel Hill: University of North Carolina Press, 2003.

Weis, Robert. *Bakers and Basques: A Social History of Bread in Mexico.* Albuquerque: University of New Mexico Press, 2012.

Weismantel, Mary J. *Food, Gender, and Poverty in the Ecuadorian Andes.* Philadelphia: University of Pennsylvania Press, 1988.

CHAPTER 7

Food and the Material Origins of Early America

JOYCE E. CHAPLIN

The most important recent development in early American food history is perfectly disgusting if also somewhat reassuring. In the spring of 2013, archeologists of the Jamestown Fort in Virginia, site of the first permanent Anglo-American settlement, introduced the world to "Jane." The female remains that went by this name are interesting for food historians because they had been cannibalized after death, with telltale signs of flesh having been removed from bone. Flesh and brains, that is, and the latter was the (faintly) reassuring aspect of the grisly case: the cannibals had twice attempted to open Jane's skull to extract her perishable yet edible brain, their clumsy multiple hacks making it apparent that they had never sought food in this way before. Colonial cannibalism was not so routine that it had established its own skill-set. And yet it existed.[1]

So much for quaint, ye olde early American food. Many scholars had dismissed narratives of cannibalism at Jamestown as propaganda directed against the ill-prepared Virginia Company; Jane's remains corroborate colonial rumor. Her scarred bones are excellent reminders of the materiality of colonial America's past. The presence or absence of food was a critical reality, and a stark measure of social status (Jane was likely an indentured servant), of cultural malleability, of the dangers of imperial overreach, of the significance of environmental conditions (Jamestown was affected by drought and, like all of the colonies, by the "Little Ice Age"), and of the fact that any kind of American-ness must have emerged as much from physical experience as from ideas. America had material as well as ideological origins.

These are important themes and food history can illuminate them, all the better to make sense of an increasingly sprawling portion of American history. For the English-speaking world (on which this essay will focus, with some glances beyond), the period roughly designated as "early America" stretches at least three hundred years, from the search for comestibles at the "lost colony" of Roanoke in the 1580s to the reestablishment of prosperity, including food production and consumption, after the War for Independence in the 1780s; some scholars allow an even longer chronology, from the Atlantic cod fishing of the sixteenth century through the arrival of new immigrant groups and foodways into the early American Republic in the early nineteenth century. Meanwhile, early America's geography typically includes regions that extended from the Newfoundland fisheries through the Caribbean sugar colonies, and from coastal areas to western frontiers, with Atlantic connections back to food hearths in Europe and Africa. The diverse parts of British America yielded quite different foodstuffs and had differing access to foreign imports, which resulted in significant variations at table, especially when compounded by the social inequalities between eaters.

The best introduction to the place of food within early American history is through historiography. A survey of the relevant literatures helps to establish not only what was eaten, when, and by whom, but more importantly, what is at stake in knowing any of that. Food history matters for itself, but also in relation to other big questions about the past, including status (race, class, and gender), power, cultural hybridity, environmental conditions, and the competing conditions of plenty and scarcity. Early American food history has touched on all of these questions though, intriguingly, not equally.

ORIGINS

It is typical to lament how food has only recently been added to the historian's repertoire, but for early American history, the problem is that food actually has a much earlier presence in the field, one dismissed as "antiquarian." At the turn of the last century, nonacademic investigators and enthusiasts explored colonial cooks and kitchens. These antiquarians looked at everyday life among free white colonists, with considerable attention to the roles of women and the texture of daily life, which professional historians for the most part disdained. In parallel, early twentieth-century decorators and antique dealers encouraged an interest in the reconstruction of "colonial" interiors. Against a rising enthusiasm for modern design, including modern kitchens, these taste arbiters looked back in time in order to create kitchens with large, open hearths hung round with a wealth of pewter implements, as well as dining rooms and kitchens decorated in a "Dutch" style, complete with the blue-and-white tiles assumed to have adorned early New York interiors. In parallel, open-air museums, especially Colonial Williamsburg, selectively introduced colonial foods to the public. The net result was both nostalgic and patriotic, representing popular interest in the sturdy origins of a United States emerging, in the twentieth century, onto the world stage.[2]

When early American history was professionalized, especially after World War II, with the rejuvenation of the *William and Mary Quarterly* in its third series and with the creation of the Institute for Early American History and Culture (both located at the College of William and Mary), scholars sought to distance themselves from the antiquarians by focusing not on the everyday life of ordinary people but on the grand narratives of politics and economic development, which they defined as more important. Those narratives were quite often constructed to explain the humble roots of the greatness of the United States (post World War II), via the American Revolution, the usual climax or even terminus for early American history as a whole.[3]

It must be said that this was an overwhelmingly successful strategy, with implications for how early American history is still written and taught. As the American Revolution became the critical watershed in American history, the colonial past went from antiquarian backwater to the very anvil on which the republic had been forged. Toward this end, early American history was interrogated for any signs of the exceptional characteristics that were thought to bring the colonists into their definitive opposition to Great Britain, not only in pursuit of their own freedom, but to establish universal liberties for all of "mankind." This gendering of American history was deliberate. Private life and female domestic activities, including cooking, were defined as nonessential within the narrative of events that turned colonists into Americans. The field of early American history was intensively nationalized, devoted to the explanation of American identity and U.S. destiny in relation to public affairs, for which diet was seen as having little explanatory power. Ideas mattered more than material circumstances, as in Bernard Bailyn's exemplary *Ideological Origins of the American Revolution* (1967), still a dominant text in the field. Early American political history, including the history of political thought, has remained largely separate from food history.[4]

At the very least, however, economic historians took seriously the topics of agriculture and trade. Their efforts resulted in foundational studies of the colonial production of fish (from New England), wheat (New York and Pennsylvania), the food-surrogate tobacco (Chesapeake), rice (South Carolina and Georgia), and sugar (the Caribbean). These analyses situated the colonies within larger worlds of empire and commerce that had been invisible in the inward-looking antiquarian picture of early America. Food has, accordingly, become a way not only to look at the American colonies as progenitors of one nation-state, the United States, but also to examine imperial and transnational geographies. Foremost in these kinds of studies were analyses of sugar plantations, the business-end of Atlantic empire, with particular attention to their disastrous demand for captive African slaves and their role in generating capital for British industrialization. Attention to these questions crowded out, however, any assessment of the ways in which colonial rice, sugar, rum, molasses, or grain-products were prepared for the table and consumed—there was little interest, that is, in the fact that these items were food.[5]

Outside academia, a variety of writers and scholars did maintain an interest in eater and eaten. From 1947 onward, in different incarnations, the magazine *American Heritage: A Journal of Community History* covered topics of popular interest, including food. In 1964, the editors produced *The American Heritage Cookbook and Illustrated History of American Eating and Drinking,* which combined a lively narrative with a cookbook of selected recipes adapted from original sources. Meanwhile, *New York Times* food writer John L. Hess and the independent scholar Karen Hess in 1972 produced their book, *The Taste of America,* which ran through multiple editions. The basic message of these and similar works of this era was nostalgic: modern food was pallid, overprocessed, and basically unsatisfactory, and a look at the fresh, wild, vital foodstuffs of the past spelled out the loss. But a gap between academic history and these works remained. *The American Heritage Cookbook* later appeared without its prefacing historical section, which the majority of readers and cooks evidently did not want.[6]

The most notable exception to these trends emerged from Latin American history, in Alfred W. Crosby's monumental 1972 contribution to food studies, *The Columbian Exchange: Biological and Cultural Consequences of 1492.* Using ideas from the very new field of environmental history, which pushed material factors to the center of historical analysis, Crosby reread the history of European colonization of the Americas as a series of powerful alterations in the natural world, whether intended or unintended. Not all of his analysis was of food; the migration of contagious diseases to the Americas was a powerful part of the Columbian exchange. But Crosby was prescient in realizing that the transfer of European food items to the Americas—including livestock—and the counterflow of American plantable commodities back to Europe (including corn and the "Irish" potato, from the Andean highlands) represented an unacknowledged reshuffling of both natural and cultural idioms. This exchange was qualitatively different from long-distance trade in edible exotics (such as spices), in which the sought-after items were rarely grown in many of the places where they were consumed. Long-distance transfer of some cultivars had happened before, but Crosby convincingly represented the era after 1492 as being on an entirely different scale of exchange, on a par with the transformations represented in the long-ago "Neolithic Revolution" in agriculture. Subsequent scholars have further speculated that the transfer of American foodstuffs to Europe (and perhaps to Africa) may have expanded food supplies that then increased population. These developments supported the consolidation of state power within the old world and outflows of people to colonized zones—the exchange was an imperial feedback loop.[7]

The "Columbian Exchange," which Crosby in 1986 stretched to a global scale in his *Ecological Imperialism: The Biological Expansion of Europe, 900–1900*, has remained tremendously influential, and a lasting reminder of the connections between environmental and food histories. (Indeed, through the popularizations of Jared Diamond and Charles Mann, the thesis has begun to be dissociated from Crosby.) Scholars of the British colonies have explained the cultural and environmental impacts of old world edible biota, from swine to wheat, as essential components of colonization. William Cronon's 1983 study of colonial New England, *Changes in the Land: Indians, Colonists, and the Ecology of New England*, provided an excellent, post-Crosby model of how environmental history and imperial history could be nearly coterminous. Food was no longer marginal to the grand narratives, but a central part of them, albeit at sub- and supra-national levels.[8]

Likewise, archeological work began to generate new information about the colonial past's materiality, often with relevance to the history of food. The sizes of colonial dwellings, the location within them of places for cooking and eating, and the disposition and contents of the inhabitants' garbage have all revealed how and what colonists ate, at different places and times. James Deetz's pioneering 1977 study, *In Small Things Forgotten: An Archeology of Early American Life* is still of remarkable value as a basic explanation of what archeologists can recover about food history, from the beginning of the eating cycle (cooking pot) to the end (chamber pot).[9]

The field of early American history was then, in the 1980s, profoundly reshaped by the series of historiographical developments associated with the Annales school in Europe and with a parallel convergence between historical and anthropological investigations into the cultures of the past. The quotidian and the material gained new importance as measures of historical changes that proceeded much more slowly than the manifest chronology of politics that led into and through the American Revolution. These analyses moved questions about social difference—class, race, and gender—firmly toward the center.[10]

Thanks to this generation of social historians, for instance, we now know that the typical early American household did not have the vast, wood-hungry open fireplace or array of pewterware that the antiquarians and antiques dealers had insisted was standard issue. Rather, even into the eighteenth century, most people cooked their meals over smaller fires, perhaps in a household's sole cooking pot, and they ate from wooden or pottery vessels, often using their hands, maybe sharing a spoon or two. Those of the upper ranks, however, ensured for themselves a remarkably ornate set of dining options, often in rooms far removed from where their meals were cooked. Atlantic trade brought them steel forks (later replaced by locally fashioned silverware), fashionable stemware for Madeira wine, porcelain teapots, and sundry other implements that would have been found on the tables of their social equals in Europe—which was the whole point. The field of material culture, and an associated convergence between academic historians and scholars who work in museums, has continued to develop an ever-more precise picture of material life in early America: how many chairs the average household had, how many napkins and tablecloths, and how much pepper or chocolate, if any. More recently, attention to the consumer revolution that radiated outward from industrializing Europe has shown the constant elaboration of everyday life in the colonies.[11]

To a great extent, the resulting picture of eating, specifically, and colonial material life more generally, has vindicated Norbert Elias's contention that modernity in the global West emerged as a performance of differentiations between polite and coarse behaviors. Within early American history, this social dynamic has been mapped over the social divisions that were, and are, thought to have informed the political disquiet that eventually fed into the American Revolution. For that reason, most new discoveries about silver wine strainers or wooden trenchers have been read against putative definitions of American identity, either as fundamentally European in its construction (which emphasizes the significance of the post-1776 rejection of Britain), or else somehow innately simpler or more egalitarian than European culture, and therefore bound to become independent from it.[12]

All the same, almost none of the social historians of early America who were influenced either by the Annalistes or by anthropologists did what could easily be labeled as food history. Quite remarkably, there was little uptake of the developments in food studies within European history that had also grown from the Annales traditions. Among Americanists, there was a lingering sense that the study of food, cookery, and eating—unless connected to recognized topics of importance to the field, such as the coming of the Revolution or the problem of social inequality—was not quite appropriate for academic scholarship. Nevertheless, early American social historians' analyses of everyday experience on a material level, including women's history and the history of slavery, had established essential bases for a subsequent generation of food historians.

INEQUALITY AMID PLENTY

The scholarship on early America continues to stress how food may be useful for explaining established trends in the larger historiography, particularly those that have been deemed characteristic of American history. These include, most notably, the unequal distribution of New World products and profits in a land that otherwise seemed naturally free from want.

Outrage at the bitterly exploitative fruits of colonization was the dominant strain of the very first analysis of early American food, the original (and possibly best) commodity study. That book was Sidney Mintz's *Sweetness and Power: The Place of Sugar in Modern History* (1985), which examined how sugar was produced in the Caribbean and consumed in Europe, with special focus on the British colonies and Great Britain, and above all with a Marxist critique of how a single food commodity became a mechanism to consolidate imperial control over working bodies on American plantations and capitalist control over their counterparts in British factories. Mintz's formula—track a single commodity to see how it made its way through the world and to see the worlds that it "made"—has been widely imitated, with scholarly studies of the potato and popular histories of salt, cod, and oysters following his model. Most of the imitators have, however, shrunk from his bold Marxist apparatus, which regarded food not merely as source of sustenance (and sometimes pleasure), but also as a means to an end: the generation of wealth for the few by the exploitation of the many.[13]

Mintz also pointed out that a great many people on either side of the Atlantic did not get enough to eat. Sugar signified a gorgeous abundance for the people who could afford the big confected centerpieces featured in Mintz's illustrations, but it grew only because underfed workers cultivated it in the West Indies and because badly nourished workers processed it in European jam factories. No one has refuted his point. Rather, his critical reading of the origins of an industrialized and standardized diet has provided an essential corrective to sunnier readings of a modern consumer revolution that brought variety to American colonists who could pay for imported delights and to Europeans who themselves imported goods from America. Those people enjoyed themselves while others barely subsisted.

Indeed, the differentiation between abundance and scarcity has been a noteworthy way to examine the greater historical meaning of New World colonization. At first, famine, which was persistent within Europe, seemed to have followed colonists across the Atlantic. The "starving times" at Jamestown in Virginia (first settled in 1607) and at Plymouth Plantation in what is now Massachusetts (1620) were particularly foreboding in this regard. In the former place, only sixty survivors from an initial group of five hundred made it to the spring of 1610; "Jane" died and was eaten during this dire period. Plymouth had lower mortality during its first winter (1620–21), only 50 percent, in part because of greater social solidarity, including the determination to grow and share food. The highest mortality, among adult women (78 percent), likely resulted because they gave their food to children, who had the lowest mortality (31 percent). The so-called first Thanksgiving at Plymouth in the fall of 1621 represented a hard-won triumph at producing food locally, and indeed might be regarded as the primordial incident of an American locavore tradition. The Pilgrims celebrated a harvest of Indian corn (from seed stolen from Indian caches) and other vegetables. Their meal was evidently filled out by game, especially venison, provided by visiting Wampanoag men, who were incredulous that such a stingy repast (what, no meat?) constituted cause for happiness.[14]

After these dramatic incidents, the starving times were over. While harvest failures and even famines recurred in Western Europe until the early 1800s, the peoples of early America did not suffer hunger from natural causes. Instead, as Mintz had already pointed out (as with Amartya Sen's critical distinction between natural versus political food shortages), material want was (and is) a sociopolitical condition. In the continental colonies, harvests were almost predictable in their bounty; failures in one place could be offset by abundance elsewhere. And yet convicts and indentured servants temporarily, and slaves persistently, continued to experience food deprivation. On Caribbean sugar plantations, food shortages could be fatal, with planters and overseers making cold-hearted calculations of expenditure on food, often when the provision trade to the islands was delayed, while forcing starving slaves to keep up production. So too did Native Americans suffer hunger and even starvation when they were forcibly removed from ancestral sites where they could plant, harvest, or hunt. White colonists endured those conditions during times of frontier war, as is evident in the captivity narrative of the persistently hungry Mary Rowlandson during King Philip's War (1675–76). The presence or absence of food can indeed meaningfully trace the material dimensions of imperialism in the greater Atlantic. That said, the specter of want and the environmental circumstances that might summon it are only beginning to be studied in any serious way.[15]

Rather than entering the general narrative of early American history, food-related problems have for the most part been segmented off into the literatures on slavery and Indian history. This is another indication of most historians' preference for an exceptionalist narrative of American history. Note that extreme deprivation has been associated with zones beyond the regions that would eventually break with Britain; the people who experienced severe food insecurity in Indian country on the continent and in the slave-majority Caribbean are outside the grand narrative in two senses. There is a factual basis to this analysis. When the English arrived in North America in the late 1500s and early 1600s, it is likely that they were shorter than American Indians, precisely because they had had less to eat as children. The situation reversed itself over the ensuing colonial period. Because they were well fed throughout their lives, except perhaps during wars, creole white colonists were, by the time of the American Revolution, taller than their British counterparts, taller than enslaved blacks, and probably taller than many of the Indians who lived in or near settlements.[16]

So important was British North America's reputation for plenty that it elicited one of history's first analyses of nature's carrying capacity, Benjamin Franklin's "Observations on the Increase of Mankind." In this demographic analysis (written circa 1751 and published in 1755), Franklin conjectured that by natural increase alone, free white Americans in North America were doubling their numbers at an unprecedented rate, every twenty years. Why? The availability of land permitted colonists to marry at younger ages than people in the "old settled" nations of Europe, and therefore produce more children. Like plants, if given "greater Ground," humans ran riot. This was, however, a naturalized analysis of an imperial situation. American land was available because, Franklin assumed, Indians, as hunters, used little of it and were doomed to diminish anyway. Nor did he think that black slaves were likely to benefit from this natural bounty, which belonged intrinsically to free farmers. In North America, Franklin predicted, in racialized terms omitted from later versions of the essay, "we have so fair an Opportunity, by excluding all Blacks and Tawneys, of increasing the lovely White and Red" complexions of Euro-Americans. He used his analysis to make an anti-imperial point. Because colonists would increase rapidly in the absence of population pressure from Indians and African Americans, they would eventually outnumber their British overlords.[17]

Franklin's thesis was arresting—and convincing. His essay ran through multiple editions and his geometrical hypothesis of population growth doubling every twenty years powerfully affected the controversy that concluded in the American Revolution. The idea that North America was undergoing a population explosion called into question British predictions of colonial weakness while heartening colonial patriots. Eventually, the idea that humans could reproduce unchecked, until they ran out of food, meaning land, would influence Thomas Robert Malthus in his *Essay on the Principle of Population* (1798; five subsequent editions to 1826). Through Malthus, Franklin's thesis about North America's fecund land and settler population would inspire the Victorian evolutionists Charles Darwin and Alfred Russel Wallace in their theories of natural selection. Fascination with American abundance has had an immense historical impact.[18]

VARIETY AND HYBRIDITY

Because abundance in some way characterized all regions of early America, however unequally over particular geographies or social hierarchies, many food historians have celebrated the regional variation in food-ways, running down the Atlantic seaboard and into the greater Caribbean. Here, the stress is not on deprivation but instead on differentiation and hybridity, the creative adoption of American staples and their amalgamation with food items and methods of cookery that had crossed the Atlantic westward.[19]

Novelty was not necessarily welcome. Histories of early American food have frequently noted colonists' conservatism. Because European medical traditions put great emphasis on physical place, with substantial suspicion that people were unwise to eat or drink the products of foreign lands, it is unsurprising that the first English settlers doubted whether Indian corn or other American staples would suit them. In his influential *Great Herbal or Generall Historie of Plantes* (1597), John Gerard declared of corn that it "yeeldeth to the body little or no nourishment . . . [and] is of hard and evill digestion, a more convenient food for swine than for man." Europeans' incredulity that settlers actually subsisted on New World products, and raised subsequent generations on them, coincided with a general prejudice against American environments as somehow too hot, too cold, too damp, or too dry to maintain animals (and therefore humans) of strength and mental capacity equal to those in the Old World. Few settlers wanted to relinquish European cultural identity by becoming natural to such environments; food xenophobia was one logical response.[20]

Indeed, it was overwhelmingly the case that the anglophone colonies retained English food preferences. The English at home and abroad may have taken to tobacco smoking with alacrity, but they did not intend to give up the meals of their nonsmoking ancestors. This included a diet of small grains baked into bread, brewed into beer, or distilled into whisky; eggs and dairy products from domesticated animals; savory herbs and vegetables cooked with meat or animal fat; and bland starches (such as dried peas) boiled into "puddings." Fish was not always highly regarded, being associated with fast days, and seafoods that are expensive and prestigious today, such as oysters and lobster, were considered trash fit for swine or the poor. Above all, entire cuts or joints of meat were the prized foodstuffs. Together, an abundance of livestock and grain signified that the continental colonies had not only replicated the material foundations of Northern Europe, but had outdone them, in harvests that almost always came without fail. Adherence to English foodways was apparent, as well, in the importation of English cookbooks, such as Susannah Carter's *The Frugal Housewife, or Complete Woman Cook* (1765), first reprinted in the colonies in 1772.[21]

There were substantial regional variations, and this has been the focus of most food studies of the past ten years. These works invite readers on a virtual tour, either of the variety that spread over the different regions of British America, or of the rich foodways within one of the regions, implicitly set against those elsewhere. Some of the differentiation can be traced back to ethnic or regional patterns within Europe. Carefully dehydrated foods (including possibly a version of cream cheese) characterized the colonial diet in Pennsylvania and the mid-Atlantic seaboard, for example, where frugal Quakers and other pietists couldn't abide waste. In contrast, wealthy and non-pietist Southern planters could afford to spit-roast meat, ostentatiously losing sizzling animal fat in the process. In the northern maritimes, colonists ate fish stews that might derive from French seafood soups cooked in large pots (*chaudières*). But in many cases, such dishes spread so quickly and distantly from any original cultural hearth that specific genealogies are rarely convincing, as the existence of various "chowders" from Halifax to Manhattan attests.[22]

Whatever the regionalisms, some colonial food was remarkably consistent across provincial lines. Dishes made from cornmeal became everyday fare throughout the continental colonies, though the regionalized forms of this daily bread were amazing. Johnny cakes or hoecakes were prepared from cornmeal mixed with water and salt, perhaps some fat, and then briefly fried. Other corn breads were made with wheat flour, milk, and eggs, even butter, depending on the region and the wealth of the household in which they were served. So-called "Indian pudding" was a New England treat that would have been unrecognizable to precontact Indians, given its milk base and heavy infusions of sugar, molasses, and Asian spices. Rye 'n Injun bread (baked from a mix of rye flour and cornmeal) and anadama (wheat flour and corn) were likewise hybrid. In similar fashion, pumpkins, Jerusalem artichokes, and persimmons took the places of Old World turnips, chestnuts, and quince. Outside urban areas, American game was prized by whoever could obtain it. Venison and game birds were common; depending on their region and class, different peoples within the British colonies also ate alligator, moose, raccoon, and possum.

Variety and hybridity also characterized the food that Native Americans and African slaves ate. By emphasizing that preference and creativity existed even within severe constraint, food historians offer an interpretation that differs from the starker contrast that other scholars have presented between colonial hunger and abundance: whatever the constraints on their choices, people always prefer some foods above others, and their choices are worth consideration.

Rather than assume that Indians resisted dietary innovation, the latest generation of Indian historians have interpreted their subjects as actors within the consumer revolution radiating outward from Europe. To be sure, most natives continued to cultivate corn, along with other traditional crops, and hunting remained a paramount way to get meat. But Indian curiosity about European foodstuffs was apparent from the first encounters. When the Indian man known as Squanto (Tisquantum) introduced himself to the settlers at Plymouth, he asked if they had any beer, for which he had evidently acquired a taste during his earlier captivity in Europe. Indian acceptance of what were for them exotics continued with a newfound appreciation of baked goods that contained white flour or sugar, alcohol distilled from grain, and flesh from domesticated animals. So called "settlement Indians" began to plant apple trees and keep herds of swine. No less than the foreigners who came to their lands, they sampled and amalgamated.[23]

Perhaps even more remarkably, enslaved Africans made clear their preference for certain foods. Consider in this regard Karen Hess's 1992 book *The Carolina Rice Kitchen: The African Connection*, which identified the creative power of slaves' taste and agency—against all odds—in the generation of a low-country cuisine. Judith Carney's *Black Rice: The African Origins of Rice Cultivation in the Americas* (2001) places at its analytical center a scenario similar to Mintz's—the production of a commodity by slaves for export to consumers elsewhere—but interprets it differently. Carney's slaves (like Hess's) have agency. They very likely brought the original seeds of the lower South's characteristic rice from Africa, and they continued to process, cook, and eat rice in ways that maintained cultural links to their homelands and introduced West African seasonings and cooking methods to the Indian and European populations of the colonies in the lower South, from southern North Carolina to northern Florida.[24]

Not all food frontiers were crossed. It is noteworthy that religion may have been the most powerful deterrent to a complete reshaping of anyone's diet. Within Europe, succeeding popes determined whether chocolate or beaver could be eaten on fast days; rabbis at some point had to decide whether manatee was kosher (no) or potatoes appropriate for Passover (yes). Similar decisions had to be made within the Americas. As he traveled the Carolina frontier in the early 1700s, the naturalist and adventurer John Lawson tended to tuck into whatever his different Indian hosts offered him. He was amused when some of his fellow travelers refused to eat fawn embryos roasted inside their "slimy" amniotic sacs within their mothers; the abstainers might have been recalling the prohibition in Leviticus against "seething" a kid in its mother's milk. For similar reasons, a South Carolina planter recorded giving one male slave rations of beef rather than of pork, probably because the man had made it clear that Islam forbade his consuming the flesh of swine, even if he starved to death. Jewish settlers quickly learned that they had to arrange their own butchering, so that their meat would be kosher.[25]

Amidst hybridity, therefore, many people continued to eat in ways that were traditional, even ceremonial. These strands of material continuity were important. Even though they were consuming American venison or American-raised beef, it was significant for white colonists that they, like their counterparts in Great Britain, were prosperous eaters of meat. So too did Indian use of alcohol significantly resemble, not the sociable tipsiness of European culture, but instead the deep and religiously inflected intoxication that had once been achieved from pre-Columbian substances, such as tobacco or *yapon* (black holly). Finally, black slaves' taste for rice and for chicken set them apart from both enslaved or free Indians, whose preferred grain was corn, and from the white settlers whose preferred meats came from animals on the hoof.[26]

If much of the hybridity of colonial foods could be interpreted as a consequence of the Columbian Exchange across and around the Atlantic Ocean, other dietary innovations must be set within even bigger geographies and imperial networks. The global dimensions of European empires have long been known, but tracing the consequences for food in this regard has been perhaps the most recent development within food studies, with some quite interesting implications for the non-American origins of typically "American" ways of eating.

Chinese tea is the best-studied global food in early America. It was the quintessential beverage of British empire, fetched to consumers in the Atlantic via India on the far side of the world. Whatever its geographically and culturally distant roots, tea proved remarkably popular within British America, and tea imports have become primary evidence of the reinforcing powers of consumer culture and of empire. Tea-drinking became a mark of cultural refinement, as did the acquisition of appropriate equipage (Asian porcelain or "china" from Asia; Spanish American silver), with clear meaning for social hierarchy. Women were particularly associated with the tea table (made of Central American mahogany). For women on both sides of the Atlantic, tea-table talk was a surrogate for political engagement, and for women who were economic consumers rather than producers, it was a way to engage with the world of commerce. Indeed, Benjamin Franklin conveniently blamed his wife for the arrival of tea (and its implements) into his household:

> My breakfast was [for] a long time Bread and Milk, (no Tea) and I ate it out of a twopenny earthen Porringer with a Pewter Spoon. But mark how Luxury will enter Families, and make a Progress, in Spite of Principle. Being call'd one Morning to Breakfast, I found it in a China Bowl with a Spoon of Silver. They had been bought for me without my Knowledge by my Wife, and had cost her the enormous Sum of three and twenty Shillings, for which she had no other Excuse or Apology to make, but that she thought *her* Husband deserv'd a Silver spoon and China Bowl as well as any of his Neighbors.

As Deborah Franklin had discovered, tea was becoming quite affordable, so much so that working people and even those one step away from slavery could indulge. A mahogany tea table has been identified as belonging to Phillis Wheatley, who was described as knowing the correct, polite behavior for taking tea.[27]

One of the reasons that tea was so affordable was that it was smuggled. Colonists preferred to buy contraband Dutch tea, which was cheaper than the British product. The Tea Act of 1773 actually lowered the price of British tea, yet was hated. The law was designed to dump cheap tea on the colonial market in order to shore up a faltering British East India Company—global politics in action. But the cut-rate tea was still more expensive than contraband, and its terms of sale were regarded as monopolistic. Coming as it did within a series of legal acts that meddled with colonial commerce, the Tea Act was considered yet another attempt to reduce the colonists to parliamentary subjection. For that reason, self-designated patriots in Boston costumed themselves as Mohawk Indians, boarded the ship that had carried East India Company tea to their harbor, and dumped it into the tidal mud. Abstaining from tea became politically virtuous; patriotic women made a point of substituting herbal infusions at their tea tables.

The colonial nonimportation movements were early instances of a lasting tendency within American food culture: moralizing abstemiousness. This was an important adjustment to the enthusiasm that early Americans seemed to have had for the consumer revolution. Temperance in the form of avoiding distilled alcohol would be an important national movement, from the nineteenth century through the Eighteenth Amendment (and its repeal), and avoidance of liquor or meat would characterize several made-in-America religions, including the Church of Jesus Christ of Latter-Day Saints, the Christian Science Church, and the Seventh-day Adventist Church. There was a secular counterpart in the antislavery movement's boycott of things produced by slaves, most notably West Indian sugar.[28]

AMERICAN SIMPLICITY, SOMETIMES

For the most part, scholarship on food within the newly independent United States has emphasized its continuity from the colonial period. The old staples were rarely replaced with new stuff; corn breads and pumpkin pie remained favorites, as can be seen in the first "American" cookbook, published by Amelia Simmons in 1796. Travelers to the new nation invariably remarked on the abundance of American food, the large meals (for free Americans), and the simplicity of the fare and of the table manners. Some crops did change; grain replaced tobacco in parts of the Chesapeake, for example. And the dynamics of marketing likewise underwent transformation, sometimes dramatically. When farmers in western Pennsylvania tried to maximize their profits by turning bulky grain into more easily transportable distilled whisky, they were so irate when the liquor came under a new tax that some led a "Whiskey Rebellion" (1791–94). Other changes in food represented an emerging similarity between the United States and older nations. The growth of existing cities and the creation of new urban centers meant that an increasing number of Americans relied on foods sold to them by strangers. The availability of wild foods likewise shrank. For the most part, however, the U.S. population was rural, and that would remain a striking feature of the nation until the early twentieth century.[29]

The most dramatic change in early American food after independence was the arrival of French cooking. It was culturally fortunate, in a way, for the newly independent Americans that France had become the Atlantic world's primary site for culinary experimentation and refinement. To follow French food fashions was, for free Americans, a way of marking a debt to their most important ally, the first nation to recognize their sovereignty, and from which they had received essential aid in their War of Independence. Eating French food could signify Americanness, and yet the new cuisine was acknowledged to be a sharp contrast to the prevailing simplicity of the traditional diet, even once France had its own revolution and formed its own republic. The resulting dilemma—which of the "sister republics" had the cuisine most appropriate to a republican citizenry?—would have a long life, from Thomas Jefferson to Julia Child (and perhaps beyond).[30]

Let's begin with Jefferson. He presided over a household that was uniquely equipped to usher French cuisine into the United States. Having become accustomed to French cookery while serving as U.S. ambassador in France, he worried about leaving it all behind when he returned to Virginia. His solution was to have one of his slaves instructed in French cuisine. James Hemings (brother of Sally Hemings, Jefferson's probable enslaved mistress) trained with a French caterer and a chef and shopped for the kitchen equipment that would help him recreate, in Virginia, the dishes he had learned to cook in Paris. Guests to Jefferson's Monticello duly remarked on their host's sophisticated offerings, from macaroni to ice cream. The amalgamation of American slavery and French cuisine is excellent, if sad, evidence of the culinary hybridity in the early Republic. So too is the fact that Jefferson's indebtedness was in part due to his expenditure on French wines, and resulted in his reluctance to free his slaves, lest his heirs be left with nothing.[31]

Even if most Americans could not sustain French cookery at home (or didn't want to eat it every day) some could enjoy it in the very newest kind of eating establishment, the restaurant. In their modern form, restaurants offered dishes from a list, essentially a menu, and served them to diners at small private tables, in contrast to the taverns or other eating houses that served only a few staples or specialties to people seated at common tables. On these lines, the Grand Taverne de Londres opened in 1782 in Paris. It is remarkable, therefore, that quite soon after that date, in 1794, the emigrant Jean Baptiste Gilbert Payplat opened Jullien's Restarator in Boston, though it is not clear how much of the new French model of eating out came with him.[32]

France was not always the source of culinary innovation, however. On the side of hearty republican virtue, the transplanted French nobleman J. Hector St. John de Crèvecœur (born Michel Guillaume Jean de Crèvecœur) extolled his status as an American farmer in upstate New York, where he produced most of his own food and drink. His *Letters from an American Farmer* (1782) praised the virtues of independent farming. "Thank God that my lot is to be an American farmer," he wrote, "instead of a Russian boor, or an Hungarian peasant," who owed their living to others. The essential food memoirist Jean Anthelme Brillat-Savarin was another Frenchman who, while in exile from revolutionary France in the 1790s, extolled the rural delights of the northern parts of the early United States, where he hunted turkey and savored squirrels cooked in Madeira.[33]

It was a food encounter in France that elicited the most poetic defense of plain American food. While serving as a U.S. diplomat and passing through Savoy, Joel Barlow partook of a quick simple peasant dish: cornmeal cooked in hot salted water, served with milk. In his mock epic *The Hasty Pudding* (written in 1793; published in 1796), Barlow recorded his rapturous recognition and homesickness:

> I sing the sweets I know, the charms I feel,
> My morning incense, and my evening meal,
> The sweets of Hasty Pudding. Come, dear bowl
> Glide o'er my palate, and inspire my soul . . .
> . . . Dear Hasty Pudding, what unpromised joy
> Expands my heart, to meet thee in Savoy!

So much for the flesh pots of Paris. Barlow's point about food was patriotic, and moralizing. "A Simplicity in diet," he remarked, "whether it be considered with reference to the happiness of individuals, or the prosperity of a nation, is of more consequence than we are apt to imagine."[34]

That's good advice to anyone interested in early American food history. The relevant primary sources, including Barlow's poem, link everyday eating to the grand narratives of American history, including the creation of the United States, and to essential questions about nation and social status, empire and liberty, hunger and abundance.

NOTES

I am extremely grateful to Paul Freedman, Ken Albala, Carla Cevasco, and the three external reviewers for their comments on this essay.

1. See www.historicjamestowne.org/jane/jane.php.

2. Alice Morse Earle, *Colonial Dames and Good Wives* (Boston; New York: Houghton, Mifflin and Co., 1895); Alice Morse Earle, *Home Life in Colonial Days* (New York, 1898); Jay Anderson, *Time Machines: The World of Living History* (Nashville: American Association for State and Local History, 1984); Richard Handler and Eric Gable, *The New History in an Old Museum: Creating the Past at Colonial Williamsburg* (Durham: Duke University Press, 1997); Annette Stott, "The Dutch Dining Room in Turn of the Century America," *Winterthur Portfolio* 37 (2002): 219–38.

3. Fredrika Teute, "A Conversation with Thad Tate," *William and Mary Quarterly*, 3rd ser., 50 (1993): 268–97; *In Search of Early America: The William and Mary Quarterly, 1943–1993* (Williamsburg, VA: Institute of Early American History and Culture, 1993).

4. See the not-quite intermeshing essays, Pauline Maier, "Disjunctions in Early American History," and James E. McWilliams, "Groping for National Identity by Forging a National Cuisine," in *Recent Themes in Early American History: Historians in Conversation,* ed. Donald A. Yerxa (Columbia: University of South Carolina Press, 2008), 9–17, 91–99. For a notable attempt to connect food to political events, see Barbara Clark Smith, "Food Rioters and the American Revolution," *William and Mary Quarterly,* 3rd ser., 51 (1994): 3–38. The edible worlds of governors' balls, diplomatic fêtes, official gifts, and unofficial bribes await their scholars.

5. Percy Wells Bidwell and John I. Falconer, *A History of Agriculture in the Northern United States* (Washington, DC: Carnegie Institution of Washington, 1925); Lewis Cecil Gray, *A History of Agriculture in the Southern United States to 1860,* 2 vols. (Washington, DC: Carnegie Institution of Washington, 1933); Wesley George Pierce, *Goin' Fishin': The Story of the Deep-Sea Fishermen of New England* (Salem, MA: Marine Research Society, 1934); Eric Williams, *Capitalism and Slavery* (Chapel Hill: University of North Carolina Press, 1944); Richard B. Sheridan, *Sugar and Slavery: An Economic History of the British West Indies, 1623–1775* (Baltimore: Johns Hopkins University Press, 1973).

6. Cleveland Amory, Helen Duprey Bullock, Helen McCully, and Eleanor Noderer, *The American Heritage Cookbook and Illustrated History of American Eating and Drinking* (New York: American Heritage and Simon and Schuster, 1964), had significant historical material; Helen McCully, Eleanor Noderer, and Helen Duprey Bullock, eds., *The American Heritage Cookbook* (New York: American Heritage, 1969), did not, nor did a subsequent 1980 reprint. See also John L. Hess and Karen Hess, *The Taste of America* (New York: Grossman Publishers, 1977), which ran through three editions.

7. Alfred W. Crosby, *The Columbian Exchange: Biological and Cultural Consequences of 1492* (Westport, CT: Greenwood Press, 1972); William L. Langer, "American Foods and Europe's Population Growth," *Journal of Social History* 8, no. 2 (1975): 51–66; Marvin P. Miracle, "The Introduction and Spread of Maize in Africa," *The Journal of African History* 6 (1965): 39–55.

8. Alfred W. Crosby, *Ecological Imperialism: The Biological Expansion of Europe, 900–1900* (Cambridge: Cambridge University Press, 1986); William Cronon, *Changes in the Land: Indians, Colonists and the Ecology of New England* (New York: Hill and Wang, 1983); Virginia DeJohn Anderson, *Creatures of Empire: How Domestic Animals Transformed Early America* (New York: Oxford University Press, 2004).

9. James Deetz, *In Small Things Forgotten: An Archeology of Early American Life* (Garden City, NY: Doubleday, 1977); see also Peter Benes, ed., *Foodways in the Northeast* (Boston: Boston University Press, 1984).

10. Joyce Appleby, "Value and Society," in *Colonial British America: Essays in the New History of the Early Modern Era,* eds. Jack P. Greene and J.R. Pole (Baltimore: Johns Hopkins University Press, 1984), 290–316.

11. John Demos, *A Little Commonwealth: Family Life in Plymouth County* (New York: Oxford University Press, 1970); Richard L. Bushman, "American High-Style and Vernacular Cultures," in *Colonial British America: Essays in the New History of the Early Modern Era,* eds. Jack P. Greene and J.R. Pole (Balti-

more: Johns Hopkins University Press, 1984), 345–83; T.H. Breen, "'Baubles of Britain': The American and Consumer Revolutions in the Eighteenth Century," *Past and Present* 119 (1988): 73–104.

12. Norbert Elias, *The Civilizing Process: Sociogenetic and Psychogenetic Investigations,* 2 vols., trans. Edmund Jephcott (Oxford: Oxford University Press, 1978–82); David Hancock, *Oceans of Wine: Madeira and the Emergence of American Trade and Taste* (New Haven: Yale University Press, 2009).

13. Sidney Mintz, *Sweetness and Power: The Place of Sugar in Modern History* (New York: Penguin, 1985).

14. Edmund S. Morgan, *American Slavery, American Freedom: The Ordeal of Colonial Virginia* (New York: W.W. Norton, 1975), 73–74; James Deetz and Patricia Scott Deetz, *The Times of Their Lives: Life, Love, and Death in Plymouth Colony* (New York: W.H. Freeman, 2000), 57.

15. Amartya Sen, "The Food Problem: Theory and Policy," *Third World Quarterly* 4 (1982): 447–59; Richard B. Sheridan, "The Crisis of Slave Subsistence in the British West Indies during and after the American Revolution," *William and Mary Quarterly,* 3rd ser., 33 (1976): 615–43; Robert A. Margo and Richard H. Steckel, "The Heights of American Slaves: New Evidence on Slave Nutrition and Health," *Social Science History* 6 (1982): 516–38; Kenneth F. Kiple, *The Caribbean Slave: A Biological History* (Cambridge; New York: Cambridge University Press, 1984); Daniel H. Usner, Jr., "Food Marketing and Interethnic Exchange in the Eighteenth-Century Lower Mississippi Valley," *Food and Foodways* 1 (1986): 279–310; Robert H. Keller, "America's Native Sweet: Chippewa Treaties and the Right to Harvest Maple Sugar," *American Indian Quarterly* 13 (1989): 117–35. On environment and food, see David W. Stahle, Malcolm K. Cleaveland, Dennis B. Blanton, Matthew D. Therrell, and David A. Gay, "The Lost Colony and Jamestown Droughts," *Science,* n.s., 280 (1998), 464–67; Thomas Wickman, "Snowshoe Country: Indians, Colonists, and Winter Spaces of Power in the Northeast, 1620–1727" (Ph.D. dissertation, Harvard University, 2012).

16. Margo and Steckel, "The Heights of American Slaves," 516–38; Richard H. Steckel, "Stature and the Standard of Living," *Journal of Economic Literature* 33 (1995): 1903–40.

17. Joyce E. Chaplin, *The First Scientific American: Benjamin Franklin and the Pursuit of Genius* (New York: Basic Books, 2006), 117–22, 196–200, 228, 232–34, 319–24; Leonard W. Labaree, et al., eds., *The Papers of Benjamin Franklin* (New Haven: Yale University Press, 1961), vol. 4, 227–28.

18. Joyce E. Chaplin, *Benjamin Franklin's Political Arithmetic: A Materialist View of Humanity* (Washington, DC: Smithsonian Institution, 2009).

19. Meta F. Janowitz, "Indian Corn and Dutch Pots: Seventeenth-Century Foodways in New Amsterdam/New York," *Historical Archeology* 27 (1993): 6–24; James McWilliams, *A Revolution in Eating: How the Quest for Food Shaped America* (New York: Columbia University Press, 2005).

20. Gerard is discussed and cited in Joyce E. Chaplin, *Subject Matter: Technology, the Body, and Science on the Anglo-American Frontier, 1500–1676* (Cambridge, MA: Harvard University Press, 2000), 196.

21. McWilliams, *A Revolution in Eating.*

22. David Hackett Fischer, *Albion's Seed: Four British Folkways in America* (New York: Oxford University Press, 1989).

23. Usner, "Food Marketing and Interethnic Interchange"; Chaplin, *Subject Matter,* 150; Anderson, *Creatures of Empire.*

24. Karen Hess, *The Carolina Rice Kitchen: The African Connection* (Columbia, SC: University of South Carolina Press, 1992); Judith Carney, *Black Rice: The African Origins of Rice Cultivation in the Americas* (Cambridge, MA: Harvard University Press, 2001).

25. Marcy Norton, *Sacred Gifts, Profane Pleasures: A History of Tobacco and Chocolate in the Atlantic World* (Ithaca: Cornell University Press, 2008); John Lawson, *A New Voyage to Carolina,* ed. Hugh Talmage Lefler (Chapel Hill: University of North Carolina Press, 1967), 58; Sylvanie A. Diouf, *Servants of Allah: African Muslims Enslaved in the Americas* (New York: New York University Press, 1998), 88–90; Marcie Cohen Ferris, *Matzoh Ball Gumbo: Culinary Tales of the Jewish South* (Chapel Hill: University of North Carolina Press, 2005), 53–54.

26. Charles M. Hudson, ed., *Black Drink: A Native American Tea* (Athens: University of Georgia Press, 1979); Peter C. Mancall, *Deadly Medicine: Indians and Alcohol in Early America* (Ithaca: Cornell University Press, 1995).

27. Alan Macfarlane and Iris Macfarlane, *Green Gold: The Empire of Tea* (London: Ebury Press, 2003), 70–75; Benjamin Franklin, *Benjamin Franklin's Autobiography: An Authoritative Text, Contexts, Criticism,* ed. Joyce E. Chaplin (New York: W.W. Norton, 2012), 77; Rodris Roth, "Tea-Drinking in Eighteenth-Century America: Its Etiquette and Equipage," in *Material Life in America, 1600–1800,* ed. Robert Blair St. George (Boston: Northeastern University Press, 1988); Margot Minardi, *Making Slavery History: Abolitionism and the Politics of Memory in Massachusetts* (New York: Oxford University Press, 2010), 97–118.

28. But see W.J. Rorabaugh, *The Alcoholic Republic: An American Tradition* (New York: Oxford University Press, 1979).

29. Amelia Simmons, *American Cookery . . .* (Hartford, Conn., 1796). See also Barbara K. Wheaton's essay in this volume, chapter 13.

30. T. Sarah Peterson, *Acquired Taste: The French Origins of Modern Cooking* (Ithaca: Cornell University Press, 1994).

31. Annette Gordon-Reed, *The Hemingses of Monticello: An American Family* (New York: W.W. Norton, 2008), 164–68.

32. On restaurants, see Paul Freedman's essay in this volume, chapter 12.

33. J. Hector St. John de Crèvecœur, *Letters from an American Farmer and Other Essays,* ed. Dennis D. Moore (Cambridge, MA: Harvard University Press, 2012), 14; Jean Anthelme Brillat-Savarin, *The Physiology of Taste, or, Meditations on Transcendental Gastronomy,* trans. M.F.K. Fisher (Washington, DC: Counterpoint Press, 1999), 85.

34. Joel Barlow, *The Hasty Pudding* ([Fairhaven, Vt.], 1796), preface, canto I.

SOURCES

If you are planning a course on early American food, you may find helpful several clearinghouses of information about teaching food history. These include the Agricultural History Society's "Food History Resource Page" and the Food Timeline, which includes a chronology of major events in food history, sample syllabi and lesson plans, definitions of key terms, bibliographies, a list of notable legal developments, and links to historical repositories. Both sites skew toward the modern period, but do include useful information on the colonial era: www.aghistorysociety.org/resources/food and www.foodtimeline.org /food2.html.

For those who would be researchers in the field, or want to invite their students to the world of research, there is good news. In contrast to the still fairly slim secondary literature on early American food, there is an abundance of primary sources, many available in handy electronic databases. Joel Barlow's "Hasty Pudding"; the first printed "American" cookbook, by Amelia Simmons; and many other texts may be found in the online Readex edition of *Early American Imprints*, if not in Michigan State University's *Feeding America: The Historic American Cookbook Project*. Google Books, it must be said, is also quite useful; there, for example, one can read *Mourt's Relation* (1622), a history of Plymouth Plantation, which includes the Pilgrims' search for food and their first "thanksgiving." The Google Ngram Viewer allows keyword and phrase searches for edible Americana. (Ask your students: Why does "turkey" spike around 1750 and 1950?) Via these websites, students can be directed to noteworthy primary texts or can do keyword searches ("rum," "beer," "tea") to find food-related patterns of their own. The *Early Encounters in North America* database contains a wealth of documents relating to interactions between Native Americans and European or U.S. explorers, missionaries, and traders between 1590 and 1860. Some of these include practical or ceremonial sharing of foodstuffs and could be used as readings for a class; with a little guidance, students could mine the database for their independent research.

A BASIC BIBLIOGRAPHY

Carson, Jane. *Colonial Virginia Cookery: Procedures, Equipment, and Ingredients in Colonial Cooking*. Williamsburg, VA: Colonial Williamsburg Foundation, 1985.

Comer, James. "North America from 1492 to the Present." In *The Cambridge World History of Food*, edited by Kenneth F. Kiple and Kriemhild Coneè Ornelas, 2:1304–23. Cambridge: Cambridge University Press, 2000.

Crosby, Alfred W. *The Columbian Exchange: Biological and Cultural Consequences of 1492*. Westport, CT: Greenwood Publishing Co., 1972.

Deetz, James. *In Small Things Forgotten: The Archeology of Early American Life*. Garden City, NY: Doubleday, 1977.

Haber, Barbara. *From Hardtack to Home Fries: An Uncommon History of American Cooks and Meals*. New York: Free Press, 2002.

McWilliams, James E. *A Revolution in Eating: How the Quest for Food Shaped America*. New York: Columbia University Press, 2005.

Mintz, Sidney W. *Sweetness and Power: The Place of Sugar in Modern History*. New York: Viking, 1985.

Norton, Marcy. *Sacred Gifts, Profane Pleasures: A History of Tobacco and Chocolate in the Atlantic World.* Ithaca: Cornell University Press, 2008.

Smith, Andrew F., ed. *The Oxford Companion to American Food and Drink.* New York: Oxford University Press, 2007.

Stavely, Keith, and Kathleen Fitzgerald. *America's Founding Food: The Story of New England Cooking.* Chapel Hill: University of North Carolina Press, 2004.

CHAPTER 8

Food in Recent U.S. History

AMY BENTLEY AND HIʻILEI HOBART

Anthropologist Claude Lévi-Strauss suggested in his 1966 essay "The Culinary Triangle" that relationships with food are one of the few universal truths of human activity.[1] Civilizations rise and fall with the success of agricultural technologies; wars are waged and won on the stomachs of soldiers; modern citizens challenge their governments through their food choices. Just as gathering, preparing, and eating food frames our daily lives, it also profoundly shapes national, global, and cultural histories. Because it is such a necessary element for life, food access has a direct link to social and political power, making its history an ideal subject to use for examining broader themes and issues. Twentieth-century food history in particular occurs against the backdrop of dramatic technological, social, political, and economic transformation. Its relevance to larger historical themes is so pervasive that it is nearly impossible to disentangle food from any narrative of modern American life. This chapter looks closely at these intersections in order to critically discuss the role that food scholarship now plays within the traditional academic discipline of history, and to affirm its place within more established frameworks for knowing the past.

"Food history" in the United States overlaps and intersects with other related topics, including histories of agriculture, the environment, nutrition, health, technology, and culture. Although food history has primarily focused on consumption, it is also an umbrella term under which falls nearly every other aspect of life. While food remained a peripheral subject within academic historical scholarship until recently, the topic of agriculture has a long scholarly tradition that extends back to the eighteenth and nineteenth centuries as an interest of early historians and gentlemen of letters. Later, in the early- to mid-twentieth century, food predominantly functioned as an indistinctive backdrop against which to examine, for example, labor relations (workers in canning factories and slaughter houses), agrarian political movements (the Grange) or industrialization (the rise of food-processing conglomerates). With the rise of academic interest in cultural history during the second half of the twentieth century, new avenues of inquiry opened up as scholars began to explore histories of the everyday. Studying the lives of women, minorities, immigrants, and the poor informed inquiry into histories of consumption in all its forms. Previously mundane and seemingly irrelevant topics, including food, became important areas of research. In retrospect, it is surprising that it took such a long time for food-centered history to emerge. After all, not only does everyone have to eat (and ideally several times a day) in order to survive, but all the great civilizations, both ancient and modern, meticulously recorded by traditional history have essentially risen and fallen according to rulers' abilities to feed their people successfully.

THE EARLY TWENTIETH CENTURY: MASS PRODUCTION HITS ITS STRIDE

An acute shift in U.S. food and consumption habits emerged in the early twentieth century with the industrialization of the food supply. New technologies such as canning, refrigerated rail cars, and pasteurization kept foods fresh for increasingly long periods of time; scientific knowledge about vitamins shifted attitudes toward diet and health; advertising enchanted the American consumer into new desires and invented needs. No longer beholden to regional and seasonal changes, people's food options exploded. Americans experienced a revolution in diet that—for the first time—was marketed, branded, and packaged for long shelf life. While food production increased and food costs declined, the ideological status of the United States as a land of agricultural plenty coalesced as citizens explored grocery aisles filled with the tastes of an everlasting summer.[2]

Between the 1880s and 1920s, Americans entered a new consumer age. Large food manufacturing corporations including Nabisco, Campbell's, the Kellogg Company, Pillsbury, and Heinz became household names as their products were mass-produced, branded, shipped, and advertised on a national scale. New packaging technologies, such as cardboard with waxed paper seals and tin cans, could be inexpensively machine-made in factories with branded labels. These companies were thus able to keep their factory-produced contents edible long enough to make it thousands of miles from the warehouse to the dinner table. Commercial canning and bottling, well established by the early 1920s and rationed during World War II, reached a "golden age" in the 1950s as new materials, new methods, and new products proliferated, and a larger percentage of household budgets went to processed foods. Consumers' use of canned foods continued to increase through the postwar era because of the convenience and stability of such products. In many rural areas still lacking refrigeration and electricity, they became integral to long-term food supply.

Between 1890 and 1950, grocery stores went from small corner shops to larger businesses often supplied by a central warehouse that offered branded food products to consumers. The cracker and pickle barrels that characterized American food shopping in turn-of-the-century general stores quickly gave way to markets stacked with individually packaged foods. Bulk purchasing in the 1800s meant that contamination and bacteria growth often compromised the quality and freshness of products, and seasonal availability controlled nonfixed prices.[3] The advent of the industrial food system gave consumers the promise of purity, consistency, and a low cost that they could rely on. For example, the National Biscuit Company (later known as Nabisco) developed "Iner-seal" packaging for its first product, Uneeda Biscuits, in order to ensure that the crackers did not go soggy or stale while waiting to be purchased. The airtight cardboard box lined in wax paper ensured that every customer received the same high-quality product at the same price, nationwide.

Changes within the domestic space were just as profound as they were in the market, particularly once freezing and refrigeration technology found its way into homes during the 1920s and 1930s. Frozen foods, especially those manufactured by Clarence Birdseye, kept highly perishable goods fresher for longer with moisture-proof packaging. Meats, vegetables, and fruits could be distributed across the country year-round in reliably steady supply. Initially hesitant consumers were persuaded with the help of advertising campaigns that promoted frozen foods' impressive new benefits.[4] The increased number of freezers in homes allowed people to buy large quantities of fresh produce to freeze for later consumption, or to store produce that they bought already frozen.

In a century of increasing international trade, where the import and export of food became a major industry, grocery store shelves put these political relationships on display. The twentieth century saw massive industrial change fueled by economic depression, two World Wars, and international aid policies that shaped American life through abundance and lack. By the advent of World War I, the eating habits of the American nation had become transformed into a modern industrial model. Dustbowls, breadlines, and Great Depression-era government legislation became major cultural touchstones for understanding this time of American hunger. As the United States forged and broke political bonds over the course of the twentieth-century, it allocated its resources towards war efforts, famine relief, and social services, thus affecting the purchasing power of its citizens.

MID-TWENTIETH CENTURY: FOOD PROCESSING'S GOLDEN AGE

The broad arc of the traditional American history narrative, grounded as it is in political history, frames our understanding of food as a vital natural, economic, and political resource. Food is central not only to domestic policy, but also to international relations. Nowhere is this more visible than throughout the Great Depression, the New Deal, and the food rationing of World War II. Following these moments of extreme oscillation between abundance and scarcity allows us to connect American history to global structures of economics and trade, national aggression, and domestic agricultural production and policy.

Much of the world's population experienced decades of economic uncertainty during this period. Countries emerged from the Great War battered and despondent, if not devastated by an unprecedented scale of death and destruction. During the worldwide depression of the 1930s, it was not clear that even the United States would survive the economic devastation of the decade. During this time the U.S. government bulldozed tons of edible grain and slaughtered thousands of pigs in an attempt to stabilize food prices, which declined dramatically in the 1930s and threatened to bring the food system to collapse. At the same time, one-third of the nation did not have adequate food. Yet even as the Depression reached its bleakest moments in the mid-1930s, the notion of the United States as a nation of agricultural plenty (or one that held the promise of agricultural plenty) remained.[5] New Deal legislation established programs, such as the Agricultural Adjustment Act (AAA), that helped stabilize prices and productions, and financed such monolithic development projects as the Tennessee Valley Authority and the Columbia Basin Irrigation Project—engineering feats that changed the nature of agriculture in these regions.

After the worldwide depression of the 1930s and faced with the devastation of World War II, the federal government in coordination with private enterprise had focused industrial and agricultural production toward a single purpose: to win this "total war." Enormous government expenditures stimulated economic production, which resulted in putting people back to work. The war accelerated and altered the production, manufacturing, and advertising of industrialized food, setting the stage for the remainder of the century. During the war, North American farmers produced food at record-breaking levels despite a smaller workforce, in part through liberal use of manufactured fertilizers and pesticides, including the new miracle insect-killer DDT. After the war, reliance on and increased use of such elements combined with increasingly sophisticated farm equipment and hybrid seeds led to even greater production (much of which was subsidized by long-held government parity agreements).[6]

U.S. farmers, agriculture scientists, and politicians turned their attention to providing adequate food for the postwar world through famine relief and crop production. The American government purchased and sent surplus food abroad to help alleviate and temper the global famine conditions wrought by drought and wartime destruction. U.S. aid under the auspices of the Marshall Plan gave billions of dollars to rebuild European and Asian economies and infrastructures. To help answer the demands of the rapidly growing global population, Rockefeller Foundation scientists engineered new seeds designed to produce significantly more grain in countries all over the world. Known as the Green Revolution, these developments seemed to work miracles by vastly increasing the amount of food available to developing countries. Yet they also put a severe strain on local economies and endangered subsistence farmers, the environment, and indigenous cultures. By the late-twentieth century large corporate farming became the norm in the United States and elsewhere.

As in farm production, World War II provided the catalyst for the postwar boom in food processing. Military quartermaster departments pounded, dried, stretched, and shrunk foods in every imaginable way in order to reduce their bulk and weight, in order to ship them overseas efficiently and in large quantities. Frozen orange juice, instant coffee and cocoa, cake mixes, "brown and serve" rolls, dehydrated soups, instant potatoes, powdered eggs and milk, ready-trimmed and packaged meats, and even the ubiquitous TV dinner all either got their start or were perfected with wartime research and technology. After the war, the food industry quickly adopted this knowledge and technology to produce food items for domestic consumers. Advertisers and enthusiastic journalists deemed the new preservation techniques "a modern miracle in the kitchen."[7] The technology permeated the global food supply so pervasively that eventually "high-quality food" became synonymous with long shelf life and low spoilage.

The advertising campaign "Kitchens of Tomorrow" promoted by large companies like General Motors and RCA/Whirlpool in 1940s and 50s played upon the efficiencies and convenience that these new food technologies promised.[8] The world watched in 1959 as American Vice President Richard Nixon and Soviet Premier Nikita Khrushchev enacted their "kitchen debate" at the American National Exhibition in Moscow, where a model kitchen and hired female actors exhibited microwave ovens as well as national ideals of freedom and modernity. Postwar housewives purchased and cooked these products—the instant mashed potatoes, the one-egg cake mixes—to feed their growing families, but with some ambivalence. Women embraced the new "package cuisine" as novel, labor-saving products that freed up a few minutes in their daily duties of feeding a family, but they also expressed a discontent over the implication of these products—and their attendant advertising—that women were somehow not up to the task of cooking from scratch.[9]

These historical arguments directly reflected the postwar political climate, where Americans defined themselves in comparative terms against their wartime allies and enemies. The United States quickly dismantled food rationing at war's end, largely at food manufacturers' insistence, while rationing continued in most European countries for several more years as nations rebuilt war-ravaged farms and transportation systems. In this postwar era the United States hoped to have it all: distribute aid to needy countries, keep farmers contented, and maintain political dominance, all the while attempting to keep Cold War politics out of domestic agriculture, processing, and consumption. Postwar American relief, whether through the auspices of the Marshall plan or through private organizations, had tremendous effect symbolically as well as materially, helping to transmit elements of American culture across the globe. Aid from CARE (Cooperative for American Remittances to Europe) became so prominent—the organization shipped thousands of food packages to war-torn Europe—that the phrase "CARE package" became a generic term.[10]

Supermarkets, hailed as the "shining food palaces of today," symbolized American political, economic, and cultural dominance in the Cold War era.[11] When foreign dignitaries, including the Queen of England and Soviet Premier Nikita Khrushchev, toured the United States, their itinerary invariably included a "typical" American supermarket.[12] The press dutifully reported the awestruck visitors' responses to the aisles and aisles of goods. "If Queen Elizabeth is a symbol of Britain," surmised one columnist, "the supermarket is a symbol of the United States."[13]

To keep up with the overwhelming number of new food products in the postwar era, grocery stores radically transformed. While larger, self-serve supermarkets existed before the war, grocery chains became a permanent fixture in the postwar landscape, eventually swallowing the older-style grocery as well as contributing to the decline of specialty stores such as butchers, fresh fruit markets, and bakeries. Supermarkets, which housed all these under one roof, offered convenience and provided a larger selection of products. Their economies of scale produced the possibility of lower prices compared with the mom-and-pop stores, but there were trade-offs, too, most notably the loss of personal service and, arguably, of quality. Supermarkets expanded in size and number to accommodate the plethora of products brought to market with regularity. Specialized supermarket departments developed to include areas for baby food, gourmet items, meat (no longer cut to order by a butcher, but prewrapped), baked goods, produce, and dairy. Because such stores allowed customers more freedom to pick up and inspect items, brand names, eye-catching labels, and advertising became prominent strategies for attracting customers.

Cold War politics that pitted capitalism against communism made the overflowing abundance of American supermarkets difficult to ignore. Processed foods exhibited on grocery store shelves became a metaphor for the political, economic, and cultural supremacy of the United States. The U.S. Department of Commerce helped American manufacturers take their wares abroad to world expositions. The "Supermarket USA" display at the 1957 International Trade Fair in Communist Zagreb, Yugoslavia stirred international interest and criticism. Over six hundred American manufacturers supplied more than two hundred thousand dollars (1.7 million in 2014 dollars) of equipment and merchandise to create a ten thousand square foot modern supermarket stocked to the gills with products. They designed the shelves, laden with all kinds of the latest products, to be a "dramatic and practical vehicle to demonstrate the America standard of living under 'people's capitalism.'"[14] While "Supermarket USA" displayed some fresh produce and dairy products, highly processed and packaged items captured the spotlight: prepared baby foods, soup mixes, canned soups, cake mixes, instant coffee and tea, juice concentrates, prepared meat loaves, cut-up chickens, and a wide range of frozen food. Highly processed food and the individual choice afforded by self-service shopping, intentionally correlated "Americanness" with large quantities of food, a symbol of personal affluence as well as of an effective industrial supply model.

In addition to supermarkets, industrially produced "fast food" became another major export of American culture; fast food chain restaurants could accomplish what locally and individually owned operations had difficulty doing: providing food that is fast, cheap, and predictable. These restaurants, run according to formulas, benefited from economies of scale by purchasing large quantities of supplies and preparing the food in a centralized kitchen to be warmed and assembled at the chain. These cost-saving techniques also meant declining food quality. Nevertheless, the "fast food taste" appealed to most customers: soft white buns, flat hamburger patties, milkshakes made with increasingly less milk and more added preservatives and flavors, all resulted in a uniformity of taste. Restaurants like McDonald's gained enormous followings and became beloved and permanent fixtures in mainstream culture. Concepts of convenience and speed became central tenets of the American diet. Although some countries, especially in Europe, protested these restaurants as an intrusion on national culture and cuisine, others, particularly in Asia, adopted and absorbed the basic concept and menu onto their gustatory landscape.[15]

HISTORIOGRAPHY OF FOOD IN THE TWENTIETH-CENTURY UNITED STATES

Few histories of food dot the historiographical landscape in the first half of the twentieth century. The most prominent example is Richard O. Cummings's *The American and His Food: A History of Food Habits in the United States*, which appeared in 1941, at a time when America was still struggling to recover from the worldwide depression of the 1930s. Growing out of the author's training in the history of science and technology, this history of food and nutrition in the United States up to 1940 tells a sweeping tale of colonial and early republic changes in the food supply as a result of scientific and technological developments and their subsequent effects on Americans' nutrition. *The American and His Food* remained perhaps the primary academic history of food in the United States for several decades and served as a model for later books covering the same terrain.

In the mid-twentieth century historians began to take greater notice of the role of food in American historical scholarship. "Consensus history," the dominant zeitgeist of the period, tended to focus on Americans' common attributes and experiences.[16] While progressive historians of an earlier generation had focused on class and cultural differences between citizens, consensus historians analyzed instead what Americans had in common. Though food is not a central component of consensus history, two prominent historians, Daniel Boorstin and David Potter, featured food in their historical analyses. Boorstin's three-volume series, *The Americans* (1958, 1965, 1973), highlighted the importance of food as a fairly significant component of U.S. growth and development. Boorstin argued that the American landscape and American citizens' material conditions of life helped produce their characteristic pragmatism, one not necessarily reproducible in other countries. David Potter's 1954 study, *People of Plenty: Economic Abundance and the American Character,* echoed this material analysis of what used to be unself-consciously called the "American character," by arguing that the United States and its citizens had been shaped, blessed, and at times intellectually and socially hindered by inhabiting one of the most resource-rich and economically successful countries in the world. *People of Plenty* was also one of the first studies to connect American abundance to increased mobility, decreased emphasis on community in favor of individualism, the rise of advertising, and the distinct nature of American democracy, including the illusion of classlessness.

Influenced by Cold War anxieties, consensus historians found a natural contrast between U.S. politics and culture and those of its rival the Soviet Union, and encouraged Americans to view themselves in terms of abundance and plenty. The "melting pot" metaphor, popular in the early twentieth century, found renewed strength when combined with an emboldened postwar notion of American exceptionalism. At the same time, advances in transportation and communications resulted in scholarship of this period frequently exhibiting elements of cosmopolitanism and an awareness of the place of the United States within a larger world.

In contrast to the consensus history of the postwar 1950s, the 1960s set in motion a period of great intellectual, social, and cultural upheaval. Spurred on by the successes of the African American civil rights movement, other marginalized groups asserted their rights to opportunity, equality under the law, and social acceptance in society. Further, in the 1970s many assumed a post-Vietnam, post-Watergate distrust of government and of institutions in general. Baby boomers, now college-aged, experimented with creative alternatives to the societal status quo, and the United States witnessed dramatic changes with regard to sexual mores, music, fashion, cultural expression, and ideology. Women and minorities asserted their right to access what had previously been the purview of mainly white middle- and upper-class males, including employment opportunities, higher education, and political office. The personal had become the political, and these social movements helped foster a new paradigm for historical scholarship, a transformation of the notion of who and what, for example, was an acceptable topic for academic study. Whereas in earlier generations "history" meant the stories of powerful men and powerful institutions, the New Social History of the 1960s and 1970s shifted the focus of the discipline to the lives of ordinary people.

The 1970s also witnessed a growing environmental movement, which fostered food history via the emerging topic of environmental history. World historian Alfred Crosby's 1972 book *The Columbian Exchange: Biological and Cultural Consequences of 1492*, focused on the environmental effects of sustained exchange between Eurasia and Africa (the "Old World") and the Americas (the "New World"). Two central chapters in particular focus on the plants and animals that made their way across the Atlantic Ocean from one continent to the other, leading to dramatic changes in nutrition, culture, and cuisine. Crosby's *The Columbian Exchange* set a new standard of method and argument that American food history writing has continued to emulate, refine, and develop.

In addition to giving increased attention to the environment, Americans during this period assumed cosmopolitan attitudes and aesthetics that left an indelible mark on the field of food studies. Inspired in part by Jackie Kennedy's attention to French haute cuisine, educated housewives bought Julia Child's *Mastering the Art of French Cooking* (1961), and engaged in what food writer and historian Betty Fussell describes as "competitive home cooking."[17] Pride in domestic kitchen work flourished, and the boom in appreciation for and experimentation with

French cuisine extended to cuisines of other countries. In the 1970s, Time-Life publishers launched a series of cookbooks, *Foods of the World,* that became immensely popular among a growing affluent, worldly, and educated middle class.[18] Several volumes in the series also covered American regional foodways, which helped Americans gain an appreciation for the importance and value of the indigenous foods and cultures of their own country.

Culinary historians during this period began to cast a critical eye at the increasingly industrialized food of the United States, scrutinizing even what passed for "gourmet" cuisine. Books like *The Taste of America* (1977) celebrated the "real" regional cuisines and dishes of the country as a critique of "fancy" food.[19] The hybrid genre of the historical cookbook also gained momentum as a category that appealed to a public interested in food and dining. Folklorists and the perspectives they brought with them also contributed significant work to the field. For example, Betty Fussell's *I Hear America Cooking: The Cooks, Regions, and Recipes of American Regional Cuisine* (1986) explored American regional cuisine through interviews and cookbooks from distinct areas of the country.[20] These books ultimately showed that an eager popular audience desired accessible, creative histories of food.

Against a backdrop of growing culinary interest, the mid- to late-1980s might be thought of as the first wave of substantial U.S. food history written by trained historians and social scientists. Food emerged as a focus of serious attention. This was the result of multiple factors: a maturing social history movement, an expansion in the breadth and depth of women's history and feminist scholarship, and the so-called cultural turn in history, which employed linguistic theory to explore the importance of beliefs and assumptions and their causal role in group behavior. The intellectual and social milieu of the mid- to late-1980s produced several strong food-focused histories in which authors creatively employed methodologies from various disciplines to craft rich cultural and social histories of food.

As a response to what many saw as the worst effects of the industrialization and globalization of the food supply, small but stubborn efforts to stem the tide emerged in the late twentieth century. Janet Poppendieck's *Breadlines Knee-Deep in Wheat* (1986) and Warren James Belasco's *Appetite for Change: How the Counterculture took on the Food Industry* (1989) both criticized the consensus narratives of abundance that had dominated mid-century scholarship. Belasco, an American studies scholar and an active participant in the counterculture about which he wrote, examined how food was central to the countercultural movement through the rise of communes, food co-ops, vegetarian restaurants, and cookbooks. Belasco is pessimistic in recounting how a corporate culture ultimately co-opted the new tastes, flavors, and dishes of the counterculture, including "ethnic" food, vegetarian items, yogurt, and herbal tea, in order to make a profit. Poppendieck similarly pushes back against previous popular understandings of American food history, chronicling the efforts of government assistance programs to restore America's economic footing, with a particular focus on farm programs such as the Agricultural Adjustment Act (AAA), which attempted to rescue a failing agricultural system that, paradoxically, produced too much food.

The strong influence of the women's movement on academic scholarship contributed greatly to the rise and development of food history in the 1980s and 1990s. The first wave of women's history in the 1970s and 1980s mainly worked to write women back into history by telling the previously ignored or underappreciated stories of women in prominent positions—a sort of "great women in history" response to traditional history. Early feminist historians generally avoided domestic subjects like food and the kitchen, which many felt had previously limited women's talents and opportunities. Yet, female daily involvement with food had remained central to women's experience for so long that feminist scholars ultimately and eventually dug into its fertile ground. Notable works from this period include Laura Shapiro's book *Perfection Salad* (1986), Joan Jacobs Brumberg's *Fasting Girls: The Emergence of Anorexia Nervosa* (1988), and Rima Apple's *Mothers and Medicine: A Social History of Infant Feeding, 1890–1950* (1987). *Mothers and Medicine* in particular employed food, in this case artificial infant formulas and infant feeding, to understand more about women's lives and the role of technology, advertising, and the medical profession on infant feeding.

Finally, in addition to social movements and the new social history, the development of cultural studies encouraged the application of linguistic and literary theory to both historical and contemporary studies and became important to 1980s food scholarship. The idea of recipes as cultural texts gained particular legitimacy in this first wave of food history. Postmodernist theory allowed scholars to "read" any number of objects and artifacts as texts: chairs, musical instruments, buildings, as well as food and recipes. Attitudes about the historical value of cookbooks gradually began to change, in part aided by literary scholar Susan

Leonardi's 1989 article "Recipes for Reading: Summer Pasta, Lobster à la Riseholme, and Key Lime Pie." Exploring the changing texts and contexts of subsequent editions of the *Joy of Cooking*, Leonardi demonstrated that recipes are a highly embedded discourse within substantial social context. This piece had a galvanizing effect on food studies scholarship by providing solid justification, as well as a template, for using recipes as texts.[21] Although other articles employing recipes and cookbooks in this way had been previously published, Leonardi's article was the first to garner enthusiastic and sustained reception.[22]

The dynamically changing historiography of food scholarship throughout the twentieth century—from ideologies of abundance, to countercultural movements, to second wave feminism—shows not only how food systems have changed over the last hundred years, but also how our understanding of them has transformed just as dramatically. Thus, the ways in which food is produced, processed, distributed, controlled, consumed, and portrayed reveal not only hierarchies of power, but also the subtle, multileveled challenges to that power by groups and individuals in society. Food can be examined both at the individual level as well as the community, national, and international levels. Since food is power, the availability of food in the twentieth and twenty-first centuries has directly influenced many nations' power and place in the world. The salience of recent debates concerning food safety, global environmentalism, the effect of food production on indigenous peoples and cultures worldwide, as well as the renewed interest in high-quality, minimally processed food, culinary tourism, and fine dining, combined with ever-rising rates of obesity and its adverse consequences, gives this history of food in the modern era rich potential.

TEACHING AND RESEARCH

Debates and divides exist among academic historians themselves over standards of evidence, thoroughness of research, historical claims, and uses of theory to inform empirical data. Historians have received cultural history and the study of popular culture, for example, with varying degrees of enthusiasm. The history profession was thrown into something of a crisis as postmodernism challenged positivism and empirical methods. Historians have gradually become more comfortable experimenting with new methods and theories and have also begun to accept as legitimate topics previously considered too mundane, such as food (though to some the subject still smacks of amateurism).

However, for historians of food, texts are only one part of a larger cadre of information that can be used to understand histories such as those discussed above. Late twentieth-century scholarship has shown us how cookbooks are valuable resources for understanding historical recipes and preparation methods. However, "reading" cookbooks can be far richer. For example, the pages of a cookbook used in the kitchen will often have splatters and food stains on heavily used sections. Some cookbooks are pocket-sized, indicating that publishers intend them to be carried in an apron for easy access. Others with glossy illustrations are printed instead as objects for admiration and fantasy, containing recipes far too challenging to be accomplished in a domestic kitchen. Menus offer another excellent example of materially important documents. Though they feature minimal text, menus reflect dining experiences through the weight of their paper, typeface, and length. Such elements reflect the history of lived experience, and how readers engage with these texts both intellectually and socially; the difference between reading a menu on a board and on a small piece of paper can be significant.

The blurry line between "thing" and "text" has been, in the past, an uncomfortable acknowledgement for traditional historians, who worried that analyzing documents through physical knowledge might compromise the scholarly value of their work. It is important to read documents contextually, not just for their words, but also in order to study what might be considered quotidian. The domestic work of twentieth-century housewives rarely came with elaborate manuals. American women did, however, read widely distributed national magazines filled with illustrated advertisements that instructed on (supposedly) ideal femininity, morality, and national identity. The image of a nuclear family sitting around the dining table expresses, on the one hand, an advertiser's method of selling consumers a product. It also suggests that consumers themselves responded to American ideals as they were portrayed in mass media. While these images may not illustrate modern realities, they show how those ideals were constructed and perpetuated through images and print media.

As food studies becomes an increasingly popular new discipline, libraries have responded by publicizing and increasing their collections of food-related materials. The substantial menu and culinary collection of the New York Public Library (NYPL) offers a web-searchable database; the Fales Library at New York University is rapidly expanding; and organizations such as the Southern Food and Beverage Museum in New Orleans have focused on establishing and enlarging a culinary library for researchers. Research collections that cater specifically to food studies scholars are now being seen as a new and exciting area of focus for special collections librarians and archivists. For example, the "What's on the Menu?" project at NYPL, launched in 2011, enlists the help of online volunteers to transcribe each digitized menu in its entirety. Of the research possibilities that this project offers to scholars, perhaps the most important is the ability to search for and aggregate information on specific dishes, ingredients, and preparation methods. While metadata for the menus has been available to researchers since the collection's beginnings, this will be the first time that the contents of the documents are searchable, allowing unprecedented electronic access.

STATE OF THE FIELD AND IDEAS FOR FUTURE RESEARCH

Few would argue with the premise that food has taken on new importance in recent decades, in large part as a reaction to the industrialization of the food supply. In many areas of the world, the last few decades have witnessed an emerging food "revolution" that has attempted to counter (or at least circumvent) the worst aspects of the industrialization of food. Yet this recent interest in food has historical roots that reach back centuries. In his 2006 book *Meals to Come*, Warren Belasco provides an intellectual history of world hunger and of the debate over providing sufficient food for all. Belasco examines in nuanced detail how each generation of Western philosophers, economists, politicians, and fiction writers has framed and evaluated that dilemma. In one camp are the pessimists, who argue that there will never be enough food to feed us all. Another group are the optimists—Belasco terms them the "cornucopians"—who see science and human ingenuity as sufficient to meet each generation's challenges and shortcomings. Finally, the "egalitarians" (William Godwin, Frances Moore Lappé) are those who see the problem as less about quantity than about equal distribution between the haves and have-nots. These basic theoretical positions have persisted across centuries. At the same time, it is important to note the culturally bound nature of these debates, especially writers' definitions of "enough food." Invariably these discussions turn to meat, and it is startling to see successive generations of European and American thinkers worrying about having enough meat, many fretting that the West will be reduced to "coolie" (grain-based) diets.[23]

Those involved in the recent food movement have worked to demonstrate the connection between good food and sustainable agricultural practices and to create better-tasting, higher-quality food. Since the late 1990s, scholarly and political attention to food matters has deepened as the academic field of food studies has emerged, and as popular books by Eric Schlosser (*Fast Food Nation*), Marion Nestle (*Food Politics* and *Safe Food*), and Michael Pollan (*The Omnivore's Dilemma*), as well as films such as *Supersize Me, King Corn,* and *Food, Inc.*, exposed to an interested public the questionable practices of the food industry and the government's willingness to accommodate food-industry demands. The list of such books is long, and the titles themselves revealing: *Stuffed and Starved: The Hidden Battle for the Food System* (Raj Patel); *Food, Inc.: Mendel to Monsanto: The Promises and Perils of the Biotech Harvest* (Peter Pringle); *The End of Food* (Paul Roberts); *Manger: Français, européens et américains face à l'alimentation* (Claude Fischler with Estelle Masson); *Slow Money: Investing as if Food, Farms, and Fertility Mattered* (Woody Tasch); *The End of Overeating: Taking Control of the Insatiable American Appetite* (David Kessler); *Food Matters: A Guide to Conscious Eating* (Mark Bittman); and *In Defense of Food: An Eater's Manifesto* and *Food Rules: An Eater's Manual* (Michael Pollan). Taken together they manifest an awareness of deep problems in the global food supply, ranging from health and nutrition, to economics and environment, to corporate control of food production, advertising, and consumption, to the peril of people and the planet. What emerges is the realization that seemingly disparate and unrelated topics (obesity, environment, flavor, family meals, hunger) are indeed interconnected. Taken together, a cluster of themes emerges. With various emphases, all address ethical, health, environmental, and aesthetic issues as well as anxieties about cultural and social reproduction that have been central to discussions about food production and consumption in the last decade.

What cultural and material currents underlie this interest in and anxiety about food? First among them is the sheer amount of food that is available, at least in the global North, with all its ramifications, positive and negative. The United States as well as other nations has become particularly adept at producing huge amounts of food, and we eat a lot more of it than we used to. The industrialization of agriculture, combined with government policies and politics encouraging the mass production of food, is a double-edged sword. While it has facilitated better overall nutrition and health, it has also allowed excess and, ironically, poor health. While some critics wonder whether the uproar over rising rates of obesity is fueled less by health concerns and more by superficial cosmetic responses and a diet and food industry that benefits from the current landscape of food consumption, there are important health concerns that cannot be dismissed, such as the startling rise in diabetes, especially among children. Combine this sheer abundance with the "omnivore's dilemma"—the anxiety created by the multitude of food options—and it is easy to understand the well-fed person's predicament in the twenty-first century.

There are also fears that industrial food culture has damaged our social fabric as well as the environment. The rise of fast food together with other social and cultural phenomena (more single-parent and two-income families, cars built with cup holders and food trays) have led to changes in domestic food practices, which have in turn been viewed as affecting family life and even civil society. While it is possible to have a meaningful meal prepared from a microwave or around a table of fast food, it is true that by its nature quickly produced and quickly eaten food changes the qualitative experience of a meal. It makes sense then that food issues are a prominent part of the public discourse in the twenty-first century. For many, careful consideration of the food one eats and serves one's family and friends helps fill a spiritual void. Only a return to more humane, more harmonious methods of growing, cooking, and eating, the thinking goes, will help restore a spiritual connection with the land, with our food, and with each other.

This is not a new idea, of course. Thinkers from Thomas Jefferson to Wendell Berry have been preaching these notions for centuries, but as we have entered the twenty-first century, they have taken a qualitatively different turn. As Jackson Lears has demonstrated about mass production in general, in the nineteenth century many people felt alienated by modernism and an industrialization that severed the connection between producer and consumer; that alienation is still palpable in our relationship to mass-produced, industrial food.[24] Seeking local, seasonal food today can be viewed as a version of the early twentieth-century critique of mass society, in which a return to artisanal food functions as a bulwark against the ease and reproducibility of mass-produced, industrial goods. For many people preparing meals from scratch for one's family using ingredients bought at a local farmer's market signifies self-reliance, a sense of simplicity, and a voluntary disconnect from the fast pace of our postindustrial, digital era. It can also result in less wastefulness. Many producers and sellers of this alternative vision of food capitalize on and cater to these kinds of desires. Indeed, marketers have learned that while the new food culture may not appeal to all (in fact, it may not appeal to the majority), it does appeal to a sizable, influential minority.

Supermarkets have become willing to stock their produce sections with organic fruits and vegetables, which, even if they do not sell readily, are attractive, powerful "loss leaders" that may draw customers into stores and bring them back again. Nonindustrial food (and industrial organic food, as Michael Pollan terms it) is simply more accessible in most parts of the industrialized world, and that availability is shaping consumption and food habits, at least in certain parts of the globe.[25]

Thus, recent discourse about food represents a genuine attempt to integrate complex issues linking aesthetics and ethics with health, the environment, family life, social issues, and notions of taste—issues the twentieth-century public might not have recognized as having much in common. Further, many today are more cognizant of the origins of their food. For most of the twentieth century, as the connections weakened between producer and consumer, many had little reason to think about and understand the origins of their food: how it was grown or raised, how it was processed, and how it reached the market or the restaurant.

If the contemporary conversation about food falls short in any area, it is in addressing the difficult but crucial issue of getting all this healthy, sustainable (more expensive, less widely distributed) food to people of little means. While many applaud the agenda of Slow Food, the work of Alice Waters, or the writings of Carlo Petrini and Michael Pollan, detractors on both the left and the right criticize this movement as elitist and unrealistic. Of course, many of the writers and activists envisioning this "grand theory of food" see little difference between science and poetry, between applying rational thought or romantic sentiment to food problems and issues. For them, all knowledge, all emotion leads to the same point: a refashioned food system incorporating sustainable practices, cultural sensitivity, good nutrition, and taste. Such a system, according to this view, is in the long run the most practical and economically viable.

These debates have produced considerable interest in food studies as an academic field. Recent work on U.S. history, like recent work on non-Western countries and populations, has focused on social and cultural history, and the histories of material culture, popular culture, ethnicity, and race. A long and varied list of food histories emanated from all of these subfields and more: social/labor history, science and technology, agricultural history, women's/gender history, race and ethnicity, and cultural history and history of consumption in its broadest sense.[26] Several university presses, including Illinois, California, and Columbia, began their own food series. In addition to the publication of several food encyclopedias and multivolume food histories numerous food histories were written with a general audience in mind, a further indication that food scholarship is entering the realm of mainstream history, both popular and scholarly.[27]

The constant popularity of food history for the general reader, and the proliferation of amateur historians writing and publishing food histories, makes for a rich and interesting mix, though one that is not without some tension. Over the decades, culinary historians (largely nonacademic) have produced a fair amount of culinary history that has mainly gone unnoticed (or ignored) by professional historians, in part because of the seemingly irrelevant nature of the topic, but also in some part because of the (perceived or real) amateurish quality of the work. This potential tension between amateur and professional standards and conventions of historical scholarship is not new, nor is it uncommon in the broader landscape of historical scholarship. For these very reasons it remains to be seen whether traditional history departments in the United States will ultimately embrace food history. In any case, given current debates concerning food safety, obesity and its health consequences, global environmentalism, the effect of food production on indigenous peoples and cultures worldwide, and with Americans' renewed interest in high-quality, minimally processed food, it is clear that food history as a focus of both scholarly and popular inquiry is a topic here to stay.

NOTES

1. Claude Levi-Strauss, "The Culinary Triangle," *The Partisan Review* 33 (1966): 586–96.

2. Susan Freidberg, *Fresh: A Perishable History* (Cambridge: Belknap Press, 2009).

3. Gabriella Petrick, "Feeding the Masses: H. J. Heinz and the Creation of Industrial Food," *Endeavour* 33, no. 1 (2009): 29–34.

4. Daniel Delis Hill, *Advertising to the American Woman, 1900–1999* (Columbus: Ohio State University, 2002).

5. Janet Poppendieck, *Breadlines Knee-Deep in Wheat: Food Assistance in the Great Depression* (New Brunswick: Rutgers University Press, 1986).

6. Amy Bentley, *Eating For Victory: Food Rationing and the Politics of Domesticity* (Urbana: University of Illinois Press, 1998).

7. Olga Curtis, "Time-Saving Modern Kitchen Miracles," *The Washington Post and Times Herald*, April 22, 1957, C2.

8. Laura Scott Holliday, "Kitchen Technologies: Promises and Alibis, 1944–1966," *Camera Obscura* 47, vol. 16, no. 2 (2001): 78–131.

9. Laura Shapiro, *Something from the Oven: Reinventing Dinner in 1950s America* (New York: Viking, 2004).

10. Bentley, *Eating For Victory*.

11. Gertrude P. Lancaster, "Emphasis on Food Quality: New Products Savor Old Standards," *Christian Science Monitor,* October 26, 1956, 10.

12. Austin C. Wehrwein, "Premier to Find Iowa Doors Open: Hosts Hope to Show Russian Cross-section View of Life Under U.S. Capitalism," *New York Times,* September 11, 1959, 12.

13. Bill Gold, "The District Line: The Queen Saw More Than Just a Store," *Washington Post and Times Herald,* October 22, 1957, B20.

14. Everett M. Smith, "Yugoslavs to See U.S. Supermarket," *Christian Science Monitor,* July 2, 1957, 14.

15. James Watson, ed., *Golden Arches East: McDonald's in East Asia* (Stanford: Stanford University Press, 2006).

16. Paul S. Boyer, *The Oxford Companion to United States History* (Oxford: Oxford University Press, 2001).

17. Betty Fussell, *My Kitchen Wars* (New York: North Point Press, 1999).

18. Craig Claiborne, "Debut for a Series of International Cookbooks," *New York Times,* February 19, 1968, 46.

19. John L. Hess and Karen Hess, *The Taste of America* (Urbana: University of Illinois Press, 2000).

20. For an important folklore perspective see Charles C. Camp, *American Foodways: What, When, Why, and How We Eat in America* (Little Rock: August House, 1989).

21. Susan Leonardi, "Recipes for Reading: Summer Pasta, Lobster à la Riseholme, and Key Lime Pie," *PMLA* 104, no. 3 (May 1989): 340–47.

22. See for example, Barbara Kirshenblatt-Gimblett, "The Kosher Gourmet in the Nineteenth-Century Kitchen," *Journal of Gastronomy* 2, no. 4 (Winter 1986): 51–89.

23. Warren J. Belasco, *Meals to Come: A History of the Future of Food* (Berkeley: University of California Press, 2006).

24. Jackson Lears, *No Place of Grace: Antimodernism and the Transformation of American Culture* (New York: Pantheon Books, 1981).

25. Michael Pollan, *The Omnivore's Dilemma: A Natural History of Four Meals* (New York: Penguin Press, 2006).

26. For social and labor history, see Daniel Rothenberg, *With These Hands: The Hidden World of Migrant Farmworkers Today* (Berkeley: University of California Press, 2000). For science and technology, see William Cronon, *Nature's Metropolis: Chicago and the Great West* (New York: Norton, 1991); and Warren Belasco and Philip Scranton, eds., *Food Nations: Selling Taste in Consumer Societies* (New York: Routledge, 2002). For agricultural history, see Julie Guthman, *Agrarian Dreams: The Paradox of Organic Farming in California* (Berkeley: University of California Press, 2004); Steven Stoll, *Larding the Lean Earth: Soil and Society in Nineteenth-Century America* (New York: Hill and Wang, 2002); and Deborah Kay Fitzgerald, *Every Farm a Factory: The Industrial Ideal in American Agriculture* (New Haven: Yale University Press, 2003). For women's history, see Amy Bentley, *Eating for Victory: Food Rationing and the Politics of Domesticity* (Urbana: University of Illinois Press, 1998); Janet Theophano, *Eat My Words: Reading Women's Lives through the Cook-*

books They Wrote (New York: Palgrave Macmillan, 2003); and Katherine J. Parkin, *Food Is Love: Food Advertising and Gender Roles in Modern America* (Philadelphia: University of Pennsylvania Press, 2006). For histories of race and ethnicity, see Hasia Diner, *Hungering for America: Italian, Irish, and Jewish Foodways in the Age of Migration* (Cambridge: Harvard University Press, 2002); and Donna R. Gabaccia, *We Are What We Eat: Ethnic Food and the Making of Americans* (Cambridge: Harvard University Press, 2000). For cultural history, see Amy Trubek, *The Taste of Place: A Cultural Journey into Terroir* (Berkeley: University of California Press, 2009); and Kathy Neustadt, *Clambake: A History and Celebration of an American Tradition* (Amherst: University of Massachusetts Press, 1992).

27. For encyclopedias, see Andrew F. Smith, ed., *The Oxford Encyclopedia of Food and Drink in America* (New York: Oxford University Press, 2004); Solomon H. Katz, ed., *Encyclopedia of Food and Culture* (New York: Scribner, 2002); and Fabio Parasecoli and Peter Scholliers, eds., *A Cultural History of Food* (New York: Berg, 2011). For popular histories, see Patric Kuh, *The Last Days of Haute Cuisine* (New York: Viking, 2001); and David Kamp, *The United States of Arugula: How We Became a Gourmet Nation* (New York: Broadway Books, 2006).

BIBLIOGRAPHY

Apple, Rima D. *Mothers and Medicine: A Social History of Infant Feeding, 1890–1950*. Madison: University of Wisconsin Press, 1987.

Beck, Simone, Louisette Bertholle, and Julia Child. *Mastering the Art of French Cooking*. New York: Knopf, 1961.

Belasco, Warren. *Appetite for Change: How the Counterculture Took on the Food Industry*. New York: Knopf, 2001. First published 1989 by Pantheon Books.

———. *Meals to Come: A History of the Future of Food*. Berkeley: University of California Press, 2006.

Belasco, Warren, and Philip Scranton, eds. *Food Nations: Selling Taste in Consumer Societies*. New York: Routledge, 2002.

Bentley, Amy. *Eating for Victory: Food Rationing and the Politics of Domesticity*. Urbana: University of Illinois Press, 1998.

Boorstin, Daniel J. *The Americans: The Colonial Experience*. New York: Random House, 1958.

———. *The Americans: The National Experience*. New York: Random House, 1965.

———. *The Americans: The Democratic Experience*. New York: Random House, 1973.

Boyer, Paul S. *The Oxford Companion to United States History*. Oxford: Oxford University Press, 2001.

Brumberg, Joan Jacobs. *Fasting Girls: The Emergence of Anorexia*. New York: Vintage Books, 2000. First published in 1988 by Harvard University Press as *Fasting Girls: The Emergence of Anorexia Nervosa as a Modern Disease*.

Camp, Charles C. *American Foodways: What, When, Why, and How We Eat in America*. Little Rock: August House, 1989.

Claiborne, Craig. "Debut for a Series of International Cookbooks." *New York Times*, February 19, 1968.

Cronon, William. *Nature's Metropolis: Chicago and the Great West*. New York: Norton, 1991.

Crosby, Alfred W. *The Columbian Exchange: Biological and Cultural Consequences of 1492*. Westport: Praeger, 2003. First published by Greenwood Press in 1972.

Cummings, Richard Osborn. *The American and His Food: A History of Food Habits in the United States*. Chicago: University of Chicago Press, 1941.

Curtis, Olga. "Time-Saving Modern Kitchen Miracles." *The Washington Post and Times Herald*, April 22, 1957.

Diner, Hasia. *Hungering for America: Italian, Irish, and Jewish Foodways in the Age of Migration*. Cambridge: Harvard University Press, 2001.

Fitzgerald, Deborah Kay. *Every Farm a Factory: The Industrial Ideal in American Agriculture*. New Haven: Yale University Press, 2003.

Freidberg, Susan. *Fresh: A Perishable History*. Cambridge: Belknap Press, 2009.

Fussell, Betty. *I Hear America Cooking: The Cooks and Recipes of American Regional Cuisine*. New York: Penguin, 1997. First published in 1986 by Viking.

———. *My Kitchen Wars*. New York: North Point Press, 1999.

Gabaccia, Donna R. *We Are What We Eat: Ethnic Food and the Making of Americans*. Cambridge: Harvard University Press, 2000.

Gold, Bill. "The District Line: The Queen Saw More Than Just a Store." *The Washington Post and Times Herald*, October 22, 1957.

Guthman, Julie. *Agrarian Dreams: The Paradox of Organic Farming in California*. Berkeley: University of California Press, 2004.

Hess, John L., and Karen Hess. *The Taste of America*. Urbana: University of Illinois Press, 2000.

Hill, Daniel Delis. *Advertising to the American Woman, 1900–1999*. Columbus: Ohio State University Press, 2002.

Holliday, Laura Scott. "Kitchen Technologies: Promises and Alibis, 1944–1966." *Camera Obscura* 47, vol. 16, no. 2 (2001): 78–131.

Kamp, David. *The United States of Arugula: How We Became a Gourmet Nation*. New York: Broadway Books, 2006.

Katz, Solomon H., ed. *Encyclopedia of Food and Culture*. New York: Scribner, 2003.

Kirshenblatt-Gimblett, Barbara. "The Kosher Gourmet in the Nineteenth-Century Kitchen." *Journal of Gastronomy* 2, no. 4 (Winter 1986): 51–89.

Kuh, Patric. *The Last Days of Haute Cuisine*. New York: Viking, 2001.

Lancaster, Gertrude P. "Emphasis on Food Quality: New Products Savor Old Standards." *Christian Science Monitor*, October 26, 1956.

Lears, Jackson. *No Place of Grace: Antimodernism and the Transformation of American Culture, 1880–1920*. New York: Pantheon Books, 1981.

Leonardi, Susan. "Recipes for Reading: Summer Pasta, Lobster à la Riseholme, and Key Lime Pie." *PMLA* 104, no. 3 (May 1989): 340–47.

Levi-Strauss, Claude. "The Culinary Triangle." *The Partisan Review* 33 (1966): 586–96.

Neustadt, Kathy. *Clambake: A History and Celebration of an American Tradition.* Amherst: University of Massachusetts Press, 1992.

Parasecoli, Fabio, and Peter Scholliers, eds. *A Cultural History of Food.* New York: Berg, 2011.

Parkin, Katherine J. *Food Is Love: Food Advertising and Gender Roles in Modern America.* Philadelphia: University of Pennsylvania Press, 2006.

Petrick, Gabriella M. "Feeding the Masses: H. J. Heinz and the Creation of Industrial Food." *Endeavour* 33, no. 1 (2009): 29–34.

Pollan, Michael. *The Omnivore's Dilemma: A Natural History of Four Meals.* New York: Penguin Press, 2006.

Poppendieck, Janet. *Breadlines Knee-Deep in Wheat: Food Assistance in the Great Depression.* New Brunswick: Rutgers University Press, 1986.

Potter, David Morris. *People of Plenty: Economic Abundance and the American Character.* Chicago: University of Chicago Press, 1954.

Rothenberg, Daniel. *With These Hands: The Hidden World of Migrant Farmworkers Today.* Berkeley: University of California Press, 2000.

Shapiro, Laura. *Perfection Salad: Women and Cooking at the Turn of the Century.* New York: Modern Library, 2001.

———. *Something from the Oven: Reinventing Dinner in 1950s America.* New York: Viking, 2004.

Smith, Andrew F., ed. *The Oxford Encyclopedia of Food and Drink in America.* New York: Oxford University Press, 2013.

Smith, Everett M. "Yugoslavs to See U.S. Supermarket." *Christian Science Monitor,* July 2, 1957.

Stoll, Steven. *Larding the Lean Earth: Soil and Society in Nineteenth-Century America.* New York: Hill and Wang, 2002.

Theophano, Janet. *Eat My Words: Reading Women's Lives through the Cookbooks They Wrote.* New York: Palgrave Macmillan, 2003.

Trubek, Amy. *The Taste of Place: A Cultural Journey into Terroir.* Berkeley: University of California Press, 2009.

Watson, James, ed. *Golden Arches East: McDonald's in East Asia.* Stanford: Stanford University Press, 2006.

Wehrwein, Austin C. "Premier to Find Iowa Doors Open: Hosts Hope to Show Russian Cross-Section View of Life Under U.S. Capitalism." *New York Times,* September 11, 1959, 12.

CHAPTER 9

Influence, Sources, and African Diaspora Foodways

FREDERICK DOUGLASS OPIE

I define foodways as the study of how recipes, cooking and eating methods, and traditions develop over time. By the 1700s, shortly after the start of colonization in the Caribbean, European planters became the minority to African slaves. In Jamaica, planters supplied slaves with weekly rations of salt cod, but slaves also negotiated access to small parcels of land set aside to cultivate produce. Many of the planters remained so focused on returning to England wealthy that they made little effort to re-create British culture and, instead, slaves were allowed to retain and cultivate an African cooking aesthetic. For years Jamaican cooks have made a variety of fish dishes from salted cod and the produce they grew, like ackee, a pear-shaped red fruit with a creamy, whitish-yellow flesh.

ACKEE AND SALT FISH[1]

1 lb boneless, skinless salted codfish fillet *(bacalao)*
1 20-oz. can ackee
4 tsp vegetable oil
½ tsp minced garlic
1 medium onion, chopped
1 large tomato, chopped
6 sprigs of thyme
¼ tsp allspice
1 cherry pepper, chopped
3 scallions, chopped

Soak the codfish overnight in a bowl of water. The next morning, drain the water from the fish and flake fish with a fork. Drain and rinse ackee and set aside. Heat oil in pan, then add garlic, onion, tomato, and thyme. Sauté for about 10 minutes on a medium fire, until the tomatoes and onions are soft. Add flaked codfish, allspice, and cherry pepper and cook for an additional 10 minutes. Add ackee and stir, being careful not to crush the fruit. Cook for an additional 5 minutes or until ackee is warmed and tender. Remove from heat and sprinkle with scallion. Serve warm.

Slave ships introduced ackee to the Caribbean from West Africa, including the Gold Coast region, during the slave trade. Today ackee and salted codfish is the national dish of Jamaica and an essential part of a special occasion breakfast for many Jamaicans.

In recent years scholars have debated which events, forces, and movements have shaped the development of African diaspora foodways. How did businesses prosper while confronting racism? What commonalities exist within African diasporas? Has the diaspora diet been healthy? To assess the development of the field over time and provide answers to these questions about African American foodways, I will explore three threads throughout this chapter. First, travel accounts and literature provide a treasure trove of answers about this rich topic. Second, I will show that Asian and Native American influences established prior to the nineteenth century have been more important than European ones on African American foodways. Third, studying African American foodways in a diasporic framework—with comparisons among Cuba, Jamaica, Brazil, Colombia, and mainland America—is far more fruitful than studying them in any area in isolation. Thus I use the term "African diaspora foodways" and start the chapter with travel literature on the Caribbean and South America before moving to mainland North America. Space constraints limit my diasporic approach to between the sixteenth and nineteenth centuries, but a short section on the twentieth century will make links back to Africa and early America. Despite the importance of this subject, historians in the academy have neglected the study of African diaspora foodways. As a result, many of the most important contributors and thought leaders have come from the fields of literature, anthropology, and American studies. Moreover, independent historians working outside colleges and universities published some of the earliest articles and books on African American foodways.

SOUTH AMERICAN INFLUENCE

Because of forced migration in the 1600s and 1700s, African immigrants outnumbered Europeans in regions dominated by slave labor.

For this reason, Africa had a stronger culinary influence than Europe on these slave-owning regions. From the beginning of the slave trade in the 1700s, Brazil received some five hundred thousand to six hundred thousand enslaved Africans. British North America received 6 percent of all enslaved Africans shipped to the Americas, as compared to Brazil, which received 40 percent. So it should come as no surprise that the African culinary retentions in Brazil are much stronger than in North America.[2] Within Brazil, the sugar-producing regions of Bahia and Pernambuco had the greatest concentration of Africans and therefore African culinary influences. "The slaves which are usually brought to Pernambuco are known under the names Angola, Congo, Rebolo [Guinea], Anjico, Gabon, and Mozambique," observed the explorer Henry Koster in his 1817 travel account.[3]

In bringing their culinary heritage with them, Africans fortified the Brazilian diet. Enslaved Afro-Brazilian women introduced nutritious ingredients from their homelands, argues the noted Brazilian historian Gilberto Freyre. Those additions include peanuts, peppers, okra, *yarb*s (inexpensive, calcium-rich, and easy-to-grow green, leafy vegetables), *dendê* (palm) oil, and coconut milk. *Yarb*s, for example, are both nutrient-rich and colon-cleansing. When making soups, Afro-Brazilian female cooks used an abundance of pepper, coconut milk, and *dendê* oil, which are rich in vitamins C, A, and E, respectively.[4] The Bahian gumbo dish *carurú* contains many of these African-introduced ingredients. "*Carurú* is a dish eaten by the Blacks, but is much esteemed by the Whites, and is, to my taste, very delicious," writes James Wetherell, the British vice consul to Salvador de Bahia, Brazil in 1860.[5]

Rice and beans are the basis of dozens of recipes from Africa and the African diaspora including New Orleans red beans and rice, hoppin' John all over the U.S. South, Caribbean peas and rice, Spanish and Latin American *moros y cristianos*, and Brazilian *feijoada*. Enslaved African women introduced rice and beans dishes to Brazil. The most popular, *feijoada*, is a dish African women made with foods they received from their owners, the plants and animals they raised, and ingredients they foraged for and/or stole. Most often they made *feijoada* with black beans, rice, and cuts of meats including pig ears. The cuts of meat in the dish have varied with the consumer's economic status. *Feijoada* made its way from pots in slave quarters, to street vendor carts, into the pots of all sectors of society. Speaking of its popularity in the nineteenth century, one travel account noted that there was "no house so rich as to exclude [black beans]." Today *feijoada* is Brazil's national dish. *Vatapa*, another popular dish, is a stew made with plants indigenous to Africa including coconut and *dendê* oil.[6]

FEIJOADA[7]

4 ½ tsp olive oil, divided
1 6-oz. package smoky pork or tempeh strips
1 medium red onion, chopped
1 rib celery, chopped
1 tsp dried thyme
4 15-oz. cans black beans, rinsed and drained
2 cups low-sodium vegetable broth
4 cloves garlic, minced
1 chipotle chile in adobo sauce, minced
¼ cup minced fresh parsley

Heat 2 tsp oil in large skillet over medium-high heat. Add meat or tempeh and sauté 2 minutes on each side, then remove from heat. Heat remaining 2 1/2 tsp oil in saucepan over medium-high heat. Add onion, celery, and thyme, and sauté 6 minutes, or until onion is golden. Stir in black beans, meat or tempeh, broth, garlic, and chipotle chile. Bring to a simmer, and reduce heat to low. Cover, and cook 45 minutes, stirring occasionally. Remove from heat, and stir in parsley. Season with salt and pepper.

Although they were enslaved people, Afro-Brazilian women entre-preneurs sold prepared foods such as *acarajé* and *milhoverde* on the streets of Bahia and Rio. *Acarajé* uses cow peas (also called black-eyed peas) brought from Africa to create a cake fried in *dendê* oil and split open like a hot-dog bun. It is filled with spicy sauces made from shrimp, cashews, and more *dendê* oil. Afro-Brazilian women street vendors continued to sell *acarajé*, first popular in Senegal, Nigeria, and Ghana, long after Brazil abolished slavery in 1888.

These entrepreneurs used street carts turned into grills to sell *mil-hoverde* (green corn), which was grown in their gardens and grilled to sweet perfection. On Sundays especially, their free day from regular labor, street vendors in Rio and Bahia hawked *acarajé, milhoverde,* fruit, "sausages, black-puddings, fried fish, oil, and sugar cakes," writes the British traveler Maria Graham in the 1820s. On the streets one could buy everything from "the most delicate preserves and candies to the coarsest preparations" made with coconut.[8] Similar scenes unfolded in sugar-based plantation societies throughout the Americas. Enslaved and free Black women in Cuba made tempting cakes and confections with coconut, sugar cane, and other plentiful and inexpensive ingredients they had on hand.

Like sugar cane, cassava is a plant native to the Americas, and after 1492 Europeans introduced it to Africa. In the viceroyalty of Peru, which included modern Colombia, Iberians in urban centers purchased a sizeable number of enslaved Africans to do cooking and other household tasks. Enslaved Africans also worked on large plantations cultivating sugar and the cacao plant, which produced the key ingredient for making chocolate. Planters set aside small parcels of land for their slaves to cultivate produce. Slaves in Colombia raised produce like cassava to supplement their rations. Cassava is a versatile plant that can be steamed and eaten like a baked potato with sea salt, pepper, and butter, fried into a tasty chip, and baked into wonderful bread. In Colombia and other places, African women incorporated local ingredients into their cassava bread recipes. Africans in colonial Colombia did a brisk business selling chocolate beverages and *enyucado*—a traditional cake from the Caribbean coast of Colombia made with shredded cassava, cheese, coconut, and star anise seeds. Today *enyucado* is a fashionable artisan curbside snack baked in a variety of ways. *Enyucado* illustrates a culinary syncretism that has emerged at the intersection of African, Indian, and Iberian influences.

ENYUCADO[9]

3 cups shredded cassava
1 ½ cups fresh grated Colombian *queso*
1 cup sugar
1 tablespoon butter, melted
¾ cup grated coconut
1 cup coconut milk
1 teaspoon ground star anise

Preheat the oven to 400. Put all the ingredients in a large bowl and mix well. Pour the mixture into a buttered baking dish and bake for about 45 minutes or until golden brown. Let cool, cut into squares, and serve.

INTO THE CARIBBEAN

When the Spanish started establishing settlements in the Caribbean, they imported large numbers of domesticated pigs that quickly became the center of the region's culinary culture.

Anthropologist Sidney W. Mintz is the most notable among those early thought leaders in food studies whose work focused on the history and meaning of food in the Caribbean. He writes that Caribbean slavery lasted from 1503 until 1886, and that during that time conservative estimates suggest that some "nine and one-half million enslaved Africans reached the Americas. Nearly a third—about 2.6 million—reached the Caribbean islands"; between the seventeenth and nineteenth centuries, merchants imported some 700,000 enslaved Africans to the island of Cuba alone.[10] Mintz documents that these enslaved Africans in the Caribbean ate a diet rich in cassava, maize, and peanuts, foods that originated in the Americas, traveled to Africa, became incorporated into aspects of African cuisine, and then returned to the New World via Africanized makeovers.[11]

European foodways had an influence on Africans in the Americas, particularly in terms of Dutch pancakes, waffles, and cookies; British puddings, pies, and cakes; and Italian pasta for macaroni and cheese. But Native American foodways had a far more significant impact. The earliest Africans learned from indigenous people about foraging, food preparation, and consumption. Native Americans taught Africans different ways to farm, including the gastronomical trinity of beans, corn, and squash. With regional differences, these three crops became staples throughout the African diaspora in the Americas.

Likewise, Africans had a tremendous impact on the regions where they disembarked. Cooks in the Hispanic Caribbean created *mofongo* from fried green plantains pounded like *foo foo* (a starch mashed into a small edible mass) with garlic, olive oil, broth, and fried pork. Africans cultivated subsistence gardens similar to those described in travel accounts from West and Central Africa. The gardens were necessary because plantation managers in the Caribbean typically distributed niggardly allotments of rations. Former slave Esteban Montejo (1860–1973) spent his formative years living and working on sugar plantations in Villa Clara, a province in the center of Cuba bordering with the providences of Matanzas, Sancti Spiritus, and Cienfuegos. He describes a slave society in Villa Clara filled with Musungo Congos, Mandingos, Gangas, Lucumis, and Carabalis Africans. Montejo recalled small gardens where "sweet potato, squash, okra, corn, peas, horse beans, beans like limas, limes, yucca [cassava], and peanuts" saved many slaves from starvation. The majority of plants that Montejo described above were cooked by Africans in West and Central Africa.[12]

Like Haiti for the French, Jamaica and Barbados were exploitation colonies in which the British remained so focused on returning to England wealthy that they made no attempt to populate the island with Europeans settlers or recreate European culture. Instead, enslaved Africans became the majority of the inhabitants in sugar-producing plantation societies and thus firmly established their African cooking aesthetic. Historian Daniel C. Littlefield estimates that "80 percent of British imports of Gold Coast slaves went to Jamaica, the largest British sugar-producing region in the eighteenth century." These enslaved Africans served as labor force as well as producers of food for the few Whites who ran the island's sugar industry.[13]

Enslaved Africans protested to gain access to small parcels of land for farming. Watermelon, peanuts, rice, okra, coconuts, yams, *callaloo* (similar to collards), and *ackee* fruit were plants brought to the Americas on slave ships. Today ackee is the national fruit of Jamaica, and cooks in many parts of the Caribbean prepare *callaloo*, a leafy green brought to the Americas from West Africa. Ackee and salted codfish, served with rice and peas (similar to hoppin' John), corn bread, and *callaloo* are essential to a festive breakfast.

Slaves sowed African legumes such as *gungo* beans, also called pigeon peas, and prepared them most often as rice and peas. "Everywhere slave traders imported Africans in large numbers—Cuba, Brazil, and South Carolina—the African developed regionally distinctive rice and beans dishes," similar to what they ate in West Africa, says food historian Karen Hess. Rice and beans provided enslaved Africans with an inexpensive and nutritious food combination that they could easily grow in their subsistence gardens.[14] Cooks seasoned rice and peas with salt, pepper, and garden-grown seasonings and simmered it in coconut milk until done. In the Caribbean and other parts of the African diaspora, enslaved Africans also planted food such as sweet potatoes, *cocoyams*, cassava, and plantains introduced to them in West and Central Africa before they boarded slave ships. In the tropical regions of the Americas, plantains became one of the first foods enslaved Africans planted in subsistence gardens and sold at market stalls and as prepared street foods in port cities like Kingston, Cartagena, Veracruz, Havana, and Port-au-Prince.[15] One seventeenth-century travel account on Barbados tells of a group of enslaved Africans who protested until their master added a regular portion of plantains to their rations.[16]

Fish consumption is also an important part of Caribbean foodways. Many of the Africans brought to the islands during the Atlantic slave trade were captured from the geographic area of the present-day countries of Burkina Faso, Senegal, Gambia, Guinea, Sierra Leone, Liberia, Ivory Coast, and Ghana. Most were subsistence farmers but those who lived in the vicinity of the large rivers worked chiefly in fishing. Jamaican plantation managers supplied slaves with weekly rations of salt cod, but slaves also made time to fish. The culinary transition to slavery in slave regions with topographies similar to Africa, such as Cuba and Jamaica, was not as difficult for enslaved Africans who had cooked similar ingredients in their homelands before captivity. For example, John Gabriel Stedman's (1744–1797) *Narrative of a Five Years Expedition against the Revolted Negroes of Surinam,* published in 1796, provides an eyewitness view with which to interpret maroon foodways during the colonial period. Stedman traversed Dutch-colonial Surinam, where escaped slaves and other fugitives lived like pirates in strongholds they purposely built in rugged terrain to resist colonial officials.[17] Stedman observed maroons barbecuing meat; cultivating gardens with rice, cassava, yams, plantains, red pepper, and palm trees; and making salt from palm tree ashes and butter from "the fat of the Palm-tree" worms and pistachio nuts.[18]

ANTEBELLUM NORTH AMERICA

By the eighteenth century, northern colonies in first Dutch and then British North America had become increasingly dependent on enslaved African laborers not only on plantations but also in the kitchens of elites and in taverns. Between 1700 and 1774 there were about sixty-eight hundred slaves in New York: twenty-eight hundred purchased directly from Africa and four thousand from elsewhere in the Americas. With them came African culinary retentions. Travel accounts tell us that "tom tom," described as "a very good Pudding Composed with the Flour of Indian Corn, and boild [sic] with Flesh, fish, Cayenne pepper," and "pepper pot" (a spicy, gumbo-like, one-pot meal featuring okra that Africans enjoyed in Africa and many parts of the Americas thereafter) were commonly sold by street venders in colonial America.[19] In addition to pepper pot, city directories tell us that African American entrepreneurs sold hominy and operated oyster houses and cellars.

During the Civil War (1861–1865), sources tell us that African-inspired pork and corn bread dishes, sweet potato, and sweetmeats represented the most requested foods among Southern troops. In the Union army, African American troops requested additional corn bread and pork as rations. When commissary officials complied, Southern-born White soldiers celebrated the change, while "their Northern-born comrades, accustomed to beef and wheat bread, complained bitterly."[20] Moreover, Union officers subjected African Americans to corporal punishment reminiscent of their enslaved experience, and assigned them to menial duties like cooking rather than combat. Today we know that during the Civil War both Confederate and Union soldiers often depended on African American cooks on the battlefield. Northern army officers put free-born Blacks and runaways into segregated regiments, paid them less than White soldiers, and fed them food inferior to that of White soldiers. A soldier's rations most often included coffee, sugar, a dried biscuit called hardtack, and salt or fresh pork or beef. Soldiers might have also received vinegar, dried fruit, and vegetables as part of their rations. On rare occasion commissaries sent fresh vegetables such as potatoes, onions, carrots, and turnips. With these food items African American camp cooks had to create meals that satisfied their regiments.

In the antebellum South, African American foodways generally had more in common, in terms of ingredients and cooking style, with Africa than with Europe. Journalist and anthropologist John Egerton insisted that for too long historians either ignored African-American cooks or had derided them as culinary geniuses void of ability to articulate their crafts to others, and people that others should not take seriously.[21] As a result, the comprehensive history of African-American culinary artists went unwritten. He writes that "from frontier cabins to plantation houses to the White House, from steamboat galleys and Pullman kitchens to public barbecues and fish fries and private homes without number, Black chefs and cooks and servants have elevated the art of American cookery and distinguished themselves in the process, and they and all other Americans need to see the story fully told."[22]

This disappearing of African influences on U.S. cooking occurred because the first wave of food historians, doing research in the 1990s, wrote primarily on French and British foodways. Eugene D. Genovese's *Roll Jordan Roll: The World the Slaves Made,* published in 1972, was the first attempt of a preeminent historian to study and interpret African American foodways. He argues that West African cooking traditions such as "highly spiced cooking" shaped U.S. cuisine and that African Americans "contributed more to the diet of the poorer Whites than the poorer Whites ever had the chance to contribute to theirs."[23]

For example, Floridians today add lime or lemon to their tomato-based barbecue sauce, like African pit masters of old, who used an abundance of hot peppers, lemon, and/or lime. Modern Carolina pit barbecue seems closest to how West and Central Africans barbecued before the start of the African slave trade. In the antebellum South, poor Whites lacked regular access to meats—"except they steal hogs which belong to the planters, or their negroes," wrote traveler Frederick Law

Olmsted—which prevented them from being thought leaders when it came to barbecuing. As for White elites like Thomas Jefferson, cooking can best be described as something they did not know how to do and left to their enslaved cooks. Virginia slave Louis Hughes maintains that "slaves could barbecue meats best, and when the Whites had barbecues slaves always did the cooking."[24]

THE RECONSTRUCTION ERA

The abolition of slavery halted the predominant influence of African cooks on the homes of Southern kitchens, but that influence resumed with the emergence of the Jim Crow political economy of the South after 1888 until 1965 and the rise of African American domestic laborers in White Southern homes. "The tables of both White and Black Southerners would never again be the same, for White households lost the skill of the Black cook, and Blacks lost both the influence of European traditions and the access to many ingredients," says Southern food writer Damon Lee Fowler. Salt pork and bacon grease became a pervasive part of Southern cooking during the impoverished years following the Civil War. Fowlers says that "a little of this seasoning had been common, though hardly universal, in Southern cooking. But with meat still scarce and poverty almost rampant, it became usual to supplement the meager diet of field peas, greens, sweet potatoes, and grits with cheap salt pork fat."[25]

W. E. B. Dubois (1868–1963) in his book *The Souls of Black Folk* may be the earliest historian to discuss African American foodways after the abolition of slavery. First published in 1903, the book is still in print and used in history courses around the world. Writing part history and part autobiography, Dubois provides descriptions of African American foodways in Tennessee where as a rural teacher he received invitations to family meals of "fried chicken and wheat biscuits, 'meat' and corn pone, string-beans and berries." He also provides a culinary interpretation of rural Black churches, maintaining that they served as the central meeting space for "entertainment, food, and religious services."[26] In some parts of the rural South, religious rituals included iconic foods with links to West Africa. One source from the turn of the century showed African Americans in rural Alabama attending church services during revival week and visiting friends who served *benne* seed wafers and cold drinks. Africans brought *benne* (Bantu for sesame) seeds to the Americas from sub-Saharan Africa in the seventeenth century during the Atlantic slave trade. Known for its mild nutty taste, benne is one of the oldest cultivated crops. Enslaved Africans planted this versatile plant around the borders of their gardens in Tuskegee, Alabama. *Benne* is high in protein, has no cholesterol, and is rich in calcium, iron, zinc, and vitamins B and E.

During the Reconstruction period (1863–1877), the various forms of debt peonage that replaced slavery throughout the South resulted in little improvement in the diet of many rural former slaves. Many migrated to Southern port cities such as New Orleans and Baltimore. At the turn of the century, the port city of New Orleans, for example, had large populations of African American workers who inhabited boarding houses, poorhouses, and hobo encampments. As a result, restaurants catering to these workers sprung up around the city. Their menus focused on the antebellum diet including the all-important three Ms—molasses, meat (salt pork), and meal (corn meal)—as well as, in the case of the Chesapeake region, terrapins that had served as rations but that enslaved Africans turned into a delicacy.

TWENTIETH-CENTURY AMERICAN INFLUENCES

One finds similar Afrocentric food iconology of the early twentieth-century South in the work of anthropologist Zora Neale Hurston (1891–1960). Her novel *Their Eyes Were Watching God* takes a fascinating look at African survival into the twentieth century and provides diasporic culinary links that connect Afro-Floridians to Blacks in other parts of the Americas.[27]

Like Arthur Schomburg, who proposed a massive survey of African and African American culinary history, Hurston actually used the study of food in her work as a new way of interpreting diasporic links throughout the Americas. For example, the first discussion of any food in *Their Eyes Were Watching God* concerns a low-country rice dish from Savannah called mulatto rice. Janie, the book's protagonist, tells the reader in the first section of the book that her grandmother, who raised her, escaped from slavery in Savannah and migrated first to Atlanta and shortly thereafter to West Florida. She tells the story while enjoying a plate of mulatto rice. Harriet Ross Colquitt includes a recipe for mulatto rice in her *Savannah Cook Book,* published in 1939. The recipe calls for frying bacon in a pan and then removing it, using the bacon grease to brown a minced onion and adding a can of diced tomatoes. Colquitt adds, "When thoroughly hot, add a pint of rice to this mixture, and cook very slowly until the rice is done."[28]

This recipe reminds me of oral histories I did with Roy Miller and Ruth Thorpe for my book *Hog and Hominy*.[29] Ruth was born in Harlem in 1932. Her mother migrated from Savannah to Harlem, where she worked as a professional cook. Ruth had vivid memories of her mother's holiday cooking including her "[Savannah] red rice, okra, and tomatoes" dish. As in Cuba and low-country South Carolina, low-country Georgia folk both Black and White viewed a huge rice dish like Savannah red rice or mulatto rice as an absolute essential at any meal.

Roy Miller, born in Harlem in 1924, found this item of culinary history "interesting because that's a crossover. Because my [West Indian] aunts used to do red rice and all of that. I can't say that is a purely West Indian dish, it may be part of an assimilation ... it emanated from the South, but my aunts used to do that beautifully also."[30] West Africans brought their way of cooking long-grain rice with them to South Carolina, Georgia, and the Caribbean. In the kitchen, the African cook and her culture made the greatest culinary thumbprint on areas where Blacks outnumbered Europeans such as Savannah and the Caribbean. My research shows that indeed Savannah red and mulatto rice has diasporic links to Africa and several regions of the Americas.[31] Both dishes seem like adaptations of a similar dish made all over West Africa, *jollof* rice. In Hurston's work the argument is that freedmen like Janie's grandmother migrated from Savannah and introduced rice dishes such as mulatto rice to Florida foodways.

In *Their Eyes Were Watching God,* Hurston brings us to West Florida where Janie's grandmother works as a cook for a White family named Washburn. Janie and her grandmother live in a house in the Washburn backyard. The Washburn's yard contains a pear tree and a "little garden" although Hurston provides no indication of who cultivates the garden and cares for the fruit tree.[32] As for prepared food, we have a description of the meal served on the occasion of Janie's marriage to her first husband Logan Killicks, a Black farmer twice her age. The two marry in her grandmother's parlor on a "Saturday evening with three cakes and big platters of fried rabbit and chicken. Everything to eat in abundance," as her "Nanny and Mrs. Washburn had seen to that."[33] Like rice, the preparation of chicken on a special occasion like a wedding also has strong diasporic roots to the Igbo, Hausa, and Mande of West Africa who ate poultry as part of religious ceremonies.[34]

As for the fried rabbit as part of the wedding reception, the inhabitants of the city of Accra, in the Kingdom of Ghana, commonly hunted and prepared rabbit. Native Americans reinforced this practice, introducing

Africans to local varieties of rabbit and the methods they used to trap and cook them. Frying became the preferred method because it is quick and requires only a large pot and few utensils. In places like the Caribbean and Brazil, enslaved Africans fried wild game in more readily available palm oil instead of pork lard.

The reference to cakes at Janie and Logan's wedding is much more complex, especially when considered in terms of links with Africa and other African diasporas. The two types of cakes one sees described in largely pre-Civil War travel accounts are everyday cakes made from corn and/or cassava and special-occasion cakes made with more refined grains like wheat flour. The Mandinka on the coast of the Gambia, for example, made "sweet cakes [from] pounded rice and honey," though there is no indication if these were special occasion or everyday cakes.[35] Most of what we describe today as cakes were prepared for events such as weddings or in smaller amounts as fast food sold on the streets in urban centers. As we have seen, in nineteenth-century Cuba and Brazil enslaved African women hawked such sweets and tempting cakes for their masters. We also have an account, from the Norwood estate in nineteenth-century Louisiana, of a slave owner who served her slaves a lavish Christmas meal including "frosted cake, and pastry of many kinds."[36] Finally, a 1904 description of a special occasion in Georgia describes a table spread with chicken, gingerbread, and "a jelly-cake."[37] So in short, the term "cake" as it appears in *Their Eyes Were Watching God* has, I would argue, tenuous links to Africa and other African diasporas in the Americas. Admittedly, there is insufficient description of the cake in Janie's West Florida wedding to be more conclusive about diasporic links and possibilities.

Janie's new West Florida husband, Logan Killicks, is perhaps twenty years her senior and an independent Black farmer with sixty acres of land free of the various debt peonage entanglements (sharecropping and the crop-lien system) that kept many Southerners impoverished. What is not clear in Hurston's picture of West Florida is how Killicks arrived at the status of prosperous farmer with an abundance of food. Killicks's kitchen has two of the three aforementioned Ms that make up the South's fundamental culinary trio. There is no molasses on hand but Killicks has "plenty" of "Ribbon-cane syrup" and "sow-belly," a type of salt pork also called streak-of-lean and used to season field peas, butter beans, and all kinds of greens. Sow belly was often fried just like bacon, as Janie does in the novel. In one exchange Logan scoffs at an increasingly estranged Janie, who is about to leave him for good, saying "A whole lot of mens will grin in yo' face, but dey ain't gwine tuh work and feed yuh." He adds, "You won't git far and you won't be long, when dat big gut reach over and grab dat little one, you'll be glad to come back here." In response, Janie says to Logan, "you don't take nothin' to count but sow-belly and cornbread."[38]

Finally let me turn to the most interesting culinary settings in *Their Eyes Were Watching God:* "the muck," or the Florida Everglades. Hurston depicts the area as a fertile Caribbean tropical region similar to the Caribbean coast of Central America.[39] My work on Caribbean Guatemala and Honduras informs my interpretation of both Jacksonville and the muck. Travel accounts from the 1920s and 1930s on Central America (written largely by White bourgeois Americans) indicate that the United Fruit Company (UFCO) of Boston and the International Railroad of Central America (IRCA) established a labor hierarchy on their Central American holdings in which Black immigrant laborers and some Ladino workers (people culturally and linguistically Spanish) served under White American managers. In 1926, U.S. author Wallace Thompson traveled by train through UFCO's Costa Rica division in Port Limón on the Caribbean coast of the country. Thompson, who had worked as U.S. consul in Mexico and for the U.S. intelligence service, described the banana-producing region as a "Latin American Black Belt" where banana plantations and Black laborers were synonymous. Black immigrants could be seen individually and in "gangs," on plantations, in "villages," and "every-where."[40] Similarly Hurston writes about the Black laborers on the muck who picked and loaded beans on trucks for White planters.

Writer Lilian Elwyn Elliott, who traveled extensively throughout Central America in the 1920s, described Black migrants in Central America loading bunches of bananas twenty-four hours a day onto UFCO boats headed for New Orleans, New York, and Boston. She wrote that "everywhere up and down the Caribbean coast of Central America" there could be no banana industry without Black immigrant laborers. If these workers had not been available, the "ports would presently disappear."[41] IRCA and UFCO commissaries in Guatemala carried imported Southern and Caribbean staples including the three Ms mentioned earlier: "The [food] stocks carried by the commissaries consist of . . . salt beef, pickled pork, salt meat, hams and bacon, [corn] meal, molasses, flour, rice, dried fish, sugar, beans, onions, potatoes, canned goods of all sorts," soft drinks, "and beer," says a 1914 business report. The report provides evidence that Black migrants had changed the culinary landscape of the Caribbean coast.[42]

On the coast of south Florida and Central America, alcohol and working class food became part of an integrated, itinerant, wild working-class milieu in which elements of the culture of the U.S. South mixed with those of the Caribbean. Historian Pete Daniel describes this kind of pleasure-seeking culture practiced by relatively autonomous single men and women—roustabouts, as it were—as "lowdown culture." These men and women entered and left railroad and/or plantation enclaves in search of high wages and plenty of time for lowdown culture, which became synonymous with eating, drinking, gambling, and sexual activity. These Black workers on the Caribbean coast of Central America had access to the three Ms and rice and beans.[43]

It's only fitting that we end this culinary read of *Their Eyes Were Watching God* the way that we started—talking about a rice dish. At almost the end of the book, in the last scene in which food is mentioned, we find Janie making pots of "black-eyed peas and rice" in the house she and Tea Cake rent in The Muck. At other times she "baked big pans of navy beans with plenty of sugar and hunks of fatback laying on top," writes Hurston.[44] One can see both these dishes, with some variation, in the pots of Black folks in different parts of the South and the Americas. As mentioned earlier, these rice-based meals are yet another example of diasporic links stretching back to Africa's rice coast and West African ethnic groups living between Cape Verde and the Gold Coast.

TEACHING

Over the years I have revised my courses to reflect my commitment to teaching food history—here I'll discuss three courses that combine diaspora history and food studies.

The first section of my African American History and Foodways course at Babson College focuses on West and Central Africa and the forced immigration and settlement of Africans in North America. I discuss creolization, arguing that when African cultures encountered multiple European and Native American cultures a new culture developed with elements of the original parts. Africans adapted agricultural practices, religious holidays, and culinary preferences from others, as others did from the Africans they encountered. Take, for example, a side dish like collard greens. The plant comes from England, but its preparation in the colonial South was distinctively African in terms of the use of hot peppers, onions, and garlic as seasoning. Today most native-born Southerners of all stripes eat greens. By the nineteenth century the majority of

Southerners ate like enslaved Africans and free African Americans, enjoying all parts of the hog, corn bread, greens, sweet potato pie, candied yams, and black-eyed peas and rice.

During the second half of the course we look at Garveyism with particular interest in Garvey's Negro Factories Corporation (NFC), which in the early 1920s had among its many enterprises three grocery stores and two restaurants in Harlem.[45] We also talk about the Harlem Renaissance using the work of writers such as Langston Hughes and Zora Neale Hurston who were foodies before the term became popular. African American foodways are prevalent in their work if you train your eyes to see them. The last section of the course relies heavily on my own book *Hog and Hominy* and talks about the Civil Rights and Black Power movements.

My African Diaspora History course blends African diaspora content on Africa, the Americas, and Europe through the lens of history and food. I use a diasporic framework to talk about colonization and migration and their impact on local food systems and consumption habits. Until I complete my own textbook for the course, I am piecing together readings.[46] The first part of the course surveys foodways and the theories of leading scholars in the field of African diaspora studies, examining the legacy of slavery, the impact of immigration, the development of discourses on race during the early twentieth century, and early responses to industrialization and modernization. The second part of the course focuses on contemporary history, examining everyday forms of racism and anti-racism, the role of the mass media in reproducing (and contesting) Eurocentric ideals, and recent organized efforts to combat racial discrimination through the lens of food. The final part of the course focuses on cultural productions such as food, music, and religion that have emerged in the twentieth century as important vehicles for identity formation, resistance, and community building among urban populations. Throughout the course, students are encouraged to think comparatively when looking at questions such as, Why is food a particularly potent symbol of personal and group identity? How does a nation-state with so much foreign migration have a national cuisine and culture? How do foreign recipes become traditional or national recipes? And what do the dietary practices of religious groups such as Rastafarians tell us about the society and culture where they live?

My upper-level seminar, Race and Ethnicity in Latin America, uses food to organically explore questions such as, What does it mean to be Black or Indian or White in Latin America? And how has the explosive growth of export-oriented economies like the banana and sugar industry transformed race relations in Latin America? I use a variety of theoretical approaches from anthropology, history, sociology, and country studies to answer these questions.

Despite the subject's importance, until recently historians in the academy have neglected the study of African and African diaspora foodways. Recent studies on the topic, drawing on a wide range of sources, including travel accounts and literature, have shown that food is an important indicator of social position, a site of community building, and a juncture where different cultural traditions can develop. Examining African diaspora foodways teaches us about the forces that have shaped the history of Black people from the Atlantic slave trade to the twenty-first century. A study of African American foodways that is diasporic in scope provides the opportunity to compare and contrast multiple points of Black identity through the lens of food. Food history also provides a new way of studying African diaspora people in an innovative approach that delves into entrepreneurship and global history.

NOTES

1. Recipe adapted from www.jehancancook.com/?p = 1679.

2. Herbert S. Klein, *The Atlantic Slave Trade* (Cambridge: Cambridge University Press, 2010), 33; James Oliver Horton and Lois E. Horton, *Slavery and the Making of America* (Oxford: Oxford University Press, 2006), 27.

3. Henry Koster, *Travels in Brazil: In the Years from 1809 to 1815: In Two Volumes* (Philadelphia, 1817), 2:2009. I have been unable to identify the area Koster calls "Anjico."

4. Gilberto Freyre, *The Masters and the Slaves: A Study in the Development of Brazilian Civilization*, trans. Samuel Putnam (Berkeley: University of California Press, 1986), 459–65.

5. James Wetherell, *Stray Notes from Bahia: Being Extracts From Letters, &c., During A Residence of Fifteen Years*, ed. William Hadfield (Liverpool, 1860), 123.

6. Wetherell, *Stray Notes from Bahia*.

7. Recipe adapted from www.vegetariantimes.com/recipe/vegan-feijoada/.

8. Maria Graham, *Journal of a Voyage to Brazil, and the Residence There, During Part of the Years 1821, 1822, 1823* (London, 1824; New York: Frederick A. Praeger, 1969), 133.

9. Recipe adapted from www.mycolombianrecipes.com/enyucado-colombian-style-cassava-cake.

10. Sidney W. Mintz, *Tasting Food, Tasting Freedom: Excursions Into Eating, Culture, and the Past* (Boston: Beacon Press, 1996), 37.

11. Mintz, *Tasting Food, Tasting Freedom*, 38–39.

12. Esteban Montejo, *Biography of a Runaway Slave,* ed. Miguel Barnet, trans. W. Nick Hill (Willimantic: Curbstone Press, 1994), 25–26.

13. Daniel C. Littlefield, *Rice and Slaves: Ethnicity and the Slave Trade in Colonial South Carolina* (Champaign: University of Illinois Press, 1991), 20.

14. Karen Hess, *The Carolina Rice Kitchen: The African Connection* (Columbia: University of South Carolina Press, 1992), 96.

15. Judith A. Carney and Richard Nicholas Rosomoff, *In the Shadow of Slavery: Africa's Botanical Legacy in the Atlantic World* (Berkeley: University of California Press, 2010), 100–8.

16. Richard Ligon, "A True and Exact History of the Island of Barbados," in *After Africa: Extracts from British Travel Accounts and Journals of the Seventeenth, Eighteenth, and Nineteenth Centuries Concerning the Slaves, their Manners, and Customs in the British West Indies,* eds. Roger D. Abrahams and John F. Szwed (New Haven: Yale University Press, 1983), 43–54.

17. J. Kunst, "Notes on Negroes in Guatemala During the Seventeenth Century; A Mulatto Corsair of the Sixteenth Century," *Journal of Negro History* 1 (October 1916): 392–98; Thomas Gage, *A New Survey of the West Indies, 1648: The English-American,* ed. A.P. Newton (New York: Robert M. McBride and Company, 1929), 205, 208.

18. John Gabriel Stedman, *Narrative of a Five Years Expedition against the Revolted Negroes of Surinam: Transcribed for the First Time from the Original 1790 Manuscript,* eds. Richard and Sally Price (Baltimore: The Johns Hopkins University Press, 1988), 410.

19. Stedman, *Narrative of a Five Years Expedition,* 536.

20. Ira Berlin, Joseph P. Reidy, and Leslie S. Rowland, eds., *Freedom's Soldiers: The Black Military Experience in the Civil War* (Cambridge: Cambridge University Press, 1998), 36.

21. John Egerton, *Southern Food: At Home, on the Road, in History* (New York: Alfred A. Knopf, 1987), 16.

22. Egerton, *Southern Food,* 16.

23. Eugene D. Genovese, *Roll Jordan Roll: The World the Slaves Made* (New York: Vintage Books, 1976), 543–45.

24. Frederick Law Olmsted, *A Journey in the Seaboard Slave States in the Years 1853–1854, with Remarks on Their Economy* (1856; repr. New York: The Knickerbocker Press, 1904), 143.

25. Damon Lee Fowler, *Classical Southern Cooking: A Celebration of the Cuisine of the Old South* (New York: Crown Publishers, 1995), 6–7.

26. W.E.B. Du Bois, *The Souls of Black Folk: Essays and Sketches* (1903; repr. New York: Barnes and Nobles Classics, 2003), 52, 137. For more on food also see page 106.

27. Zora Neale Hurston, *Their Eyes Were Watching God* (1937; repr. New York: Harper Perennial Modern Classics, 2006).

28. Harriet Ross Colquitt, ed., *The Savannah Cook Book: A Collection of the Old Fashioned Receipts from Colonial Kitchens* (New York: Farrar and Rinehart, 1933), 7.

29. Frederick Douglass Opie, *Hog and Hominy: Soul Food from Africa to America* (New York: Columbia University Press, 2008).

30. Frederick Douglass Opie, Interview with Roy Miller and Ruth Thorpe Miller, 2002.

31. Opie, *Hog and Hominy*.

32. Hurston, *Their Eyes Were Watching God*, 8

33. Hurston, *Their Eyes Were Watching God*, 7.

34. Hurston, *Their Eyes Were Watching God*, 215.

35. Alex Haley, *Roots* (Garden City: Doubleday, 1976), 2.

36. Solomon Northup, *Twelve Years a Slave*, eds. Sue Eakin and Joseph Logsdon (Baton Rouge: Louisiana State University Press, 1968), 220–21.

37. Clifton Johnson, *Highways and Byways of the South* (New York: Mac-Millan, 1904), 73.

38. Hurston, *Their Eyes Were Watching God*, 28–30.

39. Andrew Warnes, *Hunger Overcome?: Food and Resistance in Twentieth-Century African American Literature* (Athens: University of Georgia Press, 2004), 37.

40. Wallace Thompson, *Rainbow Countries of Central America* (New York: E.P. Dutton and Co., 1926), 19–20.

41. Lilian Elwyn Elliott Joyce, *Central America: New Paths in Ancient Lands* (New York: Dodd, Mead and Company, 1925), 15, 22, 150, 195, 218.

42. United States National Archives II, College Park, Maryland, Record Group 84, Correspondence American Consulate Guatemala City 1914, Part III, volume 179, Garrard Harris, Commercial Agent Yearly Business Report, Guatemala City, 1914, 3–8.

43. Pete Daniel, *Lost Revolutions: The South in the 1950s* (Chapel Hill: University of North Carolina Press, 2000), 121–25.

44. Hurston, *Their Eyes Were Watching God,* 132.

45. For more see the published volumes of *The Marcus Garvey and Universal Negro Improvement Association Papers* (Berkeley: University of California Press, 1983–2011).

46. Opie, *Hog and Hominy;* and my second book, *Black Labor in Caribbean Guatemala* (Gainesville: University Press of Florida, 2009); Judith A. Carney and Richard Nicholas Rosomoff, *In the Shadow of Slavery: Africa's Botanical Legacy in the Atlantic World* (Berkeley: University of California Press, 2011); journal articles and book chapters such as Richard R. Wilk, "'Real Belizean Food': Building Local Identity in the Transnational Caribbean," *American Anthropologist*, n.s., 101 (June 1999): 244–55; Shannon Lee Dawdy, "La Comida Mambisa: Food, Farming, and Cuban Identity, 1839–1999," *New West Indian Guide / Nieuwe West-Indische Gids* 76, nos. 1 and 2 (2002): 47–80; Ian Cook and Michelle Harrison, "Cross over Food, Re-Materializing Postcolonial Geographies," *Transactions of the Institute of British Geographers*, n.s., 28 (September 2003): 296–317.

BIBLIOGRAPHY

Bower, Anne L., ed. *African American Foodways: Explorations of History and Culture*. The Food Series. Urbana: University of Illinois Press, 2007.

Carney, Judith A., and Richard Nicholas Rosomoff. *In the Shadow of Slavery: Africa's Botanical Legacy in the Atlantic World*. Berkeley: University of California Press, 2011.

Carpenter, Frank G. *Lands of the Caribbean: The Canal Zone, Panama, Costa Rica, Nicaragua, Salvador, Honduras, Guatemala, Cuba, Jamaica, Haiti, Santo Domingo, Porto Rico, and the Virgin Islands*. Garden City: Doubleday, 1926.

Crowther, Samuel. *The Romance and Rise of the American Tropics*. Garden City: Doubleday, 1929.

Daniel, Pete. *Lost Revolutions: The South in the 1950s*. Chapel Hill: University of North Carolina Press, 2000.

Dawdy, Shannon Lee. "La Comida Mambisa: Food, Farming, and Cuban identity, 1839–1999." *New West Indian Guide / Nieuwe West-Indische Gids* 76, nos. 1 and 2 (2002): 47–80.

Egerton, John. *Southern Food: At Home, on the Road, in History*. New York: Alfred A. Knopf, 1987.

Fowler, Damon Lee. *Classical Southern Cooking: A Celebration of the Cuisine of the Old South*. New York: Crown Publishers, 1995.

Genovese, Eugene D. *Roll Jordan Roll: The World the Slaves Made*. New York: Vintage Books, 1976.

Harris, Jessica B. *Iron Pots and Wooden Spoons: Africa's Gifts to New World Cooking*. New York: Atheneum, 1989.

———. *High on the Hog: A Culinary Journey from Africa to America*. New York: Bloomsbury, 2011.

Hess, Karen. *The Carolina Rice Kitchen: The African Connection*. Columbia: University of South Carolina Press, 1992.

Hurston, Zora Neale. *Their Eyes Were Watching God*. 1937. Reprint, New York: Harper Perennial Modern Classics, 2006.

McCann, James C. *From Poverty to Famine in Northeast Ethiopia: Rural History, 1900–1935*. Philadelphia: University of Pennsylvania Press, 1987.

———. *People of the Plow: An Agricultural History of Ethiopia, 1800–1990*. Madison: University of Wisconsin Press, 1995.

———. *Green Land, Brown Land, Black Land: An Environmental History of Africa, 1800–1990*. Portsmouth: Heinemann, 1999.

———. *Maize and Grace: Africa's Encounter with a New World Crop, 1500–2000*. Cambridge, MA: Harvard University Press, 2005.

———. *Stirring the Pot: A History of African Cuisine*. Athens: Ohio University Press, 2009.

Mendes, Helen. *The African Heritage Cookbook*. New York: The Macmillan Company, 1971.

Mintz, Sidney W. *Sweetness and Power: The Place of Sugar in Modern History*. New York: Penguin Books, 1986.

———. *Tasting Food, Tasting Freedom: Excursions into Eating, Culture, and the Past*. Boston: Beacon Press, 1996.

Opie, Frederick Douglass. *Hog and Hominy: Soul Food from Africa to America*. New York: Columbia University Press, 2008.

———. "Molasses-Colored Glasses: WPA and Sundry Sources on Molasses and Southern Foodways." *Southern Cultures* 14 (Spring 2008): 81–96.

———. "Eating, Dancing, and Courting in New York: Black and Latino Relations, 1930–1970." *Journal of Social History* 42 (Fall 2008): 79–109.

Paige, Howard. *Aspects of African American Foodways.* Southfield: Aspects Publishing Company, 1999.

Pinkerton, John. *A General Collection of the Best and Most Interesting Voyages and Travels in all Parts of the World.* 17 vols. London, 1810–1814.

Stedman, John Gabriel. *Narrative of a Five Years' Expedition against the Revolted Negroes of Surinam: Transcribed for the First Time from the Original 1790 Manuscript.* Edited by Richard and Sally Price. Baltimore: Johns Hopkins University Press, 1988.

Wilk, Richard R. "'Real Belizean Food': Building Local Identity in the Transnational Caribbean." American Anthropologist, n.s., 101 (June 1999): 244–55.

Williams-Forson, Psyche A. *Building Houses Out of Chicken Legs: Black Women, Food, and Power.* Chapel Hill: University of North Carolina Press, 2006.

Witt, Doris. *Black Hunger: Food and the Politics of U.S. Identity.* New York: Oxford University Press, 1999.

———. *Black Hunger: Soul Food and America.* Minneapolis: University of Minneapolis Press, 2004.

CHAPTER 10

Migration, Transnational Cuisines, and Invisible Ethnics

KRISHNENDU RAY

Territorial presumptions about culture have been challenged by research on interconnected histories, borderlands, and oceans.[1] Drawing on that work, I contend that food traditions are as much a matter of movement and emplacement, as they are of roots. National figures often excise migrants from their cultural sphere with arguments about belonging, yet the construction of place-based food cultures, developed without acknowledging the significance of immigrant habitation, can produce virulent locavorism. For instance, Northern Leaguers in Italy mobilize around slogans of "polenta, not couscous" to exclude doner kebab sellers from the city-center in Lucca, and Mikkel Dencker, of the Danish People's Party, has bolstered his campaign against the loss of Danish identity with anxieties about a few kindergartens that have removed pork meatballs from their lunch menus.[2] It will be difficult to resist the elective affinity between the purity of local cultures and ethnic cleansing, unless transnational flows of people are accounted for in our analysis of food.[3] Within this context, the role of migrants in the U.S. food system and cultural order is evocative of the possibilities of rootlessness. This essay relies upon a number of recent studies regarding immigrant foodways in the United States to reframe the emerging conversation, and through that reorientation to make ethnic subjects legible to scholarly analysis.

The constitution of gustatory identity, typically with nation as its preeminent center and province as its conjoined peripheral twin, must elide the transient transnational to maintain a territorial focus. Dominant arguments perpetuate the idea that culture must be contained within the nation and has to be bounded at the borders, notwithstanding persistent cultural extensions: Alsace and Lorraine between Germany and France, Punjab between Pakistan and India, Mexico and New Mexico in North America, or Bengal spread out between Bangladesh and India. The examples can proliferate from almost every border-region of the world, once we take really existing societies into consideration. Nevertheless, national imaginations of taste are often constructed against the very neighboring regions that are culinarily proximate, albeit ideologically distant. Neighboring peoples and their contiguous cultures are frequently conceived as the biggest threat to national singularity. Furthermore, development bureaucracies and tourism boards now assume nations to have cuisines, as much as flags, anthems, and airlines.[4] In Sidney Mintz's cutting words, "Is having a cuisine important—is it because other people have one?"[5] This chapter questions the inevitable linking of cooking to territory so as to rethink the relationship between taste, toil, and belonging, by looking at immigrant foodways.

The idea that a civilization could be named in the spaces between territories is attributed to Fernand Braudel.[6] Braudel's work in the Mediterranean basin reconstructed the long eroded connection between the sea and the people who lived around it and recent scholarship has moved us even closer towards conceptualizing connective sensory histories beyond the Mediterranean world. Sanjay Subrahmanyan has transformed the field by drawing deep historical connections between the littoral of the Mediterranean, the Arabian Sea, and the Bay of Bengal.[7] Iain Walker's research on flows and counter-flows of Hadramis, Shimalis, and the Muwalladin traveling through networks on the Swahili coast of East Africa and Southern Yemen furthers that cosmopolitanism of the tongue woven around the wide rim of the Indian Ocean. Walker documents his subjects "slipping effortlessly from Swahili to Arabic, drinking coffee in Dar but tea in Seiyun, eating *muhogo wa nazi* [coconut cassava] in Tanga but *ruz wa dajaja* [rice and chicken] in Tarim. . . . Chewing a little qat in Shibam, quietly sipping a beer in Nairobi, assuming a tribal name in the wadi but becoming plain Awadh Salim on returning to Zanzibar."[8] In that spirit, attending to culture in the spaces between territories, this chapter examines culinary histories that have been obfuscated by methodological nationalism.

For as far back as we have records we know that immigrants have shaped the American food system at two important nodes: the farm and the kitchen. While farmworkers have received recognition since César

Chavez's movement, kitchen-workers have remained invisible.[9] Their erasure is a form of compensation for the nonnative cook's disruptive presence at the idealized housewife's hearth. The immigrant cook threatens fantasies of home and homeland, intruding into both domains of domesticity. Outside the American context we find the same invisibility of cooks and domestic servants, many of whom were rural and transnational immigrants, even in the classic work *The Making of the English Working Class* by E. P. Thompson.[10] Domestic workers are mentioned fleetingly, although by 1900 domestic service was the single largest occupation in the United Kingdom and over one quarter of the four million women in the workforce were servants. That is partly because servants, including cooks and butlers, were considered by analysts to be unheroic members of the working class, and partly because of a lack of sources. In spite of those challenges, the cook has to be accounted for in our imagination in order to expand the possibilities of a progressive food movement.[11]

Furthermore, American food culture prefigures what we have come to learn about many other contemporary cultures: the dynamics are as much about flows, friction, and fraction as they are about roots, consensus, and cultural wholes; commercialization can coexist with culture; and transactions in taste between native and immigrant are central to the production of local foodways. U.S. foodways illustrate the process by which habitual practices are made self-conscious, heightening the sense of difference, sometimes even antagonism, precisely because of their proximity to imagined others. Taste transactions—among neighbors and coworkers, friends and contested groups, between neighborhoods and within communities—all serve to accentuate differences and consciousness about them. The push and pull between current immigrants and older cohorts, resulting in processes of contestation and desperate attempts to bind communities, is what produces American foods. Millions of immigrants have settled in the United States, coming from the widest range of countries with diverse food practices. The United States is a particularly valuable location for the study of creolized foodways supported by a rich trove of sources. Generally high literacy rates, a product of state and church policy, as well as a robust historiography has enabled incomparable documentary density.[12]

Since the 1850 U.S. census, when occupation and birthplace were first recorded, data show a strong correlation between food service occupations and new immigrant groups. The foreign-born numerically dominate certain occupations, such as domestic servants, hotel and restaurant employees, hotel-keepers, saloon-keepers and bartenders, dealers in groceries, bakers, and butchers.[13] In contrast, members of the so-called white-collar occupations, such as the clergy, lawyers, school teachers, and government officials, have mostly been native-born. In New York City in 1850, for example, 70 percent of hotel and restaurant employees and 80 percent of hotel-keepers were foreign-born, mostly of Irish and German heritage. This is in a context where the foreign-born constituted about one third of the labor force. Fifty years later, according to the 1900 Census, 63 percent of hotel and restaurant employees were foreign-born (Irish and German predominated) and 65 percent of hotel-keepers were foreign-born (mostly German). Restaurant-keepers, a newly significant occupation by 1900, were 67 percent foreign-born at a time when foreign-born were about one-half of the population of New York City. Even by the 1950 census, after immigration had subsided, 64 percent of restaurant cooks were foreign-born, with Italians now at the top, followed by Greeks, Chinese, and Germans. That trend continued, according to the 2010 census, in which 75 percent of restaurant cooks and 64 percent of restaurant workers were foreign-born; the dominant countries and regions of origin were now Mexico, Central America, the Caribbean Basin, South America, China, and the former Soviet Union.[14]

PLACES OF BELONGING: TENEMENT, NEIGHBORHOOD, CITY, AND NATION

Many of these immigrant families, visible in the earliest U.S. census records, with their daily imperative of working, shopping, cleaning, and cooking, figure in Jane Ziegelman's popular book *97 Orchard. An Edible History of Five Immigrant Families in One New York Tenement.*[15] Structured as vignettes of succeeding families at one address (97 Orchard Street), and sprinkled with pictures, cartoons, menus, daguerreotypes, recipes, and census tracts, Ziegelman tells the compelling stories of the German Glockners and Irish Moores of the 1860s, the Eastern European Jewish Gumpertzs a few decades later, and the Rogarshevskys and the Baldizzis of the early twentieth century. This is a story about how immigrants have transformed American palates and food businesses.

Food is at the center but so is labor; tenement housewives were like "freight elevators, hauling groceries, coal, firewood, and children up and down endless flights of stairs."[16] Her stories maintain a crucial balance between taste and toil, without which discernment merely measures the consumption of other people's hard work. The story of food, cooking, and housework is interwoven with a history of gendered shopping in the Essex Street Market and the Fulton Market, according to sources such as Junius Henri Browne's 1869 guide to *The Great Metropolis,* and the butcher-turned-intellectual Thomas De Voe's path-breaking 1858 paper presented to the New York Historical Society.[17] *97 Orchard* is also a compelling story about public policy and how elites and commoners came to understand the city and its uses, as registered in the report of the mayor's pushcart commission of 1906.[18]

Based on Louise More's *Wage-Earner's Budget* (1907), Ziegelman's book records the conflicts and confluence of the tastes of reformers and immigrants as inscribed on the bill of fare for the Immigrant Dining Room at Ellis Island.[19] She notes how in the mid-nineteenth century, "the Irish were big in the fish and oyster business, Germans worked as dairymen, grocers, and butchers," and how immigrant food purveyors fed their own communities and the rest of the city.[20] Starting in the first decades of the nineteenth century, immigrants were peddlers of fruits, vegetables, and fish, bakers of bread, slaughterers of livestock, waiters, cooks, and brewers of beer—the last of these shifting with the shifting populace from high alcohol English ales, to the crisp, bottom-brewed, more refreshing German lagers that would come to characterize American brews. The Germans established groceries, delicatessens, beer halls, bakeries, and butcher shops, which served as both community spaces and sites of transmission for outsider cohorts, "where the native-born could sample their first bratwurst, or pretzel, or glass of lager."[21]

In his field-transforming *Revolution at the Table,* labor historian turned food scholar Harvey Levenstein reaches the conclusion that early Americans never liberated themselves from the British culinary heritage, though they tended to eat more corn, pork, and molasses, imbibe more whiskey and cider, and drink less tea and ale.[22] The potato and the tomato gained acceptance in the United States only after first entering the European diet late in the eighteenth-century. Pumpkins on the other hand found wider and quicker acceptance as analogues to European squash.[23] This pattern of culinary Anglo-conservatism "continued to be the case after 1783, even though the proportion of immigrants of non-British origin rose. Then, only the Germans could be said to have substantially influenced American cooking, and they were Northern Europeans whose cuisine resembled that of the British."[24] By the 1880s, Levenstein finds evidence of a bifurcated working class. The well-off skilled and semi-skilled comprised one side, consisting mainly of white native-born Americans and immigrants of Anglo-Saxon, Celtic, and Northern European ancestry who ate more meat, eggs, potatoes, and more fruits and vegetables, much of them canned, than their UK counterparts.[25] On the other hand, there were "New Immigrants," mostly of Central, Eastern, and Southern European ancestry, all with lower skills in the labor market, a gap that was reinforced by ethnic disdain. These latter immigrants were the target of new professionals—settlement house workers, home economists, nutritionists, and public health advocates—each seeking "to teach the immigrants how to Americanize their diets in an economical fashion."[26] Levenstein notes that this evangelical enthusiasm did *not* derive from reformers' smug self-satisfaction about their own food culture but from their scientific expertise. "Nutritional science reinforced what their palates and stomachs already told them: that any cuisine as coarse, overspiced, 'garlicky,' and indelicate-looking as the food of central, eastern, and southern Europe must be unhealthy as well."[27]

American scholarship has paid the most attention to the twenty million or so immigrants who arrived at the turn of the nineteenth and the twentieth centuries. That attention is partly driven by the density of documentary collections (powered by Progressive Era enthusiasm to reform the food habits of immigrants), and partially by the nostalgia (a term not used here merely to dismiss it) of scholars, many of whom are from the third and subsequent generations of Jewish and Italian stock. Nostalgia in this case expresses itself in a productive impulse of recuperative scholarship.

One exemplary instance of such work is Donna Gabaccia's *We Are What We Eat*.[28] Based on detailed and varied archival work that includes diaries and memoirs of plantation owners and their wives, slave memoirs produced by the Works Projects Administration, autobiographies of food businessmen, newspapers, and cookbooks, Gabaccia develops the argument that Americans have always been creoles with hybrid tastes. Interrogating these mixed diets, she shows how the relationship between food and group identity was changing, relational, and unsettled for a long time. By the end of the colonial era "region more than ethnicity defined American identities."[29]

The gradual formation of the national food market, along with transportation modernization (railroads and roadways) and the mass media revolution (print, radio, and TV), in alliance with new refrigeration technologies, produced a national diet. But the immigrant labor that made the national market possible at the end of the nineteenth and early twentieth centuries, also produced enclave eating, as racism, xenophobia, and cheap housing contained new immigrants in certain urban neighborhoods. That is also where the ethnic entrepreneur operated, supplying the produce of the old land which was often new to the rest of Americans, such as the Napa cabbage and radishes introduced by Japanese farmers in California and the broccoli, wine grapes, figs, and olive oil introduced by Italians. Sometimes small eateries and restaurants evolved from grocery stores, delicatessens, or family boarding houses.[30]

Corporate nationalization, on one hand, and ghettoization of the poor urban immigrant population on the other, produced two scripts on American cuisine. One eroded ethnic and regional accents to claim mass-produced foods as national icons, in a realm where hot dogs, Cracker Jacks, fried chicken, and Fritos lost their ethnic signifiers. Then there were ethnic enclaves, such as Chinatown and Little Italy, catering to ethnic insiders, about which I will have more to say below.

Hasia R. Diner's comparative work on immigrant cuisines, *Hungering for America,* comes at the question mostly from the other end, which is how did America transform the taste of immigrants? She crafts her project around two subsidiary queries: What is the fundamental difference between pre-immigration and post-immigration foodways of the Italians, the Irish, and Eastern European Jews in the United States; and, Why did the Italians and Eastern European Jews develop an American identity around the specificity of their foods while the Irish did not?[31] Based on a close reading of almost one hundred pieces of fiction and memoir written by immigrants and their children, *Hungering for America* is a detailed text with a social historian's eye for the perfect little instance that illuminates the bigger picture.

The most important difference between pre- and post-immigration foodways, she notes, is abundance. Rosolino Mormino, a resident of Napoleonville, Louisiana, wrote his brother in Italy with telling eloquence, "In America bread is soft, but life is hard."[32] A dietary study of Italians, done by the U.S. Department of Agriculture and Hull House in the 1890s around Chicago, reported that olive oil seemed to be essential to Italian immigrant identity, as did meat. "In Italy few from the lower classes ate [meat] more often than three times a year. In America meat appeared regularly on their menus."[33] Dishes that continued to keep their Italian names, such as *minestra* (vegetable soup) got richer and more complicated. "Pizza in Roseta Valforte [in Italy] was a flat, thin disc of bread with salt and oil. In Roseto, Pennsylvania, tomatoes,

onions, and anchovies gradually covered the dough."[34] Migration effectively elevated the cuisine of the poor Italian to that of its elite.

Class elevation also occurred with Eastern European Jewish food after
immigration. "The formerly poor started to eat *blintzes, kreplach, kasha-
varnitchkes, strudel,* noodles, *knishes,* and, most importantly, meat every
day. Their once meager cabbage or beet *borschts* now glistened with
fat."[35] Marcus Ravage, a Rumanian Jewish migrant in New York in 1900
noted with astonishment, "In New York, every night was Friday night
and every day was Saturday [sabbath], as far as food went."[36] Furthermore, a national cuisine was born in the diaspora, one which eventually
deemphasized regional styles. Angelo Pellegrini wrote that immigrants
came to America "ignorant of cuisines beyond their own regions. In the
Little Italy of the American metropolis the Southern Italian ultimately
learned about *osso buco* and *veal scaloppini,* and his neighbor . . . from
the north met up with pizza and eggplant Parmesan."[37] Furthermore, as
Niccola de Quattrociocchi, a native of Palermo, wrote in the 1920s, "One
evening [while strolling in New York], we went to an Italian restaurant
where I was introduced to two very fine, traditional American specialties
called 'spaghetti with meatballs,' and 'cotoletta parmigiana' . . . I found
both extremely satisfying and I think someone in Italy should invent them
for the Italians over there."[38] Other new elements crept into their repertoire such as the drinking of beer with their food rather than wine.[39]

Food played such an important role in Italian American identity that,
according to Diner, "even children expressed little interest in transcend-
ing the food boundaries of their families and communities."[40] She argues
that "the Italian story may best represent the experiences of most immigrants."[41] We will see below, in discussing Simone Cinotto's work how
that perspective might change if we expand the timeframe. In *The
Migrant's Table,* I show that the Bengali American immigration story, at
the turn of the twentieth and the twenty-first century, is different precisely because the respondents in my study were more affluent both in
their native contexts and in the New World.[42] The hagiography of
American abundance among Irish and Eastern European Jews or even
the muted critique of American foods and tastes by Italian Americans
stands in sharp contrast to the attitude of the Bengali American interlocutors in my study. Only two of my respondents, out of 126, mentioned abundance, while the others were highly critical of American
foods. That is due to their class background, the way they crafted
an identity that leaves behind the hunger of their poorer compatriots,
and because they take full advantage of the post-Civil Rights cultural

terrain, absorbing the current normative critique of American foods. But the case of post-1965 Bengali Americans comes long after the insertion of a much larger and an equally interesting Asian group that has changed the shape of American eating.

THE INVISIBLE CHINESE RESTAURATEUR

We are just beginning to see scholarly and serious journalistic work on the most common ethnic American cuisine—Chinese. There are more than forty thousand Chinese restaurants in the United States, more than the number of McDonald's, Burger Kings and KFCs combined.[43] Nevertheless the academic output on McDonald's and McDonaldization has been much heavier.[44] That may be because countercultural academics have come to see McDonald's as a harbinger of cultural homogenization and the shape of the neoliberal future of deskilled work, corporate control of commodity and labor markets, withdrawal of the welfare state, and the decline of taste. Unfortunately, so much single-minded attention to powerful American corporations makes the powerless even less visible. Hence it is salutary that we are finally catching up with our analysis of the Chinese restaurant in North America, the home turf of those threatening global fast food brands.[45]

The conceit behind Jennifer Lee's *The Fortune Cookie Chronicles* is to interview a wide cast of characters including an American restaurateur, Chinese restaurant worker, Korean entrepreneur, and Japanese fortune cookie maker, who were suddenly connected on March 30, 2005 when hundreds of people across the United States won the Powerball lottery.[46] It appears that these winners had all bought tickets using the same string of numbers, inscribed in fortune cookies distributed in Chinese restaurants across forty-two American states. That allowed Lee, fluent in both Mandarin and Cantonese, to get further than the usual questions asked by most Americans until then, such as why Americans eat Chinese food, or why Chinese food is popular among American Jews.[47] Her research in the digitized archives of historical newspapers and her particularly illuminating interviews with immigrant Chinese restaurateurs and workers provides an unmatched view. The limited language skills of previous Euro-American researchers and lower rates of literacy among their subjects and hence scant documentation had long precluded detailed work among the Chinese in America.

Navigating between two polarities—how the Chinese changed our food and how they got changed—Lee deftly sidesteps the issue of authenticating expatriate Chinese food by calling General Tso's chicken and chop suey "Chinese, born in America" (like herself), or "American which just looks Chinese" (like herself again). In Louisiana she tasted Szechuan alligator, which was probably unavailable anywhere in China but was still recognizably Chinese. Challenged by cream cheese wontons in the Midwest and chow mein sandwiches in New England, she comes to the brave conclusion that "Chinese food, perhaps, does not have to originate in China."[48] She then pursues fascinating tales: of the first Chinese food delivery system, developed on the Upper West Side of Manhattan in 1976; the Japanese inventor of the fortune cookie; and the early explosion of Chinese restaurants in New York City, from six in 1885 to more than one hundred in 1905.[49]

Lee concludes by pointing out that while American corporate food lore is filled with figures such as Ray Kroc of McDonald's, Howard Schultz of Starbucks, and Asa Griggs Candler of Coca-Cola, "Chinese food in America has no such dominant figures, yet it is no less a powerful presence in Americana." Rather, it is populated with micropersonalities such as Misa Chang, who redefined take-out and delivery, Edward Louie, who mastered the fortune cookie making machines, and Chefs Wang and Peng, who fabricated General Tso's chicken.[50]

The small-town Chinese restaurant is, in Lisa Cho's pointed postcolonial critique, "an awkward reminder of misplaced requiems."[51] Chinese restaurants have not died, nor have all the diasporic populations vanished into exotic but metropolitan Chinatowns. *Eating Chinese* seeks to produce an alternative history of suppressed immigrant agency.[52] These ubiquitous small-town Chinese restaurants and their menus of egg foo young, chow mein, and chop suey, according to Cho, attest to a self-conscious production of ethnicity, where the diasporic subject exploits the menu's capacity to produce a palatable ethnicity and yet frustrates the fierce white pursuit of a "knowable authentic Chinese subject" and his real food.[53] In contrast to the piercing Anglo gaze that wants to pin down authentic Chineseness once and for all, she posits an alternative possibility.[54]

Small-town Chinese restaurants are often spaces of white nostalgia that consolidate subjectivity through the production of manageable otherness, which is why we see so much memorializing and singing about them. In the latter case one can reference Joni Mitchell's "Chinese Café/Unchained Melancholy" and Sylvia Tyson's "The Night the Chinese Restaurant Burned Down."[55] One of Cho's arguments is that a certain kind of visibility produces its own shadows. She argues, insisting upon a tincture against sentimentality, that such celebration of the Chinese restaurant is a form of rationalization of domination under the guise of inclusion. Just as there would be no "Habermasian public sphere without a plantation economy," the significance of the Chinese restaurant in white bildungsroman sentimentality is a "barbed assertion of diasporic presence in the absence of any mention of diasporic subjects."[56]

Then again not all nostalgia is the same. Cho asserts that it is equally necessary to recuperate nostalgia from the strictures of white sentimentality, where the small-town Chinese restaurant is "a testament to the power of diaspora to be a force of emplacement."[57] She then goes on to discuss how small-town Chinese restaurants created a space of engagement. Yet she insists that the reader ought to be aware that one-sided memorializing of the Chinese restaurant occludes the social production of the standing spaces of the kitchen and the cash register, against that occupied by the sitting customer. Such complex accusations are typical of postcolonial theorizing, and Cho manages to unsettle the reader through high theorizing, powerful writing, and the sparse evidence of a few menus, a couple of photographs, and a handful of songs. The curse of ubiquity but invisibility dealt to the Chinese restaurateur is even more acute for another group of immigrants.

UNNAMED LATINO COOKS

Recent migrations from Latin America have drawn attention to one of the largest groups of immigrants, with the longest history within the United States. Yet that very contemporary inflow overwhelms the evidence of their ancient presence. As Zilkia Janer notes, "the cultural continuity between the two sides of the Mexico-United States border predates the arrival of Europeans and the birth of both countries."[58] The Treaty of Guadalupe Hidalgo (1848) not only transformed one-half of Mexican territory into the United States but stranded a large number of Mexicans on the wrong side of the border. Among them were ranchers, landowners, and rural workers (who would later come to be idealized as cowboys), for whom Southwestern ranch style cookery was the norm, with dried beef, fruit and vegetables, curds and fresh cheeses, pork cracklings, slow cooked stews (adobos of vinegar, garlic, and spices), and barbecues. Spanish and Native American fry breads, stews, and sausages were adopted quite early into their repertoire. And by 1895 we find evidence of food sellers serving tamales, tortillas, chiles rellenos (stuffed chilies), and *huevos revueltos* (scrambled eggs) in a plaza in San Antonio.[59] Here we witness some of the loveliest invention of traditions. The popular guidebooks produced by the Federal Writers' Project's (FWP) in the 1930s and 1940s and the archives of the America Eats project reveal the substantial presence of "Spanish-Mexican food."[60] This is also about when Tex-Mex food, with its chili con carne and combination platters of tamales, enchiladas, rice, beans, and melted cheese, became reductively associated with working-class Mexican restaurant fare, dominated by the flavors of ground chiles, cumin, oregano, and black pepper. As early as 1898 Encarnacion Pinedo was already struggling to free Mexican food from a virulent stereotype by calling her cookbook *El cocinero español* (*The Spanish Cook*), one of the earliest Spanish-language cookbooks published in California.[61]

Camille Bégin notes that the taste of race informed the taste of place as U.S. gastronomic discourse, inscribed in printed guidebooks for the newly emergent tourist trade, established Mexican food as a Southwestern regional American cuisine that "offered the sensory opportunity to perceive the race of a conquered people."[62] A potent gender dynamic also animated the sensory construction of this domestic yet exotic taste. "Daring to eat the spicy dishes prepared by Mexican women was a central experience of white male culinary tourism."[63]

There is also a process of consolidation of a cuisine that, in the diaspora, exceeds the nation-state. In North America, Mexican bakeries tend to broaden their offerings to include Salvadoran and Guatemalan breads and pastries. Sometimes what are often considered street foods, such as Puerto Rican fritters like *bacalaítos* and *alcapurrias,* are accentuated as appetizers in the menus of lunch counters and restaurants. Elaborate and occasional dishes such as complex *moles* and rich desserts often prepared only for Christmas, Lent, and family celebrations are available all the time in the post-migration context. These changes are what gives the appearance of unhealthiness to many Latino diets, along with the excessive use of soft drinks in place of fruit juices.[64]

Mexican food was for a long time hidden in plain view among migrant and expatriate population as one of the oldest regional cuisines of the Southwest, on the western end of Hispano-USA, with its distinctive avocados, sprouts, and sour cream. Next to it we had cactus fruits, green chilies, blue corn, and *pozole* around Santa Fe. It was the Civil Rights movement, and the counterculture it produced, that opened up American conceptions of legitimate palatal identities. As these variations of regional transborder cuisines come into view, the reductive archetype of Mexican food is beginning to dissipate in the eyes of many Americans. Today Los Angeles, Chicago, and even New York are beginning to see varied Mexican regional cuisines—such as Oaxacan and Poblano—and a wide range of Latin American food at restaurants, in markets, and on pushcarts populating the edges of soccer fields and street fairs.[65] Sometimes cuisines work most compellingly below national levels, in urban neighborhoods through long networks of trade, settlement, and affiliation.

One instance of this work, according to Scarlett Lindeman's study, "Alimentos Saludables," is a restaurant specializing in tamales located on Fourth Avenue in Sunset Park, Brooklyn. It is off the main commercial drag, "a bustling corridor home to dozens of Mexican restaurants, taco trucks, street vendors hawking *agua frescas, gorditas,* and *esquites,* a central social space of the predominantly Latino neighborhood."[66] The Gutierrez family has run the restaurant for eight years. Luis Gutierrez and his wife Incepción are from Puebla. They have been in the United States for more than twenty years. He initially worked in factories and "on the side helped Incepción sell tamales on the street that she made in their home. Their tamale business grew and they started renting the space."[67] Their clientele consists mostly of Mexicans and Central Americans who live in the neighborhood and some Yelpers in desperate search of authenticity.

Beginning in the early decades of the twentieth century, when more than a million migrants entered the United States, Mexicans became increasingly central to the workings of the American food system, from the agricultural laborer to the dishwasher and cook. While they became ubiquitous to the food system they and their food remained invisible to most Americans. A study of Omaha, found that Mexican food remained confined to the immigrant community until the 1950s, but then it slowly began to leak out of the immigrant population. Nationally the number of Mexican restaurants took off in the 1970s, which *preceded* the great northern migration of Mexicans by about two decades.[68] The mechanics of that transformation are unclear and remain uninterrogated.

It is worth noting that Wilber Zelinky's famous 1980 survey based on telephone directories found that the three most popular cuisines were Chinese, Italian, and Mexican, together making up 70 percent of ethnic restaurants in the United States. In that study there was an uneven regional distribution, with Mexican cuisine radiating out from the Southwest.[69] Jeffrey Pilcher's study based on 2010 data shows the continuing popularity of Mexican food in the Southwest and the West, followed by upper Midwestern cities such as Chicago, and finally the cities of the eastern seaboard. By his estimate there were about forty thousand Mexican restaurants in the United States by the year 2010, which is remarkably similar to the estimate of Chinese restaurants, all out of a national total of 579,102 restaurants.[70] We are just beginning to record the current material transformation of Latin American food reflected in the work of Meredith Abarca's *Voices in the Kitchen,* Zilkia Janer's *Latino Food Culture,* and Jeffrey Pilcher's *Planet Taco.*[71]

Yet, "one point of commonality between Mexican and U.S. versions of the *nueva cocina* has been the marginality of Mexican Americans and indigenous Mexicans" to the newly consecrated haute cuisine and related professionalizing moves.[72] Notwithstanding the popularity of the food, very few Mexican restaurants can command the price and prestige associated with Western European cuisines such as French, Italian, and Spanish, or Asian ones such as Japanese, revealing a deep-seated and insidious relationship between taste and domination.[73] The rise in prestige of Italian regional cooking since the 1980s adds another layer to that ethno-racial argument, which underlines at least two interesting peculiarities of Italian food in the eyes of American taste-makers.

WHITE BUT NOT QUITE

As Paul Freedman shows in his detailed study of the menus of elite restaurants, versions of macaroni and cheese (such as "macaroni au gratin" and "macaroni au Parmesan") were the most common elite restaurant dish in the middle of the nineteenth century, followed by escalloped oysters, baked beans and pork, oyster patties à la béchamel, and fricassee of chicken.[74] Thomas Jefferson had already popularized macaroni and cheese at the end of the eighteenth century. From that high perch in prestige, when northern Italian regional foods were seen as analogues to the Grand Tour, Italian food would be dislodged by the arrival between 1880 and 1924 of new southern Italian immigrants who were numerous and mostly poor, hence derided by the taste-making elite. That disdain spread downward. An Irish woman conceded that although she had no prejudices against her Italian neighbors, the smell of garlic made proximity difficult.[75] Italian Harlem carried the stench of poverty for middle-class visitors.[76] Northern Italians had already lent a hand in racially denigrating the diet of their southern compatriots. In one of the earliest references to the Sicilian pizza, Carlo Lorenzini (pen name Collodi), the Tuscan author of *Pinocchio,* wrote in 1886 that "the blackened aspect of the toasted crust, the whitish sheen of garlic and anchovy, the greenish-yellow tint of the oil and fried herbs, and those red bits of tomato here and there give pizza the appearance of complicated filth that matches the dirt of the vendor."[77] The reputation of Italian food recovered a little in the 1930s with the furious ascent of Italians into white racism as they sought to distance themselves from Blacks and Puerto Ricans in East Harlem, with their rhetorical embrace of *la famiglia* to stem the tide of imagined normlessness among underemployed colored households.[78] But that kind of rhetoric did not vaunt them into the elite; it just kept them treading water above the color line.

Nothing devalues a cuisine more than proximity to subordinate others. That explains not only the rise, fall, and rise again of Italian cuisine in America, but also the difficulty that Chinese, Mexican, and Soul food have faced in breaking away, in white American eyes, from the contamination effect of low-class association. Poor, mobile people are rarely accorded cultural capital. The circulation of taste through the hierarchical social architecture can sometimes allow for the creation of a subcultural niche for the best taco, dim-sum, or fried chicken but can rarely assure a position in elite food cultures. It is also a matter of timing. In twenty years from now Chinese food may be able to climb in American estimation but that depends on a lot, including the continuing economic rise of China and the decline in the flow of poor Chinese immigrants into the United States. To take a prior example, the prestige of Italian food could fully recover only by the 1980s, after the bulge of poor immigrants had dissipated over three generations, and expensive Italian restaurants and high-end chefs positioned themselves rhetorically against what they disdainfully identified as Italian-American, checkered-tablecloth, red-sauce institutions.[79]

Setting his sights on that transformation, Simone Cinotto demonstrates how race was the single most important factor in the consecration of Italian tastes in America.[80] With detailed evidence, Cinotto bleeds the story of the self-congratulation of an upwardly mobile group. And he does that by taking a scalpel to the Napa Valley Italian American wine industry, which Italians are credited with having almost single-handedly transformed "from a reserve of immigrant groups and urban Europhile elites into a mass national market." In the process he illustrates how the work of David Roediger, Matthew Frye Jacobson, and Michael Omni and Howard Winant can be deployed with empirical and conceptual subtlety to explain both the centrality of the wages of whiteness in the story of Italian winemaking, and the apparently contradictory power of the margins to explain the remarkable successes of Piedmontese wine-makers.[81] Just as the Chinese laundryman or cook did not learn his trade in China to then specialize in cooking and cleaning in California, the successes of Italian wine-makers had very little to do with the so-called Mediterranean ecology of California. Here Cinotto deals a devastating blow to the historiographical and popular claims about the successful transplantation of Old World culture and practical expertise to the New World. That sentimental comparison, he shows, is the product of a fallacious touristic gaze that hides the labor of Asian, Latino, and poor Italian coethnics in the wholesale transformation of the soil, water, hills, and valleys that made Napa's topography fit for the vine.

Yet these Piedmontese entrepreneurs were great innovators in terms of research, product development, advertising, marketing, and packaging precisely because they had very little baggage in terms of Old World traditions. From the giant size of their storage tanks, which allowed them to bear the fluctuations of the market better, electrically powered grape-pressing, portable kerosene heaters to ward off nighttime frost, the use of sulfur dioxide to counter the effects of yeasts and stabilize the wine, to industrial refrigeration, they understandably led the market. Here Cinotto breaks down another myth—of the tradition-bound Italian. What is even more counterintuitive is how he shows that apparently negative developments such as the First World War and Prohibition were turned to the advantage of the Italian wine-makers of California. His argument nicely illustrates the play of structure and contingency, race and ethnicity, culture and subculture, in the making of a self-conscious American food culture with complex routes of consolidation. In *The Italian American Table* Cinotto brings us back to Manhattan, where I began this essay. Instead of the tenements of 97 Orchard Street he takes us to East Harlem of the 1930s, where Italians were beginning to forge a gustatory identity in the crucible of race and ethnicity, setting the table for becoming white so as to relish its privileges of inclusion and exclusion.

From agricultural production, to home and restaurant cooking, immigrants have been central to the American food system in the nineteenth and twentieth centuries. Immigrants have been essential to the making of American national cuisine and to the populating of ethnic neighborhoods. A peculiar intimacy and yet polarization between the native and the ethnic has always shaped public cultures of eating and cooking in the United States. Race is embroiled in the story of American food and ethno-racial subordination drives much of the ubiquity but invisibility of the tasting and toiling ethnic subject. In the story of food that binds together the experience of home cooking and traveling cuisines, circulation matters as much as place.

NOTES

This chapter has improved substantially under criticism and with help from two anonymous reviewers, Paul Freedman, Kate Marshall, Stephanie Jolly, Liza Jennifer Howard, Esther Trakinski, and Emilie Josephine Berner. Errors of language and conception that persist are wholly mine.

1. Fernand Braudel, *The Mediterranean and the Mediterranean World in the Age of Philip II*, vols. 1 and 2 (Berkeley: University of California Press, 1949, 1996). See the concept's further development in Iain Chambers, *Mediterranean Crossings: The Politics of an Interrupted Modernity* (Duke: Duke University Press, 2008); Sanjay Subrahmanyan, *From Tagus to the Ganges: Explorations in Connected Histories* (New York: Oxford University Press, 2011); Sunil Amrith, *Crossing the Bay of Bengal: Furies of Nature and the Fortune of Migrants* (Cambridge, MA: Harvard University Press, 2013); Willem van Schendel, *The Bengal Borderland: Beyond State and Nation in South Asia* (London: Anthem Press, 2004); Gloria Anzaldúa, *Borderlands/La Frontera: The New Mestiza* (New York: Aunt Lute Books, 1987); Achille Mbembe, "At the Edge of the World: Boundaries, Territoriality and Sovereignty in Africa," trans. Steven Randall, *Public Culture* 12, no. 1 (2000): 259–84.

2. Rachel Donnadi, "A Walled City in Tuscany Clings to Its Ancient Menu," *New York Times*, March 12, 2009. Andrew Higgins, "Right Wing's Surge in Europe Has the Establishment Rattled," *New York Times*, November 9, 2013.

3. It is estimated that in 2013, remittances by labor migrants had an impact on global food security three times greater than that of official development assistance, which compels us to develop a more astute cultural politics of immigrant habitation. Food and Agriculture Organization, *The State of Food Insecurity in the World*, (Rome: FAO, 2013), www.fao.org/docrep/018/i3458e/i3458e.pdf, accessed November 11, 2013.

4. See Richard Wilk, *Home-Cooking in the Global Village: Caribbean Food from Buccaneers to Ecotourists* (London: Berg, 2006); Igor Cusack, "African Cuisines: Recipes for Nation Building?" *Journal of African Cultural Studies* 13, no. 2 (December 2000); Arjun Appadurai, "How to Make a National Cuisine: Cookbooks in Contemporary India," *Comparative Studies in Society and History* 30, no. 1 (January 1988): 3–24; Katarzyna J. Cwiertka, *Modern Japanese Cuisine: Food, Power and National Identity* (London: Reaktion Books, 2006).

5. Sidney Mintz, "Eating America," in *Food in the USA: A Reader*, ed. C. Counihan, 23–34 (New York: Routledge, 2002). Also see Michaela DeSoucey,

"Gastronationalism: Food Traditions and Authenticity Politics in the European Union," *American Sociological Review* 75, no. 3 (2010): 432–55.

6. Braudel, *The Mediterranean and the Mediterranean World*. See the concept's further development in Chambers, *Mediterranean Crossings*.

7. See for instance Subrahmanyan, *From Tagus to the Ganges*; Sugata Bose, *A Hundred Horizons: The Indian Ocean In The Age Of Global Empire* (Cambridge, MA: Harvard University Press, 2006); Thomas R. Metcalf, *Imperial Connections: India in the Indian Ocean Arena, 1860–1920* (Berkeley: University of California Press, 2007); Amrith, *Crossing the Bay of Bengal*.

8. Iain Walker, "Hadramis, Shimalis and Muwalladin: Negotiating Cosmopolitan Identities between the Swahili Coast and Southern Yemen," *Journal of Eastern African Studies* 2, no. 1 (Jan 2008): 54.

9. On the limits of that problematique see Maggie Gray, *Labor and the Locavore: The Making of a Comprehensive Food Ethic* (Berkeley: University of California Press, 2013).

10. E.P. Thompson, *The Making of the English Working Class* (New York: Vintage, 1966). See Lucy Lethbridge, *Servants: A Downstairs History of Britain from the Nineteenth Century to Modern Times* (New York: W.W. Norton, 2013).

11. Although he has little to say about immigrants, for a succinct and well articulated delineation of the American food movement see Michael Pollan, "The Food Movement Rising," *The New York Review of Books* (10 June 2010): www.nybooks.com/articles/archives/2010/jun/10/food-movement-rising, accessed October 15, 2013. See also Saru Jayaraman, *Behind the Kitchen Door* (Ithaca: Cornell University Press, 2013).

12. For two recent introductions to historical documents, processes of documentation, and historiography see Ken Albala, *The Food History Reader: Primary Sources* (London: Berg, 2013); Jeffrey Pilcher, ed., *Food History: Critical and Primary Sources* (London: Berg, 2014).

13. Occupational categories date back to the 1850 census. Cooks were first identified as a separate occupation in the detailed tables of the 1910 census and numbered 117,004. They were listed as a separate public occupation, distinct from domestic servants, only by the 1940 census, as "Cooks, except private family" (276,646). Chefs did not enter the occupational nomenclature until the 1980 census.

14. Stephen Ruggles, J.T. Alexander, K. Genadek, R. Goeken, M.B. Schroeder, and M. Sobek, *Integrated Public Use Microdata Series: Version 3.0, Machine-readable Database* (Minneapolis: Minnesota Population Center, 2004). Downloaded and processed by Sierra Burnett-Clark.

15. Jane Ziegelman, *97 Orchard: An Edible History of Five Immigrant Families in One New York Tenement* (New York: Harper Collins 2010).

16. Ziegelman, *97 Orchard*, 7.

17. Junius Henri Browne, *The Great Metropolis* (Hartford: The American Publishing Company, 1869); Thomas F. De Voe, *The Market Assistant* (New York: Hurd & Houghton, 1867).

18. City of New York, *Report of the Mayor's Pushcart Commission* (New York: City of New York, 1906).

19. Louise B. More, *Wage-Earner's Budget* (New York: Holt, 1907).

20. Ziegelman, *97 Orchard,* 27.

21. Ziegelman, *97 Orchard,* 55.

22. Harvey Levenstein, *Revolution at the Table* (Berkeley: University of California Press, 1988, repr. 2003).

23. Levenstein, *Revolution at the Table,* 3.

24. Levenstein, *Revolution at the Table,* 4.

25. Levenstein, *Revolution at the Table,* 100–1.

26. Levenstein, *Revolution at the Table,* 103.

27. Levenstein, *Revolution at the Table,* 103–4.

28. Donna Gabaccia, *We Are What We Eat: Ethnic Food and the Making of Americans* (Cambridge, MA: Harvard University Press, 1998).

29. Gabaccia, *We Are What We Eat,* 35.

30. Gabaccia, *We Are What We Eat,* 81.

31. Hasia Diner, *Hungering for America: Italian, Irish and Jewish Foodways in the Age of Migration* (Cambridge, MA: Harvard University Press 2001).

32. Diner, *Hungering for America,* 48.

33. Diner, *Hungering for America,* 56.

34. Diner, *Hungering for America,* 53.

35. Diner, *Hungering for America,* 180.

36. Marcus Ravage, *An American in the Making* (New York: Harper and Brothers, 1917), 75–76.

37. Angelo Pellegrini, "An Italian Odyssey: From Famine to Feast," in *American Cooking: The Melting Pot,* eds., James P. Shenton, Dale Brown, Angelo M. Pellegrini, Israel Shenker, and Peter Wood, 27–47 (New York: Time-Life Books, 1971).

38. Niccola de Quattrociocchi, *Love and Dishes* (Indianapolis: Bobba-Merrill, 1950), 30.

39. Diner, *Hungering for America,* 60.

40. Diner, *Hungering for America,* 81.

41. Diner, *Hungering for America,* 26.

42. Krishnendu Ray, *The Migrant's Table: Meals and Memories in Bengali-American Households* (Philadelphia: Temple University Press, 2004), 103–8.

43. Jennifer 8. Lee, *The Fortune Cookie Chronicles: Adventures in the World of Chinese Food* (New York: Ten Press, 2009), 9.

44. To point to the two most cited references here: George Ritzer, *The McDonaldization of Society* (Thousand Oaks, CA: Pine Forge Press, 1996); James L. Watson, ed., *Golden Arches East: McDonald's in East Asia* (Stanford, CA: Stanford University Press, 1997).

45. Andrew Coe, *Chop Suey: A Cultural History of Chinese Food in the United States* (Oxford: Oxford University Press 2009); Lee, *Fortune Cookie Chronicles*; Lily Cho, *Eating Chinese: Culture on the Menu in Small Town Canada* (Toronto: University of Toronto Press, 2010);

46. Lee, *Fortune Cookie Chronicles.*

47. Gaye Tuchman and Harry G. Levine, "New York Jews and Chinese Food: The Social Construction of an Ethnic Pattern," *Journal of Contemporary Ethnography* 22, no. 3 (October 1993): 382–407; S. Lu and Gary A. Fine, "The

Presentation of Ethnic Authenticity: Chinese Food as a Social Accomplishment," *Sociological Quarterly* 36, no. 3 (Summer 1995): 535–53; Lisa Hsia, "Eating the Exotic: The Growing Acceptability of Chinese Cuisine in San Francisco, 1848–1915," *Clio Scroll* 5, no. 1 (Fall 2003): 5–30. For other interesting writings on Chinese-American food-work see Louis Chu, "The Chinese Restaurants in New York City," (master's thesis, New York University, 1939); and Netta Davis, "To Serve the 'Other': Chinese-American Immigrants in the Restaurant Business," *Journal for the Study of Food and Society* 6, no. 1 (Winter 2002): 70–81.

48. Lee, *Fortune Cookie Chronicles,* 22–23.

49. Lee, *Fortune Cookie Chronicles,* 34, 45, 57.

50. Lee, *Fortune Cookie Chronicles,* 272.

51. Cho, *Eating Chinese,* 6.

52. Cho, *Eating Chinese,* 161.

53. Cho, *Eating Chinese,* 71.

54. Cho, *Eating Chinese,* 158.

55. For a cruder recent instance see Patrice Wilson and Alison Gold's embedded video here: www.thedailybeast.com/articles/2013/10/15/the-most-offensive-lyrics-and-wtf-moments-from-chinese-food.html.

56. Cho, *Eating Chinese,* 101, 103.

57. Cho, *Eating Chinese,* 108.

58. Zilkia Janer, *Latino Food Culture* (Westport, CT: Greenwood Press, 2008), 1.

59. Janer, *Latino Food Culture,* 9.

60. Camille Begin, "'The Slap Slap Motion of the Tortilla': Taste and Race in the American Southwest in the New Deal Era" (paper presented at the American Historical Association Meeting, January 2012).

61. Janer, *Latino Food Culture,* 9.

62. Begin, "The Slap Slap Motion of the Tortilla."

63. Begin, "The Slap Slap Motion of the Tortilla."

64. See Janer, *Latino Food Culture,* 102, 142.

65. Janer, *Latino Food Culture;* Jeffrey Pilcher, *Planet Taco: A Global History of Mexican Food* (New York: Oxford University Press, 2012); Sharon Zukin, *Naked City: The Death and Life of Authentic Spaces* (New York: Oxford University Press, 2010).

66. Scarlett Lindeman, "Real Tamales: Presentations and Authenticities in New York City" (unpublished paper, 2013).

67. Lindeman, "Real Tamales."

68. Pilcher, *Planet Taco,* 179.

69. Wilbur Zelinsky, "The Roving Palate: North America's Ethnic Restaurant Cuisines," *Geoforum* 16, no. 1 (1985): 51–72.

70. Jeffrey Pilcher, personal communication, October 14, 2012.

71. Meredith Abarca, *Voices in the Kitchen: Views of Food and the World from Working-Class Mexican and Mexican American Women* (College Station: Texas A&M University Press, 2006); Amy Bentley, "From Culinary Other to Mainstream America," in *Culinary Tourism,* ed. Lucy Long, 209–25 (Lexington: University Press of Kentucky, 2004).

72. Pilcher, *Planet Taco,* 176.

73. Krishnendu Ray, "Ethnic Succession and the New American Restaurant Cuisine," in *The Restaurants Book: Ethnographies of Where we Eat,* eds., David Beriss and David Sutton (Oxford: Berg, 2007): 97–114; Zilkia Janer, "The Geopolitics of Culinary Knowledge," *Seminar* 566 (October 2006), www.india-seminar.com/2006/566.htm, accessed on October 12, 2012.

74. Paul Freedman, "American Restaurants and Cuisine in the Mid-Nineteenth Century," *The New England Quarterly* 84, no. 1 (March 2011): 5–59. For a comprehensive and comparative look at menus over the centuries, see the extraordinary work of Janet Clarkson, *Menus from History: Historical Menus and Recipes for Every Day of the Year,* 2 vols. (Santa Barbara: ABC-Clio, 2009).

75. Simone Cinotto, *The Italian American Table: Food, Family and Community in New York City* (Urbana-Champagne: University of Illinois Press, 2013), 85.

76. Cinotto, *The Italian American Table,* 94.

77. Cited in Alberto Capatti and Massimo Montanari, *Italian Cuisine: A Cultural History* (New York: Columbia University Press, 2003), 27.

78. See Cinotto, *The Italian American Table,* 76–86. Also see Jennifer Guglielmo and Salvatore Salemo, eds., *Are Italians White? How Race Is Made in America* (New York: Routledge, 2003).

79. Vanina Leschziner, *Recipes for Success: Elite Chefs, Restaurateurs, and Culinary Styles in New York and San Francisco* (manuscript form of Ph.D. dissertation, University of Toronto, 2012).

80. Simone Cinotto, *Soft Soil, Black Grapes: The Birth of Italian Wine-Making in California* (New York: New York University Press, 2012).

81. Matthew Frye Jacobson, *Whiteness of a Different Color: European Immigrants and the Alchemy of Race* (Cambridge, MA: Harvard University Press, 1999); Michael Omni and Howard Winant, *Racial Formation in the United States: From the 1960s to the 1990s* (New York: Routledge, 1994); David Roediger, *The Wages of Whiteness: Race and the Making of the American Working Class* (New York: Verso, 2007).

PART TWO

Cuisine

CHAPTER 11

The French Invention of Modern Cuisine

PRISCILLA PARKHURST FERGUSON

Assigning beginnings always provokes debate, and never more so than with cultural practices and products. For strict constructionists it makes little sense to talk about the "invention" of any cultural phenomenon, much less one as complex as French cuisine. At the mere suggestion of a definitive origin, any historian worth the salt on the table will come up with a precedent or at the very least an antecedent to challenge any starting point.

Yet invention is a concept that, apparently, we cannot do without. The more significant the product, the more ardently we look for origins. Such is the case with French cuisine. In this instance, invention fits the bill. No other term expresses so well the consciousness of standing apart. No other term conveys the singular place of France in the Western food world. The customs and dishes that came to constitute French cuisine did more than innovate piecemeal: French chefs did not merely add a recipe here or a technique there. This cuisine counts as a true invention because it did more than improve on current culinary methods. French cuisine altered the way people prepared and consumed food. It changed the way people thought about and did food and not just in France.[1] French cuisine no longer governs the food world as it once did. Even so, whether praised or disparaged, imitated or rejected, it has made modern cuisine in its own image.

FRENCHNESS

From the mid-seventeenth century onward, foreigners no less than the French themselves recognized certain culinary products and rituals as different, as distinctive, and as distinctly French. That recognition, and the emulation that it sparked, made French cuisine a model for the way food was "done" far beyond the borders of France. Norbert Elias famously argued that the very idea of "civilization" expressed the "self-consciousness of the West." In much the same way, French cuisine represents the culinary consciousness of the West. More importantly for the development of sophisticated cuisines in the West, and to draw on both usages of the French word *conscience,* French cuisine also acted as a culinary conscience, rooted in a firm sense of what is right and what is wrong, what is proper and what is not, what is in good taste and what is not.

Culinary conquest was a striking feature of an emergent national consciousness. In Ancien Régime France, cuisine joined other vehicles of French glory—literature, language, music, fashion, architecture and painting. The "soft" power of culture built on the military and political power of the state even as that power, in turn, made the most of the cultural products that carried Frenchness across Europe. "Frenchness" was a positive virtue. Ever mindful of that Frenchness, chefs saw themselves as part of what the French themselves would later identify (in the different context of colonialism) as their "civilizing mission" and what Elias called the "civilizing process" of the West. "French civilization," as Elias maintains, served at once as an ideal to which everyone should aspire and an indicator of what the French had already achieved.[2]

Chefs in their kitchens were well aware of their charge as emissaries of France. The cookbooks published in ever increasing numbers beginning in the mid-seventeenth century made much of "Frenchness." François Pierre La Varenne's *Le Cuisinier françois (The French Chef)* and Nicolas de Bonnefons's *Le Jardinier françois (The French Gardener)* in 1651 were followed shortly by *Le Pastissier françois (The French Pastry Maker)* in 1653, with La Varenne's *Le Confiturier françois (The French Jelly Maker)* not far behind in 1660.[3]

Much of this conviction of superiority had to do with a conviction that cuisine had come a long way from the very different, "primitive" culinary worlds of days gone by. Cooking had indeed evolved considerably from heavily spiced medieval fare, with its strong flavors and elaborate sauces. Sauces were now simpler, prepared close to serving rather than long in advance. Some of these were not so far from those that we rely on today—*sauce mayonnaise* after all first turns up in the seventeenth century. Fresh produce figured prominently among culinary desirables—new peas were all the rage at court for a time. The culinary avant-garde of the seventeenth and eighteenth centuries made much of "natural" flavors, as would forward-looking chefs in the nineteenth century and beyond, however much the definition of "natural" varied over time and occasion.

Three recipes reveal just how much cooking had actually changed.[4] The strong tastes and spices characteristic of medieval cuisine are evident in the instructions for the popular *sauce cameline* given in the 1393 *Le Ménagier de Paris (The Parisian Household Manager)*: grind together ginger, cinnamon, saffron, nutmeg; add toasted white bread crumbs soaked in cold water and mashed; and boil (in the winter but not in the summer). After adding dark (that is, cane) sugar, serve the sauce with "a bit" more ground ginger and an "abundance" of cinnamon, covered with an "abundance" of breadcrumbs soaked in vinegar.

By contrast, the seventeenth century found less pungent flavors more to its taste. Herbs largely took over from spices. Although recipes might still call for ingredients of medieval cooking such as verjuice (an acidic juice made with sour fruit and sometimes with spices), fresh ingredients were in vogue (making reliable sources of supply all the more crucial). Two butter sauces for fresh salmon from a 1674 source reveal an emphasis on intensity of flavor and a corresponding deemphasis on spices. The white sauce calls for fresh butter, verjuice, lemon, orange, pepper, and fine salt beaten with a single crushed anchovy, a spoonful of thickener (possibly a flour roux) or, "if there is any," shrimp reduction. The more assertive version browns fresh butter, adds minced parsley, two or three anchovies prepared with "a little" fish bouillon or purée (without herbs), thickener, capers, salt, spices, a spoonful of verjuice, and half spoonful of vinegar. The sauce is to be beaten until smooth and thick and served hot.

Eighteenth-century diners consumed oysters in great quantities, and truffles were almost as popular. What more stupendously rich, flavorful sauce than these two together with a good bit of fresh butter to intensify the taste? A 1742 cookbook instructs the cook to peel and slice "beautiful truffles," half of which should be mixed with parsley, chives, shallots, salt, and pepper, then blended with butter. After layering a casserole with butter, the truffle slices, more butter, blanched oysters, and a bit of oil, the cook should let the covered casserole "sweat" for a quarter of an hour. After removing the truffles and the oysters, the rest is deglazed with a half glass of Champagne, "a bit" of highly concentrated (*quintessence*) stock, and some light veal stock. The final product should be brought to a boil, degreased, and finished with lemon juice. Luxurious, rich, certainly. Then again "you can serve [it] on anything you want" and "even serve it with croutons on its own" between regular courses (as an *entremets*).

New preparations, however natural, could not stand on their own. It was not enough to present recipes. It was necessary to promote them. Early modern French cookbook authors staked claims for their own work and for French cuisine as a whole.[5] It is striking, though not altogether surprising given the competition, how contentious and aggressive so many introductions and prefaces to these cookbooks turn out to be. In *Les Délices de la campagne (The Delights of the Countryside)* (1654) Nicolas de Bonnefons enjoined his readers to leave "depraved ragouts" to foreigners, who "never enjoy good fare except when they have cooks from France."[6] The exceptionally polemical preface to *L'Art de bien traiter (The Art of Catering)* (1674) by the unknown L.S.R. severely criticizes La Varenne for failing to distinguish between the delicate preparations suitable to France and the "villainies" (*gueuseries*) tolerated by other, benighted countries. Foreign dishes had no place in "a purified climate such as ours, where propriety, delicacy, and good taste are the object and the substance of our most solid enthusiasms."[7] The most strident case for French culinary superiority comes from François Massialot, in the preface to his 1691 cookbook, *Le Cuisinier roïal et bourgeois (The Royal and Bourgeois Chef)*. In a seamless move from Europe to France and striking a theme that will have a long life, Massialot stresses the capacity of French cuisine to transform what it takes from elsewhere into something else—something properly French. The superiority of French cuisine goes unquestioned: "Only in Europe prevail the sense of what is *proper, good taste, and flair* in preparing the foods found there; only there . . . is justice done to the marvelous gifts provided by the bounty of other climates; and only there, and *especially in France*, can one take pride in *excelling over all other nations in these matters*, as we do in manners and in a thousand other ways already familiar to us [emphases added]."[8]

The elites of seventeenth- and eighteenth-century Europe accorded unrivaled prestige to all things French, from the language and literature to the cuisine. In a 1784 prize-winning essay for a contest established by the Berlin Academy, the man of letters Antoine de Rivarol could confidently proclaim in his *Discours sur l'universalité de la langue française (Discourse on the Universality of the French Language)* that "what is not clear is not French." Like civilization itself, clarity is at once a state of perfection attained only by French and the goal for every language: "What is not clear *is still* English, Italian, Greek, or Latin [emphases added'."[9] It is indicative of French cultural hegemony that it was the Berlin Academy—not the French Academy—that set up the competition. Moreover, the Academy's questions were not whether the French language was universal but how it got to be so—and whether it deserved that privilege, or was likely to retain it.

It is not so very big a leap to the conviction of the superiority of French cuisine. A culinary rewriting of Rivarol's claim might claim that "what is not in good taste is not French." Still, like the Berlin Academy, we want to know how and why this state of affairs came to exist. So we ask, in our turn, How did French cuisine achieve its authority? Why did it deserve the privilege? In the hectic, often chaotic food world of the twenty-first century, will it retain its ascendancy?

What, then, *is* French cuisine?

SPECTACLE

Fascinated by the markers of modern social life, over a century ago the sociologist Georg Simmel pointed out the paradoxical situation whereby the most general social behavior, the activity in which every human being absolutely must engage—eating—gives rise to the most extensive and elaborate systems of social distinction.[10] Eating rituals across many cultures attest to differentiation by dining and the importance of the public manifestation of status. From the high stakes banquets in the Book of Esther to Roman orgies to great medieval extravaganzas, spectacular dining put social power on display. Even though ostentatious dining is by no means modern, spectacle nonetheless provides a key to understanding French cuisine and its impact well beyond the French court, where it was applied with the greatest determination.

More was at stake in the public aspects of dining than showing off individual status. Status determined dining; "Frenchness" demanded display. Like other consumption goods, elite foods and foodways affirmed a set of power relations even as they imposed them. Royal dining put social stratification on display. The king typically sat apart on a raised dais, sometimes with the royal family, sometimes alone. The sumptuous banquets at the seventeenth-century French court bore witness to the power of the king. At the same time, by making power relations visible, conspicuous culinary consumption helped bring them into existence. At Versailles the culinary performance joined with the great fountains and the magnificent gardens, indeed the chateau itself, as representations of the monarch and his power.

The imperatives of public consumption governed the presentation of food. Looking came before eating. Before food could be consumed, the table had to be admired. Increasingly elaborate table settings brought aesthetic considerations ever more insistently into the culinary equation. The silverware and porcelain (an important French industry since the late seventeenth century), the candles and the crystal quite literally turned dining into a brilliant parade. There was no element that did not play its part in setting the splendid scene, from intricately folded napkins to the French sequence of service—*service à la française*—that set all the many dishes for each course on the banquet table at the same time. Display dominated, and never more so than when the centerpiece was one of the outsized sugar sculptures or architectural pastry constructions that the nineteenth century called *pièces montées*.[11]

All elements of the culinary presentation favored a collective aesthetic experience, which can be shared, over the individual act of consumption, which remains idiosyncratic. The primacy of spectacle made looking essential. The aesthetics of display trumped the taste of the food. Given the logistics of service, especially with the considerable distances that typically separated the kitchen from the dining space, the hot food that modern diners routinely expect could not, and did not, figure among dining priorities. Collective appreciation won out over, and likely determined, individual preferences.

INSTITUTIONALIZATION, PROFESSIONALIZATION, CODIFICATION

The nineteenth century configured the food world that we recognize today. Instead of the grandiose spectacularity of the Ancien Régime, whose *grande cuisine* served a circumscribed elite, the nineteenth-century restaurant multiplied publics and cuisines to suit them. It also, necessarily, set up institutions to reach those publics. Fine, or what we now call upscale, dining moved into the public sphere. No longer guests selected by a host, modern diners became customers in a public eating establishment. Nineteenth-century Paris made the restaurant. Besides a fixed menu, selection of dishes, and open access, other distinctly modern features of the restaurant included extended hours, fixed prices, and individualized service. To be sure, restaurants—public eating establishments that leave the choice of dishes to the individual diner—were not new. Still, it was rampant urbanization—Paris doubled its population over the first half of the nineteenth century—that turned the restaurant of the late eighteenth century into the exemplary urban institution that it has largely remained.

In stark contrast to the overt exclusivity of Ancien Régime fine dining, the modern restaurant, in principle, welcomed all comers. Control over the meal passed from the host to the diner. Where a host defined the dinner through both the guests invited and the dishes served, the restaurant owner had to come up with dishes to attract diners. The now written menu allowed customers a say in their consumption.

Not only did the restaurant allow diners to select their meal, it required them to do so. Just as the menu laid out the offerings for individual diners to make their choices and create their own meal, the city laid out restaurants for the public at large. Choices ranged from the luxurious temples of gastronomy to neighborhood eateries that served an equally mobile but impecunious clientele. Lucien de Rubempré, Balzac's protagonist in *Lost Illusions* (1837), faces an exemplary dilemma. Newly arrived from the provinces and eager for a taste of Paris, off he goes to the elegant Véry's in the ultra-fashionable Palais-Royal. Aghast at having blown fifty francs—his whole budget for an entire month in the provinces—on a single meal, Lucien beats a hasty retreat across the Seine to Flicoteaux's, Place de la Sorbonne, celebrated among students for copious servings at a mere eighteen sous.[12]

Through the increased opportunities for work and for training that it provided, the restaurant drove the professionalization of cooking. Publication of cookbooks further expanded the opportunity structure. The expansion of the culinary field in the beginning of the nineteenth century coincided with as it profited markedly from increasing literacy (notably in urban settings), from technological advances such as roller presses and paper made of wood pulp, and from commercial innovations such as rental libraries. The publication of culinary works became an ever more important feature of the food world.

The profession of cook—with profession taken as socially organized expert knowledge—both depended on and encouraged the codification of cooking. As the great chef Marie-Antoine Carême pointed out in the preface to *Le Cuisinier parisien* (1828), the *maîtres d'hôtel* or stewards of great houses from the past wrote nothing down. In the absence of a written record, no one knew, really, how great they were. How could they? Oral tradition kept cooking in the kitchen.[13]

Carême early on grasped the significance of the written word for codifying, producing, and transmitting French cuisine. So convinced was he of the crucial importance of writing that he published his cookbooks himself. True, there were cookbooks before Carême, and he had competitors, especially the cookbooks that aimed at the rapidly expanding domestic market. But more than any other figure, Carême believed in the authority of writing. It alone would establish cooking as a profession. The greater the competition and the more numerous the competitors, the more crucial cookbooks and culinary writings became in establishing the whole profession.

Everything Carême undertook aimed to further the development of cooking as a profession: "I intend to use all means to accelerate the progress of our work by making them easier to execute."[14] He did not forget to thank the anonymous inventor of the pastry bag, was inordinately proud of his own technique to rid his ovens of bugs—1,215 of them—and bragged that his inventions alone had more than doubled the material available to pastry chefs.[15] His English translator is clear on both his success and the reasons for it: Carême "greatly enlarged the variety of *entrées* and *entremêts* previously practised," and his "clear & perspicuous details render them facile, not only to the Artist who has already an advance in his profession, but also to those whose knowledge of the higher code of the Kitchen has necessarily been limited."[16]

Carême's most important contribution to the professionalization of cooking came not from these relatively incidental innovations but from the culinary code in which they took their place. Invoking the "spirit of analysis of the nineteenth century," Carême constructed a true culinary system in which every recipe existed within a structure of interconnected parts.[17] There is, in his work, a logical culinary progression from one preparation to the next. Thus, his summa on French cuisine opens with a discussion of ordinary boiled beef, because its reduced stock supplies the essential ingredient for a vast range of preparations from soups to sauces. This foundational recipe sustains a series of bouillons, from chicken and turkey to partridge and wild rabbit. The next chapter considers consommés and fumets, lean (Lenten) bouillons, medicinal bouillons, court bouillons and marinades, that is, cooked and uncooked liquids used for poaching and marinating.

Beyond the codification of French cuisine and the professionalization of cooking, the restaurant altered consumption and redefined culinary aesthetics. Instead of a set meal determined in advance, the restaurant menu allowed customers to shape their own meals. Dining altered accordingly. Credited to the Russian ambassador to France early in the century, *service à la russe* turned the spotlight away from the host to the diner. Priorities shifted from the organization of space to the management of time. Replacing the elaborate *service à la française* where the many dishes of a single course were placed on the table all at once—making actual eating something of a catch-as-catch-can situation—*service à la russe* served dishes in sequence to the individual diner. The individualized service of single meals made hot food a real possibility. In this exemplary setting for individualized, sequential service, the restaurateur took over from the host, and guests became customers whose requirements governed the presentation and determined the timing of the meal.

In essence, the restaurant miniaturized the dining spectacle of the Ancien Régime. Small tables had no room for elaborate centerpieces or *pièces montées*. The Ancien Régime aesthetic of public display ceased to define fancy dining. As we would expect, with his roots in the Ancien Régime *grande cuisine*, Carême opposed *service à la russe* and disdained restaurants. (The financial constraints of a commercial establishment were incompatible with Carême's standards of culinary excellence.) "Our French service," he asserted in *Le Maître d'hôtel français* (1822), "is more elegant and more sumptuous. It is the model for culinary art . . . . Nothing is more imposing than the sight of a great table set out in the French service."[18] If the formal banquets that entranced Carême did not altogether disappear, dining extravaganzas remained exceptional. Sequential service became the rule. The restaurant, not the banquet, set the pattern for the fine dining of the future.

By the nineteenth century the French style of cooking had a wide international impact. French chefs had worked abroad in the Ancien Régime, but not on the scale of the nineteenth century when hotels across Europe serving an international clientele multiplied, creating sites for culinary training. Auguste Escoffier's organization of the professional kitchen into "brigades" at the end of the nineteenth century articulated the chain of command and further rationalized culinary production.

Most of all, the "fundamental principles of the science [of cooking], which we owe to Carême," as Escoffier recognized, drove French cuisine. This system had the great advantage of portability. Anyone could learn the principles, understand the rules, and work the culinary network. Escoffier boasted that his hotel kitchens had trained thousands of ambassadors, who took French culture all over the world.[19]

Had not Carême already decreed, in an update of claims from two centuries before, that "France is the only country for good food; foreigners are convinced of these truths"?[20]

CRITICISM

French culinary ascendancy has long relied on "food talk," that is, the many and varied discussions and discourses to which the preparation and consumption of food give rise. From procedures and techniques for achieving culinary excellence to declarations of belief in that excellence, food talk, most notably in its written form, spread the word and the work of French cuisine. Food talk has been around for millennia. The greatest food talker of all time is surely Athenaeus, a Greek living in Rome in the late second century C.E. whose multivolume *Deipnosophists (The Scholars at Dinner)* constitutes a compendium of ancient culinary culture as extraordinary as it is excessive. Better known were the depictions of Roman dining decadence. Petronius's depiction of an over-the-top orgy in *Satyricon* in the first century alternately haunted and enticed later civilizations. Confining ourselves to the French tradition, there's no avoiding Rabelais's iconic gluttonous giants, Gargantua and Pantagruel.[21]

Gastronomy is something else again. Countering a venerable tradition that coupled food talk of any sort with the exaggerations of comedy and satire, gastronomy signified refinement and restraint of both consumption and expression. The term emerged in the early nineteenth century to designate an increasingly salient social practice in a society that was ever more mobile, socially, geographically, and culinarily. The gastronome did not simply love food or crave food—*gourmand* or *gourmet* would have sufficed in that case—he (gastronomy was a masculine preserve) knew food. The gastronome was a connoisseur—quite the opposite of a glutton—and this connoisseur, like all committed scholars, communicated his knowledge along with his judgments.

The gastronome talked about food, wrote about it, and made his verdicts public. The postrevolutionary modern metropolis replaced the indiscriminate, insatiable glutton with the discerning gastronome, the guide to fine food that ordinary diners need and desire. Gastronomy is after all the theory or, better still, the law—*nomos*—of the stomach. The criticism and commentary that dominate the food world of the twenty-first century had their beginnings in nineteenth-century Paris where the sheer number of restaurants and purveyors made formal mechanisms of evaluation all but inevitable.

In other words, conditions were ripe for gastronomic journalism. In the annual *Almanach des gourmands* (1803–1812), A.-B.-L. Grimod de la Reynière delivered often acerbic and invariably critical judgments of restaurants, shops, and culinary customs more generally.[22] Other gastronomes turned analytical. In what soon became the bible of enlightened diners, the *Physiology of Taste* (1826) by Jean Anthelme Brillat-Savarin turned gastronomic analysis into a proto-sociological exercise.[23]

In short, nineteenth-century Paris was well on its way to the modern food world, many of its features recognizable today. In this as in so many other respects, the city was a crucible of modernity, "the capital of the nineteenth century," in Walter Benjamin's felicitous phrase, and one of the reasons was the prevalence of food talk. From the instrumental cookbook to journalistic commentary, talk about food entered the public sphere. Endowing the food world with formal mechanisms of judgment and turning ephemeral talk into the permanence of print, gastronomy turned food talk to social ends. To invoke Elias once more, gastronomy civilized appetite.

Journals, essays, and publications of every sort from novels to drama, gave form to a food world structured by intensifying competition between public eating establishments, by the professionalization of the chefs who defined those eating establishments, and, finally, by an ever-shifting, invariably choosy, often capricious, and certainly unpredictable dining public. These unstable conditions put the public at a disadvantage. Few individuals could be expected to know firsthand about the many restaurants and purveyors among which they had to choose. They needed guides, signposts, and evaluations to inform their decisions. The gastronome was just such a judge, a presumably disinterested authority who bridged the gap between producer and consumer.

Gastronomy brought the consumer into the culinary equation; discrimination in dining customs raised the individual to the higher plane of civilization. Brillat-Savarin did not mince words: "Animals fill themselves; people eat; intelligent people alone know how to eat." A twentieth-century disciple's update was even more emphatic about the connection between the French and (good) food: "Everywhere else, people eat; in France alone people know how to eat."[24]

IDEOLOGIES AND POLICIES

The culinary consciousness of Frenchness has had far-reaching effects. From support for research to protective tariffs and support for exports, modern French governments have made the excellence of French cuisine a matter of public policy. As Escoffier noted with satisfaction about his own training of chefs, "the art of cuisine is perhaps one of the most useful forms of diplomacy."[25]

That the state put itself in the position of culinary conscience also explains the initiatives of the French government to ensure the quality and the authenticity of both produce and personnel. Since the 1920s the AOCs, the *appellations d'origine contrôlées* or regulated names of origin, for wines and foods identify agricultural products, their sources, geographical origins, and mode of preparation. People get vetted as well as products. Again in the 1920s, the MOF, *meilleur ouvrier de France* or highly skilled French worker, competitions were set up to promote hand crafts, from carpentry to landscaping. Food preparation figured prominently in this landscape of closely monitored artisanal work.

During the interwar years competitive cooking realized a dream Carême had articulated over a century before. Culinary contests, he thought, would be good for French cuisine, no doubt having in mind the guilds or corporations of artisans (*corps de métiers*) that regulated so much of artisanal production from medieval times through the early modern period. To rise from apprentice to journeyman to master craftsman required the individual to undergo rigorous training and then to demonstrate competence as judged by acknowledged masters of the trade. Despite the abolition of guilds in 1791 and the consequent restructuring of workers' lives, this ideal of artisanal excellence remained in force. Today the MOF works within this same tradition that pits individuals less against other individuals than against an idea of excellence upheld by acknowledged authorities.[26]

TRANSFORMATION AND TRADITION

Culinary consciousness is a function of the *savoir faire* of the cook and the *savoir manger* of the consumer. Although spectacularity today no longer involves the magnificence of *service à la française*, there is great emphasis on the individual platings or presentations that showcase the dish and proclaim the chef's skill and imagination. The animated film *Ratatouille* (2007) dramatizes the added value of plating, namely how the dish is presented at table. Ratatouille is a familiar dish of tomatoes, onions, zucchini, and eggplant served like a stew with all the ingredients lumped together. In the film, the plating of Remy, the chef, turns this ordinary dish of everyday life into one worthy of a great chef and demanding customers. The taste is recognizable. In an update of the Proustian madeleine, one bite transports the critic back to his childhood when his mother served him this very dish. But it is the presentation that transports the dish to the higher reaches of haute cuisine.[27]

. . .

To return to the questions that opened this inquiry, will French cuisine preserve its dominance?

It will not, for in truth, it has not. In the international multiculinary food world of the twenty-first century no cuisine dominates without question. Once taken for granted, the principles, precepts, and procedures of what is now known as classical French cuisine have been questioned often and seriously. A half-century ago, the "haute-er" one got on the culinary hierarchy, the more likely one would find oneself in French territory. This is no longer the case in a food world where, to take one indicator out of many, the restaurants designated the "best in the world" turn up outside France. And if France has dominated the Bocuse d'Or competition since it began in 1987, the competition is increasingly stiff.[28] Whatever quibbles can be made over the significance of these and other potential indicators of excellence, it is clear that French cuisine today shares the spotlight on a stage where it once stood pretty much alone.

Yet talk of decline, decadence, much less demise is both excessive and premature. Even though French cuisine narrowly construed as a set of recipes and techniques must contend with ever more numerous competitors from Asia and the Americas, not to mention within Europe, the French culinary model remains a reference point. For what distinguishes this model is the compelling connection between cuisine and gastronomy, producer and consumer, cook and diner—a tie that every cuisine, every chef, every cook does well to emulate.

In November 2010 UNESCO officially recognized "the French gastronomic meal" as worthy of notice and protection as an "intangible cultural good." Along with Spanish flamenco, Mexican traditional cuisine, and Croatian gingerbread craft, the archetypal French meal, with its regulated conviviality and rules of order, joined the roster of worldwide cultural heritage manifestations. If the bid for recognition by UNESCO continues a long French tradition of claiming culinary superiority, the application for international acknowledgment also sends a signal that French culinary superiority can no longer be taken for granted—not even by the French.

Whatever the interpretation of this move, France has long made food and cuisine central to what it means to be French. The greater achievement is that France convinced so many of the rest of us that its model of cuisine and culture is central to civilization itself. French culinary nationalism shows up in the chefs who have trumpeted the virtues of French cuisine at home and abroad; it is illustrated in recipes that tout French connections and skills; it surfaces in governmental policies protecting French products and consumers; it comes out in the cooking competitions that focus on the French food world; and it turns up in films, foreign as well as French, that make the French model of conviviality more than French.[29] This manifest culinary destiny has to do with the way the French—in contrast to others, and particularly Americans—think and talk about food. These, then, are the many inventions of French cuisine, itself as much an ideal as a set of practices.

"Invention" may be off-base after all. Like every cultural good, French cuisine is the work of a long historical elaboration. Interpretation is inherently incomplete because cultural products are always in the process of becoming. The long view has the advantage of distance from the details. At the same time those details, "facts," and examples plunge us into the experience of that becoming. Every reader, every diner, must continually navigate the two.

Distance makes it clearer that when we talk about French culinary power we are not talking about a repertory of dishes, ingredients, and techniques, although that is how the term is usually taken. More accurately, French cuisine designates a distinctive mode of production, preparation, and consumption of food. "French cuisine" turns out to be shorthand for a way of thinking about and doing food that the French claimed as theirs. A skeptic might well wonder why those of us who are not culinary historians should care. The answer is that generations of French cooks, chefs, and consumers have made us care. They have worked doggedly, and with amazing success, to convince anyone with aspirations to the better things in life that cooking and eating *à la française* represent their best bet.

To have an idea how this cultural shift could occur, to understand the making and the reception of the French claims, and, finally, to grasp French culinary influence, context is everything. I have found three frames particularly useful in considering the long, slow construction of French cuisine: the social setting, which calls on political, ideological, and aesthetic movements; the meal understood as a social phenomenon; and cooking considered as an activity, an occupation and a profession.

Culinary explanations speak only indirectly to my purpose of tracing the emergence of a modern sensibility. The vast majority of the countless celebratory histories of French cuisine distract from the larger social context, fixated as they are on the particulars of recipes, ingredients, and banquets, anecdotes about chefs, and the munificence (or stinginess) of consumer-patrons. On the other hand, their often aggressive prefaces and presentations constitute a tremendous gauge of how food was thought about.

The most useful frames do not ignore these specifics of foods and individuals—far from it. Rather they put these details in the service of a larger argument. For the broadest social structural trends, I look to Elias, and to Mennell's culinary translation of his work, to lay the base for the mutability of cuisine and culinary customs.[30] Aron's pioneering study of nineteenth-century gastronomic culture is always a good place to start thinking about what makes French culinary culture so distinctive.[31] Subsequent work offers perceptive analyses of the shifts that modern institutions such as the restaurant brought for consumers as well as producers.[32]

For the meanings and functions of the meal there is no better place to begin than Simmel's provocative essay.[33] For the French conception of the meal as a crucible of conviviality, Brillat-Savarin is the work of reference.[34] There is considerable work on production and producers, notably Wheaton's pioneering culinary-cum-social history, Ferguson's reconstruction of French culinary identity, Rambourg's connection of culinary and gastronomic history with the increasing self-consciousness of practitioners, Takats's study of the contours of cooking as an occupation in eighteenth-century France, and Davis's examination of chefs' growing professional consciousness in Ancien Régime France.[35]

Any consideration of eating and cooking benefits from comparisons. Better, then, that they be explicit. Good places to start are collective works such as Flandrin and Montanari and Freedman.[36] Gigante places French and English food writers against each other, and Trubek analyzes the French influence on professional English cooking.[37]

Finally, not so much a frame as an enveloping perspective, there is food talk, that is, all the talk and writing about food, all the representations of food that make eating and cooking so much part of our lives. We do not simply eat, we talk about what we eat. In so doing we transform the material into the immaterial, the individual into the social. Thus the activity that unites us as consuming beings can also unite us as social beings—for a time at least. French culinary authority from the

seventeenth through most of the twentieth century, as well as its continued presence today, has a great deal to do with the talk that brings good
fellowship together with good food.

NOTES

1. "Innovations improve on existing ways (i.e., activities, conceptions, and purposes) of doing things, while inventions change the ways things are done. . . . the key to classifying something as an invention is the degree to which it rever-berates out to alter the interacting system of which it is a part." John. F. Padgett and Paul D. McLean, "Organizational Invention and Elite Transformation: The Birth of Partnership Systems in Renaissance Florence," *American Journal of Sociology* 111, no. 5 (March 2006): 1463–1568. Clearly, as I shall argue (after many others), the echoes of French cuisine did much to shape the larger food world.

2. Norbert Elias, "The History of Manners," *The Civilizing Process*, trans-lated by E. Jephcott (Cambridge: Blackwell, 1994), 1–256.

3. François Pierre de La Varenne, *Le Cuisinier françois*, eds. Jean-Louis Flan-drin, Philip Hyman, and Mary Hyman (Paris: Montalba, 1983); Nicolas de Bonnefons, *Le Jardinier françois* (Paris: 1651); *Le Pastissier françois* (Paris: Jean Gaillard, 1653); La Varenne, *Le Confiturier françois* (Paris: Jean Gaillard, 1660).

4. I take the sauces in the following three paragraphs from Patrick Ram-bourg, *Histoire de la cuisine et de la gastronomie françaises: Du moyen âge au XXe siècle* (Paris: Perrin, 2010), appendix 4, 364–65. Rambourg's sources are *Le Ménagier de Paris* (1393), L.S.R., *L'Art de bien traiter* (Paris, 1674), and François Marin, *Suite des Dons de Comus* (Paris, 1742). Barbara Ketcham Wheaton gives numerous recipes in the original French and in modern, usable English translation, with quantities specified. Wheaton, *Savoring the Past: The French Kitchen and Table from 1300 to 1789* (Philadelphia: University of Penn-sylvania Press, 1983).

5. The much vexed question of gender is part, but only part, of this story. In contrast to England, where Hannah Glasse's classic *The Art of Cookery* appeared in 1747, the first cookbook allegedly by a woman in France did not appear until 1795. Stephen Mennell makes the case for the masculinization of cooking in France: Mennell, *All Manners of Food: Eating and Taste in England and France from the Middle Ages to the Present* (Oxford: Basil Blackwell, 1985). Although Sean Takats argues for a more inclusive community of cooks, male and female, in eighteenth-century France, male chefs had the advantage because they took up the pen. Takats, *The Expert Cook in Enlightenment France* (Baltimore: Johns Hopkins University Press, 2011).

6. Bonnefons cited in Wheaton, *Savoring the Past*, 125.

7. L.S.R. in Gilles Laurendon and Laurence Laurendon, eds., *L'Art de la cuisine française au dix-septième siècle* (Paris: Payot & Rivages, 1995), 22–23.

8. François Massialot, *Le Cuisinier roïal et bourgeois* (Paris: Charles de Sercy, 1691), ii.

9. Antoine Rivarol, *De l'universalité de la langue française* (Paris: Cocheris, 1791), 40 (for both quotations).

10. Georg Simmel, "Sociology of the Meal," trans. Mark Ritter and David Frisby, in *Simmel on Culture: Selected Writings,* eds. David Frisby and Mike Featherstone (London: Sage, 1997), 130–35.

11. These confections now belong almost exclusively to the domain of desserts—with tiered cakes and chocolate monuments. In the nineteenth century the *pièce montée* could well be a main course, i.e., a savory dish rather than sweet.

12. Honoré de Balzac, *Illusions perdues,* in *La Comédie humaine,* 12 vols., ed. Pierre-George Castex (Paris: Gallimard: 1976–1981), 5: 271, 285, 287; on Flicoteaux, see 292, 294–96.

13. Antonin Carême, *Le Cuisinier parisien* (1828; repr. Lyon: Éditions Dioscor, 1986), 18n1. Born Marie-Antoine, Carême signed his works with the classically inflected Antonin.

14. Antonin Carême, *L'Art de la Cuisine française au dix-neuvième siècle* (Paris: Chez l'auteur, 1833), part 4, chap. 1, 288.

15. Antonin Carême, *Le Pâtissier royal parisien* (Paris, 1815), 2: 410–11.

16. William Hall, trans., *French Cookery: Comprising* L'art de la cuisine française, Le Pâtissier Royal, Le Cuisinier parisien (London: John Murray, 1836), 4–5.

17. Carême, *L'Art de la cuisine française,* t 1, lxvi.

18. Antonin Carême, *Le Maître d'hôtel français* (Paris: J. Renouard et Cⁱᵉ, 1842), 2: 151.

19. Auguste Escoffier, *Souvenirs inédits: Soixante-quinze ans au service de l'art culinaire* (Marseille: Éditions Jeanne Laffitte, 1985), 192–93.

20. Carême, *Le Cuisinier parisien,* 1, i; see also Carême, *L'Art,* 2, part 3, i.

21. Athenaeus, *The Deipnosophists of Athenaeus of Naucratis,* trans. C.B. Gulick (Cambridge: Harvard University Press, Loeb Classical Library, 1969); Petronius Arbiter, *The Satyricon* (Oxford: Clarendon Press, 1996); François Rabelais, *Gargantua and Pantagruel* (London: Penguin Books, 2006).

22. A.B.L. Grimod de la Reynière, *Almanach des Gourmands,* 8 vols (1803–1812, repr. Paris: Valmer, 1984).

23. Jean Anthelme Brillat-Savarin, *Physiologie du goût, ou méditations de gastronomie transcendante* [The Physiology of Taste, or, Meditations on Transcendental Gastronomy] (Paris, 1826), ed. and trans. M.F.K. Fisher (New York: Knopf, 2009).

24. Brillat-Savarin, *Physiologie du goût,* 11 (2ⁿᵈ aphorism); Marcel Rouff, *La Vie et la passion de Dodin-Bouffant, gourmet* (Paris: Stock, 1924), 3.

25. Escoffier, *Souvenirs,* 192.

26. Carême, *Le Pâtissier royal parisien,* 1: xii-xv. Americans will find no better introduction to the high-powered, extraordinarily stressful world of MOF competitions than the documentary film *The Kings of Pastry* (2010), directed by Chris Hegedus and D.A. Pennebaker.

27. *Ratatouille* (2007) is the most perceptive cinematic rendering of what eating and cooking mean for both the conviviality of dining and the creativity of cooking. That the film was made by Disney, the most American of production

companies, only emphasizes the authority of the French model in the modern food world.

28. For several years the annual contest for The World's Fifty Best Restaurants, produced by British magazine *Restaurant* and based on a poll of international chefs, restaurateurs, gourmands, and restaurant critics elected Ferran Adrià's El Bulli in Catalonia, Spain and René Redzepi's Noma in Copenhagen, Denmark. Both are avant garde and experimental. (El Bulli closed in 2011 to become a foundation for experimental cuisine.) On the Bocuse d'Or, see the extensive material at www.bocusedor.com/. Out of forty-two medals awarded between 1987 and 2013, France (10) is followed by Norway (8), Belgium (6), Sweden (5), and Denmark (4).

29. For a moving statement of the continued significance of the model for France, see the 2012 film, *Haute Cuisine (Les Saveurs du palais)*, directed by Christian Vincent.

30. Elias, "The History of Manners"; Mennell, *All Manners of Food.*

31. Jean-Paul Aron, *The Art of Eating in France: Manners and Menus in the Nineteenth Century,* trans. Nina Rootes (London: Owen, 1975).

32. Rebecca L. Spang, *The Invention of the Restaurant: Paris and Modern Gastronomic Culture* (Cambridge: Harvard University Press, 2001).

33. Simmel, "Sociology of the Meal."

34. Brillat-Savarin, *Physiologie du goût.*

35. Wheaton, *Savoring the Past.* Priscilla Parkhurst Ferguson, *Accounting for Taste: The Triumph of French Cuisine* (Chicago: University of Chicago Press, 2004). Rambourg, *Histoire de la cuisine.* Takats, *Expert Cook.* Jennifer J. Davis, *Defining Culinary Authority: The Transformation of Cooking in France* (Baton Rouge: Louisiana State University Press, 2013).

36. Jean-Louis Flandrin and Massimo Montanari, eds., *Food: A Culinary History from Antiquity to the Present,* trans. Clarissa Botsford, Arthur Goldhammer, Charles Lambert, Frances M. Lopez-Morillas, and Sylvia Stevens (New York: Columbia University Press, 1999). Paul Freedman, ed., *Food: The History of Taste* (Berkeley: University of California Press, 2007).

37. Denise Gigante, *Gusto: Essential Writings in Nineteenth-Century Gastronomy* (New York: Routledge, 2005). Amy B. Trubek, *Haute Cuisine: How the French Invented the Culinary Profession* (Philadelphia: University of Pennsylvania Press, 2000).

BIBLIOGRAPHY

Abramson, Julia. "Grimod's Debt to Mercier and the Emergence of Gastronomic Writing Reconsidered." *EMF: Studies in Early Modern France* 7 (2001): 141–62.

Aron, Jean-Paul. *The Art of Eating in France: Manners and Menus in the Nineteenth Century.* Translated by Nina Rootes. London: Owen, 1975.

Athenaeus of Naucratis. *The Deipnosophists of Athenaeus of Naucratis.* Translated by C.B. Gulick. 7 vols. Cambridge: Harvard University Press, 1969.

Brillat-Savarin, J.A. *Physiologie du goût, ou méditations de gastronomie transcendante* [The Physiology of Taste, or, Meditations on Transcendental Gastronomy]. Paris, 1826. Edited and translated by M.F.K. Fisher. New York: Knopf, 2009.

Davis, Jennifer J. *Defining Culinary Authority: The Transformation of Cooking in France*. Baton Rouge: Louisiana State University Press, 2013.

Elias, Norbert. "The History of Manners." *The Civilizing Process*, translated by E. Jephcott, 1–256. Cambridge: Blackwell, 1994.

Ferguson, Priscilla Parkhurst. "A Cultural Field in the Making: Gastronomy in Nineteenth-Century France." *American Journal of Sociology* 104, no. 3 (November 1998): 597–641.

———. *Accounting for Taste: The Triumph of French Cuisine*. Chicago: University of Chicago Press, 2004.

———. *Word of Mouth: What We Talk About When We Talk About Food*. Berkeley: University of California Press, 2014.

Flandrin, Jean-Louis, and Massimo Montanari, eds. *Food: A Culinary History from Antiquity to the Present*. Translated by Clarissa Botsford, Arthur Goldhammer, Charles Lambert, Frances M. Lopez-Morillas, and Sylvia Stevens. New York: Columbia University Press, 1999.

Freedman, Paul, ed. *Food: The History of Taste*. Berkeley: University of California Press, 2007.

Gigante, Denise. *Gusto: Essential Writings in Nineteenth-Century Gastronomy*. New York: Routledge, 2005.

Mennell, Stephen. *All Manners of Food: Eating and Taste in England and France from the Middle Ages to the Present*. Oxford: Basil Blackwell, 1985.

Ory, Pascal. *Le Discours gastronomique français des origines à nos jours*. Paris: Gallimard-Julliard, 1998.

Paul, Harry W. *Science, Vine and Wine in Modern France*. Cambridge: Cambridge University Press, 1996.

Pitte, Jean-Robert. *French Gastronomy: The History and Geography of a Passion*. New York: Columbia University Press, 2002.

Quellier, Florent. *Gourmandise: Histoire d'un péché capital*. Paris: Armand Colin, 2010.

Rambourg, Patrick. *Histoire de la cuisine et de la gastronomie françaises: Du moyen âge au XXe siècle*. Paris: Éditions Perrin, 2010.

Simmel, Georg. "Sociology of the Meal," translated by Mark Ritter and David Frisby. In *Simmel on Culture: Selected Writings*, edited by David Frisby and Mike Featherstone, 130–35. London: Sage, 1997.

Spang, Rebecca L. *The Invention of the Restaurant: Paris and Modern Gastronomic Culture*. Cambridge: Harvard University Press, 2001.

Takats, Sean. *The Expert Cook in Enlightenment France*. Baltimore: Johns Hopkins University Press, 2011.

Trubek, Amy B. *Haute Cuisine: How the French Invented the Culinary Profession*. Philadelphia: University of Pennsylvania Press, 2000.

Wheaton, Barbara Ketcham. *Savoring the Past: The French Kitchen and Table from 1300 to 1789*. Philadelphia: University of Pennsylvania Press, 1983.

Films

Haute Cuisine (*Les Saveurs du palais*). Directed by Christian Vincent. Wild Bunch Distribution, 2012.

The Kings of Pastry. Directed by Chris Hegedus and D.A. Pennebaker. First Run Features, 2009.

Ratatouille. Directed by Brad Bird. Disney-Pixar, 2007.

CHAPTER 12

Restaurants

PAUL FREEDMAN

The average American devotes about one-half of all his or her food expenditures to restaurant meals, and 75 percent of the population eats outside the home at least once a week. An extraordinary surge in dining out has taken place over recent decades in the United States, but the world leader is Japan, where 196 meals per year are consumed in restaurants (the figure for the United States is 119).[1] The restaurant industry hires more people in the United States than any other segment of the economy except for government. Developing (especially newly prosperous) economies have seen radical increases in dining out, even where, as in much of India for example, this had previously been almost unknown.

Dining in restaurants reflects tastes in food, but also differing definitions of sophistication, fun, and experimentation. Students in food history or social history classes are usually fascinated by restaurants as an example of a familiar but unexamined phenomenon of everyday life. The diversity of students' personal histories makes discussion interesting in itself as a sometimes uncomfortable example of class distinctions and in terms of experiences of foreign students or recent immigrants. Some students come from families that sit down at home together every day for meals, others have been extensive consumers of fast food, while still others follow the Food Network and are familiar with the latest fashions in restaurant dining.

The study of restaurants is an important part of research in food history, although historians have not until recently given attention to what people choose to eat. Restaurant-going has required a certain degree of affluence and so attention to it was regarded as a hobby rather than a serious academic interest, on the order of the "history" of shopping, decorating, or furniture. The turn towards cultural approaches to history in recent decades has drawn attention to the role of consumers and the place of desire in the introduction and promotion of commodities such as sugar or coffee. The admission of discretionary and even luxury spending as historical topics has also influenced the image of the restaurant as an expression of European bourgeois taste and institutions. Dining out is linked to the growth of the city, the expansion and display of wealth as well as culture, the creation of new gendered spaces, and the everyday implications of colonial empires. Restaurants are also important in terms of the analysis of class and discrimination made prominent by the work of Pierre Bourdieu. They have always been places to demonstrate taste and sophistication.

RESTAURANTS AS OPPOSED TO OTHER FORMS OF DINING OUT

Restaurants are not new, but in their modern articulation they go back only as far as eighteenth-century Paris and were slowly adopted elsewhere. Early nineteenth-century English guidebooks portray restaurants as among the unique attractions of Paris.[2] Thus while restaurants might now seem inevitable accompaniments to urban or even civilized life, most societies most of the time—even developed and affluent ones—managed to get along fine without them.

Naturally, provision was made in inns for travelers and others compelled by necessity to find their meals away from where they lived. Reasonably prosperous civilizations of the past (with the partial exception of Islamic realms) also had taverns and other places to drink wine, beer, or other alcoholic preparations, usually accompanied by some kind of meals or snacks. Additionally, convenience food in the form of prepared meals to take out is much older than the restaurant. In 1850 London had four thousand people selling ready-to-eat food on the street.[3]

A restaurant is more than merely a place where food is served. It is a destination rather than a convenience or accommodation. People decide to go to a restaurant in expectation of a certain kind of cuisine, a set of choices, and in hopes of a particular sort of diversion. The notion of choice is important: the customer fixes a time (based on the assurance that meals are available over a fairly extensive portion of the day), decides what to order (rather than having to be satisfied with a set meal), and sits alone or with self-selected companions in a kind of privacy within the public space. The ability of the diner to arrange his or her experience sets the restaurant apart from other places to find prepared food. Compare the restaurant's flexibility to the more structured food service at such long-standing institutions as inns, which traditionally received travelers and entertained a certain number of locals. The travelers were an essentially captive clientele; the locals were there for drink and company. The food on offer for the transients was provided as a necessity, not as a gastronomic experience. Or compare the sit-down restaurant with take-out: cities always had places that would cook food for you, either that they prepared or that you brought to them because you didn't have an oven or other equipment, or because you didn't want to bother. As in markets and souks to this day, small stands and cookshops serve rudimentary meals and carry on a take-out trade, but they are hardly white-tablecloth establishments with extensive menus.

Another earlier variation common in early modern Europe was the *table d'hôte*, which served a set meal at a particular time at a common table. The food might have been quite good, but the venue did not offer choice among menu items, dining times, or company. In contemporary society, fast food chains occupy a large role in the consumption of meals outside the home. These chains have a menu and thus the diner has choices, but brand identity at any given chain is set by one or two items: pizza, donuts, sandwiches, burgers, or tacos, to take some common examples. Features such as the absence of waiters, disposable tableware, and drive-through lanes separate fast food from restaurants properly speaking, but also demonstrate the blurred frontiers between categories. We can provisionally define the restaurant in its modern history as a semi-public and semi-private space to take meals at a choice of times, with a choice of company and dishes. It provides opportunities for business socializing, personal friendship, romance, and even companionable solitude (consider the recent vogue for eating at the bar).

RESTAURANTS BEFORE PARIS

Employing this definition of the restaurant, it is common to speak of its "invention" in the eighteenth century.[4] In the nineteenth century, the French model would be diffused throughout the world, but there were well-developed restaurant cultures earlier, especially in the ancient

Roman Empire and in China beginning in the Song dynasty (960–1279), if not earlier.

Roman sources speak of taverns, shops, and bars, but also mention sites that approximate the modern idea of restaurants.[5] The best evidence is archaeological, especially the ruins of the cities destroyed by the eruption of Mount Vesuvius in 79 C.E. No less than 158 buildings with counters facing the street have been found in Pompeii. These were mostly small structures that served as bars, food shops, and take-out places. Evidence of on-site cooking is present in 128 of them. Another 46 had four or more rooms, and food residues from drains and containers indicate that some prepared elaborate food for guests who took their meals there, reclining on the conventional dining couches.

Restaurants tend to be favored for what diners cannot easily cook at home by reason of either exotic ingredients or technology (high heat, lots of oil, long-cooking as with barbecue, to take a few examples). Restaurants in Pompeii served basic local products (fish, chicken, lentils, and the like), but also dormice, sea urchins, and even in one instance giraffe. There is not much discussion of restaurants in Latin literature, which differentiates the Roman Empire from Imperial China where not only were restaurants popular, but gourmandise was a subject for reflection, even nostalgia.

By about 1000 C.E. China developed restaurants and allied establishments such as teahouses and taverns furnished with elaborate catering and banqueting halls. In the early fourteenth century Marco Polo describes the city he knew as "Quinsai" (modern Hangzhou) as teeming and splendid. He was impressed by the gourmandise of the population, their passion for fish in particular. He was struck by the presence of meat and fish in the same meal, as medieval Europe tended to reserve fish for the numerous Catholic fast days. Marco Polo also mentions immense banqueting palaces on islands in the nearby West Lake. In the Southern Song era, preceding the Mongol conquest, teahouses provided music, wine, healthful and medicinal food, and sometimes entertainment from female singers. Taverns offered rice wine, the company of local women, and food, sometimes quite diverse and serious food. In the Song and Mongol centuries there were also large restaurants in the more populous cities that conform precisely to the definitions given above. An account written in 1275 says that customers chose where to sit, were asked what they wanted to have, and gave orders for all different sorts of food—cooked, raw, grilled, and roasted, as snacks or large meals. Some restaurants specialized in a small number of items (e.g., noodles) or the food of certain regions. One author claims, improbably, that there were restaurants in Hangzhou that specialized in "two-legged mutton" (human flesh). What is certainly true is that regional restaurants abounded, serving cuisine of Sichuan, Hopei, and provinces of northern China.[6]

Among Chinese cities Hangzhou received the most extensive attention for its food and restaurants, but it was not unique. Other imperial capitals such as Kaifeng and Beijing were famed for their restaurants of all types and levels of service and in general, as Michael Freeman remarks of the Song period, "eating at restaurants was an inescapable part of being a city dweller."[7] The history of restaurants in China is continuous from the Song Dynasty to the present, with one exception: restaurants were unknown during the rule of Mao Zedong. Although Mao and Zhou Enlai were able to offer President Nixon a lavish series of banquets during his historic visit in 1972, as late as 1980 there were fewer than ten restaurants in Beijing, and their client base was limited to foreigners and high officials.[8]

THE "INVENTION" OF THE MODERN RESTAURANT

In Europe the restaurant had different origins, although it came to fill some of the same gastronomic and social functions as it had in China. There had been luxury dining and gourmandise in the Roman Empire and, as we've seen, there were restaurants, but the splendid banquets of the premodern West took place in private villas, castles, and other sorts of great houses. The fictional banquet of Petronius's Trimalchio and the infamous parties of Nero, Cleopatra, or Elagabalus have given ancient Rome an undeservedly bad name as regards excess, and the Middle Ages, if pictured as cruder in its meal service, fare no better cinematically or in the popular imagination. With allowances for exaggeration, however, there were many opportunities for striking extravagance. A two-day banquet presented as interesting but not uniquely luxurious by Chiquart, chef to the duke of Savoy in the early fifteenth century, called for six weeks of preliminary hunting for game, thousands of pounds of spices, and the erection of edible castles with towers from which cooked fish, boar's heads, and other animals seem to breathe fire. Restaurants are not, therefore, the only way for a developed economy to display gastronomic creativity and excess.

The European restaurant arose out of needs other than ostentation, although it soon fit into the representation of high social status.

Restaurants depended for their success on the upper bourgeoisie, a class with ready money, but without palatial private entertainment spaces. Its members were sociable with regard to familial, personal, and business contacts, which they arranged in a manner distinct from the ceremonial leisure of the aristocracy.

In some respects the restaurant elaborated on the café, the location *par excellence* for socializing. In the seventeenth- and eighteenth-century coffeehouse and café, news was received, academic research was discussed, business deals were agreed upon, and friends were entertained in an atmosphere of sobriety (in contrast to taverns). The Royal Society, England's scientific academy, was established at a coffee house, as were the first insurance companies and stock trading societies. In teaching about the history of restaurants, the compatibility of dining and socializing should be readily understood by students given the way they lead their lives and in particular how they manage their friendship networks.

Restaurants in the modern Western world were developed in Paris during 1760s and 1770s. Originally their customers were persons of delicate health and disposition who were served soothing bouillon and other light fare. Restaurants (the word is derived from the physically beneficial *restauration* effected by the soup) formed part of a movement to make food more healthful and less elaborate, a campaign identified with Jean-Jacques Rousseau and the desire for a simple life. The bouillon was conceptualized as austere, but actually was time-consuming and expensive to make, much like the other dishes that started to be served: preserved fruit, stewed chicken, and other preparations of this first "nouvelle cuisine." These dishes were presented with the same ostentatious simplicity put forward by the second French nouvelle cuisine movement of the 1970s. The restaurant's extended opening hours imitated the café, but also accommodated the hypochondriac proclivities of its first clients who might feel faint, or for that matter hungry, at any time.

This may not seem a promising basis for what would become grand locales with elaborate menus, and indeed the restaurant changed character as it increased the number of dishes available and attracted hordes of people with hearty appetites who soon displaced the sickly and neurasthenic. Nevertheless, restaurants have always encouraged a sense of the human body and its satisfaction beyond mere hunger. Rebecca Spang remarks that while café patrons read newspapers and thought about the world, restaurant diners read the menu and thought about their bodies.[9]

In the early nineteenth century, the Parisian restaurant was well beyond being a quiet shop providing nourishing broths and had become a splendid site, a defining pleasure of Parisian life. As early as 1804, it was said that Paris had two thousand restaurants (undoubtedly an exaggeration) and beginning in 1803 the first guidebooks to Parisian dining establishments were composed by the indefatigable and opinionated Alexandre Balthazar Laurent Grimod de la Reynière. His *Almanach des Gourmands* was intended not for tourists but for natives; it was the first work to express the point of view of the restaurant customer, a person of taste with a desire for pleasure, not an ordinary customer looking for convenience or value. A guide of this sort now seems as natural as restaurants themselves, but both had to be created, and we in the West are the heirs of the particular formulations of restaurant, diner, and the choices among destinations established in Paris.

The end of the Napoleonic Wars in 1815 and the restoration of the Bourbon monarchy brought renewed attention to Parisian dining. Restaurants became larger, with public and private rooms, tables of various sizes, and printed summaries of offerings, *menu* from the French word for "small," that is, a condensed account of available dishes. The menu grew along with the size of the establishments. In 1820 an English traveler referring to the menu at one of the famous restaurants in the Palais Royal remarked that "Epicurus himself would stand bewildered at the sight of Véry's bill of fare."[10] An English guide to Paris published in 1837 copied the menu from Véry's, which included 250 items. The guidebook author estimated the number of restaurants at a credible and impressive 927.[11] Véry's specific dishes, although numerous, seem rather plain by later standards of "classic" French cuisine, with few sauces (and those often simple: black butter, tomato sauce, mushroom cream sauce) and a considerable amount of beef and mutton filets. But the influence of the grande cuisine created by Marie-Antoine Carême (1783–1833) is visible in the occasional mention of vol-au-vents, the more-than-occasional garnishing with truffles, and a few of the more ambitious sauces (*financière, poulette*).

THE GLOBALIZATION OF FRENCH CUISINE

By the latter half of the nineteenth century, French cuisine dominated the Western world, and gracious or at least pretentious French restaurants were found in every important city. While Carême had spent his career at princely courts and private castles, Auguste Escoffier (1846–

1935), the great codifier of French cuisine in the late nineteenth and early twentieth century, worked at hotel restaurants like the Savoy in London and other grand public establishments. French cuisine was served at royal palaces and diplomatic events from Tokyo to Washington, D.C. A dinner served to King Umberto of Italy at the Quirinal Palace in 1889 is written in French and consists entirely of French dishes including foie gras, asparagus with Hollandaise sauce, and cream of barley soup *à la reine*.[12] It was a significant gesture when just after his accession in 1888, Kaiser Wilhelm II ordered that menus for the imperial household be rendered in German instead of French.[13] Only in Bill Clinton's presidency did English definitively replace French on the menus for state occasions at the White House, and even such quintessentially English establishments as London's Garrick Club or certain Oxford and Cambridge colleges continue to provide dinner menus only in French. It is not that the food served is necessarily French, but that French has been the international language of cuisine, much as it remains the language of ballet, fencing, and heraldry.

The authority of France as culinary arbiter was hardly confined to the rituals of palaces and embassies. The success of global French haute cuisine was furthered by the power of the bourgeoisie, the well-off and status-seeking clientele of restaurants. By "bourgeoisie" I mean not literally "middle-class" in terms of income, but an elite of money rather than title, those who profited from the industrial revolution, the growth of the state, and the expansion of colonial empires. These were people of wealth, taste, and discernment in London, Paris, New York, and any place touched by the new dynamism of capitalist prosperity. But they were not operating in a stable system of social order, hereditary status, or well-protected prestige. It is wrong to see the restaurant only in terms of social aggrandizement—its real gustatory delights are not to be ignored. But in teaching about modern food history it is important to understand how restaurants have been settings for social acts and ambitions.

Fine restaurants on the French model were opened in cities outside France during the nineteenth century. In studying this development, it becomes possible for students to follow the culinary styles and the social claims of restaurants using their menus and the cookbooks that were based on their offerings. A number of menu collections are now online, notably much of the immense holdings of the New York Public Library and the nineteenth-century menus held by the American Antiquarian Society and the University of Houston. Through its Feeding America website, Michigan State University Library provides access to rare and unusual cookbooks, many reflecting restaurant service as well as chefs' recipes. There are also biographies of specific restaurants (usually in-house productions) and increasingly lavish but significant works by and about contemporary chefs such as Thomas Keller, Grant Achatz, Ferran Adrià, and René Redzepi.[14]

The initial diffusion of the French restaurant model was a slow process; the opening of Delmonico's in New York in 1830 is normally taken as the first successful American transplant of the Parisian style. Delmonico's, the creation of two brothers from the Italian-speaking Ticino canton of Switzerland, offered an impeccable setting, excellent service, and French cuisine. The introduction of French dishes was not so new, but the combination of serious attention to food (the brothers for a time owned a farm in Brooklyn because they did not like the produce available at the markets) and a gracious ambience (as opposed to the raucous atmosphere of taverns and eating houses) first set Delmonico's apart and then encouraged imitators, as its success was rapid and complete. The menu, extending at times to eleven or twelve pages, was entirely in French and although American specialties such as cooked oyster dishes, local fish, terrapin, and game (especially many kinds of duck) were included, the menus inclined to classic *grand cuisine*: foie gras, ortolans, sweetbreads, truffles, quenelles, venison, and all manner of difficult sauces (Périgord, Montpellier butter, *financière* . . .).

Delmonico's remained the most acclaimed restaurant in the United States for the entire nineteenth century. In 1884, a contributor to *Harper's Weekly* recalled that before Delmonico's, people of social prominence regarded dinner as mere sustenance. At Delmonico's, for the first time, they learned "that dinner was not merely an ingestion but an observance . . . when we compare the commensalities of our country before the Delmonico period . . . with our condition in respect of dinner now, and think how large a share of the difference is due to Delmonico's, we shall not think it extravagant to call Delmonico's an agency of civilization."[15]

Imitators of Delmonico's were everywhere, including a restaurant explicitly called Delmonico's in San Francisco. That city's first French restaurant, however, was the Poulet d'Or, opened in the Gold Rush year 1849 by François Péguillon. It quickly became known as the "Old Poodle Dog," probably as a pun or perhaps because the owner kept a white poodle.

French cuisine had been served in grand houses in England long before the first luxury restaurants were established. But the restaurant was even later in arriving in London than in New York, in part because men's clubs were the preferred setting for high-end dining.[16] The most famous (French) chef of the early Victorian period was Alexis Soyer, whose influence was at its greatest when he ruled the ultra-modern kitchens of the Reform Club (1837–1850). It was not until the establishment of the Café Royal by Daniel Nicolas Thévenon in 1865 that London had a fashionable public restaurant. The Café Royal served French food at different levels of formality. There was a glittering restaurant proper, a more relaxed Grill Room, and a downstairs Brasserie.

By the 1880s, restaurants and French cuisine had spread across the globe. Every major city had at least a first-class hotel claiming to offer French food: the Hermitage in Moscow, the Maison Dorée in Mexico City, the Union Hotel in Melbourne.[17] But money could not buy authenticity, and this was especially the case for the more remote centers of new money, such as the mining towns of the American West. Tombstone, Arizona, which was suddenly booming in the 1880s because of silver, boasted of restaurants offering Chicken à la Marengo, Salmis of Duck with Olives, Veal Fricandeau "au Meadere" (i.e. *au Madère*), as well as many items rendered in dubious French—"Glace Croquets de Voivale aux Asparagus Pointe" and "Vol au Bent des Fritters, a la Maryland" being notable examples.[18]

SOCIAL DISTINCTION AND CULINARY EXPERIMENTATION

Dining out in restaurants is a particular form of commensality, as opposed to dining at home, on picnics, or on religious occasions (church suppers or festivals). Restaurant sociability itself takes many forms and has become associated with different sorts of interactions: romance (dates, anniversaries), business negotiations, entertainment, and family occasions. The establishments tailor themselves according to these various uses. Parisian restaurants in the early nineteenth century often provided small rooms with street entrances apart from the main restaurant lobby, where men could discreetly entertain women who were not their wives. Before the 1906 earthquake and fire, San Francisco's Poodle Dog also had small upstairs rooms that could be reached by an outside staircase, for private dining. Less risqué, Delmonico's offered facilities for private parties organized around business, social camaraderie, or most often both. One of the most splendid events at Delmonico's was a dinner for 250 given on October 30, 1865 by the English railway entrepreneur Sir Martin Peto. The dinner, which apparently cost the unheard-of sum of two hundred dollars per guest, about three thousand dollars currently, was a promotional event for contacts rather than a gathering of friends. It consisted of ten courses in which elaborate presentation of game birds was especially notable, along with seven *pièces montées* (sculpted *tableaux* made of spun sugar and other malleable ingredients) representing scenes such as the ruins of Paestum and pyramids with cascading waterfalls.[19]

Restaurants also accommodated a less splashy form of sociability for both business and pleasure. The term "power lunch" was coined in 1979 in an *Esquire* piece about the Four Seasons, but the professional networking that that article lovingly detailed (complete with seating charts of the Bar Room) was not new.[20] The cementing of relationships and acquisition of contacts is encouraged by the restaurant's public but often rather clubby nature, so that the dynamic of regulars versus walk-ins can be used to create different kinds of experiences. Today, the Four Seasons has a Pool Room which, despite its grandeur, is for tourists, couples, families, and the like. The Bar Room, by contrast, was once the place for leaders of fashion, advertising, and publishing, providing a setting where they were known and cosseted. Its lunch regulars are now more likely to come from banking than from creative professions, but the distinction of being a regular and the importance of being seen to be a regular remains as strong as ever.

Restaurants furnish occasions to show (or to fail at) savoir faire and sophisticated knowledge. In William Dean Howell's novel of 1882, *A Modern Instance,* Marcia Gaylord has eloped with Bartley Hubbard and they dine at the opulent Revere House Hotel in Boston where even though they are both of modest background, Bartley is able to impress Marcia with his "nonchalant ease" and "dazzling intelligence" as he orders and supervises the meal. Knowledge is important, but so is a manner indicating negligent confidence. In recent years the more daunting test of expertise has proven to be the wine list.

The lore of gourmandise also makes it possible to accentuate social distinctions, a popular theme in films, such as *Pretty Woman* or *Titanic,* in which a lower-class person is faced with the difficulty of mastering the techniques (snail tongs) and esoteric food (caviar) that elegant dining requires. As long as the hierarchy of restaurants was clear and stable, mastery of gastronomy meant understanding an essentially French set of rules and practices. But while we have thus far concentrated on elite dining, the universe of restaurants is much larger and so is the possibility of self-improvement or self-promotion.

Of key significance in the history of dining in the United States and Britain is the advent of "ethnic" restaurants, establishments run by immigrants and offering cuisines from their countries of origin.[21] While part of their appeal was that these were less formal than restaurants of the high-end French tradition, visiting such restaurants required that nonimmigrant patrons learn new techniques (chopsticks), a new vocabulary, and most importantly an unfamiliar style of cooking.

Initially such restaurants served members of their own immigrant communities, but by the 1880s in New York and San Francisco and not much later in London, Italian and Chinese restaurants (to take two enduringly successful examples) catered to larger customer bases.[22] Experimentation with different cuisines offers opportunities for cosmopolitan but not necessarily wealthy diners to show understanding of previously unfamiliar dishes even though the proprietors of "ethnic" restaurants often provide inauthentic versions of home cooking or at least dishes only vaguely connected to anything from their countries of origin. Diners from outside the culture of a given restaurant may be aware of this to varying degrees, and may regard this "inauthenticity" with indifference or disillusionment. Chop suey eventually lost favor in Chinese restaurants in the United States, as did so-called Cantonese food as a whole; the Szechwan favorite "General Tso's Chicken" was regarded as seemingly authentic by non-Chinese diners in the 1970s and became something of a joke by 2000. In the chapter on Indian cuisine in this volume, Jayanta Sengupta recalls British Foreign Secretary Robin Cook's remark in 2001 that chicken *tikka masala* should be considered the national dish of the United Kingdom, although it is in fact an adaptation to European tastes, employing a cream and tomato base that would not have been found in India. Nevertheless, as any reader of websites such as Chowhound can readily see, the ability to trump other people's understanding of authenticity (my unknown Cambodian restaurant is better than yours) is irresistible.[23]

As early as the 1890s, New York boasted of its polyglot restaurants representing the entire globe. Paris might have greater distinction in the mastery of French cuisine, but New York offered variety.[24] The cover of *The New Yorker* for April 12, 1938, drawn by Perry Barlow, shows eight restaurant scenes—Japanese, Middle Eastern, Scandinavian, Russian, German, Chinese, Jewish, and Italian—and lists forty-seven dishes. It's interesting to see how many apparently iconic items of that period are now virtually unknown: *duck yet gram, klimsoppa,* and *kisiel.* Almost none of the Middle Eastern dishes are easily recognizable and of course Scandinavian and German restaurants have been eclipsed in the interim.

RESTAURANTS AND A WIDER PUBLIC

The first patrons of Chinese and Italian restaurants in the United States were what contemporaries referred to as "Bohemians," men and women living in cities, unmarried, with enough income to spend on small indulgences such as dining out. They were often artists or journalists with tastes for exuberance, informality, and variety and were possessed with a knowledge of urban life unknown to tourists or the upper bourgeoisie. Soon, however, they would be joined by less cultivated and more conventional middle-class diners whose increasing enthusiasm for dining out encouraged all sorts of restaurants at levels between the elite palaces of the Delmonico's type and plebian eating houses. The middle-class restaurant was not necessarily modest and sometimes provided music, dancing, or themed decor, as in pseudo-Polynesian tiki restaurants that gained favor between the wars. Above all these restaurants seemed to offer value, fun, an unintimidating environment, and novelty.

The rise of ethnic and middle-class restaurants is the major story of restaurant history in the twentieth-century United States. Their predominance is linked to the decline of formality and the proliferating of consumer niches. They did not really eliminate social distinction so much as they complicated it. The drive for new sensations, new places, and new knowledge replaced the sense of order, decorum, and predictability expressed by the encomium to Delmonico's cited previously.

Changes in restaurants at the end of the nineteenth century and the first part of the twentieth century were also related to two long-term movements and one short-term but devastating event. The two social changes are related: the increasing representation of women as restaurant clients, and developments in the location and nature of the workplace. The event was the enactment of a constitutional amendment prohibiting the sale of alcoholic beverages. Prohibition went into effect in 1920, and restaurants with any claim to fine dining found it difficult or impossible to survive without the substantial profits generated by the sale of wine and cocktails. It also would have seemed a waste of effort to serve *grande cuisine* to the accompaniment of water or fruit juice.

In Paris both men and women were admitted to restaurants although there were rules and customs about what kinds of places were appropriate for particular categories of clientele. Such relatively unconstrained mingling of the sexes was not quickly adopted elsewhere. Hotels in the United States had for a long time accommodated "respectable" women who were traveling or simply enjoying an outing in town. A New York newspaper advertisement in 1833 offered breakfast and lunch to ladies from the country or from "the upper part of the city" who might not be able to return home at midday.[25]

The grand hotels first built in the 1830s usually provided a "ladies' ordinary" dining room where women could dine without being bothered by the gazes or comments of men, the ostensible reason for providing such protected spaces.[26] An 1853 menu from the ladies' ordinary at the Burnet House Hotel in Cincinnati displays fare indistinguishable from the sort laid out for men, including an assortment of mutton preparations (mutton soup, mutton cutlets, ragout of mutton, and mutton tendons).[27] The integration of men and women in American restaurants was uneven. The luxurious Fifth Avenue Hotel, which opened in 1859, accommodated both men and women in its main dining room, but women only began to be generally welcome at the major establishments in the 1890s.

By the second half of the nineteenth century there were eateries that not only served women but catered to what were thought to be their food preferences. In the New York of 1849 ice cream saloons (as they were called) attracted ladies en route to or from Stewart's, a magnificently luxurious and immense dry goods establishment and ancestor of the department store.[28] In the *American Cookery Book* of 1866, Jennie June Croly referred to ladies' lunches, both at homes and at restaurants, that featured omelets and chicken salad.[29] The distinction between ladies of leisure who wanted lunch while shopping and working women who had a short midday break was obvious. Women of the upper classes patronized genteel tearooms, while women employed as office workers favored the speed and convenience of sandwich shops, cafeterias, and soda fountains.

The most successful establishments catering to women were those that could offer something to different classes of women and that were sufficiently robust in their atmosphere to appeal to men in a hurry as well. The ABC and Lyons teashops in Britain were early examples of restaurants emphasizing consistency, hygiene, quick service, and low prices. In the United States, chain restaurants such as Schrafft's and Child's featured caffeinated beverages, ice cream, and light lunches. The common elements among what were regarded as women's (or women-friendly) restaurants were the absence of alcohol, certain iconic ladies' dishes (tea, ice cream), and lighter fare. The notion of women preferring less elaborate or filling dishes was related both to perceived gender preferences and to the evolution of lunch as a meal taken during a break from work, in which speed should be accompanied by a modicum of graciousness not found in the hubbub, sawdust, and harsh language of men's lunch bars. Places serving sandwiches, salads, meals of few courses, and non-alcoholic beverages proliferated with the influx of women as customers and the expansion of urban clerical labor.[30]

A further encouragement for the proliferation of simpler, more convenient restaurants was the enactment of Prohibition, which had the effect of destroying the business of grand restaurants as well removing, at least from public view, the men's bars that offered substantial quantities of food and so functioned as de facto restaurants. The new model was the minimalist speakeasy on the one hand and the functional cafeteria on the other. Roadside restaurants, the ancestors of fast food establishments; diners; and restaurants with themes and entertainment were all responses to a more casual turn in manners, the official abolition of alcohol, gender integration, and a faster lifestyle.

POSTWAR CHANGES

The end of Prohibition at the depths of the Great Depression only slowly restored the grand restaurant in the United States. The establishment of Le Pavillon in New York in the seemingly inauspicious year 1941 is usually taken as marking the revival of the French restaurant as the standard in American luxury. Indeed Le Pavillon would dominate the elite dining scene for over twenty-five years, and those who trained there would extend its influence into the 1980s. In fact, New York already had a number of fine or at least glamorous French restaurants before Le Pavillon opened, places such as Voisin, the Café Chambord, Passy, and Lafayette, all of which would last into the 1960s.[31]

In 1969 the American travel magazine *Holiday* published an interview with the distinguished French food critics Henri Gault and Christian Millau asking what the best restaurant in the world was.[32] Written on the eve of the upheaval of the *nouvelle cuisine* (for which Gault and Millau became authoritative advocates), this article, seemingly an artifact from a vanished world, presents a restaurant hierarchy essentially unchanged since the previous century. After hastily, if regretfully, disposing of the rest of the world as hopelessly benighted (even Italy is considered uninteresting), the critics, with many sighs of relief, concentrate on

France and mention a good twenty-five restaurants including the Parisian shrines Tour d'Argent, Grand Véfour, and Lucas-Carton. The final competition comes down to two restaurants near Lyon, Troisgros and Bocuse. Troisgros is regarded as more traditional, intimate, and familial, while Chef Paul Bocuse is praised as a master of grandeur and creativity. As it happened, innovation à la Bocuse was to be the path to celebrity status.

In retrospect, nouvelle cuisine, while it began as a rejuvenation, marked the beginning of the end of French hegemony; the waning of French authority internationally is the major development in restaurants over the last fifty years. By elevating simplicity, intensity, flavor, and the quality of ingredients, the advocates of nouvelle cuisine seemed to be returning to the rules of the initial French culinary revolution, which ordained that food taste of its basic ingredients. At the same time they were undermining tradition and exalting the chef as creative visionary. No longer the acolyte of culinary tradition, the chef was on the way to becoming an artist—quirky, original, demanding and less and less tied to recognizable and conservative standards. Nouvelle cuisine accepted new, generally lighter flavors (less butter, fewer elaborate sauces). A Japanese aesthetic of subtlety, miniaturized beauty, and color was accompanied by tropical and international influence that expanded the ingredients and possibilities for using them. These all gave the new movement a certain style that began by foregrounding simplicity but ended up rather quickly becoming the butt of satire for its excessive elaboration, peculiar combinations (vanilla and maple syrup in everything), and overemphasis on presentation (tiny portions at high prices).

AUTHENTICITY AND INNOVATION

The message of emphasizing the primary ingredients may have taken a peculiar turn in France, but it flowered unexpectedly on what previously had been unfavorable soil. The greatest recent influence on U.S. and British restaurants has been the discovery that local produce and meat cultivated on small, less industrial farms and ranches tastes better than all the imported exotica used in previous years to cover and complicate mediocre ingredients. Chez Panisse, established in Berkeley by Alice Waters in 1971, began as a French restaurant, albeit one more focused on exuberance than on intimidation. By 1985 it became something different, more Californian, more local, more vivid in the flavors of its foods.

The 1970s, which have a bad reputation for style, are a key decade in the history of restaurants. In 1971 Chez Panisse opened in Berkeley and Le Pavillon closed in New York. The next decade saw many dubious, even atrocious innovations: the proliferation of salad bars, the rise of earnestly health-conscious vegetarian restaurants, and the complete triumph of fast food chains as the shopping mall and interstate highway took over the landscape. At the same time the 1970s also witnessed more promising tendencies, reflected in restaurants that emphasized region, locality, and ingredients.

When Calvin Trillin published his hilarious but pioneering book *American Fried* in 1974, he claimed that within the United States only in New York (and at an astronomical price) could decent French food be obtained. Instead of striving for this absurd goal, he urged Americans in the rest of the country to appreciate their neglected regional culinary treasures, emphasizing ingredients, variety, and local specificity. His assertion that the four or five best restaurants in the world were in Kansas City was not simply a comical take on claims of the Gault-Millau type, but opened up new ways of looking at pleasure in food, quality, and tradition.[33]

Chez Panisse was hardly the first restaurant in America to present French provincial food, with its emphasis on fresh, varied, and colorful primary products. It was, however, a brighter, more vibrant alternative to the elegant, old-fashioned French restaurants with their leather-bound menus, thawed meat, flambéed desserts, and formal service. Nor was Chez Panisse the first to feature American rather than French food, as it did after 1976. The Four Seasons in New York, established in 1959, was not exactly American in its cuisine, but it was at least resolutely not French. What Chez Panisse accomplished and what has made it so influential is its combination of a social agenda (against the processed foods industry and for attention to where food comes from), delight (in the primacy of taste), and the application of French notions of *terroir* to American agriculture and foraging. It is easy to satirize the kind of menu Chez Panisse made famous, one that eschews plain "pork" or "bacon" in favor of the more specific "Laughingstock Pork Chops" or "Nieman Ranch Bacon." The listings are an exercise in locavore piety and artisanal earnestness. Here again, however, it has to be emphasized how different this was, in the late 1970s and the 1980s, from the norm of American restaurants and food service generally, which was to gloss over the quality of the ingredients in favor of variety, complexity, setting, or other diversions.

Chez Panisse began as a French restaurant modeled on the gospel of the English food writer Elizabeth David, who inspired generations of home cooks with a simple, practical, yet sparkling kind of French cookery. At Chez Panisse the menu from an October 1976 dinner of regional Northern California cuisine shows the beginning of a change. All the dishes are given in English, and we see the beginnings of the provenance emphasis, with such dishes as "Big Sur Garrapata Creek Smoked Trout."[34]

The decline of French domination, however, was not caused by developments in the United States but by the difficulty of sustaining the high-end French business model with its labor costs, the de-coupling of this cuisine from real life in France (so that the grand temples of Parisian dining served affluent tourists almost exclusively), and the fracturing of a single set of standards by which to judge restaurant food. Phenomena such as globalization, the spread of wealth internationally, and post-modernism tended to break apart codes, rules, and authoritative indices of discrimination. By the 1990s it became possible to establish a reputation without having to please the French judges.

This was not a sudden revolution but rather a series of steps, visible in the rise of what would be by far the most prominent restaurant of the opening decade of the twenty-first century, El Bulli in Catalonia. Along with the Basque country, Catalonia has a tradition and reputation within Spain for innovative and intriguing cuisine, but this was beaten down by Spain's civil war, poverty, and dictatorship in the 1930s to 1960s, and then by tourism and industrialization beginning in the 1950s, which resulted in the destruction of local cultures and habitats and the desertion of the countryside. In 1983 Ferran Adrià came to an isolated cove north of Rosas on the touristy and overbuilt Costa Brava to work at a French restaurant called El Bulli. He continued as chef until he gradually reoriented it as a Catalan restaurant, in which, rather than merely reviving lost traditions, he cooked in a somewhat more expansive and eclectic style. As with Chez Panisse, therefore, the strikingly novel identity of the restaurant wasn't revealed immediately. Not until 1998 did Chef Adrià embark on an entirely new kind of cooking that relentlessly insisted on innovation, new techniques, and a rupture with traditions. Ferran Adrià marshaled his accumulated creative capital to create varied menus reflecting diverse concepts and techniques. Adrià started with the alchemical transformation of ingredients, and then elaborated permutations. Tinkering with the texture of sponges in 2000 produced "Hot Duck Foie Gras Block with Peach Caviar," "Yeast Soup with Lemon Ice Cream, Butter and Quail's Egg" and "Hot Goose Barnacle Aspic in Tea." Other innovations in 1999 and 2000 alone included agar-based cold jellies, hot jellies, clouds, new uses for microwave ovens, and cauliflower couscous.[35] Authoritative philosophical theories, such as "temperature as the most important sensation in a dish" led to soups that mingled in one serving different densities and degrees of heat. Adrià's description of experiments is quite scientific. Hot baked potato skin consommé was a side effect of experiments with potato foam. By trial and error it was determined that twenty-four hours was the ideal time for steeping potato skins in potato cooking water and that adding salt spoiled the flavor.[36]

The development of what for a time was known as "molecular gastronomy" had a paradoxical success. Sauces made of foam and other signature innovations of El Bulli began to appear everywhere, yet there have been relatively few restaurants established outside of Spain that adopted the complete experimental agenda of the Catalan *vanguardia*. New York has the energetic and talented Wylie Dufresne, but only as of this writing (in fall 2013) with the transformation of 11 Madison Park is a high-end chef and restauranteur in New York opting for this level of radical creativity. This is being done in conjunction with history and the particular local traditions of New York. A similar seemingly incongruous juxtaposition is visible in the most successful modernist restaurant in the United States, Alinea in Chicago. Its chef, Grant Achatz, not content with an exuberant scientific cuisine, has also set up a program of historical re-creation of different culinary epochs (Paris, 1906; an homage to El Bulli; et cetera) at his restaurant Next.

We end this chapter then with two seeming contradictions: between the global popularity of modernist cuisine and the simultaneous interest in locality and history; and between the avant-garde movement and the farm-to-table earnestness and simplicity that result from attempts to encourage the small, high-quality, deindustrialized food producer. What these restaurant and food philosophies have in common is a rejection of mass-market economies of scale and a reemphasis on experiencing food. Among the most acclaimed restaurants at the moment is Noma in Copenhagen whose chef, René Redzepi, combines brilliant and delightful ways of preparing even unlikely local foods such as crickets, moss, and horseradish (140 varieties of horseradish grow wild in Denmark). The local habitat is emphasized: almost everything comes from Scandinavia, mostly from Denmark. Much of this is foraged and wild, not cultivated, so *terroir* is redefined beyond the managed agricultural environment. The cooking techniques are often quite elaborate and involve modern machines, so Redzepi's cooking is not in any sense primitivist or a return to simplicity in technique. Yet a concern with the taste of the primary products remains the chief characteristic of contemporary restaurants. The extraordinary variety of international choices—the trend for every major U.S. city to have staples such as sushi, croissants, or burritos—has not yet submerged the real variety of cuisine or the role of the restaurant in presenting and changing it.

NOTES

1. Priscilla Parkhurst Ferguson, "Eating Out: Going Out, Staying In," in *A Cultural History of Food in the Modern Ages,* ed. Amy Bentley (London: Berg, 2012), 112.

2. William Francis Blagdon, *Paris As It Was and As It Is, or A Sketch of the French Capital,* vol. 1 (London: C. and R. Baldwin, 1803), 445, 447–48; Edward Planta, *A New Picture of Paris, or, The Stranger's Guide to the French Metropolis* (London: Leigh, 1837), 101–2.

3. Peter Scholliers, "Eating Out," in *A Cultural History of Food in the Age of Empire,* ed. Martin Bruegel (London: Berg, 2012), 109.

4. Rebecca L. Spang, *The Invention of the Restaurant: Paris and Modern Gastronomic Culture* (Cambridge: Harvard University Press, 2000).

5. For what follows, see Steven J.R. Ellis, "Eating and Drinking Out," in *A Cultural History of Food in Antiquity,* ed. Paul Erdkamp (London: Berg, 2012), 95–112.

6. Andrew Coe, *Chop Suey: A Cultural History of Chinese Food in the United States* (Oxford: Oxford University Press, 2009), 224–40.

7. Michael Freeman, "Sung," in *Food in Chinese Culture: Anthropological and Historical Perspectives,* ed. K.C. Chang (New Haven: Yale University Press, 1977), 158.

8. I am grateful to my colleagues Tang Li, librarian at the East Asia Library at Yale University, and Valerie Hansen, professor of history at Yale, who inform me that the Beijing Statistical Yearbook for 1980 lists fourteen hotels and restaurants and that this means that the number of stand-alone restaurants was probably in the single digits. Shanghai preserved some of its restaurant culture after the Communist regime came to power, at least until the beginning of the Cultural Revolution in 1966; see Mark Swislocki, *Culinary Nostalgia: Regional Food Culture and the Urban Experience in Shanghai* (Stanford: Stanford University Press, 2009), 176–218.

9. Spang, *Invention of the Restaurant,* 79.

10. Spang, *Invention of the Restaurant,* 184.

11. Planta, *A New Picture of Paris,* 100–6.

12. New York City, New York Public Library, Rare Books Dept., Buttoplh Collection, digital ID 4000001008.

13. Ursula Heinzelman, "German on the Menu: Serving Nationalism: Franco-German Linguistic Relations and an Evaluation of the Present Situa-

tion," in *Food and Language: Proceedings of the Oxford Symposium on Food and Cookery 2009*, ed. Richard Hosking (Totnes: Prospect Books, 2010), 153. But Wilhelm II sufficiently admired French cuisine to compliment Escoffier in 1913 with the line "I am the Emperor of Germany, but you are the emperor of chefs"; Kenneth James, *Escoffier: The King of Chefs* (London: Hambledon and London, 2002), 235.

14. Thomas Keller, *The French Laundry Cookbook* (New York: Artisan, 1999); Grant Achatz, *Alinea* (Berkeley: Ten Speed Press, 2008); Colman Andrews, *Ferran: The Inside Story of El Bulli and the Man Who Reinvented Food* (New York: Gotham Books, 2010); René Redzepi, *Noma: Time and Place in Nordic Cuisine* (New York: Phaidon, 2010).

15. Robert Shaplan, "Delmonico: I. The Rich New Gravy Faith," *The New Yorker*, November 10, 1956, 189.

16. London had many places to dine out, as revealed by a guide published in 1815, but these were modest eating houses; Ralph Rylance, *The Epicure's Almanack: Eating and Drinking in Regency London: The Original 1815 Guidebook*, ed. Janet Ing Freeman (London: British Library, 2012).

17. Rachel Laudan, *Cuisine and Empire: Cooking in World History* (Berkeley: University of California Press, 2013), 280–83.

18. Sherry A. Monahan, *Taste of Tombstone: A Hearty Helping of History* (Albuquerque: University of New Mexico Press, 2008), 134. On French in American menus, see Paul Freedman, "The Rhetoric of American Restaurant Menus and the Use of French," in *Food and Language: Proceedings of the Oxford Symposium on Food and Cookery 2009*, ed. Richard Hosking (Totnes: Prospect Books, 2010), 129–36.

19. Janet Clarkson, *Menus from History: Historic Meals and Recipes for Every Day of the Year*, vol. 2 (Santa Barbara: Greenwood Press, 2009), 675–78.

20. Lee Eisenberg, "America's Most Powerful Lunch," *Esquire* 92, no. 4 (October 1979): 34–41.

21. According to Krishnendu Ray, the first appearance of the term "ethnic restaurant" in the *New York Times* was in 1964, although the two words are found separately in the same article in 1959.

22. Coe, *Chop Suey*, 144–79; John F. Mariani, *How Italian Food Conquered the World* (New York: Palgrave Macmillan, 2011), 43–58.

23. On authenticity, adaptation, and claims to esoteric knowledge, see Sharon Zukin, *Naked City: The Death and Life of Authentic Urban Places* (Oxford: Oxford University Press, 2010), 159–92.

24. Andrew P. Haley, *Turning the Tables: Restaurants and the Rise of the American Middle Class, 1880–1920* (Chapel Hill: University of North Carolina Press, 2011), 111–17.

25. I thank Jan Whittaker for pointing this out to me.

26. Carolyn Brucken, "In The Public Eye: Women and the American Luxury Hotel," *Winterthur Portfolio* 31 (1996), 203–20.

27. From the Henry Voigt Collection of American Menus, Wilmington, Delaware. I am grateful to Mr. Voigt for access to his extraordinary collection and for his help and advice generally.

28. George Foster, *New York in Slices* (New York: W.F. Burgess, 1849), 72.

29. J.C. Croly, *American Cookery Book* (New York: American News Company, 1866), 306–7.

30. Haley, *Turning the Tables*, 141–91.

31. John Mariani, *America Eats Out* (New York: Morrow, 1991), 143–44.

32. Henry Gault and Christian Millau, "Which is the World's Greatest Restaurant?" *Holiday*, June 1969, 32–33, 76–80.

33. Calvin Trillin, *American Fried: Adventures of a Happy Eater* (New York: Doubleday, 1974), 5–14.

34. David Kamp, *The United States of Arugula: How We Became a Gourmet Nation* (New York: Broadway Books, 2006), 161.

35. Ferran Adrià, Juli Soler, and Albert Adrià, *elBulli: 1998–2002* (Cala Montjoi: elBulli Books, 2003), 450, 485–89.

36. Adrià, Soler, and Adrià, *elBulli*, 320.

BIBLIOGRAPHY

Appelbaum, Robert. *Dishing It Out: In Search of the Restaurant Experience.* London: Reaktion Books, 2011.

Beriss, David, and David Sutton, eds. *The Restaurants Book: Ethnographies of Where We Eat.* Oxford: Berg, 2007.

Beuttner, Elizabeth. "Going for an Indian: South Asian Restaurants and the Limits of Multiculturalism in Britain." *Journal of Modern History* 80 (2008), 865–901.

Bourdain, Anthony. *Kitchen Confidential: Adventures in the Culinary Underbelly.* New York: Bloomsbury, 2000.

Burnett, John. *England Eats Out: A Social History of Eating Out in England from 1830 to the Present.* Harlow: Longman, 2004.

Chang, K.C., ed. *Food in Chinese Culture: Anthropological and Historical Perspectives.* New Haven: Yale University Press, 1977.

Coe, Andrew. *Chop Suey: A Cultural History of Chinese Food in the United States.* New York: Oxford University Press, 2009.

Ehrman, Edwina, Hazel Forsyth, Jacqui Pearce, Rory O'Connell, Lucy Peltz, and Cathy Ross. *London Eats Out: Five Hundred Years of Capital Dining.* London: Philip Wilson, 1999.

Ferguson, Priscilla Parkhurst. "Eating Out: Going Out, Staying In." In *A Cultural History of Food in the Modern Age (1920–2000)*, edited by Amy Bentley, 11–126. London: Berg, 2012.

Fine, Gary Alan. *Kitchens: The Culture of Restaurant Work.* Berkeley: University of California Press, 1996.

Gabaccia, Donna. *We Are What We Eat: Ethnic Food and the Making of Americans.* Cambridge: Harvard University Press, 1998.

Jacobs, Marc, and Peter Scholliers. *Eating Out in Europe: Picnics, Gourmet Dining, and Snacks Since the Late Eighteenth Century.* Oxford: Berg, 2003.

Mariani, John F. *How Italian Food Conquered the World.* New York: Palgrave Macmillan, 2011.

Pépin, Jacques. *The Apprentice: My Life in the Kitchen*. Boston: Houghton Mifflin, 2003.

Rambourg, Patrick. *Histoire de la cuisine et de la gastronomie françaises: Du Moyen Âge au XXe siècle*. Paris: Perrin, 2011.

Scholliers, Peter. "Eating Out." In *A Cultural History of Food in the Age of Empire*, edited by Martin Bruegel, 107–22. London: Berg, 2012.

Shore, Elliott. "Dining Out: The Development of the Restaurant." In *Food: The History of Taste*, edited by Paul Freedman, 301–31. London: Thames and Hudson, 2007.

Spang, Rebecca. *The Invention of the Restaurant: Paris and Modern Gastronomic Culture*. Cambridge: Harvard University Press, 2000.

Trubek, Amy. *Haute-Cuisine: How the French Invented the Culinary Profession*. Philadelphia: University of Philadelphia Press, 2000.

Vajda, Joanne. "La construction des restaurants parisiens comme lieux d'attractivité touristique: Fin XIXe—début XXe siècle." In *Voyages en gastronomies: L'invention des capitales et des regions gourmandes*, edited by Julia Csergo and Jean-Pierre Lemasson, 74–89. Paris: Editions Autrement, 2008.

Van den Eeckhout, Patricia. "Restaurants in Western Europe and the United States in the Nineteenth and Twentieth Centuries: An Introduction." *Food and Society* 10 (2012), 143–53.

Warde, Alan. "Eating Globally: Culinary Flows and the Spread of Ethnic Restaurants." In *The Ends of Globalization: Bringing Society Back In*, edited by Don Kalb, Marcon van der Land, Richard Staring, Bart van Steenbergen, and Nico Wilterdink, 299–316. Lanham: Rowman & Littlefield, 2000.

CHAPTER 13

Cookbooks as Resources for Social History

BARBARA KETCHAM WHEATON

We humans have probably been talking about food for nearly as long as we have had language. For most of that time the conversations were not written down. Until the early modern period most of the people, men and women, who cooked and baked and preserved were illiterate or bound to silence by trade secrets. Cookbooks are the scarce, flawed, irreplaceable records of some of these voices, some of those realms of knowledge. Some cookbooks were written before any conventions established what a cookbook or a recipe should contain; some were patched together by foraging in the writings of other people. Whatever their claim to originality, they convey craft skills and cultural tradition. They instruct the young, advise caregivers, and feed ambition. In wartime and periods of economic hardship they offer survival strategies.

Cooking and eating must be studied together, and both must be understood in the context of the societies in which they happen. Some cookbooks were written by people who were watching other people cook, some by people who could cook, but were not in the habit of putting their craft knowledge into words. They contain material that cannot be found elsewhere, but they have to be read with a knowledge of their peculiarities. They are not easy to read: there is too much repetition, too many foodstuffs, and too many techniques. Reading a single old cookbook can be fascinating, but after three or four it is impossible to remember where anything is, or how to make comparisons. It is therefore advisable to approach the material in a systematic way. One such method is to begin by looking at a single facet at a time before attempting to see the book as a whole. Better still is to look at a related group of books that have been examined in this way. An inventory of the ingredients and a consideration of their qualities, an analysis of the techniques at the cook's command, a reconstruction of the kitchen and its equipment, and finally the serving and eating act that all this has led up to: this is the knowledge that will allow the researcher, teacher, or student to understand the social acts of preparing and eating meals in past times and places.

Touch, taste, and smell are the senses least used in research and teaching, and yet the experiences they convey can be remembered for decades, whether it is the first meeting with the rich aroma of a taco, the surprising heat of the ginger in Amelia Simmons's gingerbread recipe from 1796, or the salty, sticky character of a cube of pocket soup, the eighteenth-century ancestor of bouillon cubes. These experiences help people of all ages to engage with the past.

First, some definitions. A cookbook is a manuscript or printed book that contains instructions for preparing food. That is, it contains recipes and may well contain many other kinds of information. A recipe, according to the *Oxford English Dictionary,* is "a statement of the ingredients and procedure required for making something, (now) esp. a dish in cookery." It defines "receipt" similarly. "Recipe" is little used in England or America before the nineteenth century. Both "recipe" and "receipt" derive from the late Latin *recipere,* "to receive." In cookbooks, the instructions are often terse. There may well be no measurements, no information about equipment or timing. "Bukenade: Take fresh flesh, whatever it be. Seethe it with good beef, cast thereto minced onions and good spices, and thicken it with eggs and serve it forth."[1]

Authors of cookbooks have often yielded to the temptation to claim or ascribe the invention of certain recipes to themselves or to others. Such claims are frequently untrue or at least unproven. The history of particular foodstuffs has until fairly recently been filled with picturesque myths. Catherine de Medici did not arrive in France with artichokes, ice cream, or any of the other items that are attributed to her.[2] Andrew F. Smith has disproved the modern notion that nineteenth-century Americans thought tomatoes were poisonous; they were in fact widely eaten and recipes for them appear in cookbooks. The modern reader may also be distracted by unfamiliar language. A little perseverance reveals that *risshewes* are what would be called rissoles today, while *gyngautrey* turns out to be a fish stew.[3] Nevertheless, although the words sound strange they are still meaningful. The people who wrote them were not unintelligent. It is often useful to consult dictionaries that date from the time of the book to clarify puzzling instructions.

Of what use can a cookbook be to a historian or to a history teacher? There are many reasons to use them, but first a caveat: prescriptive literature always has an uneasy relationship to actuality. There are more showpiece recipes than were ever cooked. Medieval recipe collections frequently call for game, both furred and feathered, that could only have been for the tables of landowners and their fortunate guests. Swan, wild boar, sturgeon, and spices are all elite foods and flavors. Eighteenth- and nineteenth-century writers include long, complicated recipes for turtle soup, which was rarely cooked in ordinary kitchens. We cannot expect such sources to tell us about daily life for most people. The transmission of culinary knowledge then and for centuries to come was primarily through the senses and sense experience: the novice stood by the side of the expert, watching, smelling, tasting, carrying out techniques, and listening.

But the manuscripts and the printed books do tell us something of the life of cooks and their societies. Some tell us about skills and ambition and pride. Others speak of social responsibility—temperance, frugality, or community cohesiveness. There are books that tell us how to make much of little, how to deal with stale fish and wilting greens. Most say that we will do well to follow their advice.

There are a number of useful bibliographies to help the teacher or researcher find these books. Many have been reprinted in various forms. Furthermore, examples of most of the earliest printed books can be found on the Internet at the websites of national libraries such as Gallica for the Bibliothèque Nationale in Paris, scholarly collections such as Early English Books Online, and the Feeding America site at the Michigan State Library.

The best modern editions of old cookbooks present faithful images of the whole original text and may be accompanied by useful introductory material and, when necessary, a glossary. They echo the look and size of the original. The worst do not identify the edition or the source volume. They may be given a false, quaint title. In some cases publications of manuscripts rearrange the sequence of recipes according to modern ideas of how a cookbook is constructed. Since manuscript cookery and household books are usually made up of content that accumulates over time, one loses any sense of the ebb and flow of domestic interests.

Because cookbooks often bear marks of ownership, dates of use long after publication, and even comments on individual recipes, it is worth taking the trouble to look at multiple copies of the same edition. Owners sign their copies, and sometimes add notes commemorating a gift to another person. The postpublication life of some volumes can be traced via booksellers' stickers, as in the case of a late Paris edition of Menon's *Cuisinière bourgeoise* that was sold by a nineteenth-century Montreal bookseller.[4] The catalogs of dealers in cookbooks record changing values, and in the case of manuscripts, occasionally provenance. A battered copy of an 1808 edition of Simmons's *American Cookery* was bound luxuriously in gold-tooled red leather in the twentieth century, serving as an example of the changing values of old cookbooks.

There are specialist cookbooks. *A Book of Fruit and Flowers* (1653) and John Evelyn's *Acetaria* (also 1653) on salads are examples. Food writings overlap with other writings: medical, agricultural, and architectural works often include significant sections that may be small cookbooks in themselves. Books of secrets were widespread in Europe and the British Isles in the sixteenth and seventeenth centuries. They were addressed primarily to women in charge of large households, who had the responsibility of caring for the young and the sick, and often contain instructions for distilling cordials and making confectionary. Etiquette and other advice addressed to young people describe ideal behavior at ideal meals.

People buy cookbooks for many reasons: perhaps they are setting up housekeeping for the first time, or they may have become richer, or poorer. New foods arrive in their marketplace, or the shops are selling new equipment. New ideas about what constitutes a good diet lead to the avoidance of familiar foods and the acceptance of new ones.

The struggle to develop a language of cooking and eating has been long. We are fortunate to have even imperfect documentation of how people once cooked and thought about meals. In places where literacy is not the norm, even today, it is not uncommon for the first accounts of culinary practices to have been written by outsiders. These travelers' accounts, however faulty, are precious. Early manuscript recipes are often terse enough to fit inside a fortune cookie. Nonetheless we have to make do: they are as close as we can get to the skills and attitudes of the men and women who cooked in the past. If we listen to the voices in these books we may hear more than we expect. Read closely. Variations in language reflect local dialects and speech patterns. The French term "quelquechose" turns into "kickshaw" when an English cook writes it down. Twentieth-century American community cookbooks contain every imaginable variation upon the idea and the spelling of "boeuf bourguignon."

Written records of what had been a craft largely transmitted by spoken word and lived example are scarce before the late fourteenth century. They are usually written in the vernacular and emerge from courtly and monastic settings. It can be argued that the manuscript cookbook has never entirely disappeared, but has survived to the present in countless homes.[5]

In medieval Europe some culinary manuscripts, such as *Le Ménagier de Paris* (ca. 1394), existed in multiple copies but with the coming of print and the growth of literacy the supply and variety of cookbooks increased. By the seventeenth century a typical cookbook, whether French, English, or German, would be organized on one of several principles. Some are organized by season, others by the sequence of the meal, by ingredient, or by technique. As early as 1691, François Massialot's *Cuisinier roïal et bourgeois* arranges its recipes alphabetically.[6] There may be a table of contents, or an alphabetical index, although some publishers alphabetize only by the first letter. Elaborate title pages are a feature especially of seventeenth- and eighteenth-century volumes.

A few words of caution are in order. Some cookbooks stay in print for decades, slipping further and further behind real-world practices. When a cookbook goes into multiple editions the author sometimes appends new recipes at the back of the book, leaving the original text intact, as does Eliza Leslie in her *Directions for Cookery* (1837).[7]

In many parts of the world, and particularly where literacy rates for women and for the less wealthy have been low, cookbooks are rare. Even in Europe, they are rarely the prize projects of publishers. Instead, they are items that can be printed and reprinted when presses might otherwise be idle. While the first published recipes appear as early as the 1470s, there are robust cookbook-publishing traditions only in England, Germany, Italy, and France. Henry Notaker's *Printed Cookbooks in Europe 1470–1700* lists 232 different titles.[8] Some volumes appeared in a single edition, others in more than fifty (including pirated editions). His bibliography also includes agricultural and medical books that include recipes.

Quite a few of the copies of books cited in Notaker's bibliography are described as imperfect. The more medical or scientific books survive in greater numbers, probably because they were not kept in kitchens. Many editions of popular cookbooks have vanished. Some copies would have been discarded when the recipes in them became unfashionable, and others when they were simply in such poor condition as to be unusable. Andrew Pettegree, in *The Book in the Renaissance,* observes that vernacular publications before 1700 are rarer than those in Latin because they were more intensively used, and in many cases "used to destruction."[9]

The substantial growth in culinary publishing after 1700 presents a challenge. Some books, such as Menon's *Cuisinière bourgeoise,* change substantially over time, while other long-lived works remain largely unchanged. Roy Shipperbottom, in his edition of Elizabeth Raffald's *Experienced English Housekeeper,* estimates that the book went through more than thirty editions.[10] It outlived its author by more than fifty years. With the substantial growth in literacy in the eighteenth century the potential market for cookery books expanded dramatically, and publishers produced many more titles, borrowing freely from earlier works when it suited their purposes.

Cookbook authors address a variety of readers: the Parisian youth learning his trade in restaurant kitchens, the young maidservant come to Boston from a farm, the housewife with money constraints, the New York City hostess hoping to impress her guests. The writer may speak as a friend, a guide, or a stern authority. Lydia Maria Child, in her austere *American Frugal Housewife* (first edition 1829), which she speaks of as "this cheap little book," addresses the reader directly with down-to-earth language: "If your husband brings home company when you are unprepared," says she, make a rennet pudding.[11] On the other hand, Sarah Josepha Hale, writing in 1839 in *The Good Housekeeper, or the Way to Live Well and To Be Well While We Live* combines advice for "an economical dinner" with recipes for macaroons, kisses, and sugar drops.[12] It is unlikely that anyone ever cooked all the recipes in a single cookbook, but what books like this do is create expectations of what foods and what levels of complexity are appropriate in differing situations. In this sense they serve a role similar to that of etiquette books. Mrs. Cornelius calls herself, and titles her book, *The Young Housekeeper's Friend* (1846).[13]

Cooks have always made their own recipe collections, although by the nineteenth century these handwritten collections were interspersed with recipes clipped out of newspapers and magazines, and today the collections may reside in computer files and travel over the Internet. The craft of cooking has always been best transmitted by direct experience. The young girl who learns how to cook by helping her mother and the young apprentice in a professional kitchen are able to touch and taste and hear how to cook in the most precise and direct way. In such a setting, language and measurement are secondary. The novice sees how big a cupful is, feels what the texture of pastry should be, and senses how a piece of meat smells when it is done. If illiterate, she or he acquires new recipes by word of mouth. There is evidence of this in the way the names of recipes evolve over time. What is called Lombard pie in fifteenth-century England has become lumber pie in the eighteenth century, and rice pilaf can also be known as pilloe or pillow or pellaw. The naming of recipes is often arbitrary. Nineteenth-century French recipes in the haute cuisine tradition bear the names of noble families, such as the comtes d'Uxelles; chefs, such as Carême; and battles, such as Marengo. Some recipes, like one from Monsieur Marnette's *French Pastry-cook* (1656), offer a "Gammon Pastie after the Turkish mode" which is clearly culturally impossible.[14] Many dishes were named to curry favor or borrow fame. Few were invented by the people whose names are invoked. In manuscripts, named recipes can indicate social and familial networks.

A printed cookbook is not the work of a single individual. The publisher and the printer, perhaps a designer, a printmaker, or a photographer take the work of a writer and change it in ways the writer may never have intended. There may be introductory material added: a preface by one person, an introduction by another, and perhaps an index made by a specialist with no understanding of culinary naming. Stephen Mennell points out the problem in his essay "Lettre d'un Pâtissier anglois et autres contributions à un polémique gastronomique du XVIIIème siècle" concerning the introduction to *Les Dons de Comus* (1739).[15]

Even the identity of the writer may be in doubt. John Farley's *London Art of Cookery* is a fraud, as Fiona Lucraft has demonstrated in her essay "The London Art of Plagiarism."[16] Much of Hannah Glasse's *Art of Cookery* (1747) was lifted from earlier works.[17] Biographical details about authors are usually scanty, especially before the nineteenth century. A date of birth indicates whether a book is the work of a young person or an old one, whether they are preserving the past or inventing a future. Lydia Maria Child was twenty-seven when her *Frugal Housewife* was first published in 1829; Isabella Beeton published her *Book of Household Management* at the age of twenty-five, and was dead at twenty-eight. On the other hand Jos. Cooper, Robert May, and William Rabisha all based their claims to authority on having cooked at the long-gone courts of James I and Charles I. They would have been elderly men who followed their patrons to France during the Commonwealth.

If the author's name did not suffice to attract buyers, the publisher lured them with titles ranging from the terse "Art of Cookery," which was frequently used, to extensive recitals of the contents of the work. The title page of Richard Bradley's *Country Housewife* (London, 1732) runs to more than one hundred and thirty words. Frontispieces, often representing abundantly equipped kitchens added allure, as did carving and table-setting diagrams.[18]

The look, heft, quality, and typography of these volumes tell us a lot about the intended readership. The earliest American cookbook, Amelia Simmons's *American Cookery* (1796), is a modest little book, of a size that could be slipped into an apron pocket.[19] Illustrations in cookbooks are rare, with the exception of frontispieces and table-setting diagrams. Bartolomeo Scappi's *Opera* (1570) is illustrated with engravings (woodcuts in later editions) depicting cooking pots, knives, spoons, and even a fork, as well as a kitchen with a mechanical spit and a scene of men making pasta.[20] Marx Rumpolt's huge *Ein new Kochbuch* (1581) is embellished with woodcuts, but they are recycled from earlier works. It is not until the invention of chromolithography that color finds its way into print. In his *Livre de cuisine* (1867) Jules Gouffé uses color to show the reader what good and bad meat looks like, as well as to depict elaborately ornamental completed dishes.

Certain books are reprinted and sometimes revised over considerable periods of time. Menon's *Cuisinière bourgeoise* continued to be printed during the French Revolution and was still a bestseller in the early nineteenth century; it was also translated into several languages. Hannah Glasse's *Art of Cookery,* a work whose profound debts to earlier works did not prevent it from being long-lived, was far more common than better books. It was not always the best books that traveled farthest.

One would think from reading culinary bibliographies that the literature is vast. That is true for the last century or so, but is by no means the case with the earlier years. Henry Notaker, in his excellent study, *Printed Cookbooks in Europe: 1450–1700*, shows that when multiple editions of a single work, including many pirated editions and not a few translations, are grouped together the figures are surprising. During the years between 1450 and 1700, he finds one cookbook each in Catalan, Czech, Hungarian, and Portuguese; four each in Danish and Swedish; seven in Spanish; and eight in Latin. By contrast, there are twenty works in Italian, thirty-six in French, fifty-six in German, and seventy-eight in English in the same period.[21]

There is no comparable study for the years after 1700, but as literacy became more widespread among both sexes the number of cookbooks grew rapidly, and more of them were aimed specifically at one gender or the other. Lynette Hunter's seventeenth-century "Books for daily life: household, husbandry, behavior" describes the cluster of books by Gervase Markham, Hugh Plat, and Hannah Woolley that a literate Englishwoman might have used to perform her overlapping duties.[22]

After the American Civil War women raised money for charitable projects by organizing what are called "community cookbooks": collections of recipes contributed by members of a particular place or organization such as a church. We have little information about how substantial the profits were. The books are remarkable though, because they were produced at a local level, usually by women with no other publishing experience, who usually worked with printers in or near their communities. The books sometimes include pictures of churches, schools, temples, and other organizations, and short histories of the organizations themselves. Many are signed, and in some twentieth-century examples handwritten recipes are replicated in the books. Every state has produced at least a few. Some have been produced by immigrant communities in the process of acclimatizing, people who arrive with skills, ceremonies, taboos, and expectations, but who cannot be sure of finding a familiar repertory of ingredients. They adapt as best they can. Their children embrace the foods of their new country, while the grandchildren sometimes want to recreate the nearly forgotten cuisine of their grandparents.

In the United Kingdom, women's institutes produced many such community collections, for example, *Gleanings from Gloucestershire Housewives;* first published in 1927, a version was still in print in 1976.[23] In sources such as these, change over time can be observed in a fine-grained way. British citizens living in colonies of the British Empire wrote cookbooks to help their sisters adapt to life in unfamiliar places. While the majority of space was devoted to recipes from the British Isles, there were often some chapters devoted to local foodstuffs and recipes. R. Riddell's *Indian Domestic Economy* (1849), A.R. Kenny-Herbert's *Culinary Jottings for Madras* (1878), and the work of American Foreign Service wives abroad, such as *An American Accent in the Kitchen,* published by the American Women's Club of Pretoria and the American Diplomatic Wives of Cape Town in the 1950s are examples of this genre.[24] A parallel development was the publication of a number of bilingual cookbooks for people emigrating to the United States from Germany and Scandinavia; likewise, there are a few books that are intended to facilitate communication between American women employers and their domestics who did not speak English. In parts of the world where cookbook publishing has been nonexistent, sometimes shops in tourist destinations sell recipe pamphlets focusing on local specialties. The *Bermuda Recipe Book,* first published by the Warwick Branch of the Bermuda Welfare Society in 1934, and in its sixth edition in 1961, reflected a long tradition of supporting local charities with money from tourists.[25]

Cookbooks are highly interactive publications, and the signs of these interactions sometimes remain in the books. Bookplates and inscriptions of donors and owners can be helpful to the researcher. In manuscripts, if the attributions are abundant, a whole network of kinship, neighborhood, and domestic staff can be traced. However, one can go astray: "Mrs. Putnam's doughnuts" in a manuscript may well have been copied from Mrs. Elizabeth Putnam's *Receipt Book,* and not from a neighbor.[26]

Twentieth-century cookbooks emerge from the dark world of war and its aftermath. The wartime cookbooks are small and printed on bad paper. Others were compiled in situations where palatable food was only a distant dream. American prisoners of war held by the Japanese during World War II remembered the dishes they had eaten before the war. Colonel H.C. Fowler's *Recipes out of Bilibid* was compiled after his death.[27] Wilhelmina Pächter's *In Memory's Kitchen* similarly records the food memories of Jewish women in the Theresienstadt concentration camp.[28] On a somewhat less dark note, the *Operation Vittles Cook Book* was the work of American women in Berlin during the Soviet blockade.[29]

Recipes appear in places other than cookbooks—in newspapers and magazines, especially those addressed to women, and on trade cards promoting products such as Hecker's Flour, Red Star Yeast, and Liebig's meat extracts in the later nineteenth century. Food containers continue to use their packaging to supply what could be described as a user's manual for their products, such as the Ritz Crackers recipe for mock apple pie and the Baker Chocolate's recipe for German chocolate cake. American cooking school teachers, including Fannie Farmer and Mrs. Rorer, helped to introduce their students and readers to branded foods and equipment by publishing pamphlets with recipes using these products. By the end of the nineteenth century these teachers were incorporating brand names into the recipes themselves, which subsequently often traveled to the pages of community cookbooks. Publishers have advertised their other books in the back of cookbooks for centuries.

The scholar or student may well be overwhelmed by the torrent of information provided by these rich and bewildering volumes. It is best to proceed in an orderly way, considering one kind of information at a time. Ingredients, the kitchen and its equipment, techniques, the presentation and eating of a meal are best understood if they are looked at separately and systematically. Only then can the cookbook make sense as a whole, and only if it is seen with comparable works of prescriptive literature, such as craft manuals and books of advice to servants and young people.

An inventory of the ingredients in a cookbook shows what the book's author thinks might have been available to the reader. The inventory might emphasize locally produced items, or others that are rare and costly. Locally produced foods are not always eaten by the people who produce them. This is especially the case with luxury foods, such as cheeses, truffles, goose livers, and hothouse fruit, which can bring in much-needed income. Recipes using them are found not in country cookbooks, but in those written to supply wealthy urban tables.

Beyond local production, the exchange of plants and animals between the Eastern and Western hemispheres since 1492 was first described at length by Alfred W. Crosby in *The Columbian Exchange: Biological and Cultural Consequences of 1492*.[30] But there had been important movement of plants and animals in both hemispheres long before Columbus. Salt was traded over long distances in the Bronze Age; the tomato, originally from Peru, was domesticated in Central America. Southeast Asian poultry and South Asian sugar cane were in the Mediterranean in antiquity.

Geographic points of origin may be far removed from the kitchen in time as well as space. The cook's repertoire is limited by money, hunting rights, the seasons, religious observances and taboos, the commands of dietary systems, and changing fashions. In the country food can be fished, foraged, and hunted. What transportation systems are in place is a key factor in availability. Before the Industrial Revolution the presence of river systems brought seafood to Paris, but most country cookbooks emphasize freshwater, farmed, and migratory fish. Ocean fish was for the most part salted, smoked, or dried. Isochronic maps, which represent equivalences and differences in travel times rather than in space, are useful.

Foods may be gotten by work, by barter, or with money. Seventeenth- and eighteenth-century farming treatises often include a section on food, emphasizing harvesting and preserving. In addition they usually discuss varieties of plants and animals to be raised. In some cases they include recipes for other cooking techniques as well. Knowledgeable country dwellers could forage for mushrooms, greens, hedgerow berries, birds' eggs, and even lichen. They raised chickens, for their own use, to barter, or to sell. If they lived near salt water, seaweeds, such as laver, could enrich their diet. Many country people lived almost entirely outside the cash economy. Networks of bartering will not appear in the cookbooks, but were undoubtedly of great importance.

There may be other absences. In mid-twentieth-century cookbooks margarine may not be mentioned, even though it was routinely used as an economical substitute for butter. Beekeeping was a normal activity on country estates, but one rarely sees honey mentioned in recipes. Potatoes appear in English and German cookbooks in the eighteenth century, in France not until the nineteenth. An ingredient inventory will also reveal what is missing: Where are the maple syrup recipes in nineteenth-century New England cookbooks? When and why did the overwhelming preference for mutton over lamb turn completely around? Do we exaggerate the past importance of foods we now strongly associate with a region? Our expectations of what may be found in these volumes will often disappoint us because the myths that have grown up around cooking in past times have misled us.

Cookbooks reflect taste preferences as well as, indirectly, health anxieties. Consider the sensory qualities of the foods and how they varied over time. There are the basic flavors of sweet, sour, bitter, salty, and what is now called umami. What are the flavor combinations, the smells, the look of the finished dish? What are the textures and colors; how spicy or bland would the dishes be? In the Middle Ages pungent sauces using mustard, vinegar, or verjus were the norm and brightly colored dishes were admired; in the eighteenth century translucent jellies made from calves' feet were fashionable. The early nineteenth century saw a flurry of recipes for chutneys and spicy bottled sauces called soy or ketchup that were inspired by the world of the British Raj. In European haute cuisine pre–World War I, smooth textures and delicately seasoned ingredients were preferred.

Food anxiety appears again and again. In the Middle Ages fish, deemed cold and wet by followers of Galen, was sometimes made safer by adding sugar, which balanced the humors with dry heat. Melons, too, were thought to be dangerous because they were cold and wet, and tales were told of popes who died of eating them. Mid-nineteenth-century American cookbooks contain recipes that appeal to the dyspeptic, water-cure enthusiasts, and members of the temperance movement. The food theorist (or faddist) Sylvester Graham promoted the use of whole grains and the practice of vegetarianism. Graham breads are common in the cookbooks of this era. Among the informal public there was widespread distrust of the food supply. The chemist Friedrich Accum, publishing his *Treatise on Adulterations of Food and Culinary Poisons* (1820) in English and German, alerted people to the dangers threatening their diet.[31] The widespread legend in France, that butchers sold cat meat as rabbit is reflected as late as 1938, when *Larousse Gastronomique* published comparative photographs of cat and rabbit bones.

Another problem reflected in cookbooks was spoilage. Far from eating wonderful food at all seasons, our ancestors ate to keep ahead of spoilage, while still having enough left in their storerooms and root cellars until well into the spring, when the hens began to lay again, the cows to give milk, and green plants to grow. Cookbooks offer hopeful, frugal but often implausible directions: how to keep green peas until Christmas is a favorite in the eighteenth century. The labors of rural households were centered on getting food and keeping it in as edible a condition as possible. Even in cities the agricultural calendar ruled the cost and availability of food. Two domestic calendars that ran in opposite directions occupied everyone charged with supplying food for the household. The first was the cycle of the agricultural year, from the earliest spring green through to the late-autumn slaughtering of the pig. The second was the relentless slide into rottenness. Raspberries had to be preserved as soon as they were picked, no matter how hot the July day. Cheeses were made after the calves were born in the spring and the cows were giving abundant milk. The male calves soon appeared at table as veal. Once the cheeses were made they had to be inspected regularly until they were ripe and ready. Vegetables were pickled, fruit preserved by drying or with sugar. Apples were cut up, threaded on strings and dried to supply late winter pies of a rather unwelcome sort, or they could be stored on dry straw in the attic and eaten promptly when they began to wrinkle. Hams grew rusty in appearance; the spoilage was trimmed off, and the better part used at once. Hens stopped laying in the winter, and the housewife would try various methods of saving the last eggs of the laying season.

Before refrigeration the rate at which supplies deteriorated in rural households governed what was served at meals far more than did epicurean desires. Foods could be dried, salted, smoked, pickled, and preserved in sugar, if it was affordable. They could be kept in cold, dry attics, or below ground in root cellars, but few improved while they awaited use. In Northern Europe and much of North America it was well into the spring before new crops were ready for consumption. In the premodern world early spring could be a time of scurvy and starvation. Moreover, in medieval Europe food of animal origin was forbidden on fast days (Fridays, the eves of saints' festivals, and the forty days of Lent), when people could not eat meat, cheese, milk, or eggs, even if such things were available. These restrictions were eased for most of Protestant Europe in the sixteenth century. When canning came into use in the early nineteenth century, first as a commercial process and later in the home, it greatly enhanced the wintertime table.

Cookbooks arranged by month show the labors of the agricultural year as clearly as do medieval calendar illuminations. The first volume of Richard Bradley's *Country Housewife and Lady's Director* follows this plan. It is in April, when veal is plentiful, that he gives a recipe for "Veal Glue, or Cake-Soup, to be carried in the Pocket"—the ancestor of the bouillon cube.[32] The preserving of fruit during the summer and the late autumn pig slaughter, with the accompanying work of making sausages and hams, are aspects of agricultural labor that Europe and European immigrants to America have engaged in for more than a thousand years. In cookbooks written for landowners there is the added presence of game-birds and animals. The list of game items may include surprises. Surely Simmons is just showing off when, in her *American Cookery* (1796), she includes peacock in her list of birds to roast. Marx Rumpolt's *Ein new Kochbuch* (1581) offers recipes for eagle, which was probably more fantasy than practice. On the other hand, it is just barely possible that Rumpolt's aurochs recipes were used to cook those soon-to-be extinct ancestors of modern cattle. In the nineteenth century relatively modest volumes contain diagrams of how domestic animals are to be butchered, while in medieval manuscripts the writers rarely mention specific cuts of meat. On the other hand, the casual suggestion in the 1938 edition of the *Larousse Gastronomique* that the aurochs is cooked like beef has very little credibility, since the creature had by then been extinct for two centuries.

While most foodstuffs are seasonal, the kitchen, its equipment, and the cook's skills and tools are at hand all year around. Some cookbooks explicitly describe kitchens and their equipment; in others there are only clues. The kitchen as a separate room was not a feature of every household in the Middle Ages or early modern Europe. The equipment of and work performed in the French medieval kitchen are probably best evoked in the *Ménagier* manuscript from the late fourteenth century.[33] The work space would have consisted of the hearth, a big pot suspended from a crane over the fire, and andirons to hold one or more spits for roasting in front of the fire. There would have been a dripping pan underneath. By the seventeenth century kitchens in large establishments would have subsidiary work spaces: a room with a bake-oven and a cool kitchen or office, similar to the *garde-manger* in professional kitchens today. In very large eighteenth-century houses the kitchen might be placed in a side building of the principle structure, linked to it by a passageway, and balanced on the other side by the stables, thus removing noisy, smelly activities from the genteel life of the family. If the distance was great there might be an anteroom next to the dining room to reheat foods before they were served. In cities the kitchens might instead be on a basement level. In either case spaces for baking and for preparing dairy and confectionary goods might be near the principal kitchen. Most cooks worked in very modest spaces. A woodcut illustration in the 1817 edition of Juan Altimiras's *Nuevo arte de cocina* shows twenty objects, ranging from a freestanding butcher's block, long-handled frying pans for hearth cookery, a skimmer, and other readily recognizable pieces of the *batterie de cuisine* that would be normal in any European kitchen between the Middle Ages and the middle of the nineteenth century.[34] At that point the evidence for specialized equipment grows exponentially, as can be seen in the well-illustrated cookbooks by Louis Eustache Audot and Eliza Acton.[35] Both works include chapters on the changing array of recently invented devices for the up-to-date kitchen.

A close examination of a good cookbook, concentrating on the techniques and equipment used or implied will yield a picture of the cook's skills and circumstances. Recipes rarely say "take a knife," but they constantly say "cut," "slice," and so on. In other words, the equipment is invoked by the actions. So are the spaces: freshly-made sausages are to be placed "in the smoky corner of the hearth"; meats hung to dry out of doors in the breeze; fruit taken to the dry attic or set in glass jars in the sun, where they cooked from its heat. Preserves were covered with paper dipped in brandy, and we can sometimes see them in still life paintings. A gridiron might be hung from a bit of string on a nail pounded into the wall. There were also shelves on the walls to hold equipment and perhaps even a cookbook or two. In a small dwelling there might be but a single hearth, to warm the family as well as to cook the meals and light the workspace. The table where the family ate would serve as a work table as well. Such a kitchen might not have all the equipment in Altimiras's woodcut.

The price of fuels was another consideration. If there are fewer roasts in French cookbooks than there are in English it is because coal was cheaper in England than in France. In the Middle Ages and even later, ovens were often built into the sides of fireplaces, but most households well into the nineteenth century and even later baked on griddles, with wafer irons, or in covered ceramic pots or "tin kitchens" of various designs. The many recipes for pancakes, flapjacks, and other little starchy foods reflect the absence of ovens, or the cost of fuel to fire them up on a regular basis. Quick dishes such as omelets and other small egg dishes provided food with a minimum of fuel. Urban householders who lacked baking facilities used the ovens of bakers in their neighborhoods. This practice is reflected in the classic slow-baked French dishes that are typically described as being *à la boulangère*.

Eighteenth-century cookbooks will sometimes recommend using the stewing stove, or *potager*. This was a block of masonry with insets in which small charcoal-fueled fires could be made. They were, ideally, placed by windows, not only for light, but to carry off the carbon monoxide fumes that the burning charcoal produced. In northern France and the German-speaking world the hearth was raised to waist level.

In the nineteenth century the coming of cast-iron ranges, originally built into the old hearths and later free-standing, brought a change in cooking techniques, though as late as the middle of the twentieth century there were cooks in rural Europe who were still cooking at the hearth. The new equipment made some cookbooks obsolete and brought substantial changes in how people cooked. This was particularly true for baking. Further changes have been rolling in ever since: gas ranges were already being used in the late nineteenth century. With electrification, which happened at very different rates in different places, all kinds of other equipment appeared in kitchens and even in dining rooms. In the twentieth century the chafing dish, the toaster, and the waffle iron were followed by the electric refrigerator. After World War II manufacturers produced many cooking gadgets, principal among them the blender and then the food processor. Each of these devices gave rise to specialized publications, many of the earliest ones published by the manufacturers of the devices. Industrialized food producers also put out small-format recipe booklets; the gelatin companies, for example, were able to use cheap color printing to win their customers. Meanwhile, metal-stamping factories were turning out inexpensive metal molds. In earlier centuries food molds were expensive pieces of equipment, hand-hammered from sheets of copper and lined with tin. When aluminum became cheap the gelatin companies offered molds and recipes alike to encourage sales. Catalogs published by suppliers for bakers, restaurants, and confectioners are dazzling evidence of the range of materials that were actually in use at a given time.

Ice houses were built in Italy in the sixteenth century, and by the end of that century there were some in France as well. Charles II built an ice house in Hyde Park after he returned from exile in France in 1660. Ice creams were by then being frozen with a mixture of ice and salt. By the eighteenth century caterers offered them among the delicacies to be served at elaborate dinners. Before the development of the ice-exporting business in the nineteenth century, they were not normally made at home.

The basic forms of pots and pans in the ordinary domestic kitchen change slowly. Only with major changes, such as that from hearth cooking to the cast iron range does the cook need new equipment. Nevertheless, the little three-footed ceramic pipkin and the iron griddle that stood over embers on a hearth are no longer useful today, and the skills that a cook needed in order to use them are forgotten. François Massialot, in *Le Cuisinier roïal et bourgeois* (1725), when he tells the reader what would be required to cook a dinner suitable for the courtiers of Louis XIV, appends an equipment list.[36] Similarly *Miss Parloa's Kitchen Companion* (1887) lists at great length all the equipment a prosperous kitchen would need to create a fine Boston dinner party at any season of the year.[37] Pots and pans might be made of cast iron (enameled or not), tinned copper (warnings were often given about the dangers of verdigris poisoning when the tinned lining wears away), or pewter (in the earlier years containing lead). Recipes that instruct the cook to use a silver knife to cut salad greens or stir a sauce with a silver spoon date from the days before stainless steel: iron could discolor foods, and create a disagreeable flavor. Silver spoons that are worn down on one side are evidence of a cook who cared more for her sauces than for her silverware.

Cookbooks can be useful adjuncts to inventories of household goods. A surprising number of materials are routinely implied in cookbooks but are too trivial to appear on lists or in inventories. Among these are basketwork and woodenware (also known as treen) such as bowls, spoons, mortars, and pestles. Roasts are tied up with twine; metal and wooden skewers are widely used. Paper is ubiquitous. It was used to cover delicate meats as they roasted. Small pieces were folded into square boxes in which cheese was melted. Larger sheets were cut into a circle, pleated, and used to bake soufflés. This is the origin of our white porcelain soufflé dishes with their vertically pleated sides. Spices came home from market wrapped in paper or parchment cones: these may be seen in Dutch paintings of everyday life, with the remains of lost letters still on them.

Typically cookbooks assume that their readers will use many measuring systems: by weight (pounds and kilos), by volume (by cupful), and by analogy (the size of an egg). Milk for rennet pudding should be blood warm; the coffee is roasted when it can be cracked between the teeth. Teacupsful would have been customized to each kitchen. The presence or absence of exact measurements is something of a distraction for modern readers. When most ingredients used were local ones there was a lot of variation. One miller's corn meal or wheat flour would not be exactly like another's. As a cook gained experience, stopping to use measures would have been an interruption. In baking and confectionary, where the repertory of materials used is smaller and where precise measuring matters more because the materials are less forgiving, measurements are indeed more exact.

The cookbooks measure time in units ranging from seconds to years. A careful analysis of times mentioned in a cookbook will give some evidence about the housewife's day: the bread is prepared in the evening, to rise overnight to be ready for baking in the morning. Cucumbers lie in pickle for two weeks. The workflow is continuous. Lydia Maria Child advises her readers to fill "odd moments" with knitting.[38] With a pair of knitting needles and some yarn, even a young person could produce stockings and other pieces of clothing at very little cost. Mrs. Child was quite right. The work of the day, the weekly chores, the annual cleanings are all there in cookbooks, waiting to be found.

An experienced cook preparing a familiar dish will make a succession of observations and decisions as he or she goes along. Is the texture of the crust flaky? Does it need a little more flour? As the dough is rolled out, how thick should it be? The nature of the apples used must be judged. Should they be tart or sweet; how thickly should they be cut, how many are needed to fill the crust; should some starch be added to thicken the filling somewhat? How should the top crust be decorated? The experienced cook will act while at the same time keeping in mind everything necessary to get a meal on the table. An inexperienced cook, lacking a better guide, turns to a cookbook. Cookbooks idealize food preparation. The apple pie recipe conjures up a smoothly functioning world into which nothing else will intrude. Although it is therefore inherently false from the beginning, we haven't got anything better.

It is a useful exercise to use a particular book to imagine making a flowchart of a meal, from assembling the ingredients and the equipment, to the manipulations (cutting, shaping, stuffing, combining), managing the heat or the cold, assembling and perhaps decorating the finished dish, and presenting it at table. The recipe describes process. The modern recipe usually begins a list of ingredients with the quantities that are needed, listed in the order of their use. The writer usually states the number of servings that will be produced, the cooking times, and oven temperatures, and describes each stage of preparation in chronological order. There may also be a preliminary statement by the author, explaining the origin of the dish, how it can be used, and perhaps even what might be served with it. Nutritional advice is not uncommon. Recipes in older cookbooks are much looser in form and less specific in detail. The writer often assumes that the cook is already knowledgeable about his or her craft and knows how to manage a hearth or a coal stove. They demand even more of the modern reader.

As the meal ends, the dirty dishes and the debris remain. Washing up was done with soap made using leftover animal fat and with lye made with ashes from the fire. Soap was often homemade. It was supplemented with fine sand for scouring and with washing soda (sodium carbonate). Before the nineteenth century few kitchens had water piped in; it had to be drawn from wells, or, in cities like Paris, brought to the kitchen from neighborhood fountains or carried to the house by men who contracted to deliver it. Such leftovers as there were got reused within the limits of spoilage. Many recipes use them. What the residents of a household would not eat might be given to the poor; what they rejected went to the pigs and chickens.

The furnishing and arrangement of the eating space, the expected behavior of the servers and diners, the rituals of carving, and the implements used for eating are laid out in some cookbooks, and in a multitude of books of instructions to servants, to the young, and to nervous brides entering upon a lifetime of dinner-giving. Dining schedules range from two meals, one at ten in the morning and the other at four in the afternoon, in the Middle Ages, to the *ambigu,* served in the small hours of the morning at the eighteenth-century French court, and the Victorian "fork breakfast," which was more like a lunch eaten standing up. Beginning in the late seventeenth century cookbooks sometimes included printed diagrams showing how dishes should be set on tables for meals served *à la française*, often accompanied by menus. Spoons and knives are routine in the Middle Ages, while forks gradually make their way into Europe towards the end of the sixteenth century.

The rules of who sat at table, how food was distributed and eaten, and all the little niceties that were to be observed are more the province of authorities on etiquette. When the food leaves the kitchen the cook has accomplished his or her task. In the end, however, the cook and the diner together that have performed the two necessary parts of a single act.

These rich, unreliable, diverting, and moving documents challenge, surprise, and enlighten the careful reader. Speaking as they do of daily life, changing circumstances, and aspirations, they repay the effort we make to understand them.

NOTES

1. Oxford, Bodleian Library, Laud MS 553, 1430, cited in Thomas Austin, ed., *Two Fifteenth-century Cookery-books* (London: Oxford University Press, 1888), 113. I have modernized the spelling.

2. Gillian Riley, *The Oxford Companion to Italian Food* (New York: Oxford University Press, 2007), 318.

3. Harl. 4016, cited in Austin, *Two Fifteenth-Century Cookery-books*, 93–94.

4. Francois Menon, *La nouvelle cuisinière bourgeoise* (Paris: Early English Text Society, 1822).

5. Carole Lambert, ed., *Du manuscrit à la table: Essais sur la cuisine au Moyen Âge et répertoire des manuscrits médiévaux contenant des recettes culinaires* (Montréal: Presses de l'Université de Montréal, 1992).

6. François Massialot, *Cuisinier roïal et bourgeois* (Paris: Charles de Sercy, 1691).

7. Eliza Leslie, *Directions for Cookery, in its various branches,* 11th ed. (Philadelphia: Carey and Hart, 1837).

8. Henry Notaker, *Printed Cookbooks in Europe, 1470–1700: A Bibliography of Early Modern Cuisine Literature* (New Castle: Oak Knoll Press; Houten: Hes & De Graf Publishers, 2010).

9. Andrew Pettegree, *The Book in the Renaissance* (New Haven: Yale University Press, 2010), xiv.

10. Elizabeth Raffald, *Experienced English Housekeeper,* with an introduction by Ray Shipperbottom (1769; repr. East Sussex: Southover Press, 1997), xiv.

11. Lydia Maria Child, *American Frugal Housewife* (New York: Samuel S. Wood, 1844), 62.

12. Sarah Joseph Hale, *The Good Housekeeper, or the Way to Live Well and To Be Well While We Live* (Boston: Weeks, Jordan and Co., 1839), 85, 86, 98.

13. Mrs. [Mary Hooker] Cornelius, *The Young Housekeeper's Friend* (Boston: C. Tappan, 1846).

14. Monsieur Marnette, *French Pastry-cook* (London: Nathaniel Brooks, 1658).

15. Stephen Mennell, *Lettre d'un pâtissier anglois et autres contributions à une polémique gastronomique du XVIIIème siècle* (Exeter: Exeter University, 1981); François Marin, *Les Dons de Comus ou les Délices de la table* (Paris: Prault, fils, 1739).

16. Fiona Lucraft, "The London Art of Plagiarism," part 1, *Petits Propos Culinaires* 42 (1992): 7–24; part 2, *Petits Propos Culinaires* 43 (1993): 34–46.

17. Hannah Glasse, *Art of Cookery* (London, 1747). Reprinted by Prospect Books in 2004 as *First Catch Your Hare: The Art of Cookery Made Plain and Easy*.

18. Richard Bradley, *Country housewife and lady's director in the management of a house, and the delights and profits of a farm* (London: D. Browne and T. Woodman, 1732).

19. Amelia Simmons, *American Cookery* (Hartford: Hudson and Goodwin, 1796).

20. Bartolomeo Scappi, *Opera* (Venice: Michele Tramezzino, 1570). For an English translation, see *The Opera of Bartolomeo Scappi (1570): L'arte et prudenza d'un maestro cuoco / The Art and Craft of a Master Cook*, trans. Terence Scully (Toronto: Toronto University Press, 2008).

21. Notaker, *Printed Cookbooks in Europe*.

22. Lynette Hunter, "Books for Daily Life: Household, husbandry, behaviour," in *The Cambridge History of the Book in Britain, IV: 1557–1695*, ed. John Barnard and D.F. McKenzie (Cambridge: Cambridge University Press, 2002), 514–32.

23. H. Hodges and S.C. Harding, eds., *Gleanings from Gloucestershire Housewives* (Gloucester: Gloucestershire Federation of Women's Institutes, 1927; repr. 1976).

24. R. Riddell, *Indian Domestic Economy and Receipt Book* (Bombay: Bombay Gazette Press, 1852); A.R. Kenny-Herbert, *Culinary Jottings for Madras* (Madras: Higginbotham, 1885); *An American Accent in the Kitchen* (South Africa: American Women's Club of Pretoria and the American Diplomatic Wives of Cape Town, date uncertain, 1950s).

25. Committee of Warwick Branch, Bermuda Welfare Society, *The Bermuda Recipe Book: Five Hundred Tested and Specially Recommended Recipes* (Warwick: Bermuda Welfare Society, 1934).

26. Elizabeth Putnam, *Mrs. Putnam's Receipt Book and young housekeeper's assistant* (Boston: Ticknor, Reed, and Fields, 1849).

27. C.H. Fowler, *Recipes Out of Bilibid* (New York: G.W. Stewart, 1946).

28. Wilhelmina Pächter, *In Memory's Kitchen: A Legacy from the Women of Terezin* (Northvale: J. Aronson, 1996).

29. *Operation Vittles Cook Book* (Berlin: Deutscher Verlag, 1949).

30. Alfred W. Crosby, *The Columbian Exchange: Biological and Cultural Consequences of 1492* (Westport: Praeger, 2003).

31. Friedrich Accum, *Treatise on Adulterations of Food and Culinary Poisons* (London: Longman, Hurst, Rees, Orme, and Brown, 1820).

32. Bradley, *Country housewife*, I: 58–60.

33. Georgina E. Brereton and Janet M. Ferrier, eds., *Le Ménagier de Paris*, trans. Karin Ueltschi (Paris: Livre de poche, 1994). This edition includes a translation into modern French.

34. Juan Altimiras, *Nuevo arte de cocina, sacado de la escuela de la experiencia económica* (1745; repr. Madrid: Imprenta de Cano, 1817).

35. Louis Eustache Audot, *La Cuisinière de la campagne et de la ville* (Paris: L.E.A. Audot, 1818); Eliza Acton, *Modern Cookery for Private Families* (London: Longman, Brown, Green and Longmans, 1845).

36. Massialot, *Le Cuisinier roïal et bourgeois*, 25.
37. Maria Parloa, *Miss Parloa's Kitchen Companion: A Guide For All Who Would Be Good Housekeepers* (Boston: Estes and Lauriat, 1887).
38. Child, *American Frugal Housewife*, 3.

BIBLIOGRAPHY

These are the most general bibliographies and related reference works. Much more can be found in the catalogs of auction houses and booksellers, historical society publications, and the writings of food historians. Above all, there is the great exploding Internet feast.

Arndt, Alice, ed. *Culinary Biographies: A Dictionary of the World's Great Historic Chefs, Cookbook Authors and Collectors, Farmers, Gourmets, Home Economists, Nutritionists, Restaurateurs, Philosophers, Physicians, Scientists, Writers, and Others Who Influenced the Way We Eat Today.* Houston: Yes Press, 2006.

Austin, Bette R. *A Bibliography of Australian Cookery Books Published Prior to 1941.* Melbourne: RMIT, 1987.

Axford, Lavonne B. *English Language Cookbooks, 1600–1973.* Detroit: Gale Research Co., 1976.

Bagnasco, Orazio, ed. *Catalogo del fondo italiano e latino delle opere di gastronomia sec. XIV-XIX.* 3 vols. Sorengo, Canton Ticino: Edizioni B.IN.G., 1994.

Barlösius, Eva. *Man nehme . . . : Literatur für Küche und Haus aus dem Deutschen Kochbuchmuseum.* Edited by Gisela Framke. Bielefeld: Verlag für Regionalgeschichte, 1998.

Barros, Cristina. *Los libros de la cocina Mexicana.* 2nd ed. Mexico: Consejo Nacional para la Cultura y las Artes, 2008.

Blomqvist, Hans. *Mat och dryck i Sverige: Litteraturöversikt.* Stockholm: LT I samarbete med Inst. för folklivsforskning, 1980.

Brown, Eleanor Parker. *Culinary Americana: Cookbooks Published in the Cities and Towns of the United States of America During the Years From 1860 Through 1960.* New York: Roving Eye Press, 1961.

Cagle, William R. *A Matter of Taste: A Bibliographical Catalogue of International Books on Food and Drink in the Lilly Library, Indiana University.* 2nd ed. New Castle: Oak Knoll Press, 1999.

Cagle, William R., and Lisa Killion Stafford. *American Books on Food and Drink: A Bibliographical Catalog of the Cookbook Collection Housed in the Lilly Library at the Indiana University.* New Castle: Oak Knoll Press, 1998.

Cavarra, Angela Adriana, and Alberto Manodori, eds. *Le cucine della memoria: Testimonianze bibliografice e iconografiche dei cibi tradizionali italiani nelle Biblioteche pubbliche statali.* 3 vols. Rome: De Luca, 1995.

Cook, Margaret. *America's Charitable Cooks: A Bibliography of Fund-raising Cook Books Published in the United States (1861–1915).* Kent, OH: self-published, 1971.

Coron, Sabine, ed. *Livres en bouche: Cinq siècles d'art culinaire français, du quatorzième au dix-huitième siècle.* Paris: Bibliothèque nationale de France; Hermann, 2001.

Davidson, Alan, Tom Jaine, Jane Davidson, and Helen Saberi. *The Oxford Companion to Food*. 2nd ed. Oxford: Oxford University Press, 2006.

Driver, Elizabeth. *A Bibliography of Cookery Books Published in Britain, 1875–1914*. London: Prospect Books; New York: Mansell Publishing, 1989.

———. *Culinary Landmarks: A Bibliography of Canadian Cookbooks, 1825–1949*. Toronto: University of Toronto Press, 2008.

Freedman, Paul, ed. *Food: The History of Taste*. Berkeley: University of California Press, 2007.

Hieatt, Constance B. "Making sense of medieval culinary records: Much done, but much more to do." In *Food and Eating in Medieval Europe*, edited by Martha Carlin and Joel T. Rosenthal, 101–16. London: Hambledon Press, 1998.

Hieatt, Constance B., Terry Nutter, with Johanna H. Holloway. *Concordance of English Recipes: Thirteenth Through Fifteenth Centuries*. Tempe: ACMRS, 2006.

Horn, Erna. *Schöne alte Kochbücher: Katalog der Kochbuchsammlung Erna Horn und Dr. Julius Arndt*. Munich: Karl Pressler, 1982.

Hunter, Lynette. "Books for daily life: Household, husbandry, behavior." In *Cambridge History of the Book in Britain*, vol. 4, *1557–1695*, edited by John Barnard and D. F. McKenzie, 514–32. Cambridge: Cambridge University Press, 2008.

Hyman, Philip, and Mary Hyman. "Les livres de cuisine imprimés en France du règne de Charles VIII à la fin de l'Ancien Régime." In *Livres en bouche: Cinq siècles d'art culinaire français, du quatorzième au dix-huitième siècle.*, edited by Sabine Coron, 55–72. Paris: Bibliothèque nationale de France; Hermann, 2001.

Kiple, Kenneth F., and Kriemhild Coneè Ornelas. *The Cambridge World History of Food*. 2 vols. Cambridge: Cambridge University Press, 2008.

Landwehr, John. *Het Nederlandse kookboek, 1510–1945: Een bibliografisch overzicht*. 't Goy-Houten: HES, 1995.

Lowenstein, Eleanor. *Bibliography of American Cookery Books, 1742–1860*. 3rd ed. Worcester: American Antiquarian Society, 1972.

Martin, Henri-Jean, and Roger Chartier. *Histoire de l'édition française*. 4 vols. Paris: Fayard, 1989–1991.

McLean, Virginia. *A Short-Title Catalogue of Household and Cookery Books Published in the English Tongue, 1701–1800*. London: Prospect Books, 1981.

Newman, Jacqueline M. *Chinese Cookbooks: An Annotated English-Language Compendium/Bibliography*. New York: Garland, 1987.

———. *Melting Pot: An Annotated Bibliography and Guide to Food and Nutrition Information for Ethnic Groups in America*. 2nd ed. New York: Garland, 1993.

Notaker, Henry. *Fra kalvedans til bankebiff: Norske kokebøker til 1951: Historie og bibliografi / Norwegian Cookbooks until 1951: History and Bibliography*. Oslo: Nasjonalbiblioteket, 2001.

———. *Printed Cookbooks in Europe, 1470–1700: A Bibliography of Early Modern Culinary Literature*. New Castle: Oak Knoll Press; Houten, Netherlands: Hes & De Graf, 2010.

Paleari Henssler, Maria. *Bibliografia Latino-italiana di Gastronomia*. Milan: Chimera, 1998.

Parasecoli, Fabio, and Peter Scholliers. *A Cultural History of Food*. 6 vols. London: Berg, 2012.

Petit-Laurent, Dominique. *Cuisine et gastronomie: répertoire bibliophile, 1900–1960*. Bordeaux: Agora, 1996–2000.

Pettegree, Andrew. *The Book in the Renaissance*. New Haven: Yale University Press, 2010.

Régo, Manuela. *Livros portugueses de cozinha*. 2nd ed. Lisbon: Presidência do Conselho de Ministros, Secretaria de Estado da Cultura, Biblioteca Nacional, 1988.

Riley, Gillian. *The Oxford Companion to Italian Food*. New York: Oxford University Press, 2007.

Rodinson, Maxime, A. J. Arberry, and Charles Perry. *Medieval Arab Cookery: Essays and Translations*. Totnes: Prospect Books, 2001.

Simón Palmer, María del Carmen. *Bibliografía de la gastronomía y la alimentación en España*. Gijón: Ediciones Trea, 2003.

Smith, Andrew F., ed. *The Oxford Encyclopedia of Food and Drink in America*. Oxford: Oxford University Press, 2004.

Törmä, Topi, and Inari Liinamaa. *Suomalaista gastronomista kirjallisuutta, 1735–1974*. Helsinki: Suomen gastronomien seura, 1975.

Vicaire, Georges. *Bibliographie Gastronomique*. Paris: P. Rouquette, 1890.

Weiss, Hans U. *Gastronomia: Eine Bibliographie der deutschsprachigen Gastronomie 1485–1914: Ein Handbuch für Sammler und Antiquare*. Zurich: Bibliotheca Gastronomica, 1996.

Westbury, Richard Morland Tollemache, Baron. *A Handlist of Italian Cookery Books*. Florence: L. S. Olschki, 1963.

White, Eileen, ed. *The English Cookery Book: Historical Essays*. Leeds Symposium on Food History. Totnes: Prospect Books, 2004.

Willan, Anne, Mark Cherniavsky, and Kyri Claflin. *The Cookbook Library: Four Centuries of the Cooks, Writers, and Recipes that Made the Modern Cookbook*. Berkeley: University of California Press, 2012.

Witteveen, Joop, and Bart Cuperus. *Bibliotheca Gastronomica: Eten en drinken in Nederland en België, 1474–1960*. 2 vols. Amsterdam: Linnaeus Press, 1998.

PART THREE

Problems

CHAPTER 14

The Revolt against Homogeneity

AMY B. TRUBEK

This essay focuses on the modern tensions between defining food (and drink) as a commodity versus as a good, as well as the implications of that choice for practices and perceptions.[1] Defining food as a commodity uses the narrow lens of modern capitalist economics: a commodity is something produced to be bought and sold in the marketplace purely as an economic transaction, providing profit for the producer and a needed service for the consumer. When food is defined solely as a commodity, use value and exchange value are conflated, whereas considering food as a good permits greater diversity of meaning. Scholars have sought to define the persistent "nonmarket" qualities of goods using definitions such as "the social life of things," "economic embeddedness," and "food culture."[2] The problem of definition when food is solely considered as a commodity has also occurred on the ground; the scholarly debate is a reflection of many *in situ* concerns about the organization of food, from production through consumption, in modern life.

The lack of distinction between use value and exchange value is due in part to historical transformations in the organization of food and drink. Although the legacy of competing definitions and practices can be traced back to the early days of conquest and colonialism, this essay will focus on the past century. The changing, or perhaps increasingly invisible, "biographies or 'social lives' of production" have accelerated as food and drink are increasingly globally sourced and traded.[3] The organization of the modern food system reflects and shapes other persistent structural shifts in the organization of everyday life: the increased movement of people from rural to urban areas, the industrialization of food production from farm to table, the expansion of food exchanges, and the rise of technology in all forms of food work. This long-term transformative process results in many competing realities as to on-the-ground decisions about what to grow, harvest, ship, eat, and drink.

Globalization and industrialization preoccupies many scholars in the humanities and social sciences looking at all manner of modern social, cultural, and economic issues. Some look broadly at macro-level transformations, and some examine these transformations by closely considering microprocesses.[4] Food has functioned as an instrumental element in the development of these systems, but food is also a good lens for understanding their present functioning. Many food scholars have argued that the notable food-related events and actions of the twentieth century share characteristics resulting from the increasingly global reach of an "industrialized agricapitalist food system."[5] One result of such integration has been the emergence of "global food regimes" focusing not just on food as a commodity that can be bought and sold in marketplaces of any scale, but also on food as an object requiring standardized oversight, including such twentieth-century developments as food safety regulations, packaging requirements, global supply and distribution channels, and more. However, investments in preserving, promoting, and protecting those forms of food and drink that continue to exist somehow outside (or at least in spite of) such regimes also characterize this time period. Over the past twenty years, a number of food scholars have looked at smaller-scale actions—the development of place-based policies in Europe, the rise of organic modes of production in the United States and beyond, the persistence of subsistence-based food systems—to demonstrate that sweeping claims about the hegemony of the global-industrial food system may lead to the neglect of vibrant traditions and powerful protests around the globe.[6] Another scholarly approach has been to examine the intersections between food as commodity and as a public good, to demonstrate the possibly hegemonic power of the industrialized agricapitalist system to absorb other approaches, or, conversely, the limits of new modes of production in transforming the present system.[7]

Another issue to consider involves the continuities and disjunctures between an "industrialized agricapitalist system" and people's everyday lives. For example, the global demographic shift of people from rural to urban areas accelerated the movement of some domestic culinary tasks out of the household or village milieu; in the twentieth century bread baking was generally seen as the work of laborers outside the home, unless an individual *choose* to bake at home. By 1920, an increasing number of people were living in urban areas, often residing in small, cramped quarters with little kitchen space. Thus numerous adaptive methods of procuring and preparing food were required. These shifts were not identical in every place; time frames vary widely. By 1960, new technologies—from tractors to pesticides—transformed the scale of possibility for many farming systems. The ubiquity and necessity of food to everyday life means that what is happening at any moment is characterized by fluidity.

Among contemporary college students, seeking to make sense of an increasingly interdependent and interconnected world, the tension between how food and drink are *created* and what this process of creation *means* is potent and compelling. They, too, see the limits of defining food and drink as homogeneous commodities. At this juncture, however, those involved in the revolt against homogeneity (farmers, chefs, students, parents, public health officials) seem preoccupied with looking backward and looking to other cultures, in order to identify more pristine times and places as well as morally pure beliefs and actions. The challenge of teaching about the present revolt involves engaging students about their own romancing of the past. A trail of food scholarship now exists that addresses the importance of not falling into either romantic nostalgia or moral absolutism when looking at food and drink—be it that of yesterday, today, or tomorrow.

In this sense, considering the contemporary food revolt could easily involve comparisons with other recent social movements, most notably the environmental movement. Fifteen years ago, environmental historian William Cronon called on those in the environmental movement to reconsider their assumption that the goal of their particular revolt should be to create (or recreate) the ideal of a pristine wilderness. He asserted that wilderness is "quite profoundly a human creation—indeed, the creation of very particular human cultures at very particular moments in human history."[8] Focusing solely on a vision of pristine farms or perfect meals may interfere with our ability to figure out how to properly feed ourselves in the twenty-first century. As Cronon says: "If living in history means that we cannot help leaving marks on a fallen world, then the dilemma we face is to decide what kinds of marks we wish to leave." What are the principled positions that need to be adopted in order to build a better food system for all? And how do we encourage students to see these principled positions as extending across space and through time? The compelling reasons for rejecting food and drink as only involving use value might also explain the temptation of an analysis based on romance and nostalgia. As anthropologist Heather Paxson puts it, "Food offers a strong anchor for identity because eating well—adequately, appropriately—holds not only the promise of being well (healthy) but also being good (moral)."[9] Teaching about the tensions inherent in the contemporary global and industrial food system alongside the many interventions and alternatives to that system is exciting and rewarding work. Protests against the powerful modern impulse to focus on homogeneity and consistency have long arcs into the past, but also can be cast anew in the future.

There are so many opportunities to engage passionate students and take them on an intellectually complex and rewarding journey. This essay examines the contemporary struggle between food as a commodity and food as a good by following particular foods or drinks. These claims are considered by examining scholarship that looks at activities and events from throughout the past century. This approach grounds the very broad and complex systemic forces that create the juxtapositions between, for example, slow-fermented, wood-fired baguettes and Wonder Bread, providing concrete examples and particular stories.

FOLLOWING WINE, CHEESE, AND COFFEE THROUGH TIME AND SPACE

Using case studies permits a consideration of both breadth and depth, providing better illumination of the long-term tensions between food as a commodity and as a good. The first case will be about modern wine production, illuminating the problem of boundaries around practices and perceptions. The second case will consider cheesemaking, since two of the vexing issues for modern cheese are the scale of production and the role of industrial technology. The final case examines coffee production and trade, as the emergence of global coffee production and consumption are directly linked to colonial and postcolonial politics and regimes of power. In teaching about food, case studies provide great scaffolding for broader theoretical discussions about globalization, industrialization, power, and the implications for modern food systems. Numerous other cases studies can also be compiled from the burgeoning literature looking at the exchange value of food and drink, including sugar, tomatoes, fish, and more.[10]

Wine

Wine, the naturally fermented juice of fresh grapes, is today a globally consumed alcoholic beverage that has long held strong associations with certain natural and cultural environments. The earliest archaeological evidence of cultivated grapes for winemaking dates to 5000–7000 B.C.E. in what is now the Eurasian state of Georgia. The ancient Babylonian and Egyptian civilizations made wine, but it was the ancient Greek and Roman civilizations that embraced viticulture and viniculture, spreading grapes and winemaking knowledge to their far-flung colonies. The Greeks are known to have brought grapes to southern Italy, Sicily, and southern France.[11] Wine growing moved further north with the Roman Empire, helping to create wine cultures in all of Europe, especially what is now France, which was long the major producer of wine in Europe (and sometimes beyond European borders as well). By the Middle Ages, wine was France's premier export crop, and by the 1800s most regions of the nation boasted vineyards. Natural disasters, especially the phylloxera epidemic, wreaked havoc on French viticulture and viniculture during the nineteenth century. Many winemakers and vineyards became increasingly vulnerable to competition from other parts of Europe and beyond. By 1900 wine production had extended to North and South America, South Africa, and other areas; these wine producers relied on the traditions of French winemaking for their own practices.

These threats to the livelihoods of French peasants, vignerons, and *negociants* alike led to protests against the increasingly commodified definition of wines, the most notable being the global adoption of the name "champagne" for sparkling wine, rather than reserving it for a wine made in the Champagne region of France (the original site of production). By the 1890s, producers of French Champagne wanted to retain control over the production process and protect champagne's reputation as a unique good.[12] The increasingly elevated status of Champagne amongst the international bourgeoisie during the Belle Epoque did little to contribute to the livelihoods of the laborers in the fields and much to threaten their identity. The vignerons wanted to retain some proprietary rights to the name "champagne," by then used all over the globe, so they turned to the soil, *terroir,* fighting for Champagne as a product of the soil rather than a placeless pretty label. In 1908 Champagne was the first region to be awarded an *appellation* or controlled delimitation by the French state. This French legislation links a specific food or drink to a region, a bond described as "local, loyal and constant."

The initial, regional legislation was to protect Champagne from international fraud; another outcome was to help launch a series of efforts to create national legislation to preserve and promote food and drink from different regions. By the time the final national legislation was passed in 1935, creating the quality label *appellations d'origine controlées* (AOC), and the governing body to oversee the label, the Institut des Appellations d'Origine Controlées, the concern extended to concepts of uniqueness and quality. Joseph Capus, an agronomist who became a member of the French Senate in 1930 and drafted the final legislation, said, "It is not sufficient simply to guarantee the product's authenticity, but also to ensure *quality* in so far as it can be measured by soil and grape variety."[13] The AOC quality label went on to inspire an Italian variation (*denominazione di origine controllata*), which passed into law in 1963, as well as other versions in Spain and Portugal. The AOC quality label now includes numerous other products beside wine, including cheeses, olives, honey, and fruits. Quality labels are an intervention by the state that assumes the importance of "biography" to a food or drink, and so provides an early example of nonmarket principles being introduced into the global agricapitalist food system. An unusual aspect of the AOC intervention is that the laws protect *both* the natural and human elements involved in producing distinctive food and drink.

The link among taste, place, and quality, together understood as *terroir*, remains a compelling claim about how wine is produced and consumed in France. Almost a century after the enactment of the first AOC legislation, the French wine industry still relies on such claims, although the practice of drinking wine every day as a part of rural life has shifted to drinking wine to commemorate special occasions or to demonstrate connoisseurship. In fact, globalization now means that the AOC label is not just a guarantee of authenticity but part of a set of larger socioeconomic transformations that has helped propel a shift in the production and marketing of wine for consumers. Regionalism and regional identity within the context of globalization now operate as the most powerful influences on future wine consumption in France. This is seen in the emergence of the wine grower as a new cultural icon, representing the best of rural, agrarian France, as well as the resurgence in the importance of *terroir* as an indicator of wines of quality.[14]

Cheese

The process of transforming fluid milk into cheese first emerged in the Fertile Crescent during the Neolithic period. The first cheeses were made using acid coagulation, which occurs when milk is heated to a certain temperature and an acid is added, causing curds to form and separate from the whey. By 4500 B.C.E., cheesemaking knowledge and technology had spread to the Mediterranean basin, Europe, and the Middle East. In Mesopotamia, the worship of the Sumerian goddess Inanna involved daily offerings of butter and cheese.[15] By 1500 B.C.E. cheesemaking was part of daily life in South Asia, as can be seen in the revered status of cheese in the Vedas. Making cheese eventually became part of any food system relying on domesticated animals; cheese is much easier to preserve and store than fluid milk, which requires storage at cold temperatures to last for any length of time.

Cheesemaking, initially an innovation to help deal with excess milk, became part of people's daily diet in Europe. Over the course of the Roman Empire, cheese transformed from a byproduct of subsistence farming to part of an agricultural economy involved in feeding both rural and urban citizens. Roman cheesemaking techniques spread beyond Italy to France, England, and beyond, and cheese became a central part of European agriculture and cuisine. By the Middle Ages, two parallel sets of practices emerged: peasant cheesemaking on a small scale on a single farmstead and manorial cheesemaking on a much larger scale on a manor or in a monastery. This pattern dominated throughout Europe through the twentieth century, allowing for the development of a wide array of cheese types, emerging from the particularities of natural environment, cultural values, and organization of production.

During the nineteenth century in much of Europe, cheesemaking became more than a convenient process of farm-based food transformation and preservation, but also a crucial component of regional and national cuisines. To have cheese as part of a meal became crucial not just to the farm families of Normandy, but also to the laborers and bourgeoisie residing in Paris. An increased urban demand for cheese required new organization of production. The case of Camembert reveals the interdependence of urban consumer demand and the transformations in the organization of cheese production. Camembert is a soft, bloomy rind cheese that was long produced in the Auge region—and consumed primarily within the region.[16] The development of rail lines directly to Paris opened up a new means of successfully transporting this quite delicate cheese to market. By the late nineteenth century, this very localized cheese had become widely available in major French cities, including Paris and Lille. The increased demand and complex production involved in making Camembert led to the concentration of cheese manufacture in centralized cheese factories. Camembert requires immediate molding after curdling. According to Pierre Boisard, "if molding is begun too early, the curd will be too fragile and will break apart in the mold. However, if it is delayed too long, the draining process will be slowed down by overly clotted curds. Ladle-molding therefore takes place as soon as the curdling process is complete."[17] Problems with damage during shipping lead to the development of special wooden boxes to facilitate transport Camembert. Other fragilities, including the development of unwanted molds on the rind, led to changes in manufacturing, including in some cases pasteurizing the milk used to make Camembert. New technologies were introduced to facilitate production; by the 1920s, "steam boilers now produced the steam for heating the milk and the water needed for cleaning."[18] Over the course of the twentieth century Camembert came to define a certain style of French cheese writ large, extending demand far beyond the shores of France. New technologies were incorporated in attempts to stay true to the original recipe of making Camembert, while also increasing the volume of cheese made every day. The delicate process of ladling the cheese into molds can now be done by a machine, a "robot molder" that has ladle arms which move across twenty molds at a time, pouring the curds into each mold with mathematical precision.

In the United States, with a food system dominated by industrial agricultural practices, on-farm subsistence cheesemaking fairly quickly transformed to purchasing milk and making cheese in cheese factories. The first American cheese factory was founded in 1851 in upstate New York. By 1900 about ten million pounds of cheese were produced per year on farmsteads and three hundred million pounds in cheese factories. By 1930 there was very little cheese produced on farmsteads, and by midcentury most cheese produced on a small-scale consumed by Americans was imported from Europe.[19] By the end of the twentieth century, over nine billion pounds of cheese were produced annually, almost exclusively in large manufacturing facilities, with the majority of this cheese consumed on pizza or in other melted forms.

Over the past forty years, cheese as an easily meltable commodity has been joined by a new type of American cheese, a food inscribed with multiple exchange values. An artisan cheese movement has emerged; a growing group of small farmstead cheese makers are dedicated to an "ethos of craftsmanship" and carefully consider each step of the process of making cheese—the pasture where animals graze, the breed of animal, the type of cheese, the separation of curd from whey, the place to age—hoping to adopt good practices, but also to be good citizens.[20] To take one regional example, Vermont has over forty artisan cheesemakers, all of whom are first-generation cheese makers, and they have become a dynamic force in the conversation about dairy farming in the state. Artisan cheese operations, unlike the faltering dairy farms that produce fluid milk for a commodity market, are flourishing. Much of the success of Vermont artisan cheese, both within the state and also in urban areas such as Boston and New York, is due to the *meaning* seen to reside in these cheeses. The meaning varies depending on interpreter, but in most cases, as Paxson puts it, "artisanal cheese contributes a new chapter to the American Pastoral."[21] The difficulty lies in the modern distance between the aspiration to make and eat food that holds more than commodity value, and the actual reality of industrial food production. We want to find purity and beauty in our cheese, but the agreed upon best practices—pasteurization, HACCP principles, national shipping and distribution—are ruled by practicality and efficiency.

Coffee

Coffee can easily be identified as a commodity. It is harvested from a plant that only grows in a tropical climate but is consumed globally. In fact, coffee is now second only to petroleum in global trade in terms of movement of goods. The coffee plant is an evergreen shrub that for proper growing conditions needs to be planted at 1,800–3,600 feet of altitude in areas characterized by good rainfall or at 3,000–6,300 feet in equatorial regions. *Coffea arabica* is indigenous to Ethiopia, and the first center of commercial production was Yemen. The early commercial trade for coffee did not involve the fully integrated supply chains that characterize the modern period, but rather involved numerous small producers, transporters, and retailers. There have long been complex social, political, and economic networks involved in moving coffee from the farm to the cup—in fact it can be argued that coffee production has always been embedded in a transnational landscape, operating at both local and global scales. Coffee has always been a luxury product with ubiquitous demand.

Coffee became an important part of colonial trade; the first colonial coffee plantations were developed by the Dutch in Indonesia, and coffee was first planted in the Americas as a colonial crop in the 1700s. By 1800 coffee was the third most valuable traded global commodity. Colonial coffee production revolved around the creation of large plantations, often relying on slave labor or indentured servitude. In the postcolonial period, nations such as Columbia and Brazil became major producers of coffee; production systems varied from nation to nation, with both small holders and large plantations increasingly involved in the global marketplace.

By the twentieth century the global North processed and consumed coffee and the global South grew it. Over the past thirty years, however, new interventions into the dominance of the North in the global coffee market have emerged, involving the creation of alternative global supply chains in order to better benefit coffee farmers in the global South. A notable issue for coffee farmers trying to navigate a global supply chain involves the relatively small scale of much coffee farming and the much larger scale of the entities involved in shipping, roasting, and selling the coffee beans to consumers. On average, the grower only receives seven cents out of a one-pound bag of coffee that consumers purchase for nine dollars and fifty cents.[22] The majority of the money earned goes to those who provide transportation, processing, and roasting. These components of the global coffee supply chain are dominated by multinational corporations and national cooperatives.

Coffee has become an important part of the fair trade movement, which began to focus on food and drink twenty-five years ago. This intervention into the modern market system "began as an initiative to improve market access and trading conditions for small-scale producers in the south who were considered 'disadvantaged.'"[23] Early attempts to launch fair trade networks developed in the 1960s and 1970s in response to trade embargoes due to political sanctions (notably in Nicaragua and Cuba). These efforts converged with initiatives attempting to address underdevelopment in the global South. The notion of fair trade came to be organized around third-party certification that guaranteed that the purchased product was produced according to a set of core principles, including trade at above-market prices, direct trade, financial support for producers, and democratic organization of producers to promote sustainability.[24] The main goal of fair trade is to change the parameters of trade between North and South in order to guarantee better livelihoods for producers. Coffee, the second most traded commodity in the world, was an early choice for the fair trade community, with early initiatives developed in the Netherlands and the United Kingdom. For example, Cafédirect in the United Kingdom involved a collaboration between four alternative trade nongovernment organizations (NGOs). Most early coffee interventions were collaborations of farmers with NGOs that could bridge the gap between them and suppliers, roasters, and marketers.

The fair trade coffee movement has moved far beyond the early efforts of advocates and NGOs. Purchasing fair trade coffee has now become intrinsic to the social entrepreneurship models of coffee companies large and small, including Douwe Egberts in the Netherlands and Starbucks in the United States. This had led to concerns that fair trade, initially a form of resistance to the dominant system and founded on nonmarket principles, has now been absorbed by the global agricapitalist food system. This could create erosion in one of the principled claims of the movement: fair prices for growers and a socially based system of coffee distribution.

THE REVOLT AGAINST HOMOGENEITY: ENGAGING ETHICS, AESTHETICS, OR BOTH?

Despite the many pronouncements about the eventual triumph of progress through better living with machine-made, scientifically produced, and globally sourced food, in reality we still aren't quite sure how we should feed ourselves. The tension between aspirations (consistency versus diversity; convenience versus connection), as well as between methods (machine- versus hand-made; organic versus chemical inputs; small- versus large-scale) remain. This makes for fruitful teaching opportunities; examining the history of progress, protest, and principles shaping food can lead to larger considerations of meaning in modern life.

Our contemporary confusion about how we should feed ourselves has helped to propel a food movement that revolts against the consequences of the increasing scope and scale of the global agricapitalist system. In the United States, this newest version of a long century of protest engages people with many different agendas and goals for the future. The combined frustrations of farmers, environmental activists, nutritionists, parents, youth, and other groups has led to a remarkably large and robust call for large-scale systemic change in the organization of food, from production through consumption. Journalists have been particularly effective in announcing a call to arms; Michael Pollan's extremely influential book *The Omnivore's Dilemma,* which reported on the industrial logic behind raising larger numbers of animals on feedlots and adding extra calories from high fructose corn syrup to myriad processed foods, was joined by other journalistic critiques.[25] New modes of communication on the Internet, including social marketing and social media, have been particularly effective with young people. Finally, a series of widely popular films have also raised awareness of the consequences of using a strict commodity interpretation of making, moving, and eating food and drink.[26]

Close examination of the myriad interventions into our "industrialized agricapitalist food system" leads to larger intellectual questions: What makes food good? What makes food sustainable? What makes food virtuous? And why do these groups of people, right now, care to answer such questions with such actions? Taking our present concerns with food and teasing out the meaning behind any number of current small innovations can reap rich pedagogical rewards. What of the desire to sail to the Dominican Republic to pick up a supply of cocoa beans for a small business that sells eight-dollar chocolate bars (as in the case of Mast Brothers Chocolate in Brooklyn)? And what of the decision to run a solar-powered goat farm that only milks twenty goats and sells in local farmers' markets and food co-ops (as in the case of Lazy Lady Farm in Westford, Vermont)? And what of the coffee farmer cooperatives in El Salvador trying to create a direct market with American consumers for their coffee beans (as in the case of the Community Agroecology Network in Santa Cruz, California)?

Attempting to answer these broader questions can lead in diverse scholarly directions. One approach is to consider the contributions of contemporary philosophers. In the current revolt, there is a desire to "be good" with food in a way that bypasses the earlier signposts of agrarian and culinary progress. So instead of better living through long-distance trade and nifty machines, there is a desire for minimal chemical inputs, ad-hoc domestic organization, et cetera. This desire becomes cast as an ethical stance; in particular, there is a tendency to create a dichotomy between "good" and "bad" foods. The problem with such a dichotomy, as philosopher Lisa Heldke points out, is that "dichotomies tend to erase nuance; to eliminate the possibility of anything existing in between their poles; to purify . . . ambiguous cases." Dichotomies are difficult to sustain in our current system. Sauerkraut, essentially processed cabbage, might be a virtuous food if made under certain conditions (organic? small-scale? living wage?), but it is always a processed food, considered a "must avoid" in some versions of good versus bad foods. Even within the realm of virtuous foods much sorting occurs: among activists the juxtaposition of "big" and "small" organic farms or the boundaries of local sourcing (fifteen miles versus one hundred miles) are often invoked as moral problems. Another excellent area of inquiry, one that has preoccupied ethicists for some time, involves the rights of and the humane treatment of animals. Is it more ethical to slaughter a "happy" cow that has grazed on open pasture than a "sad" cow that ate feed corn from a trough on a feed lot?[27]

And what of history? When considering the various protests against changes that have made growing, transforming and eating food more consistent and homogenous, an invocation of the past often explains what has been lost. Contemporary protests, though, are notably characterized by a *dualistic* engagement with the past. For example, agrarian philosopher Wendell Berry creates this stark juxtaposition: "The food industrialists have by now persuaded millions of consumers to prefer food that is already prepared. They will grow, deliver, and cook your food for you and (just like your mother) beg you to eat it . . . . The industrial eater is, in fact, one who does not know that eating is an agricultural act, who no longer knows or imagines the connections between eating and the land, and who is therefore necessarily passive and uncritical—in short, a victim." Discontent with the present food system points to the past for an explanation of our present predicament but it also creates a wellspring of ideas and examples about the future. In the writings of many who critique the food system lies the landscape of another era, an earlier time when there was a connection between eating, tasting, and the land. In Berry's analysis, and those of many others, there exists an assumption that we once had it right, but industrialization and globalization have allowed (or perhaps forced) us to lose our way.

Among people engaged with making and promoting the "good" foods that define alternatives to the dominant industrial global food system, the good also increasingly involves an aesthetic dimension. The *quality* of food has become increasingly central to the emerging definition of food and drink that attempts to transcend a definition of food as a commodity. Philosopher Carolyn Korsmeyer calls this "ethical gourmandism." Focusing on taste sensation, she uses recent research in psychology to point out that taste sensations are never solely bodily experiences but are mediated by moral and other concerns, such that "tastes are always tastes of."[28] The emerging notion of quality is still vague, but most often involves a connection between sensory tastes, moral values, and an ethic. Such food tastes better. Scores of U.S. citizens are presently engaged in humanely raising pigs, carefully planting greens, and precisely making cheese that combines aesthetic and moral ideals about food that tastes good, intervenes in the corporate industrial food system, and is good for the planet.

Anthropologists have done fieldwork among groups protesting or responding to a food system increasingly defined by industrial modes of production and by scopes and scales that are global in reach. Much of their focus is on fine-grained analysis of how "nonmarket" ideas, aspirations, and values shape perceptions and practices.[29] The central conflict for people engaged in preserving traditional practices or inventing new virtuous practices lies in whether to, or how to, engage with the global or industrial qualities of the dominant food system. Most often, these are not practices embedded in long-standing immutable cultural traditions, but rather activities that in some way are responding to the dominant system. These "tastemakers"—the chefs, cheese makers, vignerons, and others involved in such work—tend to vacillate between market pressures and ethical and aesthetic aspirations. These are also the struggles of committed consumers, like those involved in fair trade, organics, or slow food. These consumers see food purchasing decisions as "voting with your fork," staking claims for shifting the marketplace in the direction of nonmarket principles that can help promote and preserve cultural and agricultural diversity. In this view, each "vote" for Mast Brothers chocolate bars or fair trade coffee potentially reorients the larger system.

CONCLUSION

Food always functions as far more than mere biological and physiological sustenance. Food is pleasurable, meaningful, hospitable, personal, social, spiritual. Food simply matters. In any place or time, food can also create social, political and/or economic conflicts, or symbolize these conflicts. Otherwise, why eat the cake? Why dump the tea? In the modern period, conflicts about the meaning of food—for ourselves, for nations, for nature, for principles and practices—increasingly involve an engagement with the globally dominant system of making and moving food. At the same time, dominance does not have to mean absolute hegemony. Tracing the many ways people negotiate, navigate, and protest our increased reliance on food as a commodity reveals new levels of complexity and possibility, both in the past and the present.

NOTES

1. For the remainder of this essay, it will be assumed that all manner of alimentation, including all libations, can be categorized as food.

2. There are numerous social science studies that look at the exchange value of globally traded commodities, including and extending beyond food and drink. Notable examples include Arjun Appadurai, ed., *The Social Life of Things: Commodities in Cultural Perspective* (Cambridge: Cambridge University Press, 1988); and Karl Polanyi, *The Great Transformation* (New York: Rinehart, 1944). More recent scholarship has looked specifically at food and drink, such as Elizabeth Barham, "Translating Terroir: The Global Challenge of French AOC Labeling," *Journal of Rural Studies* 19 (2003): 127–38; and Marie-Christine Renard, "Fair Trade: Quality, Market and Conventions," *Journal of Rural Studies* 19 (2003): 87–96.

3. Heather Paxson, *The Life of Cheese: Crafting Food and Value in the United States* (Berkeley: University of California Press, 2012), 14.

4. Jurgen Habermas's work is an example of considerations of macro-level transformations; see Habermas, *The Structural Transformation of the Public Sphere: An Inquiry into a Category of Bourgeois Society,* trans. Thomas Burger (Cambridge, MA: MIT Press, 1991). The work of English social historians, for example E.B. Hobsbawm, provides examples of micro-level manifestations of larger changes; see Hobsbawm, *The Age of Empire: 1875–1914* (New York: Vintage Books, 1989).

5. The work of critical sociologists on the emergence of an increasingly integrated global agrifood system has been instrumental in the growing critique of our contemporary food systems. Some early and important scholarship that helped to build this argument are Harriet Friedmann, "The Political Economy of Food: The Rise and Fall of the Postwar International Food Order," *American Journal of Sociology* 88, supplement (1982): 248–86; Harriet Friedmann, "The International Relations of Food: The Unfolding Crisis of National Regulation," in *Food: Multidisciplinary Perspectives,* eds. Barbara Harriss-White and Raymond Hoffenberg (Oxford: Blackwell, 1994), 174–204; Alexander Bonanno, "Liberal Democracy in the Global Era: Implications for the Agro-Food Sector," *Agriculture and Human Values* 15, no. 3 (1998): 223–42; Michael Watts and David Goodman, "Agrarian Questions: Global Appetites, Local Metabolism," in *Globalizing Food: Agrarian Questions and Global Restructuring,* ed. David Goodman and Michael J. Watts (London: Routledge, 1997), 1–23.

6. For example, Amy Trubek, *The Taste of Place: A Cultural Journey into Terroir* (Berkeley: University of California Press, 2008).

7. In this next generation of critical sociology, emerging interventions into the global agrifood system are examined closely for the potential of structural transformation, for example, Julie Guthman's analysis of the organic movement in California: Guthman, *Agrarian Dreams: The Paradox of Organic Farming in California* (Berkeley: University of California Press, 2004) and Patricia Allen, ed., *Together at the Table: Sustainability and Sustenance in the American Agrifood System* (University Park, PA: Pennsylvania State University Press, 2004).

8. Cronon's seminal article, "The Trouble with Wilderness," inspired new considerations of the goals of the environmental movement. William Cronon, "The Trouble with Wilderness; or, Getting Back to the Wrong Nature," in *Uncommon Ground: Rethinking the Human Place in Nature,* ed. William Cronon (New York: W.W. Norton, 1996), 69–90.

9. Paxson, *The Life of Cheese,* 4.

10. See Sidney Mintz, *Sweetness and Power: The Place of Sugar in Modern History* (New York: Penguin Books, 1986); Deborah Barndt, *Tangled Routes: Women, Work, and Globalization on the Tomato Trail,* 2nd ed. (Lanham: Rowman & Littlefield, 2008); Barry Estabrook, *Tomatoland: How Modern Industrial Agriculture Destroyed Our Most Alluring Fruit* (Kansas City, MO: Andrews McMeel, 2011); Mark Kurlansky, *Cod: A Biography of the Fish That Changed the World* (New York: Penguin, 1998).

11. Jancis Robinson, *The Oxford Encyclopedia of Wine* (Oxford: Oxford University Press, 1999), 330.

12. For more detailed historiography, see Kolleen Guy, *When Champagne Became French: Wine and the Making of a National Identity* (Baltimore: Johns Hopkins University Press, 2003).

13. From the website of the Institut National des Appellation Controlée, www.inao.gouv.fr, accessed March 2013.

14. For more on the changing face of wine connoisseurship in France, see Marion Demoissier, *Wine Drinking Culture In France: A National Myth or a Modern Passion?* (Cardiff: University of Wales Press, 2010).

15. For a very detailed analysis of the historical emergence of cheesemaking, see Paul Kindstedt, *Cheese and Culture: A History of Cheese and Its Place in Western Civilization* (White River Junction: Chelsea Green Publishing, 2012).

16. The material on Camembert comes from Pierre Boisard, *Camembert: A National Myth,* trans. Richard Miller (Berkeley: University of California Press, 2003), 35–55.

17. Boisard, *Camembert,* 62.

18. Boisard, *Camembert,* 133.

19. See Kindstedt, *Cheese and Culture,* 206–207.

20. For more on the contemporary artisan cheese movement, see Paxson, *The Life of Cheese.*

21. Paxson, *The Life of Cheese,* 15.

22. For more details, see Catherine Tucker, *Coffee Culture: Local Experiences, Global Connections,* Routledge Series for Creative Teaching and Learning in Anthropology (New York: Routledge, 2010), 124–26.

23. Caroline Wright, "Fairtrade Food: Connecting Producers and Consumers," in *The Globalization of Food,* eds. David Inglis and Debra Gimlin (Oxford: Berg, 2009), 140.

24. Wright, "Fairtrade Food."

25. In many ways, the investigative journalism on the contemporary food system has tried to marry the critiques of critical sociologists with the utopian calls for food versions of "pristine wilderness." For other examples see Raj Patel, *Stuffed and Starved: The Hidden Battle for the World Food System* (New York:

Melville House, 2008) and Paul Roberts, *The End of Food* (New York: Houghton Mifflin, 2008).

26. Some notable films are *Food, Inc; Super Size Me; Fresh;* and *Mondovino.*

27. Philosopher Peter Singer's arguments in *Animal Liberation: The Definitive Classic of the Animal Movement* (1975; repr. New York: Harper Perennial, 2009) have influenced other considerations, both in scholarly and journalist circles, such as Jonathan Safran Foer, *Eating Animals* (New York: Little, Brown and Company, 2010) and Temple Grandin and Catherine Johnson, *Animals Make Us Human: Creating the Best Life for Animals* (Boston: Houghton Mifflin Harcourt, 2009).

28. Carolyn Korsmeyer, "Ethical Gourmandism," in *Philosophy of Food*, ed. David Kaplan (Berkeley: University of California Press, 2011), 87–102.

29. Examples include Trubek, *The Taste of Place;* Alison Leitch, "Slow Food and the Politics of 'Virtuous Globalization,'" in *The Globalization of Food*, ed. David Inglis and Debra Gimlin (Oxford: Berg, 2009), 45–64; Paxson, *The Life of Cheese;* Demoissier, *Wine Drinking Culture in France.*

BIBLIOGRAPHY

Allen, Patricia, ed. *Together at the Table: Sustainability and Sustenance in the American Agrifood System.* University Park, PA: Pennsylvania State University Press, 2004.

Appadurai, Arjun, ed. *The Social Life of Things: Commodities in Cultural Perspective.* Cambridge: Cambridge University Press, 1997.

Barham, Elizabeth. "Translating Terroir: The Global Challenge of French AOC Labeling." *Journal of Rural Studies* 19 (2003): 127–38.

Barndt, Deborah. *Tangled Routes: Women, Work, and Globalization on the Tomato Trail.* 2nd ed. Lanham: Rowman and Littlefield, 2008.

Belasco, Warren. *Meals to Come: A History of the Future of Food.* Berkeley: University of California Press, 2006.

Berry, Wendell. "The Pleasures of Eating." In *What Are People For?* San Francisco: North Point Press, 1990.

Boisard, Pierre. *Camembert: A National Myth.* Translated by Richard Miller. Berkeley: University of California Press, 2003.

Bonanno, Alessandro. "Liberal Democracy in the Global Era: Implications for the Agro-Food Sector." *Agriculture and Human Values* 15, no. 3 (1998): 223–42.

Cronon, William. "The Trouble with Wilderness; or, Getting Back to the Wrong Nature." In *Uncommon Ground: Rethinking the Human Place in Nature,* edited by William Cronon, 69–90. New York: W.W. Norton, 1996.

Demossier, Marion. *Wine Drinking Culture in France: A National Myth or a Modern Passion?* Cardiff: University of Wales Press, 2010.

Foer, Jonathan Safran. *Eating Animals.* New York: Little, Brown and Company, 2010.

Friedmann, Harriet. "The Political Economy of Food: The Rise and Fall of the Postwar International Food Order." *American Journal of Sociology* 88, supplement (1982): 248–86.

———. "The International Relations of Food: The Unfolding Crisis of National Regulation." In *Food: Multidisciplinary Perspectives,* edited by Barbara Harriss-White and Raymond Hoffenberg, 174–204. Oxford: Blackwell, 1994.

Grandin, Temple, and Catherine Johnson. *Animals Make Us Human: Creating the Best Life for Animals.* Boston: Houghton Mifflin Harcourt, 2009.

Guthman, Julie. *Agrarian Dreams: The Paradox of Organic Farming in California.* Berkeley: University of California Press, 2004.

Guy, Kolleen M. *When Champagne Became French: Wine and the Making of a National Identity.* Baltimore: Johns Hopkins University Press, 2003.

Habermas, Jürgen. *The Structural Transformation of the Public Sphere: An Inquiry into a Category of Bourgeois Society.* Translated by Thomas Burger. Cambridge, MA: MIT Press, 1991.

Heldke, Lisa. "Down-Home Global Cooking: A Third Option between Cosmopolitanism and Localism." In *The Philosophy of Food,* edited by David Kaplan, 33–51. Berkeley: University of California Press, 2011.

Hobsbawm, Eric. *The Age of Empire: 1875–1914.* New York: Vintage Books, 1989.

Inglis, David, and Debra Gimlin. "Food Globalizations: Ironies and Ambivalences of Food, Cuisine and Globality." In *The Globalization of Food,* edited by David Inglis and Debra Gilman, 3–42. Oxford: Berg, 2009.

———, eds. *The Globalization of Food.* Oxford: Berg, 2009.

Johnson, Hugh. *Vintage: The Story of Wine.* New York: Simon and Schuster, 1989.

Kaplan, David, ed. *The Philosophy of Food.* Berkeley: University of California Press, 2011.

Kindstedt, Paul. *Cheese and Culture: A History of Cheese and Its Place in Western Civilization.* White River Junction: Chelsea Green Publishing, 2012.

Kingsolver, Barbara. *Animal, Vegetable, Miracle: A Year of Food Life.* New York: HarperCollins, 2009.

Korsmeyer, Carolyn. "Ethical Gourmandism." In *Philosophy of Food,* edited by David Kaplan, 87–102. Berkeley: University of California Press, 2011.

Leitch, Alison. "Slow Food and the Politics of 'Virtuous Globalization.'" In *The Globalization of Food,* edited by David Inglis and Debra Gimlin, 45–64. Oxford: Berg, 2009.

Mendez, V. Ernesto. "Farmers' Livelihoods and Biodiversity Conservation in a Coffee Landscape in El Salvador." In *Confronting the Coffee Crisis: Fair Trade, Sustainable Livelihoods and Ecosystems in Mexico and Central America,* edited by Christopher M. Bacon, V. Ernesto Méndez, Stephen R. Gliessman, David Goodman, and Johnathan A. Fox, 207–34. Cambridge, MA: MIT Press: 2008.

Mintz, Sidney. *Sweetness and Power: The Place of Sugar in Modern History.* New York: Penguin Books, 1986.

Patel, Raj. *Stuffed and Starved: The Hidden Battle for the World Food System.* New York: Melville House, 2008.

Paxson, Heather. *The Life of Cheese: Crafting Food and Value in the United States.* Berkeley: University of California Press, 2012.

Polanyi, Karl. *The Great Transformation.* New York: Rinehart, 1944.

Pollan, Michael. *The Omnivore's Dilemma: A Natural History of Four Meals.* New York: Penguin, 2006.

Renard, Marie-Christine. "Fair Trade: Quality, Market and Conventions." *Journal of Rural Studies* 19 (2003): 87–96.

Roberts, Paul. *The End of Food.* New York: Houghton Mifflin, 2008.

Robinson, Jancis. *The Oxford Companion to Wine.* Oxford: Oxford University Press, 1999.

Singer, Peter. *Animal Liberation: The Definitive Classic of the Animal Movement.* New York: Harper Perennial, 2009. First published in 1975 by Avon Press.

Trubek, Amy. *The Taste of Place: A Cultural Journey into Terroir.* Berkeley: University of California Press, 2008.

Tucker, Catherine. *Coffee Culture: Local Experiences, Global Connections.* New York: Routledge, 2010.

Watts, Michael, and David Goodman. "Agrarian Questions: Global Appetites, Local Metabolism." In *Globalizing Food: Agrarian Questions and Global Restructuring,* edited by David Goodman and Michael J. Watts, 1–23. London: Routledge, 1997.

Wright, Caroline. "Fairtrade Food: Connecting Producers and Consumers." In *The Globalization of Food,* edited by David Inglis and Debra Gimlin, 139–57. Oxford: Berg, 2009.

Films

Food, Inc. Directed by Robert Kenner. Magnolia Pictures, 2009.

Fresh. Directed by Ana Sophia Jones. 2009.

Mondovino. Directed by Jonathan Nossiter. ThinkFilm, 2006.

Super Size Me. Directed by Morgan Spurlock. Samuel Goldwyn Films, 2004.

CHAPTER 15

Food and Popular Culture

FABIO PARASECOLI

Few drinks can claim a more iconic and enduring presence in popular culture and the global imagination than champagne. This product has been the object of historical analyses of its origins, the changes of its flavor profile over time, the heated political debates that accompanied the definition of its area of production, and the role played by economics and global trade in determining its success. However, aspects of champagne's unique story would risk being overlooked if research neglected its presence in popular culture, which has reflected and reinforced its prestige. Mentioned in theatrical productions as early as 1698, in the comedy *Love and a Bottle* by George Farquhar, champagne also appeared in visual representations as diverse as paintings, advertising posters, and trade cards. Its qualities were extolled in cookbooks, printed tracts, auction catalogues, and agricultural and oenological treaties, while remaining constantly present on menus of court banquets, restaurants, and all sorts of drinking establishments. Its fame determined the success of the Champagne area as a tourist destination, generating economic revenue from activities ranging from hotels to museums. These wide-ranging images, oral and written texts, practices, and institutional arrangements have determined champagne's connotations as a symbol of refinement and wealth, which also resonate in photography, movies, as well as rap lyrics and music videos. The example of champagne highlights some of the research venues that can open up to historians—and in particular food historians—who engage with popular culture. This chapter suggests that this kind of inherently multidisciplinary exploration can offer access to the life-worlds, the mental universes, the daily practices, and the embodied experiences of individuals and communities, and to the ways these interact and influence each other at determined historical moments.

WHAT IS POPULAR CULTURE?

Due to its ever-changing and disparate objects, its varied actors, and its constant expansion, popular culture comes across as a slippery and hard to delimit field of research. For the purposes of this article, popular culture is defined as the totality of ideas, values, embodied experiences, representations, material items, practices, social relations, organizations, and institutions that are conceived, produced, experienced, and reciprocally connected within environments influenced by markets and consumption, with or without the specific economic goal of reaping a profit. This definition includes what at any given moment is perceived as mainstream, together with alternative or oppositional subcultures, as well as the evolving dynamics through which the mainstream is constantly defined, reinforced, negotiated, or resisted. The study of popular culture also examines subgroups that establish forms of expression directly or indirectly criticizing or opposing the mainstream, and the dynamics through which elements of their cultural production can be taken out of context, integrated, and given new life and meaning by the very mainstream apparatuses that they initially aimed to undermine. From the methodological point of view, this kind of research requires a productive dialogue with various disciplines (anthropology, sociology, political science, economics, media, and communication) and fields (food, gender, ethnicity, and cultural studies).

For instance, looking at a common item such as apple pie, we can identify a set of environments, practices, values, and institutions both in the present and the past that large segments of the population have considered—and largely still consider—as normal and culturally acceptable, including domestic and community kitchens, bakeries, supermarkets, corner stores, diners, high-end restaurants, roadside food areas, cooking classes, home deliveries, potluck dinners, Sunday meals, church gatherings, bake sales, weekend outings, and holiday parties, where the item is routinely produced, bought, consumed, discussed, and represented. In addition to observing how the pie is made and served, the quality, availability, and accessibility of its ingredients, its price point, attitudes and relationships among producers and consumers, quantity provided, and so on, it is possible to analyze the very diverse and changing practices, norms, and representations in which the dessert is enmeshed and which are in turn connected to larger social and economic issues. At different points in time and in different environments within American culture, apple pie has been considered high-brow or low-brow, healthy or excessive, comforting or boring, authentic or inauthentic, traditional or innovative, gourmet or ordinary, unique or mass-produced. These perceptions have been predicated on their participation in a wide network of ever-changing textual, visual, and aural representations and ideas created, reflected, circulated, reproduced, reinforced, and resisted through food advertising, commercials, TV cooking shows, podcasts, radio interviews, cookbooks, restaurant reviews, recipes, cookbooks, packaging, and design. We might encounter environments, practices, and ideas that revolve around apple pie to express different degrees of countercultural attitudes. For instance one consumer might choose to buy apple pies exclusively made with organic ingredients; another might opt for a vegan version; yet another might decide to shop for the dessert at a stall at a farmers' market rather than at the supermarket or at a bakery. For historians, new and original insights about specific places and periods can be gained through the examination of these behaviors, their representations and cultural evaluations, and the material objects around which they are constructed, as well as the social and institutional practices they sustain and are shaped by.

It is possible to identify aspects of the dynamics and the phenomena that we consider as food-related popular culture in very diverse and somewhat unexpected historical periods and geographical locations, often coinciding with bourgeoning consumer cultures, expanding trade, processes of urbanization, the growing availability of disposable income among certain segments of the population, and the consequent diffusion of forms of conspicuous consumption. When investigating food customs in the great cities of the Roman Empire, for instance, archeological findings such as graffiti and sketches on walls of brothels and taverns, the material objects and practices of daily consumption connected with the market, the networks of actors and institutions involved in food provision and distribution, and representations in literature, theater, and other forms of entertainment can all be considered and investigated as forms of popular culture that had some impact on the mental world and the daily lives of the inhabitants of those urban centers. The same could be said of Hangzhou during the Song dynasty, Florence in the

Renaissance, or prerevolutionary Paris. Unfortunately, we do not have access to the totality of the rich and effervescent oral culture that undoubtedly blossomed in those environments, thriving on the proximity of individuals of different origins, social extractions, and educations. Only echoes have reached us, usually filtered by upper-class testimonies and mostly available through pictorial representations and written texts—the latter only accessible to the very limited alphabetized segments of the population. Much material is likely to have been considered as unworthy of conservation due to its categorization as common and undignified, uncomfortably connected with the lives and mores of the lower strata of the population, and was often treated with disdain by the guardians of cultural canons and proper cultural reproduction. In other instances, traces of material objects and practices may have been destroyed because they were deemed morally offensive or even socially dangerous, as in the case of erotic pictures, advertisements and ephemera connected to vaudeville and burlesque acts, as well as marketing material like posters and trade cards.

Contemporary popular culture can be distinguished from similar phenomena in the past in terms of speed and intensity in the exchange of ideas, people, goods, and money, together with the increasingly rapid technological advances in food production, transportation, and communication. In the past it took centuries for items like coffee, chocolate, tea, and sugar to achieve a truly global diffusion and to penetrate into practices, discourse, representations, and ideological debates. In more recent times, it took a few decades for hamburgers and the fast food industry to become an international phenomenon, and only few years for bubble tea to spread from East Asia to diasporic communities in metropolitan centers all over the world.

Today, objects and practices bounce around quickly, reflected and possibly distorted between distant places and different media. Their life may be shorter, but their temporary interactions within the global networks of media, communication, trade, behaviors, and ideas can be intense: the ripples travel faster and wider in the global pond of popular culture. Items are likely to acquire a wide variety of new meanings in the process, a phenomenon that Arjun Appadurai and Igor Kopytoff have analyzed as "the social biography of things."[1] Through cultural and social negotiations, food-related meanings and behaviors can be embraced, selectively adopted, or transformed and directed to different goals. For instance, the shape of a traditional cheese, its milk and fat content, or its aging modalities can evolve over time because of economic constraints, environmental and climate variations, and cultural and social factors involving manufacturers, distributors, and consumers. These shifts in material objects, their production environments, and their uses can foster even more noticeable changes in meaning when negotiated through different forms of communication and practices. A slice of the above-mentioned cheese may appear in an organized farmhouse tour for out-of-town visitors, in an upscale gourmet shop, in scene signaling gourmandise in a movie with a famous star, in the hands of a political lobbyist defending local agriculture, in a pamphlet by industrial cheese producers lamenting the hygienic dangers of artisanal cheese-aging methods, in the pages of a cookbook, and last but not least, in the logo of an association for the defense of traditional foods.

Cultural norms, expectations, and context greatly affect the use and understanding of culinary systems in popular culture. For instance, chitterlings (cooked pig's intestines) from the U.S. South are often identified with African American culture and one of its culinary expressions, soul food. However, this traditional dish was talked about, prepared, experienced, and represented quite differently in antebellum America, after emancipation on the occasion of African American family reunions, and when cooked by rural black immigrants moving into Northern cities during the Great Migration. In more contemporary times, it acquires specific meanings when featured on the menu of a fundraising event for a folklore museum, or when placed on the menu of a hip soul-food restaurant in New York trying to profit from the renewed interest in old-style dishes. In Spain, paella has run the gamut from peasant tradition to family comfort food to tourist fare to a tongue-in-cheek, sophisticated touch in a fancy meal. These dynamics also take place with industrial products. The cocoa-and-hazelnut spread Nutella was launched in the late 1950s in Italy and welcomed as a symbol of the economic development that finally made chocolate, until then considered a luxury, accessible to many consumers. Over the years the product, promoted and made popular by intense advertising, acquired emotional connotations that enshrined it as a cherished childhood food for generations of Italians. Nutella's specific place in consumer culture was reflected in music, movies, pop art, street performances, and comedy.[2] In more recent years, Nutella events in dance clubs have featured little bites of bread or cookies covered with the chocolate spread, served together with alcoholic drinks. Even Nutella sex parties are known to have reached a certain underground appeal. At the same time, as the product began to be marketed outside Italy, it came to occupy completely different spaces in the global imagination. Its recent involvement in a lawsuit for false health-related advertising claims in the United States projected Nutella into discourses about nutrition and children's diet completely different from those of its Italian origins, while also having an impact on the perception of Italian products in general.

MULTIDIRECTIONAL ANALYSIS

The above examples suggest different approaches for food historians when exploring popular culture. Food-related objects, behaviors, and representations can be analyzed in their synchronic dimension, considering them as components in complex and sprawling networks of simultaneous relations with not only other objects, behaviors, and representations, but also with norms, values, discourses, embodied experiences, social relations, organizations, economic and political structures, and so on. This approach can be metaphorically compared to taking a snapshot of the topic of research at a specific moment in time, temporarily suspending connections with its past and future. This momentary erasure of history allows the researcher to apply a semiotic analysis, emphasizing the cultural and social meanings and uses of the elements she is exploring as signs. One of the basics tenets of semiotics is that everything in a culture can be considered as carrying meaning and that as humans we are constantly engaged in semiosis, the process of making sense of the reality that surrounds us. Signs need to be considered within their context, as parts of a system, in which each component's role is somehow defined by the other elements in it. Structuralism actually pushed this argument to claim that no constituent of a system has any meaning in itself, but is instead defined by what it is not, in terms of relations, difference, and oppositions. We can define these networks of meaning as "signifying," insofar as they are experienced and interpreted by different actors seeking to comprehend cultural environments and negotiate their rules and boundaries.

Representations and practices around food are so ramified that it can be daunting to follow all the connections across fields of research that are often the domains of specific disciplines with well-defined methodologies. How can we deal with this huge amount of material? It can be useful to approach the very diverse aspects of popular culture as expressions of a single "code," in the sense introduced by film theorist Kaja Silverman: "A code represents a sort of bridge between texts. Its presence within one text involves a simultaneous reference to all of the other texts in which it appears, as to the cultural reality which it helps to define—i.e. to a particular symbolic order . . . The codes which manifest themselves through connotation function endlessly to repeat what has been written in other books and portrayed in other films, and so to reproduce the existing cultural order. Repetition does the same thing for that order as constant re-interpellation does for the subject. It creates the illusion of stability and continuity."[3] Roland Barthes had already provocatively put forward the propositions that texts—in their traditional interpretation as individual "works"—are actually a cultural illusion. In the famous 1968 essay "The Death of the Author," often read as a precursor of poststructuralist theory and a founding text for cultural studies, he stated:

> The birth of the reader must be at the cost of the death of the author and that as a matter of fact there is no author speaking, but just language. A text consists of multiple writings, proceeding from several cultures and entering into dialogue, into parody, into contestation; but there is a site where this multiplicity is collected, and this site is not the author, as has hitherto been claimed, but the reader: the reader is the very space in which are inscribed, without any of them being lost, all the citations out of which a writing is made; the unity of a text is not in its origin but in its destination, but this destination can no longer be personal: the reader is a man without history, without biography, without psychology; he is only that someone who holds collected into one and the same field all of the traces from which writing is constituted.[4]

As a consequence, single works must be distinguished from texts. The work "is a fragment of substance, it occupies a portion of the spaces of books (for example, in a library)," while "the text is a methodological field."[5] It is evident that the concept can be applied to the study of popular culture. We can look at our object of interest as a text whose fragments surface in diverse media, discourses, practices, and institutions.

In the case of Nutella, which we already introduced, investigation would focus on the product's place in the food culture of the time and place when it first became popular, in the early 1960s in Italy, exploring what food was considered nutritious, comforting, and affordable at the time. Further insight could be gained by identifying competitors who manufactured similar products and understanding the company's marketing and advertising strategies to reach the target consumers. What values, goals, and behavior did marketers exploit to reach audiences? How did these forms of advertisement relate to the mediascape of the time? Were visual, aural, textual, or narrative elements from Nutella advertising and commercials integrated in other media, performances, or practices? How did consumers actually receive the product? What embodied and emotional experiences did they construct around it? What was the role of the product in shaping the budding consumer society?

While so far our attention has concentrated on synchronic analysis, snapshots of the same object or practice, like the one we constructed about the postwar Nutella, could be taken at various intervals, then compared with each other to see how and why meanings and social uses have shifted, if they have. The comparison of snapshots from different periods brings history and change back into the exploration of popular culture. Such a diachronic dimension can highlight how the systems of meanings hinging on food have evolved and continue to evolve.

Let's take sugar as an example: its availability, its role in various culinary systems, and its social and cultural signification have visibly mutated over time and space. With the arrival of sugar into Western Europe during the Middle Ages, courtly culinary systems created a specific role for the new substance, which was considered a spice, and presented as such in the artistic and folkloric production of the time. As new techniques from the Muslim world were integrated in the Western culinary world, starting in the Renaissance sugar was employed to produce candied fruit, sorbets, and all kinds of dessert, playing an important and quite visible role in the spectacular banquets organized by and for the upper classes of the time. When production increased in the Caribbean sugar plantations, desserts slowly became a separate part of the meal in Western society, and pastry developed as a codified set of techniques that started trickling down to the lower classes. Starting in the nineteenth century, sugar became available to the masses, assuming for instance a fundamental role in the nutritional patterns of British industrial workers. At the same time, it acquired heavy political connotations in the debates surrounding the abolition of slavery and in all the forms of popular culture that reflected them, from pamphlets to satiric cartoons. Today sugar is singled out as the main reason, together with fat, for the obesity epidemic that has struck many Western countries and is the subject of popular discourses that range from cooking to fashion, from health to ethics.

Building on the French psychoanalyst Jacques Lacan's observations, we could argue that signifiers are actually more stable than signifieds: in other words, the material and formal element of a sign (an object, practice, or visual or textual element that carries meaning) stays the same, while its meaning and social uses can shift. These changes, however, are not random; rather they constitute the result of underlying dynamics that submit cultural elements to constant negotiations among social forces. In the analysis of these dynamics, however, it is crucial to maintain a distinction between the images and practices projected by popular culture, media, and commercial entities and the realities of the everyday lives of people in all walks of life all over the world. Although the two dimensions are certainly linked and influence each other, those connections need to be examined in their historical and social contexts.

Representations do have the potential to be inscribed as norms, ideals, and expectations onto bodies that exist in families, armies, factories, and kitchens, interacting with the way individuals construct and experience their identities. Anthropologist Arjun Appadurai noted in his 1996 *Modernity at Large* how imagination and fantasy have become a fundamental social practice, offering many individuals and communities throughout the world new filters through which they can reflect on their daily lives and interact with other spheres of cultural, social, and political life.[6] From this point of view, popular culture is particularly relevant because it constitutes a sort of open and ever-growing warehouse for visual and aural elements, narrative components, and embodied practices that can be borrowed by individuals, subcultures, and whole communities to make sense of the everyday experience.

However, as cultural studies theorist Stuart Hall has argued, there are huge possibilities for disruption in communication processes in many food-related aspects of popular culture, as members of communities sharing the same set of signifying networks can approach the same elements in very different ways. Meanings and uses can be interpreted, misunderstood, distorted, adapted, and selectively embraced depending on the cultural, social, and political background of the actors involved.[7] The observations about audiences expressed by film theorists Stam and Spence can be extended to the phenomena we are examining: "The film experience must inevitably be infected by the cultural awareness of the audience itself, constituted outside the text and traversed by sets of social relations such as race, class, and gender. We must allow, therefore, for the possibility of aberrant readings, reading which goes against the grain of the discourse. Although fiction films are persuasive machines designed to produce specific impressions and emotions, they are not all-powerful; they might be read differently by different audiences."[8] We need to keep in mind these caveats when proceedings with our analysis of food in popular culture. Only empirical research, surveys, and spectatorship analysis can ascertain how the repository of images, sounds, and narrative elements turns into actual perceptions, ideas, values, and practices.

WHY SHOULD WE CARE ABOUT POPULAR CULTURE?

Popular culture is not a mere reflection of reality; it can be used ideologically to reinforce power structures and cultural biases. However, it can also provide ammunition for subtle provocations and real attacks against the status quo as viewers know and perceive it. The way we conceptualize and experience our physical needs—including the way we choose, store, prepare, cook, ingest, and digest food, and excrete waste—is far from being neutral or normal. As part of the realm of personal and social experiences that are usually considered a mere expression of "natural" instincts and mundane needs, eating and thinking about food have become politically and culturally sensitive. Food's neutrality and ordinariness can normalize various cultural and social dynamics, making them invisible and allowing ideologies to operate more efficiently, extending their reach to the most intimate aspects of individual lives.[9] Eating and cooking, seemingly trivial and familiar acts, offer an apt environment for the embodiment and the actualization of values, attitudes, and behaviors that reflect widely accepted and culturally sanctioned templates. In the body, ideology achieves material existence. All food-related practices share an ideological function in the sense that they tend to introduce, legitimize, and strengthen specific values and goals for society at large by repetition of gestures and behaviors.

Interesting case studies illustrate the ideological use of food in popular culture. Certain ingredients, dishes, or traditions enjoy a special position in the definition of individual and communal identities, such as pasta for Italians, beer for Germans, kimchi for Koreans, sake for the Japanese, or champagne for the French. These occurrences are particularly interesting for the historian, as they constitute examples of how popular culture has interacted with media, politics, economics, and institutions to mark items and practices as symbols of tradition (albeit often invented), community (at times imagined), and authenticity.[10] It is important to understand how the specialties involved have been recognized and interpreted at different times by different actors, whose own identities have been constructed and performed precisely in their use of these meaningful elements and in their interaction and negotiations with others actors around them. These dynamics affect the image that members of a culinary community nurture of themselves and their social position.

Continuous negotiations define and redefine these "identity foods" both within and outside the communities that produce them. Power and the ideals it promotes—such as tradition and authenticity—are not always imposed on individuals from the outside, but are embodied autonomously through norms and practices. No government could convince its citizens that a new ingredient or dish is part of their traditions: the Dutch would not buy into any media campaign trying to impose blue corn as a national product any more than Belgians could be convinced by a popular movie that reindeer is a common source of meat protein.

However, although tradition and authenticity, as cultural constructs, cannot be considered as a direct consequence of political, economical or social forces, they are influenced by them. Tradition and authenticity are the result of the reiteration of highly regulated and ritualized practices, norms and processes that respond to ideals and cultural models, and acquire material reality, visibility, and cultural intelligibility in the very body of each individual. Italians—or at least large segments of the Italian population—are often represented as great pasta consumers, to the point that these customs have often been employed as negative stereotypes. However, pasta has become a widespread dish only relatively recently: until the nineteenth century, it was still perceived as a regional dish. Mechanization of production, developments in transportation, and changes in distribution networks in Italy made pasta available all over the country. Marketing played an enormous role in solidifying the image of the dish as a national institution, and price subsidies during World War I made it affordable for almost everyone. After the food scarcity during World War II, pasta constituted a relatively cheap source of energy, and it is represented as such in, for instance, Neorealist cinema and comedies from the 1950s. Over time industrial pasta companies managed to market their product as a symbol of Italian identity, a position reinforced by media, newspapers, and cookbooks. TV commercials underlined its function as the center for family meals, and highlighted elements of emotional nostalgia. The repetition and pervasiveness of these practices and representations, the social and political discourses constructed around them, and even foreign perceptions and prejudices contribute to define norms and ideals that underline and reinforce national identities, which in turn can be exploited by different interest groups and political factions toward their specific agendas.

Food is pervasive in contemporary postindustrial popular cultures, influencing the way we perceive and represent ourselves as individuals and as members of social groups. However, the ubiquitous nature of these cultural elements makes their ideological and political relevance almost invisible, buried as it is in the supposedly natural and self-evident fabric of everyday life. Meanwhile, our own flesh becomes fuel for all kinds of cultural battles among different visions of personhood, family, society, and even economics.

TEACHING FOOD HISTORY THROUGH POPULAR CULTURE

The exploration of popular culture, with its physical, emotional, and symbolic resonance, can allow us to approach complex problems and understand phenomena in food history that directly impact our daily lives, choices, and agency as citizens. Looking at practices, representations, and objects that fall under the heading of popular culture can provide an excellent introduction to how global politics and economics have shaped the most basic practices of everyday life and the mentalities of different communities throughout history.

For this reason, this approach can be introduced with success in the classroom to help students hone critical thinking and engage with the most tangible and material aspects of society, aspects that are often taken for granted. These reflections can stimulate students to develop more articulated outlooks on pressing issues concerning production, distribution, and consumption of food, as well as their own connection with the environment and the global realities they inhabit. They can learn to integrate the often homogenized and economy-driven spaces of contemporary life with a more personal and attentive connection to their local milieus, giving them the tools to make informed decisions.

The use of popular culture as a pedagogical tool is particularly effective given that students are increasingly immersed in a heavily visual and multimedia environment. Visual elements are increasingly understood as effective—although not unequivocal—entryways into societies and the way they articulate cultural dynamics, everyday life, and communication. Jeremy Stoddard and Alan Marcus contend that "film and similar media serve a larger role as historical sources for the public at large. We now know that many people outside the classroom are not learning about history from reading books or from engaging in primary sources research; instead, they are learning what they know about the past from engaging with media such as film, web based media, or video games."[11] Images and sounds from the past can be interpreted as repositories of memories to be accessed by subsequent generations, but at the same time their use requires students to become familiar with important processes and methods of interpretation. As with any other historical source, no images or objects in popular culture can be taken at face value. Their possible "low brow" status at the time of their production does not make them more innocent or more trustworthy reflections of the reality in which they were embedded. On the contrary, they incorporate the dynamics of their production, diffusion, and consumption, including the techniques available at the time, modes and environment of use, choices of subjects and themes, and intended audiences. Furthermore, sources from popular culture have the potential to retrieve material from the past whose choice and utilization is influenced by motives and sensibilities embedded in present contexts, requiring additional levels of interpretation.[12] In discussing the transformations in the current understanding of cultural processes, historians Joeri Januarius and Nelleke Teughels point out that "post-structuralists recognized the role of the reader in the making of meaning, which led to an understanding of interpretation as a process in which meaning is produced rather than simply uncovered. Interpretation is an act happening in the present, which aims to make sense of the material culture of the past. Not only can artifacts assume multiple and sometimes even contradictory meanings according to their historical and social contexts, different people will interpret them in very distinctive ways, depending on their own backgrounds and research questions."[13]

Students need to develop the analytical and critical tools to unpack these elements in ways that allow them to understand the relevance of interpretive work in studying history. The advantage of using popular culture is that these seemingly theoretical and abstract procedures can be brought down and made accessible to students by introducing material that they can easily relate to. For example, a reflection on representations of bananas in U.S. popular culture can help students understand important issues of globalization, cultural and material imperialism, and postcolonial dynamics. Bananas have been frequently used in the construction of colonial and subaltern subjects whose existence is perceived in connection with the entertainment and the satisfaction of white audiences in the global North. By analyzing images, advertising materials, objects, videos, songs, and practices developed around bananas, students can not only question their immediate surroundings but also examine their own attitudes, perceptions, and biases about the object of their study. The exploration can start, for instance, with the visual materials produced at the turn of the century, which includes photographs of various phases of cultivation, collection, and transportation of bananas in

Caribbean and Central American plantations commissioned by the production companies, as well as posters and trade cards. Students could reflect on why these materials were produced, what their intended function was, and who the target audiences were supposed to be. Is a photograph of workers gathering bananas a more reliable historical source than an advertising poster depicting banana workers? In what kind of communication were they embedded? How would different kinds of viewers interpret them? Students could also look at how bananas were featured in photographs of people on excursions or gathering on social occasions, showing their function as status symbol at a time when their consumption was still limited and their price quite high. Images from different periods can be provided to show how the use of the fruit changed over time, and how it surfaced in quite unexpected places, from Josephine Baker's skirts for her dance numbers at the Folies-Bergère in Paris to Carmen Miranda's hats in her 1940s movies and Bugs Bunny's drag performances in cartoons. Most students are likely to be familiar with Chiquita Banana, both as a brand and as a popular culture icon. The examination of how Miss Chiquita was created and developed over the years can raise issues about consumerism, global trade flows, and labor exploitation in developing countries. At the same time, these images and representations can be approached to assess the state of the political and economic relationships between the United States and its southern neighbors.

The Caribbean is particularly interesting in the study of popular culture in food history because of its long-term visibility in English-language cultural environments as a place of origin for many familiar and unfamiliar foods. It is also as a space of exoticism, relaxation, and exploration that has loomed large in visual and textual representations, as well as practices that include tourism, resorts, and cruise ship travels. Ian Cook and Michelle Harrison's work on Caribbean products such as hot sauces provides a good model of how the examination of such everyday objects, their meaning, and their use in various contexts can shed light on social, political, and economic dynamics that would otherwise come across as too remote for many students, especially younger ones.

A similar approach can be applied to all sorts of objects, practices, and representations that students may be familiar with, including aspects of popular culture that can be problematic or culturally sensitive. A good example of this kind of work is provided by Psyche Williams-Forson's eloquent documentation in her book *Building Houses Out of Chicken Legs: Black Women, Food, and Power* of the importance of chicken to African American women in the Southern United States from slavery to present times.[14] Through the examination of textual and visual sources, Williams-Forson acknowledges how Black culture was negatively portrayed through racist chicken imagery, and how such racism has been parodied by comedians like Chris Rock and emotionally explored by artists like Kara Walker. She also successfully demonstrates how black women defied these representations and used chicken to exercise influence in food production and distribution, from sales at train stations to larger businesses. Race issues in the nineteenth-century United States are also successfully tackled through the examination of nineteenth-century trade cards, nursery rhymes, and theatrical performances in Kyla Wazana Tompkins's *Racial Indigestions: Eating Bodies in the Nineteenth Century.*[15] Working on these materials may force some students out of their comfort zone, but at the same time it can provide a safe environment in which to examine historical dynamics around race, ethnicity, and migration.

In *Meals to Come: A History of the Future of Food,* Warren Belasco provides a template for the use of sources as diverse as pictures, world fair exhibitions, supermarkets, and restaurants to assess how ideas about the future of food—its increasing abundance or the looming specter of famine—have influenced political debates about larger societal issues.[16] The analysis of domestic and public spaces, from kitchens to different kinds of eateries and shops, can also provide valuable insights on how food was thought of, discussed, and experienced at different times and in different environments. A good example of this kind of analysis is offered by the essays in collections such as *Eating Architecture* and *Food: Design and Culture.*[17]

Looking at their own environment under a new light, students can explore practices, representations, objects, and places they are familiar with to discover how their daily lives are actually shaped by past events and dynamics. Food and eating provide a particularly effective field for reflection as they are aspects of the human experience that everybody shares, and precisely because of their apparent normality and banality they can create, reinforce, hide, or question ideas, norms, and values that characterize present and past societies.

NOTES

1. Arjun Appadurai, ed., *The Social Life of Things: Commodities in Cultural Perspective* (Cambridge: Cambridge University Press, 1986).

2. Bernard Cova and Stefano Pace, "Brand Community of Convenience Products: New Forms of Customer Empowerment: The Case 'My Nutella the Community,'" *European Journal of Marketing* 40, no. 9/10 (2006): 1087–1105.

3. Kaja Silverman, *The Subjects of Semiotics* (New York: Oxford University Press, 1983), 239.

4. Roland Barthes, *The Rustle of Language,* trans. Richard Howard (New York: Hill and Wang, 1986), 54.

5. Barthes, *The Rustle of Language,* 57.

6. Arjun Appadurai, *Modernity at Large: Cultural Dimensions of Globalization* (Minneapolis: University of Minnesota Press, 1996).

7. Stuart Hall, "Encoding/Decoding," in *Culture, Media, Language,* eds. Stuart Hall, Dorothy Hobson, Andrew Lowe, and Paul Willis, 107–16 (London: Unwin Hyman, 1980).

8. Robert Stam and Louise Spence, "Colonialism, Racism and Representation," *Screen* 24, no. 2 (March/April 1983): 19.

9. Sherrie Inness, ed., *Kitchen Culture in America: Popular Representations of Food, Gender, and Race* (Philadelphia: University of Pennsylvania Press, 2001); Sherrie Inness, ed., *Pilaf, Pozole, and Pad Thai: American Women and Ethnic Food* (Amherst: University of Massachusetts Press, 2001).

10. Benedict Anderson, *Imagined Communities: Reflections on the Origin and Spread of Nationalism* (London: Verso, 2006); Regina Bendix, *In Search of Authenticity: The Formation of Folklore Studies* (Madison: University of Wisconsin Press, 1997); Eric Hobsbawm and Terence Ranger, eds., *The Invention of Tradition* (Cambridge: Cambridge University Press, 1992).

11. Jeremy D. Stoddard and Alan S. Marcus, "More Than 'Showing What Happened': Exploring the Potential of Teaching History with Film," *The High School Journal* 93, no. 2 (2010): 84

12. Sarah Barber and Corinna Peniston-Bird, eds., *History Beyond the Text: A Student's Guide to Approaching Alternative Sources* (London: Routledge, 2009); Peter Burke, *Eyewitnessing: The Use of Images as Historical Evidence* (Ithaca: Cornell University Press, 2001).

13. Joeri Januarius and Nelleke Teughels, "History Meets Archaeology: The Historical Use of Images: A Survey," *Revue Belge de Philologie et d'Histoire* 87, no. 4 (2009): 676.

14. Psyche Williams-Forson, *Building Houses Out of Chicken Legs: Black Women, Food, and Power* (Chapel Hill: University of North Carolina Press, 2006).

15. Kyla Wazana Tompkins, *Racial Indigestions: Eating Bodies in the Nineteenth Century* (New York: New York University Press, 2012).

16. Warren Belasco, *Meals to Come: A History of the Future of Food* (Berkeley: University of California Press, 2006).

17. Jamie Horwitz and Paulette Singley, *Eating Architecture* (Cambridge, MA: MIT Press, 2004). Claire Catterall, *Food: Design and Culture* (London: Laurence King Publishing, 1999).

BIBLIOGRAPHY

Anderson, Benedict. *Imagined Communities: Reflections on the Origin and Spread of Nationalism.* London: Verso, 2006.

Appadurai, Arjun. *Modernity at Large: Cultural Dimensions of Globalization.* Minneapolis: University of Minnesota Press, 1996.

———, ed. *The Social Life of Things: Commodities in Cultural Perspective.* Cambridge: Cambridge University Press, 1986.

Ashley, Bob, Joanne Hollows, Steve Jones, and Ben Taylor. *Food and Cultural Studies.* London: Routledge, 2004.

Barber, Sarah, and Corinna Peniston-Bird, eds. *History Beyond the Text: A Student's Guide to Approaching Alternative Sources.* London: Routledge, 2009.

Barthes, Roland. *Elements of Semiology.* Translated by Annette Lavers and Colin Smith. New York: Hill and Wang, 1977.

———. *The Rustle of Language.* Translated by Richard Howard. New York: Hill and Wang, 1986.

Belasco, Warren. *Meals to Come: A History of the Future of Food.* Berkeley: University of California Press, 2006.

———. *Appetite for Change: How the Counterculture Took on the Food Industry, 1966–1968.* Ithaca: Cornell University Press, 2007.

Bendix, Regina. *In Search of Authenticity: The Formation of Folklore Studies.* Madison: University of Wisconsin Press, 1997.

Burke, Peter. *Eyewitnessing: The Use of Images as Historical Evidence.* Ithaca: Cornell University Press, 2001.

Catterall, Claire. *Food: Design and Culture.* London: Laurence King Publishing, 1999.

Cook, Ian, and Michelle Harrison. "Cross over Food: Re-Materializing Postcolonial Geographies." *Transactions of the Institute of British Geographers* n.s. 28, no. 3 (2003): 296–317.

———. "Follow the Thing: 'West Indian Hot Pepper Sauce.'" *Space and Culture* 10, no. 1 (2007): 40–63.

Cova, Bernard, and Stefano Pace. "Brand community of convenience products: new forms of customer empowerment—the case 'my Nutella The Community.'" *European Journal of Marketing* 40 (2006): 1087–1105.

Cramer, Janet M., Carlnita P. Greene, and Lynn M. Walters, eds. *Food as Communication: Communication as Food.* New York: Peter Lang, 2011.

De Certeau, Michel. *The Practice of Everyday Life.* Translated by Steven Rendall. Berkeley: University of California Press, 1984.

Douglas, Mary. "Deciphering a meal." *Daedalus* 101, no. 1 (Winter 1972): 61–81.

Eco, Umberto. *A Theory of Semiotics.* Bloomington: Indiana University Press, 1976.

Fischler, Claude. *L'Homnivore: Le goût, la cuisine et le corps.* Paris: Editions Odile Jacob, 2001.

Hall, Stuart. "Encoding/Decoding." In *Culture, Media, Language,* edited by Stuart Hall, Dorothy Hobson, Andrew Lowe and Paul Willis, 107–16. London: Unwin Hyman, 1980.

Hobsbawm, Eric, and Terence Ranger, eds. *The Invention of Tradition.* Cambridge: Cambridge University Press, 1992.

Horwitz, Jamie, and Paulette Singley. *Eating Architecture.* Cambridge, MA: MIT Press, 2004.

Inness, Sherrie, ed. *Kitchen Culture in America: Popular Representations of Food, Gender, and Race*. Philadelphia: University of Pennsylvania Press, 2001.

———, ed. *Pilaf, Pozole, and Pad Thai: American Women and Ethnic Food*. Amherst: University of Massachusetts Press, 2001.

Januarius, Joeri, and Nelleke Teughels. "History Meets Archaeology: The Historical Use of Images: A Survey." *Revue Belge de Philologie et d'Histoire* 87, no. 4 (2009): 667–83.

Johnston, Josée, and Shyon Baumann. *Foodies: Democracy and Distinction in the Gourmet Foodscape*. New York: Routledge, 2010.

Korsmeyer, Carolyn. *Making Sense of Taste: Food and Philosophy*. Ithaca: Cornell University Press, 1999.

LeBesco, Kathleen, and Peter Naccarato. *Edible Ideologies: Representing Food and Meaning*. Albany: State University of New York Press, 2008.

Long, Lucy M., ed. *Culinary Tourism*. Lexington: University Press of Kentucky, 2004.

Mauss, Marcel. "Techniques of the Body." *Economy and Society* 2, no. 1 (1973): 70–88.

Parasecoli, Fabio. *Bite Me: Food in Popular Culture*. Oxford: Berg, 2008.

Silverman, Kaja. *The Subjects of Semiotics*. New York: Oxford University Press, 1983.

Stam, Robert, and Louise Spence. "Colonialism, Racism and Representation." *Screen* 24, no. 2 (March/April 1983): 2–20.

Stoddard, Jeremy D., and Alan S. Marcus. "More Than 'Showing What Happened': Exploring the Potential of Teaching History with Film." *The High School Journal* 93, no. 2 (2010): 83–90.

Tompkins, Kyla Wazana. *Racial Indigestions: Eating Bodies in the Nineteenth Century*. New York: New York University Press, 2012.

Watson, James L., and Melissa L. Caldwell, eds. *The Cultural Politics of Food and Eating: A Reader*. Malden: Blackwell, 2005.

Williams-Forson, Psyche. *Building Houses Out of Chicken Legs: Black Women, Food, and Power*. Chapel Hill: University of North Carolina Press, 2006.

CHAPTER 16

Post-1945 Global Food Developments

PETER SCHOLLIERS

This chapter focuses on one big question: How can we possibly seize the fast and wide-ranging changes of our food since the late 1940s? Keywords of this chapter would indeed lead to an endless enumeration because of the richness, coverage, and complexity of reflecting on foodways since 1945. To illustrate these changes, I have used the hundreds of keywords that typify the papers that deal with the twentieth century published in 2010, 2011 and 2012 in two journals: *Food, Culture and Society* and *Food and History.* The outcome is far-reaching and truly mixed, but also somewhat discouraging precisely because of this richness and diversity. Here is a (severe) selection of keywords: Advertising, Artisans, Authenticity, Banquets, Body, Branding, Canning, Charity, Childcare, Citizenship, Class, Consumers, Diaspora, Famine, Fasting, Feast, Gender, Health, Heritage, Identity, Inequality, Legislation, Malnutrition, Market, Migration, Monitoring, Nazism, Obesity, (Post)colonialism, Poverty, Quality, Racism, Religion, Safety, Sociability, Supermarkets, Supply, Taste, *Terroir,* and TV-Cooks. Predictable keywords, such as Recipes, Dieting, Eating Out, and Overweight abound, but peculiar keywords, like Nullification, Cosmology, Cubism, or Polygamy (all of which I find quite puzzling in relation to food) are present too. Considering some life-science journals, like *Appetite* and *British Food Journal,* which now and then publish papers with an historical perspective, yields keywords such as Sustainability, Time Budget, Naturalness, Organic Food, and Genetic Modification. Some of the abovementioned keywords refer to the big problems of today and tomorrow, particularly hunger and obesity, which form a very perplexing pair that characterizes our present world.

Taken together, these keywords encompass dozens of current scientific interests and approaches that, in turn, testify to small and big changes since World War II in the way people farm, shop, cook, eat, think, write, and talk about food. Surely, considering any other time period would also yield an impressive list of keywords, which would refer to other points of attention such as guilds, price control, rituals, or the so-called Columbian Exchange (the transfer of goods between the Old and New Worlds that brought, for example, the potato to Europe and the domesticated pig to the Americas). However, following many authors I argue that post-1945 developments in food evolve faster, have a broader reach, are more international, and cause irrevocable transformations for more people than ever before. This causes unease among consumers and makes them search for ways to feel safe, which leads some to eat abundantly, others to explore gourmet cuisine or turn to organic food, and still others to revisit their grandmother's recipes or become adepts of (more or less healthy) diets. The velocity and scale of transformations since 1945 lead to complications with regard to studying and interpreting the global foodscape. The answer to my question in the first sentence of this chapter will consist of considering a couple concepts and approaches by which modifications in the global landscape of food since 1945 may be interpreted, which I will exemplify by means of the history of eating out.

SPEED AND SCALE OF CHANGE

Claiming that the speed and scale of change with regard to our food has increased since the end of World War II needs clarification. In the context of spectacular changes in earlier periods, for example the diffusion of cocoa in Europe in the seventeenth century or that of the potato in the eighteenth century, this claim may seem overstated. It is, however, not my aim to negate or belittle the impact of food innovations prior to 1945 or to overstress changes since that year. I just wish to argue that the pace and scale of change increased because of a combination of diverse and continuous transformations in various segments of the food provisioning chain. This implies that, on the whole, new food items in whatever form were much faster and more generally diffused and adopted in the second half of the twentieth century than before. I will try to clarify this by referring to the concepts of productivity, real prices, and Engel's law.

The concept of productivity, or the output per time unit and person, is key to interpreting the increasing speed of changes in the landscape of food. In a world of little or no productivity change, few or no changes occur in terms of output, unless more time or people are involved (situations which of course occurred). In a world of increasing productivity, output grows continuously, which has a direct influence on the price, significance, and usage of goods or services. Productivity growth is not new, but two elements seem decisive in claiming its weightier role since 1945: its intensification and its occurrence over all links of the food provisioning chain. There are plenty of examples that show the increasing rate of productivity growth in agriculture since the early nineteenth century. The productivity of potato growing in the Netherlands, for example, rose in the second half of the nineteenth century (0.7 percent per year between 1851 and 1900), but accelerated in the first half of the twentieth century (1.5 percent) to surpass this high rate between 1950 and 1980 (1.6 percent). The growth weakened between 1980 and now (0.5 percent).[1] In actual quantities, this represents a progress from 10,900 kilos per hectare (i.e., per 2.47 acres) in 1900 to 44,600 in 2010. Figure 1 shows the year-to-year evolution between 1961 and 2010, with the doubling of output between the early 1960s and late 1990s, and the decline since the latter date. Note, too, some sharp fluctuations in particular years (noticeably, 1998).

The consequence of increased productivity was the availability in local markets of plenty of potatoes as well as the large-scale export, the price decline (taking inflation into account), the changing application of the product (for example, its upgrading through transformation into crisps, dried mashed potatoes, or deep-frozen chips), and the change of the image of the tuber. The causes of this growing productivity rate are manifold, but continuing mechanization and chemical fertilization are decisive. With regard to the latter, it should be mentioned that, overall, Dutch agriculture used about 100 million tons of chemical nitrogen in the late 1930s, but had quintupled this by 1985, lowering it somewhat since then. Certainly, Dutch agriculture was very advanced, but it was not exceptional. A heavy ecological cost accompanied this process though, as has become evident since the late 1960s. For example, the 1972 Club of Rome's report *Limits to Growth* not only dealt with population, pollution, and natural resources, but also and very insistently with food production and consumption. The conclusions were pessimis-

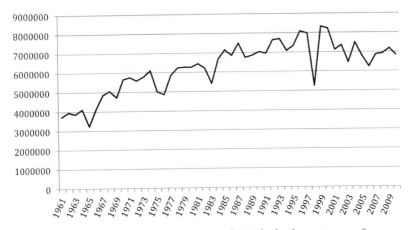

FIGURE 1. Annual output of potatoes (in tons), the Netherlands, 1961–2010. Source: "Production: Crops," FAOSTAT, http://faostat3.fao.org/, accessed September 15, 2012.

tic and were contested into the late 1990s, but seem to have gained support in recent years (to which the 2004 updated Club of Rome report testifies). Productivity gains in agriculture cannot be detached from (supranational) policies, power relations, ideology, or consumers' attitude, although technology, efficiency, and labor input are fundamental.

Rapid productivity growth also occurred in the transporting, storing, manufacturing, packaging, and retailing of food, although in some of these sectors productivity rises prior to 1940 were quite important too. For lack of space, I will confine the discussion to retailing in order to underline the importance of the most recent changes. Productivity growth in food retailing may be illustrated by referring to the efficiency rise in U.S. food and beverage stores since the mid-1980s, which reached 1 percent per year between 1987 and 1995, but attained 3.2 percent between 1995 and 2005. The introduction in the 1980s of EPOS (electronic points of sale) technology that included electronic cash tills and scanning, helps explain this fast growth in the 1990s. As a consequence, shoppers' queues were shortened, employment and wage costs were cut, and shelves were efficiently filled. New technology embracing food packaging, form, color, taste, and ingredients also encouraged the introduction of novel food products. Supermarkets could decide whether or not to offer new foodstuffs in an extremely flexible way. A 2006 report of the Food and Agriculture Organization (FAO) noted that every year, supermarkets in the United States and Europe add between five hundred and one thousand new products to their stockpile (or about 5 percent of their total supply), which demonstrates the rapidity of product innovation in food retailing. Although only 1 percent of these new foodstuffs are still on the shelves after five years, consumers have become used to this non-stop supply of new goods, which creates an impression of endless choice.

Before discussing the consequences of productivity gains in agriculture, transport, stocking, and retailing, I briefly come back to FAO's databank. As shown in figure 1, this databank offers year-to-year development of agricultural output since 1961. The databank's content, however, is much richer, and anyone studying the world's food production and consumption since 1960 may use it with great benefit. One component, the Food Balance Sheets, for example, provides the available food by country, expressed in kilocalories, proteins, and fat per day and person. Limitations on the use of this data include the lack of consideration for national character (no regional or social diversity), the theoretical approach (the quantities produced are *not* actually entirely consumed), and the emphasis on staple foods (e.g., no data on bread consumption). The balance sheets have been used before, by David Grigg in 1999 among others.[2] Grigg, a geographer, questioned the appearance of the so-called European food model in other regions of the world after World War II. This model connects income levels to food consumption: when income increases, people will initially eat more of the basic food (e.g., grain in Europe), but when income growth persists, people will eat less of the staple food and diversify their diet (more meat and dairy products). Grigg used FAO's Food Balance Sheets to investigate his hypothesis and found that this model actually emerged in many but certainly not all countries with rising income, and that more than just income was involved: the composition of households, work conditions and, especially, culture (e.g., decline of religion or a growing interest in healthy food) were important factors. In particular, the Food Balance Sheets allow one to follow developments in specific countries, as well as comparing between them (data are standardized). Figure 2 compares the yearly intake of kilocalories in Angola, China, and the United States between 1961 and 2010, and shows year-to-year fluctuations within each country, with an important decline in Angola in the 1980s, and a general rise in all three countries between 1961 and 2010, particularly with the Chinese Great Leap Forward. It also reveals persisting gaps despite agricultural "miracles."

Let me return to the consequence of productivity gains in agriculture, transport, stocking, and retailing. These gains greatly influenced the

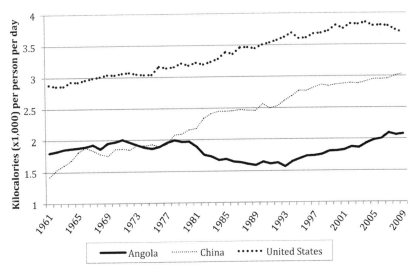

FIGURE 2. Availability of kilocalories (x 1,000) per day and person in China, United States, and Angola, 1961–2010. Source: "Food Balance Sheets," FAOSTAT, http://faostat3.fao.org/, accessed September 20, 2012.

price of food and, hence, the cost of living. The cost of food may be set alongside the rise of wages during the second half of the twentieth century in order to assess improvements in purchasing power and shifts in overall consumption. This connection may be made in two ways: by using the real wage or the real price. The former is the well-known concept of purchasing power, calculated by dividing the average wage (or income) by the price of a representative basket of goods and services in consecutive time periods (mostly by using annual index numbers). Since the end of World War I, real wages have been uppermost in the considerations of social researchers, trade unionists, managers, politicians, and many consumers. Looking back at the past fifty years, a worldwide increase of the real wage may be observed, as well as a smoother, less volatile evolution of wages compared to the decades prior to 1940 (however, the real wage also fell regularly, as in the United States in some years of the 1980s and 1990s). Here, I will use the less familiar concept of the real price, to show the effect of changes in productivity on particular foodstuffs. The real price is the outcome of the division of the price of a good or service by the hourly wage of a typical blue-collar worker in the same period; it is expressed in units of time (mostly, minutes of work to buy a particular good or service). It allows for a clear assessment of changes in the actual price of goods and services through-out time and space. For example, today it takes the average Parisian male worker twelve minutes of work to purchase a loaf of bread, but it took him twenty-two minutes in 1975, thirty-eight minutes in 1950, and forty-five minutes in 1930. Disregarding the altered quality and composition of bread (from *pain de ménage* to *baguette* to *baguette artisanale*), the decrease of the real bread price led to a radical change in the significance, image, and usage of bread, as well as to a definite trans-formation in the structure of household expenditure. The example of the real bread price also confirms the increasing velocity of change after 1945: this real price dropped by 0.8 percent per year between 1930 and 1950, but by 2.1 percent between 1950 and 1975, and by another 1.7 percent between 1975 and 2010. There are plentiful examples of declin-ing real prices of food thanks to the work of the French economists Jean and Jacqueline Fourastié, who collected hundreds of prices of all kinds of goods and services. For example, a liter of ordinary red wine required the Parisian worker forty-six minutes of work in 1950, but only four-teen in 1975, and seven in 2003; one kilo of butter cost eight hours of work in 1950, but only ninety minutes in 1975, and thirty minutes in 2003; and one kilo of meat (*faux filet*) required eight hours of work in 1950, but four hours in 1975, and merely eighty minutes in 2003. This simple method also helps in making international comparisons. For example, in 2002, one loaf of bread cost thirteen minutes of work to the average male worker in the United States and Canada, twenty minutes in France, twenty-nine minutes in Bulgaria, and almost one hour in Argentina. Bread being crucial nutrition in all of these countries, it goes without saying that overall diet differs radically according to the bread's real price. Obviously, changes in the real price are not identical for all goods and in all countries, but almost all foodstuffs are captured in the productivity rationale (some exceptions are, for example, truffles and, as will appear below, gastronomic dining).

Changes in real prices of food revolutionized the structure of average household expenditures in many countries: the share of food in total family spending dropped and gave way to spending for other goods and services such as transportation, dwelling, or leisure. The gradual but definite fall of real food prices thus co-created and was even a condition of the so-called era of mass consumption in many countries after 1950. Again, this change is part of a continuous process that began in some regions of the United States and Europe in the late nineteenth century, but accelerated in many countries after World War II. In the 1890s, the

Prussian statistician Ernst Engel noticed a comparable phenomenon when studying the expenditures of various income groups, which led him to posit a social law: the richer the people, the lower the share of food in total family spending. As many nations have become wealthy, it appears that Engel's formula is valid through time and social and geographical space. The example of the United States demonstrates this well: in this highly market-oriented economy, the share of food in total expenditure fell from 30 to 14 percent between 1950 and 2010 (it had been 42 percent in 1900 and 34 percent in 1935).

Considering the share of food in total household spending thus suggests the general wealth of a nation. Table 1 shows the share of food in total family spending in a couple of countries in selected years. The gap between France, Portugal, and the United States in 1950 reflects quite different living conditions and diets, but the closing of the gap between France and the United States in the 1960s and 1970s, and with Portugal after 1980 equally shows the convergence of consumer patterns in these three countries. Naturally, there are still differences today, but fewer than in 1950.[3] The data with regard to Algeria, Bangladesh, and Peru since 1990 suggest the overall poverty of these countries as well as their limited spending power on goods and services other than food. Yet, Bangladesh's and particularly Peru's data indicate an important change in the 1990s, while Algeria's data show a diminishing share of food expenditure only in the 2000s. The gap in 2010 between these three countries and France, Portugal, and the United States, however, is still large. These data allow very crude comparisons through time and space: for example, the share of total family expenditure spent on food in Algeria in 2010 equals that of France in 1950 and that of the United States in 1900. This, of course, does not mean that diets in these places were similar.

This relationship between income and share of food in total spending is explained by the low elasticity of food expenditures, meaning that food has to be obtained in *all* situations whatever its price. When the real food price decreased and more diverse food became available at affordable prices, flexibility of food expenditures rose, meaning that the share of food in total family spending could diminish.

National data refer to the average household, which conceals important differences according to the composition of the family, age, dwelling place, or income, as Engel demonstrated in the 1890s. Differences within a nation are telling. For example, in the United States in 1950 the lowest income groups' spending on food reached 32 percent of total household expenditure, whereas the highest income group spent

TABLE I SHARE OF FOOD AND DRINKS CONSUMED AT HOME AND AWAY IN
TOTAL HOUSEHOLD SPENDING (IN PERCENT)

	1950	1960	1970	1980	1990	2000	2010
France	45	33	26	21	19	21	22
Portugal	58	–	–	–	32	31	28
United States	30	24	20	17	18	14	14
Algeria	–	–	–	–	52	53	44
Peru	–	–	–	–	62	36	32
Bangladesh	–	–	–	–	63	55	54

Based on the databases of Eurostat, FAO, and national statistical bureaus. Food consumption expenditure refers to the monetary value of food, including all beverages and food consumed both at home and away from home.

22 percent; in 2003, the figures had diminished to 22 and 5 percent, respectively.[4] Accepting the link between wealth and the share of food in total expenditure, the latter data suggest improvement for both income categories between 1950 and the 2010s, but marked polarization.

In absolute terms, rich households spent more on food than other families. Moreover, and very notably, this cannot be viewed in terms of quantity alone: rich and poor people (and rich and poor nations) *buy* different food. In general and in the long run, the richer a household (or nation) is, the higher the share of food of animal origin. Yet, in rich countries differences tend to fade away if only big product categories (for example, meat) are considered. Belgian household budget surveys demonstrate this: working-class families spent 32 percent of their total food expenditure on meat in 1974, whereas white-collar families, having in general higher incomes than the former group, spent 2 percent less on meat. Differences appear on a more detailed level: for example, in 1974 the white-collar households spent more money on chicken and beef than working-class families did. Tellingly, white-collar households' share of fresh fish was higher than that of blue-collar families (3.5 and 2.7 percent respectively), which reflects the growing appreciation of fresh fish in the 1970s, as well as the slightly diminishing interest of the middle and upper classes in all sorts of meat.[5]

FURTHER INTERPRETATIVE CONCEPTS

The above section highlighted economic features of the development of the landscape of food since 1945, but hardly mentioned politics, culture, social relations, or preferences. This present section puts the economy in context by referring to broad concepts that may help interpret recent food developments. I will do so by paying attention to the actors who assign meaning and by considering the concept of the food system.

"Inside meaning" and "outside meaning" are notions used by anthropologist Sidney Mintz when trying to streamline interpretations and discussions about recent food changes. "Meaning" stresses the actors' perceptions, interpretations, and creation of values. People assign meaning to objects, events, institutions, ideas, and relationships, and, by so doing, co-shape these objects, events, institutions, ideas, and relationships. Emphasis is put on actor-oriented perspectives (or "lived experience"), as distinguished from the tendency of historians to question from a distance why and how things happen. "Outside meaning" comprises "grand changes" that set boundaries, which include the functioning and perception of the economy, industrial relations, the state and its actions, school systems, the type and place of work, overall gender relations, political rights, and other such big issues, which are given meaning by various actors. These actors may have opposite views, which brings power relationships into the concept of meaning. "Inside meaning" is closely linked to these grand changes, but evolves on a micro scale that may be labeled the "daily life" of a community or a household. Mintz illustrates inside and outside meaning by referring to the British working-class *high tea:* this practice emerged when workers actually created it ("inside meaning," referring to particular foods, time allocation, use of tableware, et cetera), but only when conditions ("outside meaning," referring to jobs, income, trade) were advantageous, conditions over which the workers had little or no control. If the division between "grand changes" and "daily life" is not easy to maintain, it is nonetheless an adequate way of interpreting changes in the landscape of food, because actors appear very clearly when they assign meaning to foodstuffs, leisure time, grocers, feasting, advertisements, wages, eating out, dieting, or whatever development is happening in and outside the landscape of food. Yet, if dividing our attention between grand changes and daily life simplifies the way we interpret food changes, it does not facilitate the study of these changes. Conceiving of food within a chain of provisioning, or a system, may be of help. In these terms, incorporating Mintz's anthropological approach into the concept of food systems may offer a very promising prospect.

When dealing above with productivity growth, I mentioned various domains such as agriculture, transport, storage, retailing, et cetera, as though these operate separately from each other. They do not: these domains are closely connected. What good would increasing productivity in agriculture do if the produce could not be adequately transported, stocked, manufactured, sold, cooked, and consumed? This "land-to-plate" approach leads to conceiving of a food provisioning system that consists of interconnected chains. I will use it to suggest a frame of approaching and interpreting global changes in the landscape of food in the past fifty years. However, this approach is debated, and it is of course not the only possible way to assess global food developments.[6]

One way of looking at recent changes and at the integration of the food industry is commodity system analysis, which first appeared in agro-food studies that connected agriculture to agribusiness. Later, sociologists applied the notion of the animal food chain to human consumption, and social researchers started to link production to distribution and consumption, joining physical places and actors (farm, market, kitchen, and table; worker, retailer, cook, and diner) or introducing particular categories such as social class, advertising, food advice, or preferences. Economist Ben Fine revisited the concept in the early 1990s by situating it in the emerging field of consumption research. Stressing the necessity of conceiving of food within a chain, he concluded that each foodstuff evolves in a specific system because of differences in modes of production, retailing, marketing, and consumption. Hence, he refers to the "meat system," "sugar system," or "dairy system" (and one might add, for example, the "cheese system," "soft drinks system," "biscuit system," et cetera). The crucial idea of thinking in "food systems" is not about merely linking production to consumption, but about the fact that production and consumption are part of a chain whose various links influence each other. This interconnectivity makes a particularly difficult but promising subject of research, because it raises key questions such as how advertisement influences consumption, or how consumers influence the agro-industry. There is a shifting balance of power in the food chain. If large landowners decided what to produce in the nineteenth century, today big retailers seem to decide what is being produced and when. Some other recent characteristics of the food chain: it has become longer (there are more components between land and plate); it has become much more complex (each link is caught in technologies); and the connections between some links have narrowed (agribusinesses owning farmland; supermarkets owning transport firms).

If the concept of the food system has recently gained popularity among sociologists and economists, historians have applied it only rarely. The latter willingly connect two components, as for example

TABLE 2   COMPONENTS OF THE FOOD CHAIN

Activities	Places	People
Researching and developing	Farms, laboratories	Farmers, scientists
Producing (farming, fishing, hunting, gardening, gathering)	Farms, gardens, woods, seas, rivers	Farmers, gardeners, fishers, landowners, speculators
Preserving (salting, drying, heating, cooling)	Farms, storages, cellars	Farmers, gardeners, fishers, home cooks
Trading (import, export, wholesale)	Warehouses, packaging, transport systems, harbors	Merchants, truckers, harbor workers
Manufacturing (transforming, upgrading)	Factories, shops (bakeries, butchers), packagers	Workers, entrepreneurs, the self-employed
Preserving (canning, freezing)	Factories, homes	Workers, entrepreneurs, the self-employed, home cooks
Distributing (retailing)	Shops, (super)markets, street stalls	Retailers
Mediating (advertisements, recommendations, education)	Public space (schools, streets, radio, television)	Marketers, teachers, scientists
Preparing (cleaning, cooking)	Commercial kitchens, home kitchens	Commercial cooks, waiters, home cooks
Eating (breakfasting, lunching, snacking, dining; eating away from home, eating at home; eating alone, entertaining)	Private and public space (kitchens, dining rooms, restaurants, cafeterias, stalls)	Diners, family members, guests
Wasting (leftovers, fodder, losses)	Kitchens, wastebins	Diners, dishwashers, home cooks

farming with farmers' lobbying groups, or retailing with retailers' man-ufacturing of store brands, but they seldom situate these components within the entire process from land to plate. This avoidance may be due to the complexity of addressing the whole food chain. Above, I mentioned four categories (farm, market, kitchen, and table), but actually, each single component of the chain should receive proper attention. A full food chain might look as shown in table 2.

Three observations should be made when considering this table. First, relations between each component must be studied: it does not suffice to assume that, for example, the breakthrough of the supermarket transformed shopping and eating; how and when this precisely operated should be considered. Second, although each link influences the whole chain, it is clear that any given link may have more weight in a particular period and for a particular food. This, too, should be studied in detail. Third, and most important, referring to Mintz's view, it is clear that "meaning" pervades all activities, places, and people that appear in this table. "Meaning," linked to both daily life and grand changes, determines whether money is invested in research and technology, whether diners decide to go to a restaurant, or whether people prefer one brand to another.

Thinking about food in terms of a system has the advantage of putting seemingly detached features within context. The large-scale emergence of the refrigerator in Europe around 1960, for example, can only be interpreted with reference to its diminishing production cost, intensifying promotion, growing supply in supermarkets of fresh products (e.g., yoghurt and desserts), and approval by consumers. David Gentilcore's *Pomodorro!* gives a pertinent example of applying the concept of the food chain (without taking it as the initial theoretical frame). He studies the tomato in Italy (with excursions to the United States); explicitly refers to the concept of the food chain; pays attention to meaning, research and development, production, canning, trade, advertisements, retailing, cooking, and eating; and investigates links between these domains.

DINING OUT SYSTEMS

This section applies a food systems approach to one of the key features of recent worldwide food developments: dining out. Eating out may be seen as the end of the chain where the food is actually consumed (in table 2, these places might appear as "restaurants, cafeterias, stalls, and take away"). Yet many of the components of the chain in this table can be applied to the world of eating out.

To show the growing importance of dining out since the 1950s, I refer again to the changes in household expenditures during this period. The share of money spent on food eaten at home dropped significantly between 1950 and today. But investigators also paid attention to money spent on food "eaten outside the home" (as it was first defined in the United Kingdom), "not from the household stock" (later definition in the United Kingdom), "eaten away from home" (the United States), or "purchased in restaurants and hotels" (many European countries' description, accentuating leisurely consumption). Research on restaurants and other public dining spaces has appeared only recently, although various forms of eating out have long existed, as Paul Freedman emphasizes in chapter 12 of this book. By 1950, most cities offered a dozen or so public eating-out forms, each with specific connotations ranging from necessity to pleasure, from fancy to basic. Family spending on eating out, however, was still extremely low. In Belgium in 1957, for example, working-class families spent 0.6 percent of their total expenditure on eating out, farmworkers 0.2 percent, and administrators and managers 1.3 percent (in money, this came to 560, 120, and 3,000 francs respectively, which highlights the gap between the three social categories).[7] Industrial workers spent a tiny 0.1 percent of their total expenditure on meals in the factory, meaning that they brought along most food from home, but administrators and managers spent 0.6 percent of their total spending on food at their work place, which means that they regularly bought food in snack bars or simple eateries. Differences with regard to restaurant dining are very telling: farmworkers spent 58 francs per year and per household (0.1 percent of the total), industrial workers 165 francs (0.2 percent), but administrators and managers 1,473 francs (0.7 percent), or almost nine times more (in money) than blue-collar workers. Interestingly, the Belgian investigators did not comment on eating out or on this large divergence, as if money spent on eating out was totally insignificant even among well-off administrators and managers.

Eating out in other countries differed from the Belgian experience in the late 1950s. In Great Britain in 1960, for example, the average share of total family expenditure spent on eating out attained almost 10 percent (all forms of eating away from home are included). This doubled between 1960 and 1990 via smooth and regular annual growth. In the 1990s, however, it rose brusquely from almost 21 percent to over 33 percent. The small decrease between 2000 and 2009 seems to have come to a stop in 2010.[8]

The remaining part of this section offers an attempt to interpret this tripling of the share of money spent on eating away from home in the past fifty years, a shift that occurred in many countries of the world. Of course, income, family structure, and location differ between and within countries. With regard to the latter, well-to-do urban dwellers between twenty-five and sixty years old, without children and/or living alone, eat out much more than a poor, elderly couple living in the countryside.

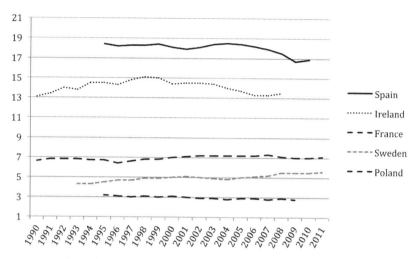

FIGURE 3. Share of money spent in restaurants and hotels by average households in five European countries, 1990–2010, in percent. Source: "Final consumption expenditure of households, by consumption: Restaurants and hotels," Eurostat, http://epp.eurostat .ec.europa.eu/tgm/table.do?tab=table&init=1&plugin=1&language=en&pcode=ts dpc520, accessed September 23, 2012.

With regard to differences between countries, statistics show large disparities within the same geographical space. Figure 3 illustrates this for five European countries, showing the average family expenditure in restaurants and hotels from 1990 to 2010 (note the narrower focus compared with the data for the United Kingdom). Averages evolve on quite different levels in the five countries, with the extremes in 2010 being Spain (17 percent) and Poland (3 percent), but fluctuations within one country are limited, showing persistent habits. Interpreting these fluctuations would require thorough knowledge of national developments (income, structure of catering business, habits, et cetera). For example, the increase in Ireland in the 1990s and the decline in 2000 and again in 2005 may be linked to the country's economic performance during that time, via income, (un)employment, and feelings of (in)security. Naturally, the lasting disparities among these five countries reflect radically different meanings and practices related to eating. I should emphasize that spending on eating out has tended to rise or at least stagnate in most countries, as opposed to spending on food eaten at home. I should also point out that a slight change, even just 0.1 percent of the average household expenditure, means a lot of money in terms of the national gross domestic product.

Before I start exploring the eating away from home system by assessing its significance in 1950, I should emphasize that the number and variety of eating out places rose considerably throughout the world after 1950. Data about Amsterdam exemplify this: in 1964 there were eighteen eateries per ten thousand inhabitants, in 1975 this rose to thirty, and in 1995 there were fifty-five eateries per ten thousand Amsterdammers. Since then the number has stagnated. This increase is largely explained by rising numbers of visitors, but thriving tourism has also had an effect on the city's catering facilities and the inhabitants' eating out habits. Between 1950 and 1980, the number of sandwich bars, lunchrooms, and fries booths diminished, whereas the number of proper restaurants grew tenfold. Since the 1970s, the Amsterdam catering sector has seen one of the city's highest bankruptcy rates. A similar evolution occurred in most major cities of the world, entailing the clustering of eateries in particular areas, as well as the forging of the culinary reputations of particular cities (for example, at present there is debate whether Paris, Lyons or Strasbourg should be called France's gourmet capital, although Bordeaux, Dijon, Brest, and Toulouse are also in the running).

As I mentioned above, in the early 1950s various types of eateries were well established in towns and cities all over the world. Next to mundane booths that sold sandwiches and fish and chips, there were pubs that supplied simple dishes, alongside fancy restaurants that offered outrageously expensive meals. People knew about the convenience, luxury, status, ease, and even adventure represented by each of these places. Thus, eating out had various and clear meanings around 1950: to many people it signified an inconceivable practice, to some it had become a workday routine, and to others leisurely dining out was a longing on the verge of becoming attainable.

The growing accessibility of various forms of eating out in the 1960s and thereafter was the consequence of intertwined changes of the entire system of eating away from home. Food prepared in the kitchens of public eateries was mostly fresh, but increasingly more treated food was used. Since the 1910s, canned food and ready-made sauces, produced by big international companies, had been familiar in kitchens of most luxury and ordinary eateries. These products necessitated little additional work and, moreover, reduced the effects of the seasons in cooking. Frozen ingredients were new in the 1950s (for example, Birds Eye fish fingers: "No bones, no waste, no smell, no fuss," according to an advertisement of those days). At first quite expensive, but later within reach of all *restaurateurs*, frozen food got a reputation for keeping flavor better than canned or dried food. Precooked ingredients burgeoned in the 1970s. This was the consequence of fast-growing agribusinesses that supplied prepared food in very diverse forms: frozen fries, sliced meats, dried sauces and herbs, canned vegetables, ready-to-bake dough, and cleaned fish. Nearly all restaurant kitchens began to utilize these conveniences more and more. Additionally, many kitchens called upon subcontractors to supply bread, pastries, or desserts. This time-saving and cost-lowering logic meant that, in the 1990s, in some commercial kitchens (particularly in cafeterias of schools, firms, hospitals, and other institutions) hardly any cooking was done, except for dressing and heating. However, fresh (and, later, organic) food regained full importance in gastronomic restaurants in the 1970s and spread to many eateries in the 1990s, when it even could appear in the simplest sandwich bar. Today, some high-end restaurants and bars explicitly refer to locally produced food, emphasizing the season and taste, connecting to both the producers' supply and the diners' demand. The Parisian daily food market, the Marché International de Rungis, opened in 1969 and is allegedly the biggest wholesale fresh food market in the world: it illustrates well the constant expansion of the wholesale trade in fresh food. Meat, fish, fruit, dairy products, and vegetables arrive from all over France (and the world) and leave Rungis for international destinations, via waterways and the railroad, but increasingly also by plane (from nearby Orly airport) and by trucks (the latter using motorways that expanded dramatically in the 1970s). The increased reputation of this market is demonstrated by the fact that today tourist visits are organized in seven languages.

Since the 1950s, chefs and cooks have increasingly used utensils driven by electricity, such as heaters, refrigerators, blenders, peeling and cleaning machines, and automatic dishwashers, which facilitate and quicken work. These tools were specially manufactured for kitchens of big (institutional) restaurants and made their way to smaller kitchens quite quickly. Also, the diffusion of stoves and ovens run on gas or electricity, replacing those run on coal, changed cooking techniques. This technology was particularly present in new types of eateries, such as fast-food outlets, where food was being prepared on the spot, and efficiency and time (or productivity) were crucial. McDonald's appeared in its present form in the United States in 1948, and Wimpy in Britain in 1954. Via franchising (and hence, limitations of risk for the company), both developed quickly, but Wimpy collapsed in the 1980s, whereas McDonald's flourished: from one hundred eateries in 1959 in the United

States, to seven thousand in 32 countries around 1980, and about thirty-three thousand in 119 countries today. This success caused protest in some European countries, as for example in 1999 the violent assault of a McDonald's under construction in the town of Millau (in the South of France) by José Bové, who since 2009 has been a member of the European Parliament. Nevertheless, today, McDo (as the company is known in France) has one of the densest branch networks in Europe.

Installation of ever more technology required vast investments, which led proprietors of restaurants to adapt new business forms, sometimes establishing international chains. For example, the Brussels-based Chez Léon expanded to France in 1989 and to the United Kingdom in 2012, taking the form of a stockholding company. French gastronomic restaurants such as Paul Bocuse and Alain Ducasse internationalized as well (expanding to the United States and Japan in the 1990s, to South Korea, China, and Russia more recently).

The technological-industrial turn in professional cooking did not lead to a drastic change in the skills required of restaurant staff. However, alongside the well established (intense and often harsh) on-the-spot training necessary to become an artisan, cooking schools expanded and specialized. Already prior to 1914, some countries had tried to develop formal education in catering and hotel service, but this was rarely successful until the 1950s. The Ecole hôtelière de Lausanne, Switzerland, founded in 1893 and the world's oldest hospitality school, expanded its enrollment from sixty students per year in the 1920s, to five hundred (from thirty countries) in 1950 and seven hundred (from eighty-two countries) in 2008. Some big restaurants, such as Bocuse or Ducasse, now also offer advanced classes. Still, it was the talent and courage of individual chefs, with or without formal training, that changed the preparation and presentation of the food in restaurants. Innovative preparations came along with changes on the plate and in the dining room, thus underlining the novelty of the cuisine (big, square plates, or meat or fish placed on top of the sauce in the nouvelle cuisine of the 1960s; food in glasses of all types or foams in the molecular gastronomy of the late 1990s).

Changes in the preparation and presentation of food occurred on various levels during this period. In general, the notion of safe, hygienic food became much more pressing. The concept was not new (in Brussels a chemical laboratory for testing food had existed since 1856), but local, national, and international regulation aimed at ensuring safe food. Regular control of public eateries is part of such attention: to take just one example, the French Contrôle sanitaire department inspected twenty-two thousand restaurant kitchens in 2011, finding at least one problem in 12.5 percent of them. Some eateries emphasized their hygienic way of preparing food, as does McDonald's India today: "A hygienic and well-organised kitchen is the heart and soul of our restaurants." This slogan is embedded in broader attention for health and the optimal diet, about which an increasing stream of books appear in every country.

Chefs, too, write books, thus codifying the gastronomic and bourgeois cuisine of their time. Since the early 1960s, however, this genre has proliferated, with dozens of cooks publishing their recipes and philosophies, while trying to build a niche in this blooming market. National, regional, international, healthy, organic, fusion, or other cookery books appeared, regularly yielding worldwide bestsellers. Moreover, restaurant cooks appeared in newspapers and magazines first as expert authors, but since the 1970s increasingly also as acclaimed stars, a status most chefs readily promoted, leaving their kitchens and entering dining rooms and television studios, as did, for example, Chef Tell (F.P. Erhardt) who appeared on U.S. television for the first time in 1974.

Information about eating out, however, was particularly a matter of restaurant and travelers' guides. Again, this was not new. Since 1920 the *Guide Michelin* has advised travelers where to eat in several European countries, introducing a classification of restaurants. Today, each year Michelin categorizes restaurants in twenty-three countries, including Japan, Italy, and (some parts of) the United States. Its publication is an annual event in the press. This form of rating creates or ruins reputations of restaurants, cities, and regions. The power of restaurant guides is perhaps best demonstrated by what happened in the 1960s when two journalists, Henri Gault and Christian Millau, invented *nouvelle cuisine*. Of course, certain young French chefs had already started to emphasize freshness, natural taste, lightness, and presentation on the plate, but Gault and Millau actually *created* this cuisine by classifying and codifying it. During the post-1945 period, restaurant guides thrived (e.g., the UK's annual *Good Food Guide* started in 1951), specialized magazines appeared (e.g., *Bon Appetit* in the United States was founded in 1956), and television shows were broadcast (e.g., Julia Child's *The French Chef* in the United States from 1963 to 1972). Alongside this type of mediation of fancy eating out, other media continued and developed, such as exhibitions and contests. With regard to the latter, the highly publicized and dazzling Bocuse d'Or may be mentioned. Since 1987, this biennial contest between chefs of several nations has taken on the atmosphere of a football game between Madrid and Barça. Today, there are Bocuse d'Or contests in Europe, Asia, and Latin America. Interestingly, for the last couple of years the restaurant guides' classification of eating places is no longer limited to fancy dining, but also includes brasseries, cafés, bars, and even street vendors. Of course, it is no longer necessary to wait for professionals to pass judgment: with the arrival of social media and blogging platforms, every diner can become a critic.

The dozens of restaurant guides that have appeared all over the world since the 1950s have been successful because they met with the diverse expectations of a growing public of enthusiastic diners. Public life transformed rapidly in many ways after 1945: many more men and women got jobs in the service sectors, moved into cities and, later, into suburbs, spent less time at home, lived in smaller households, and earned more money. Obviously, this did not occur all at once in all countries: rates of urbanization, individualization, and enrichment varied highly, with fluctuating inequality between and within countries. In many countries, dining out increased as part of a generally growing interest in leisure activities. So, the *nouveaux riches* of the 1960s delightedly joined the wealthy in fancy restaurants, but the latter looked for even more exclusive experiences in new places in order to maintain social boundaries. They gladly paid for meals that cost, in real-price terms, exactly as much as they had in the 1950s, 1970s, or 1990s. In the 1970s, middle-class Americans and Europeans coming back from voyages abroad tried to retain a holiday feeling by patronizing local ethnic restaurants. In the same decade, many children, who now got more pocket money, deserted the school canteen to lunch in fast food eateries, whereas businessmen more and more often signed contracts in the dining rooms of grand hotels. In the 1980s, working-class families no longer celebrated only at home, but more and more they went out to dine in restaurants. And since 1950, because of constant changes in the usage of time related to work, transport, or leisure, an ever-growing number of men and women lunched habitually in sandwich bars, fast food eateries, pizzerias, street stalls, and other relatively cheap places to eat away from home. In short, diverse people took a keen interest in eating out, and for diverse reasons. They could pay for it and found the experience fun and convenient.

With regard to waste, the final component of the restaurant chain, a 2011 FAO report estimates that losses in retailing and restaurants have increased since 1990, explaining that "a lot of restaurants serve buffets at fixed prices, which encourages people to fill their plates with more food than they can actually eat." The throwing away means, for both patrons and restaurant owners, that the West can afford this. The remedy is education.[9] Yet, waste and losses are not only the diners' responsibility: even more food may be lost during preparation. In its 2010 survey, the Sustainable Restaurant Association (UK), for example, noted that 65 percent of restaurant waste is generated in preparing (peeling, clumsy cooking, poor planning), 30 percent comes from customers' plates, and only 5 percent is spoilage (out-of-date and unusable food). Its recommended remedies are, among others, "careful ordering and menu planning" or "keeping skins on vegetables."[10]

Since 1945, dining out has become quite common for many people in many countries, whether for work or pleasure. All sorts of people eat out in very diverse places with very diverse expectations. Clearly, the significance of this act is extremely varied; moreover, it changes constantly. In interpreting dining out, considering only one or two components does not suffice: the whole chain has to be considered, with attention to each link and their relations. Even a simple question, such as why top chefs valued fresh vegetables in the 1960s, benefits from this food chain approach: looking at the entire chain we can see that important factors included not only the chefs' talent, but also the general cultural concern about health, the reaction against the success of treated foods, the existence of a gourmet group of rich patrons, the expanding and more flexible supply of vegetables, and the cooks' and restaurants' image in the media. These are all interconnected: discard one of them, and the (sub)system of the fancy restaurant would no longer function. All components should also be dealt with in interpreting institutional catering, fast food outlets, street vendors, and any other form of public eating out. These are all caught in the big restaurant system.

TEACHING POST-1945 FOOD HISTORY

Studying the global landscape of food since 1945 is complex and, as I argued, increasingly complicated because of ever-faster changes that affect an ever-growing group of people in ever more regions of the world. The idea that food can be conceived of as part of a system, where each component between agriculture and plate influences all the others, is a possible approach to this complexity. The process of giving meaning encompasses the whole chain, which includes cultural aspirations, economic decisions, and local, national, and international policies. Eating out, the example at hand, has illustrated this complexity and touched upon production and manufacturing of food, its transport and whole-sale trade, the way restaurant kitchens operate, the training of cooks, the roles of mediators, the expectations of very diverse customers, and their purchasing power and interests. In this chapter, I did not pose one central question to encompass post-1945 food developments, nor did I survey the vast literature that deals with this period, nor did I reflect on historians' methodologies, sources, or approaches; I took a didactic line by exploring some concepts and sources, and by giving one example.

NOTES

1. "Landbouw, Cijfers, Historische reeks," Centraal Bureau voor de Sta-tistiek, www.cbs.nl/nl-NL/menu/themas/landbouw/cijfers/default.htm, accessed September 4, 2012.

2. David Grigg, "The Changing Geography of World Food Consumption in the Second Half of the Twentieth Century," *The Geographical Journal* 165, no. 1 (1999): 1–11.

3. Recent information on household expenditures is to be found at the Inter-national Labor Organization, http://laborsta.ilo.org/, containing data per coun-try (access via "Household Income and Expenditure").

4. Data for 1950: *Historical Statistics of the United States: Colonial Times to 1970*, Vol. 1 (Washington: Bureau of the Census, 1975), 320; data for 2003: International Labour Organization, *Household Income and Expenditure Statis-tics*, http://laborsta.ilo.org/STP/guest, accessed March 23, 2014.

5. Lode Quintens, "Het verbruik van voeding en dranken door de Belgische gezinnen," *De Gids op Maatschappelijk Gebied* 76, no. 2 (1985): 167–69.

6. See Ben Fine's 2004 paper for bibliographic references and replies to criti-cism against this concept: Fine, "Debating Production-Consumption Linkages in Food Studies," *Sociologia Ruralis* 44, no. 3 (2004): 332–42. One alternative could be to conceive of "food regimes," a chronological division based on agri-cultural developments (land ownership, technology, labor, output, et cetera).

7. Pierre De Bie, *Budgets familiaux en Belgique 1957–1958: Modes de vie dans trois milieux socio-professionnels* (Louvain: Editions Nauwelaerts, 1960), 110, 118, 124.

8. Data for 1960–1990 are based on Alan Warde and Lydia Martens, *Eating Out: Social Differentiation, Consumption, and Pleasure* (Cambridge: Cam-bridge University Press, 2000), 34; data for 2000–2010 are based on "Food and Drinks Expenditure (average pence per person and per week)," Department for Environment, Food and Rural Affairs (DEFRA), Family Food Dataset, www .gov.uk/government/organisations/department-for-environment-food-rural-affairs/series/family-food-statistics, accessed May 25, 2013.

9. Jenny Gustavsson, Christel Cederberg, and Ulf Sonesson, *Global Food Losses and Food Waste* (Rome: Food and Agriculture Organization, 2011), www.fao.org/docrep/014/mb060e/mb060e00.pdf.

10. "Too Good to Waste," Sustainable Restaurant Association, www.thesra
.org/wp-content/uploads/2012/02/SRA002-SRA-Food-Waste-Survey-Full-
Report.pdf, accessed September 30, 2012.

BIBLIOGRAPHY

Bardi, Ugo. *The Limits to Growth Revisited*. New York: Springer, 2011.
Bentley, Amy, ed. *A Cultural History of Food in the Modern Age*. London: Berg, 2012.
Bieleman, Jan. *Five Centuries of Farming: A Short History of Dutch Agriculture, 1500–2000*. Wageningen: Wageningen Academic Publishers, 2010.
Block, Daniel. "Food Systems." In *A Cultural History of Food in the Modern Age*, edited by Amy Bentley, 47–67. London: Berg, 2012,
Claflin, Kyri W., and Peter Scholliers, eds. *Writing Food History: A Global Perspective*. London: Berg, 2012.
De Bie, Pierre. *Budgets familiaux en Belgique 1957–1958: Modes de vie dans trois milieux socio-professionnels*. Louvain: Editions Nauwelaerts, 1960.
Ferguson, Priscilla Parkhurst. "Eating Out: Going Out, Staying In." In *A Cultural History of Food in the Modern Age*, edited by Amy Bentley, 111–26. London: Berg, 2012
Fine, Ben. "Debating Production-Consumption Linkages in Food Studies." *Sociologia Ruralis* 44, no. 3 (2004): 332–42.
Fine, Ben, Michael Heasman, and Judith Wright. *Consumption in the Age of Affluence: The World of Food*. London: Routledge, 1996.
Fischler, Claude, and Estelle Masson, eds. *Manger: Français, Européens et Américains face à l'alimentation*. Paris: O. Jacob, 2008.
Fourastié, Jacqueline. "Le progrès technique a-t-il encore une influence sur la vie économqiue?" *Sociétal* 50 (2005), www.societal.fr/ael/50/p4.htm#12.
Fourastié, Jean, and Jacqueline Fourastié. *Pouvoir d'achat, prix et salaires*. Paris: Gallimard, 1977.
Gentilcore, David. *Pomodorro! A History of the Tomato in Italy*. New York: Columbia University Press, 2010.
Grigg, David. "The Changing Geography of World Food Consumption in the Second Half of the Twentieth Century." *The Geographical Journal* 165, no. 1 (1999): 1–11.
Historical Statistics of the United States: Colonial Times to 1970. Vol. 1. Washington: Bureau of the Census, 1975.
Jacobs, Marc, and Peter Scholliers, eds. *Eating Out in Europe: Picnics, Gourmet Dining, and Snacks Since the Late Eighteenth Century*. Oxford; New York: Berg, 2003.
Meadows, Donella, Jorgen Randers, and Dennis Meadows. *Limits to Growth: The 30-Year Update*. London: Earthscan, 2005.
Mintz, Sidney W. *Tasting Food, Tasting Freedom: Excursions into Eating, Culture, and the Past*. Boston: Beacon Press, 1996.
Quintens, Lode, "Het verbruik van voeding en dranken door de Belgische gezinnen." *De Gids op Maatschappelijk Gebied* 76, no. 2 (1985): 157–72.

Ritzer, George, "The McDonaldization of Society." *Journal of American Culture* 6, no. 1 (1983): 100–7.

Sarasúa, Carmen, Peter Scholliers, and Leen Van Molle, eds. *Land, Shops and Kitchens: Technology and the Food Chain in Twentieth-Century Europe.* Turnhout: Brepols, 2005.

Scholliers, Peter. "Novelty and Tradition: The New Landscape for Gastronomy." In *Food: The History of Taste,* edited by Paul Freedman, 333–57. London: Thames and Hudson, 2007.

Trubek, Amy. "Kitchen Work: 1920–present." In *A Cultural History of Food in the Modern Age,* edited by Amy Bentley, 127–44. London: Berg, 2012.

U.S. Department of Labor and U.S. Bureau of Labor Statistics. *100 Years of U.S. Consumer Spending: Data for the Nation, New York City, and Boston.* Washington: U.S. Department of Labor; U.S. Bureau of Labor Statistics, 2006.

Van den Eeckhout, Patricia. "Restaurants in Western Europe and the United States in the Nineteenth and Twentieth Centuries: An Introduction." *Food and History* 10, no.1 (2012): 143–53.

Warde, Alan, and Lydia Martens. *Eating Out: Social Differentiation, Consumption, and Pleasure.* Cambridge: Cambridge University Press, 2000.

Winger, Ray, and Gavin Wall. *Food Product Innovation: A Background Paper.* Agricultural and Food Engineering Working Document 2. Rome: Food and Agricultural Organization, 2006. www.fao.org/docrep/016/j7193e/j7193e.pdf.

Contributors

KEN ALBALA is a professor of history at the University of the Pacific in Stockton, California and director of the University of the Pacific's food studies program in San Francisco. He is the author or editor of eighteen books on food including *Eating Right in the Renaissance, Food in Early Modern Europe, Cooking in Europe: 1250–1650, The Banquet, Beans: A History, Three World Cuisines,* and two cookbooks: *The Lost Art of Real Cooking* and *The Lost Arts of Hearth and Home.* He was coeditor of the journal *Food, Culture and Society* and is series editor of Rowman and Littlefield Studies in Food and Gastronomy. His course *Food: A Cultural Culinary History* can be purchased on DVD from the Great Courses company. He is currently working on a book about fasting in the Reformation.

E. N. ANDERSON is Professor Emeritus of Anthropology at the University of California, Riverside. He received his PhD in anthropology from the University of California Berkeley in 1967. He has done research on ethnobiology, cultural ecology, political ecology, and medical anthropology in several areas, especially Hong Kong, British Columbia, California, and the Yucatan peninsula of Mexico. His books include *The Food of China* (Yale University Press, 1988), *Ecologies of the Heart* (Oxford University Press, 1996), *Political Ecology of a Yucatec Maya Community* (University of Arizona Press, 2005) and *The Pursuit of Ecotopia* (Praeger, 2010). He has five children and five grandchildren. He lives in Riverside, California, with his wife Barbara and three large dogs.

WARREN BELASCO is Professor Emeritus of American Studies at the University of Maryland, Baltimore County, where he taught for thirty-two years. He has also been a Visiting Professor of Gastronomy at Boston University. He is the author and editor of several books, including *Appetite for Change: How the Counterculture Took on the Food Industry* (1990), *Food: The Key Concepts*

(2008), and *Meals to Come: A History of the Future of Food* (2006). He is currently working on a culinary history of Washington, D.C.

AMY BENTLEY is an associate professor in the Department of Nutrition, Food Studies, and Public Health at New York University. A historian with interests in the historical and cultural contexts of food, she is author of *Inventing Baby Food: Taste, Health, and the Industrialization of the American Diet* (University of California Press, 2014). Bentley is cofounder of the Experimental Cuisine Collective, an interdisciplinary group of scientists, food studies scholars, and chefs who study the intersection of science and food, and also cofounder of the NYU Urban Farm Lab. She serves as editor of *Food, Culture, and Society: An International Journal of Multidisciplinary Research*.

JOYCE E. CHAPLIN is the James Duncan Phillips Professor of Early American History at Harvard University. She is the author, most recently, of *Round about the Earth: Circumnavigation from Magellan to Orbit* (2012) and editor of Benjamin Franklin's *Autobiography: A Norton Critical Edition* (2012). She is currently coauthoring a book on Thomas Robert Malthus called *Malthus and the New World* (Princeton University Press, forthcoming).

PRISCILLA PARKHURST FERGUSON is a professor in the Department of Sociology at Columbia University. After work on French literary identity in *Literary France: The Making of a Culture* (1987), she focused on the modernizing urban culture of Paris in *Paris as Revolution: Reading the Nineteenth-Century City* (1994). Her early work on cuisine and food culminated in *Accounting for Taste: The Triumph of French Cuisine* (2004). Her most recent book, *Word of Mouth: What We Talk About When We Talk About Food* (2014), looks at how we use food to construct our lives and our cultures.

PAUL FREEDMAN is a professor of history at Yale University. He is the author of several books on medieval Catalonia, the church, and the peasantry. In 2007 Freedman edited *Food: The History of Taste*, which was nominated for a James Beard award. His *Out of the East: Spices and the Medieval Imagination* (2008) considers the desire for spices in medieval Europe and its historical impact. His current food history research is on American restaurants. His article on "Women and Restaurants" appeared recently in the *Journal of Social History*. He is writing a book to be called *Ten Restaurants That Changed America*.

JESSICA B. HARRIS is the author of fifteen books, including twelve cookbooks, documenting the foods and foodways of the African diaspora. Her most recent is *High on the Hog: A Culinary Journey from Africa to America*. A culinary historian, Harris has lectured at institutions throughout the United States and abroad, and is an award-winning journalist who has written extensively about the foodways and culture of Africa in the Americas. Harris was the inaugural Scholar in Residence in the Ray Charles Chair in African-American Material Culture at Dillard University in New Orleans. She is currently a professor at Queens College/C.U.N.Y.

HI'ILEI JULIA HOBART is a doctoral candidate in the NYU Food Studies program. She holds an M.A. in decorative arts, design and culture from the Bard Graduate Center and an M.L.S. in archives management and rare books from the Pratt Institute. Her research is concerned with how food and print media frame territorial occupation in nineteenth-century settler colonial contexts. Her dissertation research uses frozen water, or ice, to explore the politics of ingestion, representation, and materiality in colonial Hawai'i.

FREDERICK DOUGLASS OPIE is a thought leader on food traditions and how and why they change. Opie is the author of several books and articles, and he frequently appears on radio and television. He is a professor of History and Foodways at Babson College and the author of the forthcoming book *Upsetting the Apple Cart: Black and Latino Coalitions in New York From Protest to Public Office* (Columbia University Press, 2014). He recently completed a manuscript on Zora Neale Hurston through the lens of food. You can read more work on food history and recipes on his blog, www.foodasalens.com.

FABIO PARASECOLI is an associate professor and the coordinator of Food Studies at the New School in New York City. His research explores food in media, popular culture, and politics. He studied East Asian cultures and political science in Rome, Naples, and Beijing. After covering Middle Eastern and Far Eastern political issues, he was the U.S. correspondent for *Gambero Rosso*, Italy's authoritative food and wine magazine. His publications include *Bite Me! Food in Popular Culture* (2008) and *Al Dente: A History of Food in Italy* (2014). He is general editor with Peter Scholliers of the six-volume *Cultural History of Food* (2012).

CHARLES PERRY majored in Middle East Studies at Princeton University and the University of California, Berkeley. After graduation he pursued a writing career, serving as an editor and staff writer at *Rolling Stone* from 1968 to 1976 and a staff writer at the *Los Angeles Times* Food Section from 1990 to 2008. He began collecting medieval Arab cookery manuscripts in 1980 and has published widely on Middle Eastern food history. His most recent book is *Scents and Flavors the Banqueter Savors*, a translation of a thirteenth-century Syrian cookbook to be published by New York University Press, Abu Dhabi.

JEFFREY M. PILCHER, a professor of history and cultural studies at the University of Toronto, has taught classes on food and drink in world history for more than twenty years. His books include *Planet Taco: A Global History of Mexican Food* (2012) and *The Oxford Handbook of Food History* (2012). He coedits the journal *Global Food History*.

KRISHNENDU RAY is an associate professor in Food Studies and Chair of the Department of Nutrition, Food Studies, and Public Health at New York University. Prior to joining the NYU faculty in 2005, he was a faculty member and an acting associate dean for curriculum development at The Culinary Institute of America (CIA). A food studies scholar with interests in the social and historical contexts of food production and consumption, he is the author of *The Migrant's Table* (Temple University, 2004) and the coeditor of *Curried Cultures: Globalization, Food and South Asia* (University of California Press, 2012).

PETER SCHOLLIERS teaches European history of the nineteenth and twentieth centuries, with an emphasis on labor, industrial heritage, inequality, and food. His research focuses on the history of shopping, cooking, and eating, with particular interest in the history of nutrition. He is coeditor of *Food and History*, and a member of the board of editors of *Food, Culture and Society*, and *Appetite*. Most recently he coedited, with Fabio Parasecoli, *A Cultural History of Food* (6 vols., Berg, 2012) and, with Kyri Claflin, *Writing Food History* (Berg, 2012), and wrote, with Patricia van den Eeckhout, "Feeding Growing Cities in the 19th and 20th Centuries," in *The Handbook of Food Research*.

JAYANTA SENGUPTA was educated in the Universities of Calcutta and Cambridge. He has taught at Jadavpur University, Kolkata, and the University of Notre Dame, and held visiting appointments at the Universities of Pennsylvania, Calcutta, Cambridge, and Heidelberg, and at Utah State University. His primary research interests are the social and cultural history of modern India, transnational intellectual history, and the culture and politics of food. His first book, *At the Margins: Discourses of Development, Democracy and Regionalism in Odisha*, was published by Oxford University Press in 2014. He is currently the Director of the Victoria Memorial Hall, Kolkata, India's leading museum of Indo-British history.

AMY B. TRUBEK is an associate professor in the Nutrition and Food Sciences department at the University of Vermont and Faculty Director of the Food Systems graduate program. Trained as a cultural anthropologist and chef, her research interests include the history of the culinary profession, the globalization of the food supply, the relationship between taste and place, and cooking as a cultural practice. She is the author of *Haute Cuisine: How the French Invented the Culinary Profession* (2000) and *The Taste of Place: A Cultural Journey into Terroir* (2008), as well as numerous articles and book chapters.

BARBARA KETCHAM WHEATON is Honorary Curator of the Culinary Collection at the Schlesinger Library at the Radcliffe Institute for Advanced Study at Harvard University. Her book *Savoring the Past: the French Kitchen and Table from 1300 to 1789* was published by the University of Pennsylvania Press in 1983. She taught French food history courses at the Radcliffe Seminars and continues to teach a seminar on the systematic reading of early cookbooks. At present she is working on a database project intended to assist this process.

Index